Canada's Resource Economy in Transition:

THE PAST, PRESENT, AND FUTURE OF CANADIAN STAPLES INDUSTRIES

EDITED BY

Michael Howlett

Department of Political Science
Simon Fraser University
Burnaby, British Columbia
Canada

Keith Brownsey

Department of Policy Studies
Mount Royal College
Calgary, Alberta
Canada

2008
Emond Montgomery Publications Limited
Toronto, Canada

Emond Montgomery Publications Limited
60 Shaftesbury Avenue
Toronto ON M4T 1A3
http://www.emp.ca/university

Printed in Canada.

We acknowledge the financial support of the Government of Canada through the Book Publishing Industry Development Program (BPIDP) for our publishing activities.

Acquisitions developmental editor: Mike Thompson
Marketing coordinator: Kulsum Merchant
Editorial assistants: Samantha Waldie, Nick Raymond
Copy editor: Mariko Obokata
Proofreader: Claudia Kutchukian
Production editor: Jim Lyons, WordsWorth Communications
Text designer: Tara Wells, WordsWorth Communications
Indexer: Paula Pike, WordsWorth Communications
Cover designers: Stephen Cribbin & Simon Evers

Library and Archives Canada Cataloguing in Publication

Canada's resource economy in transition : the past, present, and future of Canadian staples industries / edited by Michael Howlett, Keith Brownsey.

Includes index.
ISBN 978-1-55239-255-3

1. Natural resources—Canada. 2. Industries—Canada. 3. Canada—Economic conditions—1991– 4. Canada—Economic policy—1991–
I. Howlett, Michael, 1955– II. Brownsey, Keith, 1955–

HC113.5.C244 2008   338.0971   C2007-906603-8

Contents

PART I Introduction

Chapter 1   Introduction: Toward a Post-Staples State?
Michael Howlett and Keith Brownsey

PART II The Post-Staples State in Theory and Practice

Chapter 2   The (Post) Staples Economy and the (Post) Staples State in Historical Perspective
Adam Wellstead

Chapter 9   A New Staples Industry? Complexity, Governance, and Canada's Diamond Mines
Patricia J. Fitzpatrick

Chapter 10   Knotty Tales: Forest Policy Narratives in an Era of Transition
Jocelyn Thorpe and L. Anders Sandberg

Chapter 11   The Future of Non-State Authority in Canadian Staples Industries: Assessing the Emergence of Forest Certification

Benjamin Cashore, Graeme Auld, James Lawson, and Deanna Newsom

PART V   Transmission Industries: Oil & Gas and Water

Chapter 12   The New Oil Order: The Staples Paradigm and the Canadian Upstream Oil and Gas Industry

Keith Brownsey

List of Figures

Preface

This volume is the product of a multi-year collaborative effort among the contributors who contemplated, conceptualized, and analyzed the changes each saw occurring in the contemporary Canadian "staples" or primary resource–driven political economy. Each contributor is an expert in a specific sector—from agriculture to fisheries, forests, mines, and energy issues. All contributors describe a period of transition in which "their" sector was moving from an older, "classic" model of staples development to either a mature-staples or a post-staples mode of production. At the outset of the project, however, it was unclear exactly how similar the sectors were, and whether their collective changes added up to a significant overall shift in the nature of Canada's primary resource industries and economy.

Beginning with several concurrent workshops held at the 2003 annual meeting of the Canadian Political Science Association in Halifax, the contributors to this volume set out to answer these questions. The first step involved understanding the history of the various staples economies in Canada. Specialists in each area undertook to provide detailed overviews of the past and present developments of the main primary staples commodities found in Canada: agriculture, fish, forests, mines, oil and gas, and water/hydroelectricity. These overviews are complemented by the identification of specific contemporary issues that mark a distinct break from how things were done in the past and serve as indicators of future development: genetically modified foods, aquaculture, forest certification, First Nations' and public participation in mining project development, the growth of the offshore oil and gas industry, and the potential for bulk water exports. Several scholars were recruited to discuss these issues. Their thoughts on the emerging post-staples economy helped to develop the concept of a post-staples transition. Finally, authors who had contributed elsewhere to the formulation of the post-staples concept were invited to submit chapters—specifically Tom Hutton, who writes on transitions to a post-staples political economy in Canada, and Adam Wellstead, who addresses the differences between "Ricardian" (or rent extraction economic development) and "Schumpeterian" (or production innovation–oriented) state systems involved in the conscious "steering" or direction of staples-based political economy.

Together, these elements combined to create a unique description, evaluation, analysis, and critique of the trajectories and development of both individual staples industries and the overall Canadian primary resource sector. Although the pattern of change uncovered in each primary industry was found to be unique, similarities were also evident. In each case, the "old" staples experience of rapid growth was followed by maturation and resource depletion. Similarly, each sector faced new challenges, not just from resource depletion but also from a more complex regulatory and production environment. Among these new challenges were concerns with First Nations' rights; with enhanced consultation and participation in decision making; with pressures both domestically and internationally toward the attainment of some level of environmental protection and sustainability; with the integration of high-technology inputs, such as biotechnology; and with the effects of the negotiation and implementation of free trade treaties on industries and governments, including open competition from lower-cost suppliers in other countries.

Some of these concerns are long-standing issues that have always faced staples industries, whereas others are much newer. They have, however, added new dimensions to the current and future prospects of these key sectors of the Canadian economy. This volume marks a first step in coming to terms with both ongoing and novel concerns and issues and with not only their impact on the future of Canada but also their impact on the future of other countries—from Norway and Saudi Arabia to Venezuela, New Zealand, Australia, and others—that similarly rely on bulk resource commodity exports for their economic well-being and for the health of their societies and ecosystems.

Acknowledgements

The authors of this volume collectively owe a debt of gratitude to the Toronto school of political economy; to authors such as Harold Innis, Arthur Lower, W.A. Mackintosh, Vernon Fowke, V.W. Bladen, Donald Creighton, and others whose analysis of Canada's place in North America and the world has provided a framework for understanding the significance of staples exports for Canada's economic and political development. We also owe a collective debt to those who followed in the footsteps of these pioneers, from Mel Watkins and H.V. Nelles to Daniel Drache, Wallace Clement, John Richards, Glen Williams, and others who resurrected and improved upon staples theory in their writings from the 1970s through to the present day.

More specifically, our thanks are extended to Robert Finbow who encouraged and helped organize the first meeting of authors at the Canadian Political Science Association meetings in Halifax in 2003 and to the many reviewers and commentators on the manuscript who helped focus its discussion and integrate its analysis. Our colleagues Luc Bernier and Jeremy Rayner sat through many evenings where the topic of conversation was the nature of a post-staples Canada. They have our gratitude. Thanks are also due to the highly professional team at Emond Montgomery Publications who shepherded the final manuscript to press, including Mike Thompson, Jim Lyons, and Mariko Obokata.

Finally, we must thank our families for their patience and good humour. Without their support, this project would not have been completed.

About the Authors

Graeme Auld is a PhD candidate at the Yale School of Forestry and Environmental Studies in New Haven, Connecticut.

Keith Brownsey teaches in the Department of Policy Studies at Mount Royal College in Calgary.

Benjamin Cashore is a Professor of Environmental Policy and Governance at Yale University's School of Forestry and Environmental Studies in New Haven, Connecticut.

Peter Clancy is a Professor of Political Science at St. Francis Xavier University in Antigonish, Nova Scotia.

Patricia J. Fitzpatrick is an Associate Professor in the Department of Geography at the University of Winnipeg.

Gunhild Hoogensen is an Associate Professor in the Department of Political Science at the University of Tromsø in Tromsø, Norway.

Michael Howlett is Burnaby Mountain Chair in the Department of Political Science at Simon Fraser University.

Thomas A. Hutton is a Professor at the Centre for Human Settlements at the University of British Columbia.

James Lawson is an Assistant Professor in the Department of Political Science at the University of Victoria.

Mary Louise McAllister is an Associate Professor in the Department of Environment and Resource Studies at the University of Waterloo.

John N. McDougall is a Professor of Political Science at the University of Western Ontario.

Elizabeth Moore is an Associate Director at Agriculture and Agri-Food Canada in Ottawa.

Alexander Netherton is a Professor at Malaspina University-College in Nanaimo, British Columbia, and a Research Associate with the Centre for Global Political Economy at Simon Fraser University.

Deanna Newsom is a researcher and long-term consultant for the Rainforest Alliance. She is based in Montreal.

Jeremy Rayner is an Associate Professor of Political Science at the University of Regina, where he also serves as Department Head.

L. Anders Sandberg is an Associate Dean and a Professor of Environmental Studies at York University in Toronto.

Grace Skogstad is a Professor in the Department of Political Science at the University of Toronto.

Jocelyn Thorpe is a PhD candidate in the Faculty of Environmental Studies at York University in Toronto.

Adam Wellstead holds a PhD from the University of Alberta and is a Forest Social Scientist with the Canadian Forest Service of Natural Resources Canada.

PART I
Introduction

CHAPTER 1

Introduction: Toward a Post-Staples State?

Michael Howlett and Keith Brownsey

For generations, provinces such as British Columbia and Quebec were known for their forestry resources, whereas others, such as Prince Edward Island, Saskatchewan, and Manitoba, were known for their farms. Ontario mining was legendary, as were the oil and gas wells of Alberta and the fisheries of Newfoundland, New Brunswick, and Nova Scotia (Howlett 2006). It was common wisdom, for example, that 50 cents of every dollar in British Columbia came from the forestry industry and that sawmills, pulp and paper, shingle mills, and other related industries employed hundreds of thousands of people in cutting, hauling, and producing various wood products. Those days are gone.

The Douglas fir no longer reigns in British Columbia's economy; in its place tourism, film and television production, aquaculture, and other industries have taken a strong if not leading role in the province's economy (Luke 2002; Howlett and Brownsey 1996). Although still important to British Columbia's economy, as with most other provinces, the original "staples" resource industries of farming, fishing, mining, and forestry have given way to service and other types of business. The wheat economy of the Prairies has similarly diversified into the production of a wide range of agricultural products, from canola seed to cattle, and wheat producers have been consolidated into large agribusiness. On the east coast, the Atlantic cod fisheries have vanished due to overfishing and poor management; on the west coast, the Pacific salmon stocks have dwindled. In the energy sector, the staples of hydroelectricity, crude oil, and natural gas have been transformed by environmental regulation, the decreasing conventional reserves of liquid hydrocarbons, conflict over land use, new technology, and scarcity of supply. As well, a security premium on oil and gas reserves adds to the final production and consumption cost. Mining, too, now relies on sophisticated non-traditional products, such as diamonds, for much of its growth.

No longer tied exclusively to the original staples industries, Canada is an advanced economy but one that remains different from the typical model of advanced manufacturing and services found in Europe, the United States, and Japan. The base of the Canadian economy retains its roots in early staples industries but with many new activities grafted into, and onto, those traditional sectors (Watkins 1997). At the same time that this transformation of the old staples political economy has ushered in some elements of a new political and social order, it has exacerbated or worsened many elements of the old (Clarkson 2001).

Changes in the staples economy are linked to the rise of new social movements, urbanization, and an increasingly disconnected regional politics. These changes are a product of the globalization and regionalization of markets, as the transformation of the staples economy can be attributed to such factors as industrialization and urbanization, resource depletion, increasing competition from low-cost producers, immigration from non-European countries, the regionalization of markets and industrial restructuring, and the rising importance of new social movements and knowledge elites (Howlett 2003; Hessing, Howlett, and Summerville 2005). Simply put, the traditional staples industries within Canada have been affected by a variety of factors, which together have transformed the Canadian political economy, moving it in the direction of a "new" or "post"-staples political economy (Hutton 1994); that is, one still very much linked to primary natural resource production, but in new forms and combinations.

The contributors to this volume provide an overview of these changes in the political economy of Canada's contemporary primary sector. Each tries to answer a series of questions with respect to a specific sector of the economy and its overall trajectory. First, what was the traditional staples economy in that sector? Second, how were the various staples industries organized within the centre–periphery or "metropolis–hinterland" model that characterized Canada's period of staples-led development? Third, how has each sector changed in recent years, and fourth, what factors led to change within each particular industry? Ultimately, taken together, the book addresses the larger issues set out by Thomas Hutton in his earlier work (Hutton 1994) and in chapter 3 of this volume: "How has a staples political economy evolved in Canada? And if a new post-staples political economy has emerged, how does it differ from a traditional staples economy?"

OVERVIEW: THE EVOLUTION OF A STAPLES POLITICAL ECONOMY

A *staple* refers to a raw or unfinished bulk commodity product that is sold in export markets. Timber, fish, oil and gas, and minerals are typical staples, usually extracted and sold in external markets without significant amounts of processing, but so are most agricultural products, energy, and, increasingly, water (Innis 1930, 1933). Clapp (1998) has argued that specific resource sectors typically follow a similar pattern of development caused by a fall in profits and dislocations, after the exhaustion of easily accessible resources and their "replacement" by dwindling or more difficult-to-access supplies.

In this view, individual staples sectors typically follow four phases as they grow and evolve. The first phase is a period of rapid expansion as the new staple is developed using easy-to-access, plentiful natural resource supplies. The second phase is a maturing phase as the limits of easily accessible, low-cost resource supplies are reached and/or increased competition limits both market growth and the rate of the expansion of the sector. The third phase is one of disequilibrium as the state and private sector respond to the slowing of growth by trying to force expansion through subsidies, weaker regulations, or the search for new resource supplies. These efforts at expansion can create some growth, but it is usually short-lived as subsidized supplies are again depleted and costs rise. The fourth phase is one of either decline or crisis as the subsidized expansion is shut down and the industry downsizes, moves to other countries still offering plentiful cheap supplies, or makes a transition to a new form of resource activity, as when aquaculture activities increase to offset declines in the wild fishery (Clapp 1998).

An economy based on a single or a multiple set of "primary" or resource industries has been a common feature at various points of their histories for many countries, ranging from the United States (North 1961), to Argentina, Chile, New Zealand, Australia, Canada, Brazil, Norway, and many others (Hirschman 1958; Watkins 1997); and many countries still rely on a single resource industry, including oil-reliant states in the Middle East and central Asia and agriculture- and mineral-reliant countries in Africa (Freudenburg 1992). Some of these countries have evolved from a staples base to a manufacturing or service base, but others have not, or have only partially done so (Watkins 1963, 1977; Freudenburg 1992). An economy reliant on a single staple would be expected to follow the same four stages, overall, as its dominant industry. Countries based on multiple staples, of course, could have more complex patterns of development but, ultimately, would also be expected to pass toward the final post-staples stage.

Thus, in historical terms, we can construct an ideal-typical sequence of staples-based political economic regimes:

1. First, there is the "frontier staples state." In this initial period of staples development, easily available bulk commodities (for example, fisheries, furs, and timber) in the period of European exploration and the colonial enterprise are exported to metropolitan countries. The extraction of these resources in raw or unprocessed form acts as a leading influence on social formation and settlement patterns, characterized by conflict between both contending

powers (for example, France, Britain, and the United States) and trading companies over territory and resources, and marked by widespread displacement of Aboriginal societies (Innis 1956; Lower 1973).

2. Second, there is the archetypal or classical expanding staples state. In Canada, this state developed with the expansion of agriculture, forestry, fisheries, and mining in the 19th and early 20th centuries, based on comparative advantage in natural resource endowments; incorporating the formation of a national core–periphery staples economy described in compelling terms by Harold Innis (1933) and Donald Creighton (1937); dominated by the industrial metropolises of Montreal and Toronto and their satellites; and with the extraction of staples constituting a lead *development* sector (that is, investment, employment, and community formation) for the national periphery (Watkins 1963; Bertram 1963; Buckley 1958).

3. Third, there is the "mature staples state." Here, the rapid expansion of staples extraction dating from the First World War is facilitated by new industrial production technologies and Fordist labour organization, stimulated by both domestic and export market demand and coincident with the growth of "core" cities linked to resource peripheries at the national *and* provincial scales (Clarke-Jones 1987).

4. Fourth, there is the new or post-staples state. This state shows signs of emerging in the late 20th century and early 21st century in many countries as a set of new conditions influences the trajectory of staples development. In Canada, since the 1980s, this state was characterized by increasing pressures on resources and allied staples sectors and on communities derived from resource depletion, global market pressures, the relentless substitution of capital for labour, social factors (notably environmentalism and its variants), and a context of increasing metropolitan hegemony and transnational urbanism (Hutton 1994).

As Hutton has observed, several possible permutations can occur on the general staples "theme." Thus, in addition to the frontier and "classic" staples political economy—based on easily accessible and ample resource supplies, labour-intensive means of production, social insurance, and export-enhancing infrastructural investment—the "mature, advanced" staples political economy also exists, characterized by a substantial depletion of original resource endowments and consequent increasing pressure on the part of industry to access more costly or protected stocks and supplies. In most countries, this intensification is resisted by environmental groups originating both in urban centres divorced from the resource economy and in hinterland communities desiring to replace "exploitation" with "sustainability" as the operating motif of their livelihood. Mature staples economies feature the increasing capital- and technology-intensiveness of resource extraction processes and consequent decreases in employment in the staples sector, the evolution of development from "pure" extraction to increased refining and secondary processing of resource commodities, and the diversification of economic structures in cities and small towns with growth in non-staples-related areas, such as tourism, local administration, education, health, and other social services (Hutton 1994).

Although a mature staples political economy may still be characterized as resource-dependent, such an economy is more diffused and diversified than in the past. As Clapp (1998) and Hutton (1994) suggest, if this diffusion, diversification, and resource depletion continue, the result may be an economy that evolves even further toward a post-staples economy; that is, an economy characterized by critical resource sectors under extreme pressure and the likelihood of even greater contractions in the near future. Under such conditions, production costs increase and unprocessed bulk commodities often can no longer compete with low-cost suppliers in traditional export markets, resulting in an economy's internal reconfiguration toward growth and development. For the countries concerned, such a transition typically involves a significant increase in the metropolitan shares of population and employment; the emergence of regional economic centres; the decline of smaller resource-dependent communities; the increased prominence of the internal market for the remaining smaller-scale resource industries; and the transition of existing staples sectors toward hi-tech, higher-value-added activities and products (Hutton 1994).

For countries such as Canada, Australia, New Zealand, Chile, and others that remain based on multiple staples resource extraction (Hessing, Howlett, and Summerville 2005), knowing how these transitions are occurring is critical, as is knowing to what extent each component primary industry, and thus the country as a whole, has approached Clapp's (and Hutton's) final phase. This book contributes to discussion of this key issue in studies of political economy and economic development (Williams 1983; Britton 1996; Niosi 1991b; Clarkson 2001).

THE SIGNIFICANCE OF A TRANSITION TO A NEW OR POST-STAPLES POLITICAL ECONOMY

The significance of having an economy based on exporting unfinished bulk goods is manifold. First, such an economy creates continuing issues with respect to resource technologies, supplies, profits, rents, location, and availability (Hessing, Howlett, and Summerville 2005). As Naylor (1972) and others have also shown, the development of a staples-based economy can trigger government and private sector investments in large-scale infrastructure activities, such as transportation and communications facilities required to coordinate the extraction and shipment of bulk commodities to markets in distant lands, as well as provisions of export subsidies and credits designed to facilitate trade and the distortion of the banking and financial system away from consumer and small business credit to a concentration on large industrial loans and profits (Naylor 1972; Stone 1984; Whalley 1985). This development can constitute, as Watkins (1963) and Freudenburg (1992) have noted, a "staples trap" or an "addictive economy," in which a cycle of large-scale resource exploitation is entrenched, with one staple succeeding another as supplies diminish or worldwide demand declines.

Second, the characteristics of natural resource exploitation or harvesting affect activities in related areas, such as education and training. As the Toronto school of staples theorists noted many years ago when undertaking their pioneering studies of Canada's primary sector (Fay 1934), frontier staples economies, for example, have only a limited need for education and technical skills and entrench a system of metropolitan–hinterland links in both economy and culture (Watkins 1963; Freudenburg 1992). The impact of natural resource exploitation on the structure and organization of public services as a whole is no less telling (Hodgetts 1973).

Third, the relative success or failure of a natural resource or primary industry–based economy also indirectly affects many other areas of social life, such as the ability of governments to pay for or support welfare, health and social policies, or economic diversification and regional development (Howlett, Netherton, and Ramesh 1999). That is, basing a country's wealth on foreign markets also requires populations, governments, and industries to anticipate and react to their continued vulnerability to international market conditions. The fact that staples-reliant countries have tended to focus on markets in foreign lands is significant in itself. Because most staples-based countries have a monopoly or near-monopoly on the production of only a very few resources or agricultural goods, producers must sell at prices set by international conditions of supply and demand. Although international demand for most resources—outside of wartime—has increased at a relatively steady but low rate, world supplies of particular primary products are highly variable. A good harvest, the discovery of significant new reserves of minerals or oil, or the addition of new production capacity in the fishery or forest products sectors can quickly add to world supplies and drive down world prices until demand slowly catches up and surpasses supplies, resulting in sudden price increases that trigger a new investment cycle and a subsequent downturn (Anderson 1985; Webb and Zacher 1988). As Cameron (1986) has noted, these fluctuations in international supplies account for the "boom and bust" cycles prevalent in most resource industries and, by implication, most resource-based economies, and lead affected populations to press governments to provide a range of social, unemployment, and other types of insurance schemes and to invest large-scale public expenditures in areas of job creation and employment.

Most observers would agree that Canada can be historically characterized as having had a staples economy, which has had a significant impact on the evolution of Canada's resource regimes and practices (Wilkinson 1985). As the discussions in other chapters of this book show, however, considerable disagreement exists over whether this depiction continues to apply to all of Canada's primary industries and hence, overall, whether it continues to characterize the general Canadian economy and to what extent it will continue to do so in future years (Howlett 2003). Earlier debates within the staples school centred on whether Canada had emerged as an industrial power in the wake of the wheat boom and manufacturing activities associated with the First World War. However, the failure of the manufacturing sector to grow outside of wartime led to the re-emergence of staples analysis in the 1960s and 1970s (Drache 1978; Williams 1983). Current debates focus less on the impact of a transition from primary to secondary activities than on the undeniable growth in service-sector employment and production in the post–Second World War era (Clement and Williams 1989; Clement 1997)[1] and the transition of many staples industries toward more capital- and technology-intensive forms of production—undermining the association of large parts of the population directly with staples-extraction activities and exacerbating urban–rural divides. The idea that significant parts of the economy have entered a new post-staples mode has led to a variety of debates in Canada concerning the consequences of such a development for government policy-making, society, culture, the environment, and the economy.[2]

This book helps to shed light on these questions by carefully assessing the development of traditional staples, such as farm products, fish, minerals, trees, oil and gas, and hydroelectricity, as well as by chronicling the rise of new variations on these traditional themes or industries, such as genetically modified foods, aquaculture, diamond mines, offshore oil and gas, eco-forestry, and water exports. The authors in this collection examine the development of Canada's primary industries and provide an extensive elaboration and critique of the post-staples thesis. They look for evidence of the transition of traditional resource sector activity from a mature to a post-staples phase but find this transition to be the case in only several specific sectors, whereas most sectors continue to exist in a mature (although sometimes depleted) staples configuration. Overall, the authors of this book find that the evidence for a general transition to a post-staples state is mixed, with some trends apparent in this direction, but other industries remaining in a mature staples mode.

ORGANIZATION OF THE BOOK

The book is organized into pairs of chapters examining different Canadian primary industries. The first chapter in each pair provides an overview of the development of a sector in terms of the industry involved, government regulations, and the major problems the sector has faced. The second chapter in the pair examines a specific contemporary issue in the sector, which reveals much about the nature of any transitions occurring in that sector. This analysis of the sectoral structure of Canada's primary industries supports the idea that Canada is involved in a very uneven transitional process in a movement from a staples state to a post-staples state.

The book begins, however, with two chapters that review the classic staples approach to political economy as defined by Harold Innis in the 1920s and 1930s and set out the principle elements of the evolutionary model of staples industry development described above. Adam Wellstead surveys the Innisian approach to political economy, while Thomas Hutton identifies the central elements of any emergent post-staples regime. Wellstead uses the concept of the competitive state to examine the link between state and industry in contemporary Canada. In his chapter, Hutton argues that the resource economy is indeed in decline, supplanted by the rise of not simply urban regions but also international or metropolitan cities as generators of wealth and employment.

Grace Skogstad and Elizabeth Moore then begin the examination of specific staples resource, or primary, sectors by examining the changes occurring in the Canadian agricultural sector. Skogstad's overview of this staple industry discusses the programs and problems facing the farming and ranching communities in an increasingly competitive international marketplace and the federal state's policy response to this situation. Arguing that agriculture—specifically grain production—is a mature staples sector, Moore provides a detailed examination of the federal government's support for genetically engineered crops as a possible technological solution to the economic problems facing the industry. Her conclusions cast doubt on decades of national agricultural policy and suggest a move toward a post-staples future in this sector.

Gunhild Hoogensen, Jeremy Rayner and Michael Howlett then focus their attention on the Atlantic and Pacific fisheries. One of the oldest extractive industries in the country, the fishing industry faces historically low levels of stocks at the same time as international competition has increased. Hoogensen discusses the problems facing the creation of a sustainable Canadian fishery and the political, social, and economic impact of the moves toward free trade in goods and services on the prospects of reversing the declines in traditional fisheries. Rayner and Howlett assess the possibilities and problems facing fin and shellfish aquaculture on both coasts, a new staples industry developed in order to offset declines in wild harvests. They conclude that environmental and market issues have restricted the expansion of this technologically based post-staples industry, limiting its ability to completely offset declines in the wild fishery.

Forestry, another traditional staples industry, has also undergone extensive change through resource depletion, international competition, and technological change. Jocelyn Thorpe and L. Anders Sandberg argue that in many communities and jurisdictions the response has been to try to change the nature of the forest from being the basis of extractive industries to "attractive" industries, such as eco-tourism. The rise of the environmental movement, Aboriginal land claims, and immigration have fundamentally altered the conditions necessary to maintain the traditional forest industry, but the new attractive model is also much more ecologically and culturally damaging than many allege. In their chapter on forest certification, Benjamin Cashore, Graeme Auld, James Lawson, and Deanna Newsom look at new non-state forms of governance that have emerged as the traditional forest industry has tried to move beyond its "cut and run" past and assuage the concerns of environmentalists and "green" consumers. They study the emergence of forest certification schemes in Canada and the impact of international environmental groups and voluntary regulatory regimes on the way Canadian resources are managed. The authors claim that the international certification movement has provided a new model for the regulation of forest staples extraction, one that has altered the political and social context of the industry in its very late mature phase.

Mary Louise McAllister tackles another old traditional staples industry—mining. Despite its declining importance in the overall Canadian economy, the mineral sector remains an important industry for many rural communities. But low-cost competition, environmental concerns, new technologies, and innovative labour processes such as long-distance commuting have transformed both the industry and the communities that depend on it. The industry has responded to these challenges with innovative programs in community partnerships, sustainability, and new work relations. However, McAllister finds the mining sector continues to operate in a pattern consistent with a mature staples economy. While McAllister focuses on the entire mineral sector, Patricia Fitzpatrick provides a case study of the development and regulation of the new and important diamond mining industry in Canada's northern territories. She finds the governance structures, environmental concerns, and Aboriginal land claim framework within which the diamond mining industry operates have created a very different model of development from the old pattern of company towns and mine tailings dumps. The attempt to manage the pressure of resource extraction, minimize adverse social and environmental impacts, and balance the economic benefits among various groups describes the current situation in this mature staples industry.

In his chapter, Keith Brownsey looks at the oil and gas sector and argues that the upstream industry in the western sedimentary basin has followed a similar pattern to other mature resource industries. With the decline of conventional reserves, non-conventional resources, such as the oil sands and coalbed methane, have become increasingly important. Technology, skilled labour, and massive infusions of capital are all required to keep the industry operating. Small producers, however, have aligned themselves with provincial governments—especially in Alberta—to push back against the regulatory and environmental incursions of the

federal state because they simply do not have the ability to meet the new requirements and requisites for continued growth. As a result of these political alignments,
the producing provinces find themselves in conflict with the federal government
over a range of issues, from the Kyoto Protocol to worker training. Peter Clancy's
study of the Atlantic offshore examines another aspect of this industry. Here, various
local interests compete with national and international forces to develop and regulate the industry. However, unlike in the western provinces, while local interests
have struggled to have a voice in resource development, the federal government
has extended its offshore jurisdiction, and small capital is insufficient to provide
both the technology and the expertise required for offshore exploration and production. The influence of metropolitan and post-materialist political forces, such as
environmental concerns, workplace health and safety, and Aboriginal land claims,
illustrate the continuing problems facing this advanced, mature staples sector.

Finally, John McDougall tackles the issue of water. Although not yet a staple
product due to bans on exports, as a "potential staple" water has quickly become
an issue both for Canadian–American trade relations and domestic politics. Comparing water with oil and gas exports to the United States, McDougall makes the
claim that liquid hydrocarbons and water have many market similarities. The
convergence of the political economy of oil and water are illustrated, he states, by
aspects of free trade policy regimes that despite Canadian domestic, political, and
environmental concerns, the United States may use to put pressure on the Canadian
state to allow exports of fresh water through massive diversion projects or open
up water services to foreign competition. Alex Netherton expands the theme of
water in his study of hydroelectricity generation in Canada. He traces the evolution
of Canadian hydroelectric power production, from a privately owned industry to
an agent of provincial economic development and finally to its current status as an
export commodity tied to international distribution systems or grids. Regulatory
reform in the United States, Netherton claims, has forced the restructuring of the
Canadian industry, and a new technology-based export product has emerged in
a post-staples environment.

Together these chapters present a detailed picture of a changing Canadian staples
political economy. No longer on the periphery of empire, Canada has become a
mature staples state, and many of its regions—urban and rural—and resource
sectors have developed elements of a post-staples political economy. These chapters begin the process of explaining and understanding the political, social, and
economic impact of this situation.

NOTES

1. On the service sector specifically, see Warton 1969 and Grubel and Walker 1989.

2. Many of these discussions centre on the role of technology in driving service-sector development. See Anderson et al. 1998; Niosi 1991a and 1991b.

REFERENCES

Anderson, F.J. 1985. *Natural resources in Canada.* Toronto: Methuen.

Anderson, R., Cohn, T., Day, C., Howlett, M., and Murray, C., eds. 1998. *Innovation systems in a global context: The North American experience.* Montreal and Kingston: McGill-Queen's University Press.

Bertram, G.W. 1963. Economic growth and Canadian industry, 1870–1915: The staple model and the take-off hypothesis. *Canadian Journal of Economics and Political Science* 29(2): 162–84.

Britton, J.N.H., ed. 1996. *Canada and the global economy: The geography of structural and technological change.* Montreal and Kingston: McGill-Queen's University Press.

Buckley, K. 1958. The role of staple industries in Canadian economic development. *Journal of Economic History* 18(4): 439–50.

Cameron, D.R. 1986. The growth of government spending: The Canadian experience in comparative perspective. In *State and Society*, ed. K. Banting, 21–52. Toronto: University of Toronto Press.

Clapp, R.A. 1998. The resource cycle in forestry and fishing. *Canadian Geographer* 42(2): 129–44.

Clarke-Jones, M. 1987. *A staple state: Canadian industrial resources in Cold War.* Toronto: University of Toronto Press.

Clarkson, S. 2001. The multi-level state: Canada in the semi-periphery of both continentalism and globalization. *Review of International Political Economy* 8(3): 501–27.

Clement, W., ed. 1997. *Understanding Canada: Building on the new Canadian political economy.* Montreal and Kingston: McGill-Queen's University Press.

Clement, W., and Williams, G., eds. 1989. *The new Canadian political economy.* Montreal and Kingston: McGill-Queen's University Press.

Creighton, D.G. 1937. *Empire of the St. Lawrence.* Toronto: Macmillan.

Drache, D. 1978. Re-discovering Canadian political economy. In *A Practical Guide to Canadian Political Economy*, eds. W. Clement and D. Drache, 1–53. Toronto: Lorimer.

Fay, C.R. 1934. The Toronto school of economic history. *Economic History* 3(1): 168–71.

Freudenburg, W.R. 1992. Addictive economies: Extractive industries and vulnerable localities in a changing world economy. *Rural Sociology* 57(3): 305–32.

Grubel, H.G., and Walker, M.A. 1989. *Service industry growth: Causes and effects.* Vancouver: Fraser Institute.

Hessing, M., Howlett, M., and Summerville, T. 2005. *Canadian natural resource and environmental policy: Political economy and public policy.* Vancouver: University of British Columbia Press.

Hirschman, A.O. 1958. *The strategy of economic development.* New Haven, CT: Yale University Press.

Hodgetts, J.E. 1973. *The Canadian public service.* Toronto: University of Toronto Press.

Howlett, M. 2003. Canadian environmental policy and the natural resource sector: Paradoxical aspects of the transition to a post-staples political economy. In *The Integrity Gap: Canada's Environmental Policy and Institutions,* eds. E. Lee and A. Perl, 42–67. Vancouver: University of British Columbia Press.

Howlett, M. 2006. De-mythologizing provincial political economies: The development of the service sectors in the provinces, 1911–2001. In *Provinces: Canadian Provincial Politics,* ed. C. Dunn, 261–83. Peterborough, ON: Broadview Press.

Howlett, M., and Brownsey, K. 1996. From timber to tourism: The political economy of British Columbia. In *Politics, Policy and Government in British Columbia,* ed. R.K. Carty, 18–31. Vancouver: University of British Columbia Press, 1996.

Howlett, M., Netherton, A., and Ramesh, M. 1999. *The political economy of Canada: An introduction.* Toronto: Oxford University Press.

Hutton, T.A. 1994. *Visions of a "post-staples" economy: Structural change and adjustment issues in British Columbia,* working paper PI #3. Vancouver: University of British Columbia Centre for Human Settlements.

Innis, H.A. 1930. *The fur trade in Canada: An Introduction to Canadian economic history.* Toronto: University of Toronto Press.

Innis, H.A. 1933. *Problems of staple production in Canada.* Toronto: The Ryerson Press.

Innis, H.A. 1956. *Essays in Canadian economic history.* Toronto: University of Toronto Press.

Lower, A.R.M. 1973. *Great Britain's woodyard: British America and the timber trade,* Montreal and Kingston: McGill-Queen's University Press.

Luke, T.W. 2002. The uneasy transition from extractive to attractive models of development. In *A Political Space: Reading the Global through Clayoquot Sound,* eds. W. Magnusson and K. Shaw, 91–92. Montreal and Kingston: McGill-Queen's University Press.

Naylor, R.T. 1972. The rise and fall of the third commercial empire of the St. Lawrence. In *Capitalism and the National Question in Canada,* ed. G. Teeple, 1–42. Toronto: University of Toronto Press.

Niosi, J. 1991a. Canada's national system of innovation. *Science and Public Policy* 18(2): 78–90.

Niosi, J., ed. 1991b. *Technology and national competitiveness: Oligopoly, technological innovation and international competition.* Montreal and Kingston: McGill-Queen's University Press.

North, D.C. 1961. *The economic growth of the United States.* Englewood Cliffs, NJ: Prentice Hall.

Stone, F. 1984. *Canada, the GATT and the international trade system.* Montreal: Institute for Research on Public Policy.

Warton, D.A. 1969. The service industries in Canada, 1946–1966. In *Production and Productivity in the Service Industries,* ed. V.R. Fuchs, 158–73. New York: Columbia University Press.

Watkins, M.H. 1963. A staple theory of economic growth. *Canadian Journal of Economics and Political Science* 29(2): 141–58.

Watkins, M.H. 1977. The staple theory revisited. *Journal of Canadian Studies* 12(5): 83–95.

Watkins, M. 1997. Canadian capitalism in transition. In *Understanding Canada: Building on the New Canadian Political Economy,* ed. W. Clement, 19–42. Montreal and Kingston: McGill-Queen's University Press.

Webb, M.C., and Zacher, M.W. 1988. *Canada and international mineral-markets: Dependence, instability and foreign policy.* Kingston: Queen's University Centre for Resource Studies.

Whalley, J. 1985. *Canadian trade policies and the world economy.* Toronto: University of Toronto Press.

Wilkinson, B. 1985. Canada's resource industries. In *Canada's Resource Industries and Water Export Policy,* ed. J. Whalley, 1–159. Toronto: University of Toronto Press.

Williams, G. 1983. *Not for export: Toward a political economy of Canada's arrested industrialization.* Toronto: McClelland & Stewart.

PART II
**The Post-Staples
State in Theory
and Practice**

CHAPTER 2

The (Post) Staples Economy and the (Post) Staples State in Historical Perspective

Adam Wellstead

INTRODUCTION

This chapter examines the evolution of the contemporary staples state. It first outlines the economic importance of contemporary staples production at both the national and the provincial levels. The next section chronologically defines the staples state in relation to popular characterizations of its pre-20th-century form to its present competitive state. The third section discusses the importance of governance and the forms of coordination within competitive states.

Two forms of competitive states are relevant to a discussion of the Canadian (post) staples state: the Schumpeterian and Ricardian competitive states. The main characteristics of the Schumpeterian competitive state and its development closely correspond to Hutton's discussion of a post-staples state (see chapter 3). The importance of the Schumpeterian competitive state is the focus of Jessop's (2002a) *The Future of the Capitalist State*. The Ricardian competitive state receives only a passing reference (one paragraph) in that work; however, its characteristics support the argument that the contemporary staples states that continue to flourish throughout many parts of Canada are in fact Ricardian competitive states. Below, we describe these two images of the competitive state and their relation to the contemporary Canadian staples context.

THE ORIGINS OF STAPLES POLITICAL ECONOMY: HAROLD INNIS AND THE TORONTO SCHOOL

The staples approach was developed primarily by Canadian economists and historians whose works are rooted firmly in the historical examination of the development of the Canadian economy. They describe the effects of this development on Canadian social and political life. Originally, the staples thesis set out an export-led model of economic growth and attempted to describe how regional natural resource endowments led to the autonomous demands for and dependence upon exports, their spreading effects (linkages) to the rest of the economy, and technological changes. The school derives its name from the emphasis on staples industries, which, following Gordon Bertram (1963, 75), are defined as those industries "based on agriculture and extractive resources, not requiring elaborate processing and finding a large portion of their market in international trade." Staples theorists view Canadian political economy as having been shaped by the export of successive staples over the course of Canadian history, from the earliest colonial times to the modern era.

The staples approach has its origins in research into Canadian social, political, and economic history carried out in Canadian universities, roughly between 1920 and 1940, by members of what were then known as departments of political economy. The two most prominent scholars following this approach were Harold Innis and W.A. Mackintosh. Numerous other scholars during the same era arrived at similar conclusions regarding the significance of the resource industries and their impact on Canadian settlement (Innis 1943), including, most notably, Arthur Lower, a Queen's University historian; Donald G. Creighton, a University of Toronto historian; and S.A. Saunders, a Dalhousie University historian. Lower (1938) explored the origins and impact of the lumber industry on Canadian development, whereas Creighton (1937) adopted several staples tenets in developing his Laurentian thesis of Canadian history (Berger 1987). Saunders examined the development of the Maritime provinces using a staples framework (Saunders 1939).

By the mid-1930s, a sufficient number of scholars were working in a similar vein to allow the publication of a nine-volume *Frontiers of Settlement* series on the history of Canadian economic, political, and social development. Between 1934 and 1938, this series of books published some of the finest writings in this tradition, including submissions from Lower (1938), Innis and Lower (1936), Mackintosh (1934), and Morton (1938). In 1939, major submissions by Saunders (1939) and Mackintosh (1939) to the Royal Commission on Dominion–Provincial Relations (known familiarly as the Rowell-Sirois commission) presented the development of the Canadian economy in staple terms; and in 1943, V.W. Bladen (1943) relied on a staples framework to write the first textbook on Canadian political economy.

Harold Innis, an economist at the University of Toronto and one-time head of the American Economics Association, wrote a series of books discussing the significance of various early resource industries to the development of different parts of Canada. Published from the 1920s to the 1940s, this series comprised numerous essays and edited writings, including the classic works *A History of the Canadian Pacific Railway* (1923), *The Fur Trade in Canada* (1930), and *The Cod Fisheries* (1940).

Innis argued that the political economy of Canada was shaped by the successive concentration on exports of cod, fur, lumber (and pulp and paper), agricultural products (principally wheat), and minerals, which were all destined for the metropolitan economies of Europe and later the United States. As Innis summarized his staples thesis:

> The economic history of Canada has been dominated by the discrepancy between the centre and the margin of western civilization. Energy has been directed toward the exploitation of staple products and the tendency has been cumulative. The raw material supplied to the mother country stimulated manufacturers of the finished product and also of the product which were in demand in the colony. Large-scale production of raw materials was encouraged by improvement of technique of production, of marketing, and of transport as well as by improvement in the manufacture of the finished product … Agriculture, industry, transportation, trade, finance, and governmental activities tend to become subordinate to the production of the staple for a highly specialized manufacturing community. (Innis 1956, 385)

Innis argued that Canada's export of staples products in unprocessed or semi-processed forms was necessitated by the lack of technological capability to process these products within Canada and that exports were also essential to supporting the improved living conditions that had brought Europeans to Canada in the first place. The exportation of staples and the importation of consumer goods, although satisfying the needs of the immigrants, primarily benefited the interests of the industrialized nations, which secured a cheap and reliable supply of raw materials. The domestic commercial interests involved in the movement and financing of the export–import trade also benefited from the process.

With the passage of time, Innis argued, increasingly larger local resources had to be devoted to resource exports, which exacerbated the staples orientation of the political economy. The railways built to transport wheat and lumber could not pay for themselves, which made it necessary to export pulp, paper, and minerals to take advantage of the railway's unused capacity (Innis 1956). The increasing dependence on staples correspondingly widened Canada's technological backwardness, which only deepened the country's dependence on unprocessed or semiprocessed raw materials. This situation was different from that in the United States, where a less harsh geography and a larger population enabled the economy to depend less on staples exports and to develop a large and prosperous agriculture sector capable of supporting both a large domestic population and an industrial sector to serve the growing domestic market.

Climatic and topographical difficulties prevented Canada from undergoing a similar process of development, and the resulting dependence on staples exports, according to Innis, doomed Canada's chances of developing a domestic industrial base. Reliance on staples exports necessitated increasingly large investments in building a transportation infrastructure. The heavy debt-servicing charges of such investments diverted funds from other areas of the economy, including manufacturing. The dependence on staples export also increasingly exposed the Canadian economy to the vagaries of international commodity markets, which tend to witness violent fluctuations as a new capacity comes on stream in different countries, lowering world prices until world demand catches up with global supplies and prices rise accordingly. The cumulative impact, according to Innis, was that the Canadian economy became caught in what Mel Watkins (1963) would later call a "staples trap." This form of economic life could provide relatively high standards of living to citizens of exporting countries, but only as long as domestic resource supplies and world demand either remained constant or increased. Any declines in demand or increases in supply would have drastic consequences for the domestic political economy, which would be poorly placed to respond to the challenge of finding a new economic base. As a result, Innis and most staples political economists following his lead were pessimistic about Canada's future as a reasonably wealthy "developed" country.

After a slowing down of scholarly work during the Second World War, more work in the staples tradition emerged following the war, including works by Vernon Fowke (1946) and Kenneth Buckley (1958). Both point out the tremendous economic spinoffs to the Canadian economy that had accrued as a result of booming wheat exports between the 1890s and 1920s. They argue that a large proportion of the benefits did not flow to the western wheat producers but to Canadian manufacturers, most of them located in central Canada.

By the 1950s, many different aspects of Canada's resource-dependent economy were being investigated (Easterbrook 1959), including the impact on provincial development (Dales 1957) and the impact of U.S. investment in key industries (Aitkin 1959, 1961). The high point in the staples analysis, in a practical political sense, likely occurred in the late 1950s when the Royal Commission on Canada's Economic Prospects (known familiarly as the Gordon commission) focused its efforts on planning for and controlling the various effects of resource-led economic growth on Canadian society (Canada, Royal Commission on Canada's Economic Prospects 1957).

Shortly thereafter, the staples thesis received its clearest formulation in Watkins's staple theory of economic growth. Watkins makes it clear that the staples approach applies only to "new" countries, such as those in North and South America, Australia, and New Zealand. The distinguishing feature of these nations is their favourable ratio of natural resources (staples) to labour and capital, which makes it obvious that staples necessarily form the cornerstone of their economies.

> The limited … domestic market, and the factor proportion—an abundance of land relative to labour and capital—create a comparative advantage in resource-intensive exports, or staples. Economic development is a process of diversification around an export base. The central concept of a staple theory, therefore, is the spread effects of the export sector, that is the impact of export activity on the domestic economy and society. (Watkins 1963, 153–54)

The extent to which the spread effects are realized depends on three kinds of "linkages" in the export of particular staples: "backward linkage, forward linkage, and final demand linkage" (ibid., 155). The forward linkage involves investments to further process the staples, such as the converting of lumber into pulp and (preferably) paper. The backward linkage involves investments in production of the inputs required by the staples sector, such as railways to move wheat or machinery used in mining and logging. The final demand linkage is created by the expenditure of incomes generated in the production and export of staples; this linkage exists to the extent that those incomes are used to invest in manufacturing of the goods consumed in the home country.

The establishment of these three linkages cannot be taken for granted. Much depends on the nature of the staple itself. Cod fishing afforded few linkages because, at the end of the season, the fishermen tended to return to their homeland after they had caught and cured their fish; they didn't invest in backward or forward industries. Wheat, in contrast, attracted permanent immigrants who established, for example, an agricultural machinery industry (backward linkage) as well as food milling, processing, and preserving industries (forward linkages). Wheat production also automatically led to some degree of final demand linkage as industries were established to supply basic needs, such as clothes, shoes, and toiletries, to farmers and other members of the agricultural community.

The importance of final demand linkage is clearly the greatest if the economy is to diversify. But the full realization of this linkage remains elusive if the staples exports are in the hands of foreign investors who siphon their profits to their home countries, leaving little behind to invest in local manufacturing. Besides, it is easier and more profitable for foreigners to supply manufactured goods to the local economy from their home country, thus making profits in both the export of staples and the import of manufactured goods. The most significant problem, however, is that staples dependence fosters an "export mentality, resulting in an overconcentration of resources in the export sector and a reluctance to promote domestic development" (Watkins 1963, 152). If this overconcentration happens, the economy is caught in the "staples trap": it becomes dependent on the economies that receive its exports and supply its manufactured goods. Toward the end of his article, however, Watkins (ibid., 157) indicated that he was optimistic that eliminating the "inhibiting export mentality" is within the means of policy-makers.

Ultimately, following Gordon Laxer (1989, 180–81), we can identify four main "analytical assumptions of the staples school." First, staples theorists believe that the key to understanding Canadian history is to discover the export commodity that the economy depends on. They argue that the Canadian state and Canadian capital have devoted themselves single-mindedly to discovering and extracting bulk resource commodities or staples that have a ready export market. The money thus derived is used to pay wages to Canadian workers and finance imports of goods demanded by Canadian consumers. Canadian economic growth, then, is intimately linked to the demand for staples in the industrialized nations, and this demand has shaped economic development in Canada: any shift in demand for the staple in question, although inconsequential for the importing country, has a pervasive impact on the local economy, which is dependent on its export. For example, the fading of the fashion in beaver-felt hats in Europe had a serious, de-bilitating effect on the early 19th-century Canadian economy, which was almost completely dependent on the export of furs (Innis 1956).

Second, staples political economists argue that Canadian political life is heavily influenced by the country's staples export–dependent economy because economic wealth and political power are concentrated in Canadian business and political elites—often the same people—who act as the instruments of interests in the in-dustrialized countries importing the staples. According to this idea, the Canadian business community has been more interested in promoting continued and ex-panded staples-resource exports than in acting as entrepreneurs to develop an industrialized Canadian manufacturing economy.

Third, the staples school emphasizes history as a key to understanding the Canadian political economy. A study of the actual history of Canadian economic development enables these scholars to overcome the limitations of other models developed to understand the industrialized economies of Europe. They clearly understand that Canada and many other "new world" economies have unique features that the most traditional theories cannot account for.

Fourth, analysts in this school argue that the need to overcome geographical impediments to the expansion of staples exports helps explain the state's role in a staples-dependent market economy. They argue that confronting the harshness of the Canadian terrain and the physical distances that had to be traversed to transport staples from the hinterland to ocean-loading ports required a transportation and communications infrastructure, but Canadian business could not afford such a large capital expenditure. Instead, projects such as canals and river improvements, railway construction, and the establishment of telephone, electrical, and airline systems were all undertaken by the Canadian state.

THE POST-STAPLES THESIS

The prevailing view of Canada's economy, as well as some provincial economies, is that a shift from dependence on staples production began in the 1960s, leading to the emergence of a new form of political economy. Exactly what this political economy is, however, remains uncertain and controversial. One view, suggested by Thomas Hutton (1994 and chapter 3) in his work on the development of the British Columbia political economy, is that signs in some regions indicated the emergence of a post-staples-based economy and with it, new forms of governance. Differentiating a post-staples political economy from a "mature" staples economy, Hutton argues that substantial natural resource depletion, increasingly capital- and technology-intensive resource extraction from lower-cost staples regions, and the transformation from pure extraction to increased refining and secondary processing of resource commodities were characteristic of a mature staples environment. If these changes persisted, he argues, a sectoral shift from natural resources to the service sector, and from periphery to centre, as the focus of economic growth could occur, ushering in a new post-staples political economy. Similar observations about the evolution of British Columbia's forest economy were made by Barnes and Hayter and their colleagues (Barnes and Hayter 1997; Hayter 2000).

The Empirical Situation

Figure 2.1 supports the argument that Canada's resources are declining in their overall national economic importance. Less than 7 percent of Canada's workforce are employed in natural resource sectors, and they contribute to only 13 percent of national gross domestic product (GDP), despite the fact that Canadian exports of resources more than doubled between 1990 and 2001, growing from $72.0 billion to $167.5 billion, for an annual rate of growth of just under 8.0 percent for the period (Canada, Department of Foreign Affairs and International Trade 2003). However, this resource-based growth rate was less than the 10.7 percent average annual rate recorded by non-resource exports, which increased from $76.9 billion to $234.8 billion (ibid.).

A provincial consideration of natural resource–related trade—the heart of staples-based research—reveals a greater dependence on the natural resources sector. The role of resources in the various provinces is best demonstrated by two sets of statistics in figure 2.2. The first set of statistics, revealed comparative advantage, shows the ratio of the provincial share in resources trade to the national share of resources in total trade. If this statistic is greater than one, then the province trades relatively more in natural resources than it does for all other commodities. Conversely, if the ratio is less than one, resources are less important for the overall scheme of the province's trade. The second set of statistics is a dependency ratio that shows the share of natural resources in total provincial trade. This statistic

Figure 2.1   Economic Indicators for Canada's Natural Resource Sectors

Year (2005)[a]	Forestry	Minerals	Energy	Geomatics[b]	Total natural resources	Canada
Gross domestic product ($ billions)	$37.6 (3.0%)	$50.7 (4.0%)	$75.2 (5.9%)	$2.4 (0.2%)	$165.9 (13.1%)	$1,276.6 (100%)
Direct employment (thousands of people)	340 (2.1%)	388 (2.4%)	250 (1.5%)	27 (0.01%)	1,005 (6.0%)	16,169 (100%)
New capital investments ($ billions)	$3.5 (1.3%)	$7.4 (2.8%)	$56.4 (21.3%)	n.a.	$67.3 (25.4%)	$265.5 (100%)
Trade ($ billions) Domestic exports (excluding re-exports)	$41.9 (10.3%)	$62.1 (15.2%)	$84.8 (20.8%)	$0.5 (0.1%)	$189.3 (46.4%)	$408.1 (100%)
Imports	$10.2 (2.7%)	$56.7 (14.9%)	$34.1 (9.0%)	n.a.	$101.0 (26.6%)	$380.8 (100%)
Balance of trade (including re-exports) . . .	+$31.9	+$7.5	+$50.7	n.a.	+$90.1	+$55.2

[a] The data reported for each of the natural resource sectors reflect the value of the primary industries and related downstream manufacturing industries as of September 2006. "Minerals" include uranium and coal mining. Balance of trade is the difference between total exports and imports of goods. Services and capital flows are not included.
[b] 2005 estimates for the geomatics industry.

Source: Natural Resources Canada. 2007. Statistics on natural resources. Online at http://www.nrcan.gc.ca/statistics/factsheet.htm.

indicates that trade in resources accounts for a certain percentage of total provincial trade. Both Ontario and Quebec had revealed comparative advantage scores less than one (0.46 and 0.99 respectively) and an export dependency less than 40 percent (18.6 percent and 39.99 percent respectively).

High revealed comparative advantages and export dependencies were evident in nearly all the other provinces and territories. In the case of the Prairie provinces, both Alberta and Saskatchewan are highly dependent upon natural resource sectors. Their sources of dependency are highly differentiated. The oil and gas sector dominates Alberta's natural resource sector, while agriculture is the leading sector in Saskatchewan. Manitoba, on the other hand, has a comparatively diversified economy and diversified natural resource sector. Although Manitoba is still dependent on natural resources, its economy includes strengths in agriculture, forestry, mining, and hydropower. Furthermore, Manitoba is a crucial transportation hub. As a consequence, transportation, an indirect but important staples-related service

Figure 2.2   The Role of Resources in Provincial Exports: 1997–2001 Averages

	Revealed comparative advantage	Export dependency
British Columbia	1.87	75.87
Alberta	1.97	79.95
Saskatchewan	2.19	88.56
Manitoba.	1.42	57.41
Ontario	0.46	18.60
Quebec	0.99	39.99
New Brunswick	2.24	90.60
Nova Scotia	1.59	64.30
Prince Edward Island.	1.94	78.76
Newfoundland & Labrador.	2.38	96.48
Yukon	2.13	86.20
Northwest Territories	2.45	99.08
Nunavut.	2.46	99.64

Source: Department of Foreign Affairs and International Trade. 2003. Fourth annual report on Canada's state of trade. Online at http://www.dfait-maeci.gc.ca/eet/trade/sot_2003/SOT_2003-en.asp.

sector, plays an important role in Manitoba's economy (4.7 percent of GDP and 20 percent of foreign-based commodity exports) (Manitoba 2004). The variety of economic compositions and natural resource endowments in the three Prairie provinces suggests that state responses will also differ. The most surprising statistics were the results for British Columbia, which revealed high comparative advantage (1.87) and (75.87) export dependency scores. However, as argued earlier, the province's transformation to a post-staples economy should suggest lower scores. Recently, *The Economist* reported that the natural resource "sunset" had "given way to a new dawn," driving a revival in British Columbia's economy (Coal's Chinese dawn 2005, 23).

DEFINING THE STAPLES STATE

Conceptualizing the capitalist state's evolution is a critical starting point to developing an understanding of the evolution of Canada's overall and regional political economies. The evolution of the state in Canada has moved through four generalized forms as staples production has advanced (see figure 2.3): the minimalist state, the emergent state, the Keynesian welfare state, and the competitive state.

The Minimalist State
The pre-20th-century period defined the classic staples political economy, in which state involvement was sparse to non-existent in nearly all staples-based sectors.

Figure 2.3   Historical Evolution of the State in Response to Canadian Economic Organization

Type	Minimalist state		Emergent state	Keynesian welfare state	Ricardian and Schumpeterian competitive state
	Interventionist–Mercantilist state	UK free trade state–early Canadian state			
Time period	1600s–1840s	1840s–1900	1900–1945	1946–1970s 1970s–1990s	1990s–present
Characteristics	Colonial control and mercantilist expansion Trading preference for colonial goods	Free trade Industrialization Responsible government National Policy	Core-periphery relationships, industrialization, staples traps, rise of protest movements Key path dependencies are developed	US branch economy, regional economic development policies, state expansion and then retreat Federalism	Globalization and re-scaling, environmental protest movements
Organizations	Few—mainly companies	Few—mainly companies	Rise in government agencies and pressure organizations	Organizational state	Organizational state Transnational organizations
Coordination	Market-hierarchical	Market-hierarchical	Market-hierarchical Early policy communities	Hierarchical, regulatory policy communities	Hierarchical-network, non-state governance
Dominant staples	Fur, fish, forestry (timber), agriculture	Forestry, agriculture	Multiple agriculture, forestry (pulp and paper), mining	Multiple—oil and gas, hydroelectricity	Multiple Water exports (potential)

Conversely, staples defined Canada's overall economic growth (Hessing and Howlett 1997). The state and its actions revolved around the facilitation of, or impacts on, resource development for colonial or mercantilist interests. For example, the impact of a particular colonial policy decision, such as the 1831 *Colonial Trade Act* or the 1854 Reciprocity Treaty, defined the extent of state involvement in the economy. In *The Fur Trade in Canada: An Introduction to Canadian Economic History*, Innis (1930) noted that the administration of the early fur industry revolved around the interaction of the early traders with two large mercantilist companies and their officials, namely the North West Company and the Hudson's Bay Company. He noted (ibid., 387) that "it was significant, however, that business organization was of vital importance [to the development of Canada's fur trade]." In the conclusion, Innis acknowledged (ibid., 393) the staples-related business linkages with the early Canadian state: "The lords of the lakes and forests have passed away but their work will endure in the boundaries of the Dominion of Canada and in Canadian institutional life."

Similarly, in the forest sector, the Department of the Interior's Dominion Forestry Branch, the precursor of today's Canadian Forest Service, was established in 1899. However, rapid commercial timber harvesting had been underway and proceeded unabated for nearly a century prior, particularly during the early 1800s.[1] In eastern Canada, concern over the depletion of forested lands precipitated calls for timber regulations (Ontario, Royal Commission on Forest Reservation and National Park 1893). The Forestry Branch was charged with the monumental task of the "protection of standing forests on Dominion lands" (Whitford and Craig 1918, 145). In western Canada, the Forestry Branch reported that in 1918 it employed 562 members, of which only 44 were "technically trained foresters" (Whitford and Craig 1918, 115). The Commission of Conservation Committee also highlighted the challenges of forest administration:

> In the early stages, forest matters were dealt with by the officials of the Department of Lands. The work centred chiefly in Vancouver, at the office of the timber inspectors. A forest ranger with a launch patrolled the 700 miles of coast-line between Vancouver and Prince Rupert. The forests of the interior country were administered by collectors, who paid occasional visits in quest of royalty due from operators who had cut Crown timber. In those days, even though logging operations were conducted on a small scale, this slender staff was unable to cope with the situation effectively. (Whitford and Craig 1918, 115)

Prior to the First World War, state involvement by either level of government in forest matters was very limited. A newly emerging cadre of forest professionals first seriously raised the concerns about the depletion of forests at the 1906 Canadian Forest Convention in Montreal and the 1909 North America Conservation Conference (Burton 1972). State involvement within the natural resource sector was very limited. The state's focus during the latter half of the 19th century was the expansion and settlement of Canada's hinterland (for example, the construction of the Canadian Pacific Railway).

The Emergent State and New Industrialism: The Staples State's Golden Era

The minimal state can be contrasted with the emergent industrialized capitalist state (1900–1945) and the growth of a "new generation of staples," particularly the expansion of prairie-based agriculture development but also the development of the pulp and paper industry, efforts at oil and gas extraction, and the foundation of the hydroelectric industry. The role of the state in staples production in all provinces and sectors developed rapidly during this period—which Nelles (1974) refers to as the "new industrialism." One of the driving factors behind economic growth was a booming population as a result of the federal government's immigration policy.[2]

Accompanying the demographic and economic expansion of the agriculture sector was increased political activity in the form of protest movements. This emergence was most profoundly shown by the formation of the agricultural co-operative movements and many of the prairie agricultural organizations, such as the Manitoba Grain Growers' Association and the Alberta Farmers' Association, some of which continue be in operation today. Grace Skogstad's discussion of the initial early 20th-century struggles by farmers to form agriculture co-operatives (see chapter 4) underlies the longstanding history of the political and policy interaction between farmer-based organizations and the state. According to her chapter, the growth of organizational activity on the prairies outlined the importance of these organizations in developing early agricultural policies. The role of producer-based groups continues to dominate current agricultural policy-making.

Whereas the issue of marketing and prices dominated the early 20th-century agriculture sector, conservation came to the forefront of the burgeoning Canadian forest sector and was the reason for the rise in the "emerging state." Forest-related industrial activity, particularly after the First World War, was spectacular. Between 1918 and 1922, pulpwood production quadrupled, and more than 300 pulp mills were established throughout Canada. As a result of this economic growth, many tracts of land in the western provinces had been cut over, as noted by the 1924 Royal Commission on Pulpwood (Howlett 2001). The push for conservation-oriented policies was a predominant concern among civil servants within the Dominion Forestry Branch (Gillis and Roach 1986). This matter also resonated from within newly formed prairie provincial departments of forests that were established as a result of the 1930 *Natural Resources Transfer Agreement* that transferred the ownership of resource rights from the Dominion government to the provinces. The prominence of provincial forestry responsibilities and the concern over long-term sustained timber yields signalled the beginning of extensive state involvement throughout the Canadian forest sector. Regarding the mining sector, McAllister (see chapter 8) also highlights the influence of scientific management, business, and liberalism on the political culture of 20th-century public and private mineral organizations. A notable aspect of this period is the number of institutional and structural outcomes and developments that continue to influence natural resource sectors today. In forestry, for example, an initial event, namely the transfer of forested Crown lands to provincial governments, eventually led to the creation of large-scale industrial tenure arrangements. Such path dependencies (Goldstone 1998) are exhibited across all natural resource sectors and continue to shape the state's response to the challenges of Canada's primary industries.

The Keynesian Welfare State

The 1946 to 1990 period marks a decline in the dominance of staples within the Canadian political economy. During the previous emerging state period, staples activities were defined along the lines of the classic staples core–periphery relationship, the focus of Innis and other staples theorists. This uneven relationship was built on the extraction of staples and their transportation to the centre for processing. Periphery-based producers then purchased capital from the centre. This unequal relationship produced the rise of prairie political protest movements in the early part of the 20th century, chronicled in such seminal works as C.B. Macpherson's *Democracy in Alberta* (1953).

During the Keynesian welfare state (KWS) period, the relationship between the core and periphery changed.[3] The periphery retained and attempted to foster industrial growth. Provincial states developed strategies and ambitions of their own (Richards and Pratt 1979; Cairns 1977). Conversely, economic activity was no longer linked to the domestic centres for financial and other service-related sectors (Krugman 1991). Between 1940 and 1994, the percentage of Canadian exports to the United States increased from 41.1 percent to 81.4 percent. However, the growths in exports (both in total dollar value and as percentage of exports) were for manufactured goods. This period marked the debate regarding Canada's "branch plant" relationship with the United States (Levitt 1970; Watkins 1970).

In the area of staples dependence, provincial and federal governments made concerted efforts to overcome a common problem, namely the "staples trap." Staples dependence, it is argued, could lead over a long period of time to well-established investment and market patterns (path dependencies) that are difficult to change (Marchak 1983). In some cases, regional decision-makers can become "addicted" to resource extraction, with little opportunity to escape (Freudenburg 1992).

According to Marchak (1983), escape from the staples trap can take a number of different forms, and national and provincial governments during the KWS period pursued three notable strategies. The first strategy was to do nothing, or rather to simply continue historical resource exploitation patterns, which led to resource exhaustion and permanent underdevelopment. Such a strategy was undertaken in Atlantic Canada, leading to both the exhaustion of its key resources, the fisheries and coal, and the subsequent decline of its economy (Organisation for Economic Co-operation and Development [OECD] 2002).

The second strategy was to promote a new or existing staples base. McAllister (see chapter 8) details the use of a national flow-through share program that allows a company to flow a 100 percent tax deduction for the cost of eligible exploration expenses, an example of a state subsidy to this sector. Pratt and Urquhart (1994) similarly chronicle the province of Alberta's role in expanding its forest sector through the use of generous government land tenure arrangements and favourable loans to multinational forestry corporations in the 1980s.

The third and most prevalent strategy during the KWS period was the diversification of resource-dependent regions. For a number of decades, this strategy has been an ongoing policy direction of both the federal and the provincial governments. For example, the Pearson government established the Department of Regional Economic Expansion (DREE) and the Department of Regional Industrial Expansion (DRIE) to pursue this goal.

The Mulroney Conservative government began to both gradually reduce the level of industrial incentives and promote a knowledge-based industrial strategy coupled with an emphasis on free trade (Doern and Phidd 1992). Federal agencies, such as the Atlantic Canada Opportunities Agency (ACOA) and Western Economic Diversification (WED), remained in order to tap into "insufficiently exploited local competitive advantages" but were a shadow of previous attempts to enhance regional development (OECD 2002, 3). The shift to efforts to promote a knowledge-based economy marked the beginning of the emergence of the competitive state in Canada in a "post-staples" era.

The Competitive State: A Reconsideration of the Staples State in the Contemporary Era

Jessop (2002a, 2002b) argues that since the early 1970s the postwar Keynesian welfare state has been destabilized by crisis and is in decline. In its place has emerged the Schumpeterian competitive state (named after the Austrian political economist Joseph Schumpeter). The "generalized" Schumpeterian competitive state's orientation is "the concern with innovation, competitiveness and entrepreneurship tied to long waves of growth and pressures for perpetual innovation" (Jessop 2002a, 112). Such a state must facilitate one of the key features of nearly all capitalist economies: the transformation from an industrial or commodities-based economy to an economy based on knowledge.

Key characteristics of the Schumpeterian competitive state include changing regulatory frameworks to facilitate market flexibility and mobility; liberalizing and deregulating foreign exchange (to facilitate the internationalization and acceleration of capital flows); modifying institutional frameworks for international trade (the harmonization of technological, economic, juridico-political, socio-cultural and environmental issues); promoting national-level industries and their "global spread"; and engaging in place-based competition in an attempt to fix mobile capital within the state's own economic spaces, thereby enhancing inter-urban, inter-regional, or international competitiveness (Jessop 2002a). Hutton (see chapter 3) also discusses the growing importance of transnational urbanism as the leading agency of economic growth and change and the movement away from a policy emphasis on resource development. Although Jessop dedicates most of his discussion to the Schumpeterian competitive state, he does highlight other forms of competition that may lead to other forms of political action. One such state directly linked to staples production is the Ricardian competitive state.

Unlike its Schumpeterian counterpart, the Ricardian competition state (named after the British economist, David Ricardo) stresses the importance of a comparative advantage and/or relative prices (Jessop 2002a). Such competitiveness depends on exploiting the most abundant and cheapest factors of production in a given economy and exchanging products embodying these factors for products from other spaces with different factor endowments. Ricardian competitiveness depends on a static or stable level of efficiency in the allocation of resources to minimize production cost with a given technical division of labour and on the assumption that current economic conditions will continue (Oser and Blanchfield 1975). Because of the importance of natural resources to nearly all of Canada's provinces (see figure 2.2), some provincial states will continue to promote their natural resources (their abundant factors of production) and will retain this Ricardian competitive state.

CONCLUSION

This chapter sought to reconsider the recent history of the staples state. As Hutton (see chapter 3) discusses, natural resources within some provinces face widespread resource depletion and competition from lower-cost staples regions, regional markets (for example, the Pacific Rim), and growth of city regions. This situation may be the case for Canada as a whole and in some provinces, such as British Columbia, Ontario, and Quebec. However, many provinces and territories continue to remain staples-dependent.

Throughout Canada's history, the match between the staples political economy and a generalized state-type economy has been uneven. Until the dawn of the 20th century, state involvement was minimal. However, the emergent state was present during the golden age of the staples era. During this period, Canada's economy centred on natural resource exploitation, and the emergent state facilitated its growth and expansion. This scenario contrasts with the shift to the Keynesian welfare state's strategy of increasing industrial capacity and providing a social safety net for workers. As the KWS has, in turn, declined, the competitive state has emerged. This state is involved both in the trend toward new post-staples economies and in the perpetuation of staples-dependent trajectories in some provinces and regions. Whereas the Schumpeterian version stresses the importance of knowledge and innovation in developing new industries to augment or replace staples dependency, the Ricardian state continues to rely on the exploitation of resources for its comparative advantage.

NOTES

1. The British placed heavy tariffs on Baltic and American timber, in favour of Canadian timber (Marr and Paterson 1980).

2. Canada's net migration increased in the 1901–1911, 1911–1921, and 1921–1931 periods by 716,000, 232,000, and 229,000 respectively (Marr and Paterson 1980). The influx of immigrants is largely attributed to the prairie wheat boom (Marr and Paterson 1980). That is, Manitoba's population increased from 152,506 to 461,394 between 1891 and 1911; Saskatchewan's grew from 91,279 to 492,432 between 1901 and 1911; and Alberta's grew from 73,022 in 1901 to 374,295 in 1911 (Innis 1943). Because settlers were attracted to free or inexpensive landholdings, the area of prairie land in farm holdings grew from 5.9 percent in 1881 to 52.9 percent in 1911.

3. Ample scholarly analysis and debate address the KWS and its subsequent crisis (see Crozier, Huntington, and Watanuki 1975; Gough 1979; Offe 1984; Esping-Andersen 1990 for extensive overviews of the welfare state).

REFERENCES

Aitkin, H.G.J. 1959. *The state and economic growth.* New York: Social Science Research Council.

Aitkin, H.G.J. 1961. *American capital and Canadian resources.* Cambridge, MA: Harvard University Press.

Barnes, T., and Hayter, R. 1997. *Troubles in the rainforest: British Columbia's forest economy in transition.* Victoria: Western Geographical Press.

Berger, C. 1987. *The writing of Canadian history,* 2nd ed. Toronto: University of Toronto Press.

Bertram, G.W. 1963. Economic growth and Canadian industry, 1870–1915: The staple model and the take-off hypothesis. *Canadian Journal of Economics and Political Science* 29(2): 162–84.

Bladen, V.W. 1943. *An introduction to political economy.* Toronto: University of Toronto Press.

Buckley, K. 1958. The role of staple industries in Canadian economic development. *Journal of Economic History* 18(4): 439–50.

Burton, T. 1972. *Natural resource policy in Canada: Issues and perspectives.* Toronto: McClelland & Stewart.

Cairns, A. 1977. The governments and societies of Canadian federalism. *Canadian Journal of Political Science* 10(4): 695–725.

Canada, Department of Foreign Affairs and International Trade. 2003. Fourth annual report on Canada's state of trade. Online at http://www.dfait-maeci.gc.ca/eet/trade/sot_2003/SOT_2003-en.asp.

Canada, Royal Commission on Canada's Economic Prospects. 1957. *Final report.* Ottawa: Queen's Printer.

Coal's Chinese dawn: British Columbia's new, old economy. 2005. *The Economist,* March 10: 23.

Creighton, D.G. 1937. *Empire of the St. Lawrence.* Toronto: Macmillan.

Crozier, M., Huntington, S., and Watanuki. J. 1975. *The crisis of democracy: Report on the governability of democracies to the Trilateral Commission.* New York: New York University Press.

Dales, J.H. 1957. *Hydro-electricity and industrial development in Quebec, 1898–1940.* Cambridge, MA: Harvard University Press.

Doern, G.B., and Phidd, R.W. 1992. *Canadian public policy: Ideas, structure, process,* 2nd ed. Toronto: Nelson Canada.

Easterbrook, W.T. 1959. Recent contributions to economic history: Canada. *Journal of Economic History* 19(1): 76–102.

Esping-Andersen, G. 1990. *The three worlds of welfare capitalism.* Princeton, NJ: Princeton University Press.

Fowke, V. 1946. *Canadian agricultural policy: The historical pattern.* Toronto: University of Toronto Press.

Freudenburg, W.R. 1992. Addictive economies: Extractive industries and vulnerable localities in a changing world economy. *Rural Sociology* 57(3): 305–32.

Gillis, R.P., and Roach, T. 1986. *Lost initiatives: Canada's forest industries, forest policy and forest conservation.* New York: Greenwood Press.

Goldstone, G. 1998. Symposium on historical sociology and rational choice theory: Initial conditions, general laws, path dependence, and explanation in historical sociology. *The American Journal of Sociology* 104(3): 829–45.

Gough, I. 1979. *The political economy of the welfare state.* London: Macmillan.

Hayter, R. 2000. *Flexible crossroads: The restructuring of British Columbia's forest economy.* Vancouver: University of British Columbia Press.

Hessing, M., and Howlett, M. 1997. *Canadian natural resource and environmental policy: Political economy and public policy.* Vancouver: University of British Columbia Press.

Howlett, M. 2001. Introduction: Policy regimes and policy change in the Canadian forest sector. In *Canadian Forest Policy: Adapting to Change,* ed. M. Howlett, 3–22. Toronto: University of Toronto Press.

Hutton, T.A. 1994. *Visions of a "post-staples" economy: Structural change and adjustment issues in British Columbia*, working paper PI #3. Vancouver: University of British Columbia Centre for Human Settlements.

Innis, H.A. 1923. *A history of the Canadian Pacific Railway.* Toronto: University of Toronto Press.

Innis, H.A. 1930. *The fur trade in Canada: An introduction to Canadian economic history.* Toronto: University of Toronto Press.

Innis, H.A. 1940. *The cod fisheries: The history of an international economy.* New Haven, CT: Yale University Press.

Innis, H.A. 1956. *Essays in Canadian economic history.* Toronto: University of Toronto Press.

Innis, H.A., and Lower, A.R.M. 1936. *Settlement and the forest frontier in Eastern Canada.* Toronto: Macmillan.

Innis, M.Q. 1943. *An economic history of Canada.* Toronto: The Ryerson Press.

Jessop, B. 2002a. *The future of the capitalist state.* Cambridge, UK: Blackwell.

Jessop, B. 2002b. Capitalism, steering, and the state. Online at http://www.ru.nl/socgeo/ colloquium/CapitalismSteeringState.pdf.

Krugman, P. 1991. *International trade: Theory and policy.* New York: HarperCollins.

Laxer, G. 1989. The schizophrenic character of Canadian political economy. *Canadian Review of Sociology and Anthropology* 26(1): 178–92.

Levitt, K. 1970. *Silent surrender: The multinational corporation in Canada.* Toronto: Macmillan.

Lower, A.R.M. 1938. *The North American assault on the Canadian forest.* New York: Greenwood Press.

Mackintosh, W.A. 1934. *Prairie settlement: The geographical setting.* Toronto: Macmillan.

Mackintosh, W.A. 1939. *The economic background of dominion-provincial relations.* Ottawa: King's Printer.

Macpherson, C.B. 1953. *Democracy in Alberta: Social Credit and the party system.* Toronto: University of Toronto Press.

Manitoba. 2004. Budget paper A: The economy. Online at http://www.gov.mb.ca/ finance/budget04/papers/economy.pdf.

Marchak, P. 1983. *Green gold: The forest industry in British Columbia.* Vancouver: University of British Columbia Press.

Marr, W., and Paterson, D. 1980. *Canada: An economic history.* Toronto: Gage.

Morton, A.S. 1938. *A history of prairie settlement.* Toronto: Macmillan.

Natural Resources Canada. 2007. Statistics on natural resources. Online at http://www .nrcan.gc.ca/statistics/factsheet.htm.

Nelles, H.V. 1974. *The politics of development: Forests, mines and hydro-electric power in Ontario, 1849–1941.* Toronto: Macmillan.

Offe, C. 1984. *Contradictions of the welfare state.* Ed. J. Keane. Cambridge, MA: MIT Press.

Ontario, Royal Commission on Forest Reservation and National Park. 1893. Papers and reports upon forestry, forest schools, forest administration and management, in Europe, America and the British possessions, and upon forests as public parks and sanitary resorts. Online at http://www.ourroots.ca/f/toc.aspx?id=3829.

Organisation for Economic Co-operation and Development. 2002. *OECD territorial reviews: Canada.* Paris: Organisation for Economic Co-operation and Development.

Oser, J., and Blanchfield, W. 1975. *The evolution of economic thought,* 3rd ed. New York: Harcourt Brace Jovanovich.

Pratt, L., and Urquhart, I. 1994. *The last great forest: Japanese multinationals and Alberta's northern forests.* Edmonton: NeWest Press.

Richards, J., and Pratt, L. 1979. *Prairie capitalism: Power and influence in the New West.* Toronto: McClelland & Stewart.

Saunders, S.A. 1939. *The economic history of the Maritime provinces.* Ottawa: King's Printer.

Watkins, M.H. 1963. A staple theory of economic growth. *Canadian Journal of Economics and Political Science* 29(2): 141–58.

Watkins, M.H. 1970. The dismal state of economics in Canada. In *Close the 49th Parallel Etc.: The Americanization of Canada,* ed. I. Lumsden, 197–208. Toronto: University of Toronto Press.

Whitford, H.N., and Craig, R.D. 1918. *Forests of British Columbia.* Ottawa: Commission of Conservation Canada, Committee on Forests.

CHAPTER 3

The Reconstruction of Political Economy and Social Identity in 21st-Century Canada

Thomas A. Hutton

INTRODUCTION: THE POST-STAPLES HYPOTHESIS IN CONTEXT

Staples extraction has been central to Canada's development, dating from the age of European exploration and the early colonial period, and has constituted a foundation of the national economy throughout the 19th and 20th centuries.[1] Forestry, mining, fishing, and agriculture (included here in a generous definition of staples production) evolved as key elements of regional growth and comparative advantage throughout much of Canada. Associated resource processing, manufacturing, and ancillary industries represented critical features of regional development, with respect to higher-value-added output, labour formation, and economic base (export trade) impacts. Beyond the sites of staples extraction in the peripheral regions, resource development contributed to the growth of allied industries and employment within Canada's cities. This growth was evidenced in specialized service industries, such as banking and finance, business services, and transportation, and in the secondary manufacture of resource commodities.

This resource-led development trajectory in Canada, together with its characteristic socio-economic features and spatial asymmetries (as Wellstead has argued in the previous chapter), was powerfully captured in the theoretical scholarship of Harold Innis fully seven decades ago. Innis identified the recurrent pattern of staples extraction and export to distant markets as the defining attribute of the Canadian economy, with the "result that the Canadian economic structure had the particular characteristics of areas dependent on staples—especially weakness in other lines of development, dependence on highly industrialized areas for markets and for supplies of manufactured goods, and the dangers of fluctuations in the staple commodity" (Innis 1933, 6). Further, the staples development experience incorporated regional disparities within the Canadian economy, depicted in the classic core–periphery model as comprising an industrialized, urban core region and highly dependent staples regions within the national periphery. At the national level, Innis described the key asymmetrical features of the core–periphery model as comprising the dominance of the industrial metropole expressed in terms of corporate "command and control" functions, flows of capital and financial returns favouring the core region, and the relatively truncated nature of peripheral economies mired in the "staples trap."

Throughout the 1960s and 1970s, a new generation of Canadian scholars synthesized the Innisian model of staples dependency with a Marxist posture, then in vogue within the academy, to explain persistent underdevelopment. These proponents of the "new political economy" abandoned the idea of the state as an essentially neutral factor in the national development trajectory, concerned primarily with basic administrative and technical functions, and instead positioned the state in relation to structures of class and corporate power. Leading figures in this new political economy discourse (notably Watkins 1963; Mackintosh 1964; Naylor 1972; Clement 1975) proposed a strongly nationalist policy response to the agendas of global capital.

These views represent problematic features of the staples economy structure as seen from a historical perspective. From a contemporary vantage point, the resource economy (and many dependent primary regions and communities) in Canada seems to be clearly in a position of secular decline vis-à-vis the advanced industrial (and post-industrial) sectors concentrated within the larger city-regions (Coffey 1994). However, it is possible to overstate this "staples in decline" syndrome in the Canadian context. After all, a number of resource sectors, notably oil and gas, forest products (including highly engineered, high-value wood and paper products), and high-quality grains represent important export commodities and generate considerable earnings, incomes, and tax revenues. Among the four western provinces, a large proportion of export revenues continues to be derived from staples exports, and the resource trade values for other provinces are by no means negligible. Encouraging new opportunities are also available for staples-led development, including diamond extraction in the Northwest Territories (see Fitzpatrick, chapter 9) and (perhaps more environmentally problematic) oil and gas deposits in British Columbia's offshore zone (see Clancy, chapter 13).

Despite this reality, the rhetoric of development for Canada as a whole in the early years of the 21st century emphasizes the centrality of advanced industrial activity, specialized services, and "knowledge production" (both theoretical and applied) to national economic progress. Broadly, this hegemony of high-value goods and services (and implicit subordination of staples production) within the national development trajectory is commonly attributed to (1) the role of Canada's cities as sites of leading-edge growth and change, and more particularly the *urbanization–industrialization* development nexus, reflecting the centripetal tendencies of urban agglomeration, scale economies, and human and social capital factors among advanced economies; (2) the problems of regional staples production in situ, including resource depletion, overall environmental degradation, cost factors, and out-migration; and (3) a range of *exogenous* factors, including competition from resource-rich (and typically lower-cost) regions, changes in staples consumption patterns among principal export trade customers, the globalization of commodity production and markets, and declining terms of trade for staples exports relative to industrial end-products and specialized services.

No doubt these factors account for a large measure of the relative decline in the position of Canada's staples sectors and dependent regions, as addressed in many of the substantive chapters of this volume. But in this essay I will be advancing an argument that the national development trajectory is in transition from a "mature staples" phase to a "post-staples" era,[2] signifying not only a new phase of industrial restructuring but also profound shifts in social development and the structures and operations of the state. This emergent development trajectory is shaped by a mélange of influences that include new rounds of industrial restructuring, the repositioning of cities and settlements within the Canadian urban hierarchy and (more decisively) international networks, and influential social movements (including multiculturalism and environmentalism). More specifically, we can acknowledge cultural change as a cardinal influence both on Canada's emerging development modality and on the structures and orientation of the state. Successive inflows of international immigration, especially since the mid-1980s, have produced an increasingly multicultural society, fundamentally reconfiguring regional labour and housing markets and reinforcing the competitive advantage of city-regions by enhancing the entrepreneurial potential of the urban economy and the city's linkages with international markets and societies.

"Transnational urbanism," as defined by the political scientist Michael Smith (2001), with its emphasis on complex, multi-layered social, economic, political, and cultural networks linking international cities, has largely supplanted both the "regional central place" concept and the "national core–periphery" framework as the situating spatial matrix for Canada's largest city-regions. The cumulative force of these processes serves to underpin the ascendancy of new epistemic communities (including policy professionals, the scientific community, and other knowledge elites), which increasingly privilege cities and urban interests over the interests of resource industries, settlements, and allied constituencies. In the aggregate, these new (or reconfigured) processes serve not only to diminish the status and prospects of resource regions and communities but also to marginalize the staples economy in the shaping of the public consciousness, in the ordering of priorities within the agencies of the state and among influential policy communities, and in the formation of social identity.

It is important to recognize, however, that this post-staples political economy is not a "non-staples" economy. That is, as Wellstead has discussed (see chapter 2), many regions of the country remain at the stage of a mature staples political economy, functioning under a Ricardian state system. Moreover, despite the many efforts of Canadian governments to promote "knowledge-based" industries, such as the production of software and computer games, which have few if any material inputs, most of the industries and activities toward which knowledge has been directed in Canada are classic staples industries, such as agriculture (genetically modified foods), forestry (new pulp and paper techniques, biologically enhanced silviculture), fisheries (aquaculture), mines (enhanced reclamation), and energy (hydrogen fuels, renewables, offshore drilling, and tar sands production). The post-staples direction of Canada's political economy, then, is complex and nuanced but represents significant continuity with earlier stages in Canada's economic history, not a total break from the past.

Following this introduction, the paper offers a restatement of the "conditions of mature staples economies," extending conceptual work undertaken a decade or so ago in the British Columbia context (Hutton 1994), but seeking, as well, broader Canadian applications. Next, an inventory and elaboration of new social, cultural, and political processes are presented, together with an articulation of some defining outcomes and issues for Canada's prospective development as a post-staples state. Finally, the conclusion will set out some implications for development policy, in part as an acknowledgement of the deeply problematic and socially divisive outcomes of the "post-staples consciousness" of 21st-century Canada.

THE "STATE" OF THE "ADVANCED STAPLES STATE": DEFINING CONDITIONS

Before advancing to an articulation of the new (or emergent) processes influencing the fortunes of Canada's resource sector and its dependent regions and communities in a post-staples development scenario, it may be worth briefly restating some of the defining conditions of "advanced" or "mature" resource economies, as follows.

1. Spatial recalibration of the core–periphery framework
The Innisian analysis applied categorically to the national scale, where Canada's extensive peripheral regions supplied resources (minerals, forest products, energy, foodstuffs, and water) to the manufacturing and commercial heartland of Canada, largely concentrated (then as now) in the metropolitan Toronto and Montreal

regions and their industrial satellites. As a corollary of this asymmetrical relationship, these peripheral regions and constituent communities served as "captive markets" for end products (goods and services) from the industrial metropolises in central Canada (Innis 1933). Over the last century, the core metropolitan regions in Canada have experienced considerable (if temporally and spatially uneven) *development*, as well as growth. Development in this context connotes transformative industrial change, transitions to higher levels of human capital formation, more specialized employment and occupations, and a richer, more diverse sociocultural base. Most peripheral regions, in contrast, tended to achieve far more limited development outcomes and have been subject to deeper and more recurrent recessions.

By the middle of the 20th century, this core–periphery construct could also be discerned at the provincial scale (Ley and Hutton 1987). To illustrate, the author has proposed a model of core–periphery relations in British Columbia comprising linkages between metropolitan Vancouver as the provincial core and "industrial metropolis" and the "periphery" (or more pejoratively "hinterland") regions. These linkages include not only "control functions" (that is, head offices and financial and business services) but also *production linkages*, incorporating Vancouver's role as processing and secondary manufacturing centre for resource commodities; a *strategic transportation role*, notably the export of some 40 million to 50 million tons of staples commodities annually; *consumption interdependencies*, including a considerable flow of staples from the province's interior to the consumer markets of its Lower Mainland; and *socio-cultural relationships*, including the influence of the staples economy and resource industries on the formation of class and community structures in Vancouver (Hutton 1997, 70–71). The parameters of this provincial core–periphery framework are neither universal nor immutable,[3] but some of the basic linkage patterns described in the British Columbia case can be discerned in the Prairie provinces, in the Maritime provinces, and in Quebec.[4]

2. Problems of resource endowment depletion

Although Canada's natural resources have been subject to extraction for several centuries, rates of depletion for many key staples have accelerated markedly since the mid–20th century: first, with the stimulus of industrial production and derived demand for resources during the Second World War, 1939–1945, including key minerals and timber required for the production of wartime *matériel* for Canada and its allies; a second resource boom occurring during the period of postwar reconstruction, exemplified by the greatly increased harvest of softwood timber for new housing in an increasingly urban Canadian society; and third, a heightened demand for Canada's natural resources associated with the rapid growth of manufacturing industry in Canada over the third quarter of the 20th century, and with growth in export markets.

By the end of the last century, numerous key staples stocks in Canada, both in renewable and non-renewable resources, had been seriously depleted following these cycles of accelerated exploitation. In the case of mining, depletion has often meant reliance upon lower-grade ores; whereas in forestry, severe depletion of high-quality fibre has forced an exploitation of second- and third-growth timber, often in less accessible areas, as in the examples of Quebec and British Columbia. Some important fisheries, exemplified by the fate of the historic Newfoundland cod fishery, had been effectively exhausted by the 1990s (see Hoogensen, chapter 6). Typically, mature resource economies, such as Canada's, are characterized by increasing resource management problems in the face of mounting pressures on the resource stock, often (as in the case of the New Brunswick and British Columbia salmon fisheries) from multiple user groups.

3. Increasingly capital-intensive resource extraction processes
A salient feature of advanced, mature staples economies is the relentless application of capital and technology to extraction and processing, in order to (1) increase production efficiency (as in investments in seed grain research and in harvesting technologies among the Prairie provinces) (see Moore, chapter 5); (2) extract greater value from resource inputs (exemplified in the forestry and forest products sectors of Quebec, Ontario, New Brunswick, and British Columbia); (3) access resources requiring technologically advanced extraction systems (for example, petroleum deposits embedded within the Alberta tar sands) (see Brownsey, chapter 10); and (4) compete effectively in increasingly globalizing commodity markets. This capital intensification is required to sustain Canada's competitiveness in resource extraction; however, these advanced production technologies have tended to displace labour within the resource economy over the past quarter-century. Increasingly, the survival of staples communities implies acceptance of a Faustian bargain of continuing rounds of plant contractions and layoffs as the price of new investments in leading-edge production technologies.

4. Increasing competition from foreign staples producers
Canadian staples industries and their constituent producing regions operate under increasing pressure, both from other advanced staples producers (as in the case of highly engineered, high-value-added wood products from Germany and Scandinavian countries), some of which also exhibit lower-cost profiles (as in the case of the southeast US softwood lumber producers); as well as from jurisdictions with huge, largely untapped natural resource endowments and significantly lower labour costs (notably Russia). In the case of mineral exploration and mining, Mary Louise McAllister (see chapter 8) has observed that new competitors in the world market—for example, those in Latin America—present a serious challenge by offering rich, readily accessible deposits and an inexpensive labour force and by welcoming

governments anxious to attract investment in these countries to build their developing economies. As Michael Porter (1990) has stated, staples regions within developed societies can thrive in the global economy, but to do so they need to be at the leading edge of productivity; that is, they must be technologically advanced and thoroughly embedded in the latest scientific developments. Stated starkly, Canadian staples producers must increasingly compete within global commodity markets both on price *and* quality.

5. Evolution from "pure" extraction to secondary processing and manufacturing

Over time, advanced staples economies tend to engage more in secondary processing, specialty resource production, and allied service industries, as exemplified by the high-technology paper and wood product industries in Quebec, British Columbia, and New Brunswick; in the production of high-value specialty grains in Saskatchewan and Alberta; and in the expansion of organic agriculture in Ontario, British Columbia, and other provinces. Grace Skogstad (chapter 4) offers a compelling illustration of this tendency to favour downstream manufacturing and service industries in Canada's agricultural sector, noting that, in economic importance, food processing now exceeds primary (commodity) production in all provinces east of Manitoba. While acknowledging the finding by Agriculture and Agri-Food Canada (2006) that food processing constitutes the third-largest manufacturing industry in Canada (and the largest in no fewer than seven provinces), Skogstad underscores the rapid rise of allied service-sector industries and employment by noting that Canadian retail, wholesale, and food services employ a greater number of Canadians and contribute greater amounts to gross domestic product (GDP) than do food production and processing combined (see Skogstad, chapter 4). At the same time, however, the globalization of some principal commodity markets has retarded the development of advanced resource processing, as illustrated by the export of raw logs to the United States.[5]

6. Industrial diversification within resource communities

Over time, some resource communities among advanced staples economies achieve a measure of industrial diversification, including higher-value-added industries linked to local staples production. These notable success stories of diversification include producers of high-quality wines in southern Ontario and in the Okanagan Valley of British Columbia, tourism (including eco-tourism), and the expansion of regional administration and public services, including higher education. In these cases, favourable developmental factors can include high levels of local amenities (for example, Kamloops and Kelowna in British Columbia, Red Deer in Alberta, Niagara-on-the-Lake in Ontario, and Lunenburg in Nova Scotia) and public investments in higher education in support of regional development in the periphery (such as the University of Northern British Columbia in Prince George and the recent establishment of an Okanagan campus of the University of British Columbia in Kelowna).[6]

7. Pressure from environmental groups

Environmental advocates and effective lobbying have served to promote greater constraints on staples industries and regions in Canada, as seen in the creation of new wilderness areas, the reduction of allowable resource yields in key staples sectors, and the introduction of higher standards of resource extraction and processing. Some of this pressure derives from concern about specific depletion effects, while at a more general level environmental advocacy includes an insistence upon principles of "full cost accounting" (including social and environmental costs) of resource development. Broadly, too, the public appreciation is generally higher for the "existence values" of natural resources, including the increasing utility of natural resources in tourism, observation, scientific research (including medicine as well as fundamental or basic research), and regional cultural expression.[7]

8. Search for resource substitutes and "synthetic" stocks

Concern about the depletion of major resource stocks in Canada, an attribute of mature (or advanced) staples economies, has stimulated an aggressive exploration of artificial or man-made stocks and resources. These alternatives include substitutes for key mineral resources and more contentious interventions, such as plantation-style cultivation of softwood timber and coastal and estuarine aquaculture. Each of these substitutes may relieve stresses on extant natural stocks to a degree, but they also generate their own sets of problems and pressures, as evidenced in the debate about the impact of Atlantic salmon farming on wild salmon stocks on the southern coast of British Columbia. To elaborate, Jeremy Rayner and Michael Howlett (see chapter 7) describe aquaculture as an archetypical post-staples resource industry, incorporating high capital intensity and sophisticated technology, but point to factors perpetuating the classic problems of the staples economy: the hinterland location and heavy export reliance.[8]

This inventory of the defining attributes of advanced resource economies and illustrative applications to the Canadian experience is by no means exhaustive, but indicates some basic typological parameters for understanding the state of the mature staples state. The overall profile is strongly suggestive of a marked *progression* of largely problematic features of the Canadian staples economy: increasingly capital-intensive production, with attendant and ongoing *contractions of labour*; serious depletion (and in some cases near-exhaustion) of key resource stocks; exposure to increasing *competition* from both other advanced staples producers and lower-cost regions with major untapped endowments; exigencies of increasingly forceful and complex *regulation* (including significant yield adjustments); and increasing *conflicts* among diverse user groups. Evidence of industrial diversification exists among some resource regions and communities in Canada. But this diversification has tended to be a highly selective experience, favouring settlements situated within the "urban field" of large cities; smaller communities possessing high levels of natural, recreational, and cultural amenities; and cases of successful local entrepreneurship and innovation.[9]

NEW DYNAMICS OF REGIONAL DIVERGENCE IN THE POST-STAPLES STATE

The subordination of Canada's staples economy to the advanced industrial and post-industrial trajectories associated with city-regions has been a salient feature of national development for at least several decades. This profile is familiar enough and can be seen as a feature of other advanced staples economies, notably in resource-dependent regions of the United States and Australia. But I argue that in the last decade or so a dramatic and profound reshaping of development factors has further marginalized Canada's staples economy and its constituent regions and communities. In the early years of the 21st century, we are at the advent of a post-staples state, in which resource extraction is increasingly seen by policy-makers and the broader public as a *residual* of the national economic structure, a vestige of a historical development path that sustained many Canadian regions and communities. The historical staples economy construct was spatially represented by a system of inter-regional and inter-industry linkages and by patterns of co-dependent social constituencies, which to some extent connected the fortunes and public consciousness of Canada's diverse regions and legitimized the state's commitment to national support and stewardship programs. These traditional linkages—substantive and symbolic—are appreciably diminished and continue to weaken in the face of social, cultural, market, and policy factors operating at the global, national, and regional scales. Some of the more consequential forces underpinning regional divergence and the formation of the post-staples state may be described as follows.

1. The power of city-regions: from urbanization to "metropolitanization"

The growth of cities in Canada (and more specifically the shift of population and labour from rural to urban areas) is often cited as a marker of the diminished role of the staples sector and the constituent producing regions in Canada. Against this backdrop of a secular process of urbanization in Canada is a current need to underscore the particular significance of *metropolitan* cities (or city-regions) in the national economy, society, and state. Here, the descriptor *metropolitan* signifies not simply attainments of crude population thresholds but also expressions of corporate power, industrial scale and specialization, multicultural values and cosmopolitan sensibilities, and a growing, complex global–local interface and interdependency.

At the peak of the national urban hierarchy, Canada's city-regions encompass disproportionately large and growing shares of the national population, skilled labour, propulsive-scale corporations, knowledge-intensive firms, leading educational institutions, innovative production spaces (including science parks), media (including "new media"), and global connectivity (as measured principally by international air connections and the quality of telecommunications infrastructure and systems). These metropolitan cities also confront serious problems and adjustment issues, but their populations, electoral constituencies, and growing political representation provide a growing platform of influence within public and private sector executive bodies and bureaucracies. Cities within this echelon of dominant metropolitan city-regions indisputably include Toronto, Montreal, and Vancouver. Over the last decade or so, additional city-regions have achieved a compelling metropolitan character in terms of population and economic development, notably Ottawa (population just over 1 million) and Calgary (population just under 1 million), while other city-regions (such as Edmonton and Halifax, with important university, research, and government clusters) may be at a threshold of influence and power. Over time, this process of metropolitanization will increasingly dominate the development fortunes of Canada at large and will indirectly suppress the status of staples regions and industries within Canadian society.[10]

This growing structural disparity in the political influence of regions in Canada is also likely to be exacerbated by the development of *executive government* at the federal level, in which power is increasingly concentrated within the cabinet (and more particularly the Prime Minister's Office [PMO]), relative to members of Parliament (MPs), even those in the governing party. The locus of power in this executive government model is heavily weighted toward the interests and constituencies domiciled within the major metropolitan cities (Ottawa, Montreal, and Toronto and, to a lesser extent, Vancouver, Calgary, and Edmonton), which in turn tend to narrow the "scope of vision" of the federal government across Canada's society and space-economy in policy-making processes and in the allocation of the state's discretionary resources.[11]

2. New rounds of regional industrial restructuring

Since the 1970s, resource and urban regions alike have been subject to wrenching experiences of industrial change, including reorganizations that are *cyclical* (short-term shifts) and *structural* (more far-reaching shifts in the composition of industry and labour). In some serious recessions, such as those experienced in British Columbia in the early 1980s, and in the greater Toronto and Montreal regions in the early 1990s, downturns encompassed both cyclical and structural elements. Restructuring in many resource regions has entailed major plant closures (associated with resource depletion, plant obsolescence, the rationalization of production capacity, and corporate downsizing) and attendant contractions in employment and household income, typically followed by difficulties in securing new industries and investment, although (as noted earlier), successful diversification has led to some spectacular exceptions to this syndrome.

Canada's urban regions have experienced negative consequences of industrial restructuring, exemplified most notably by the collapse of the traditional Fordist industry in the 1970s and 1980s, as well as the dot-com boom and bust of the late 1990s and the early years of this decade. These restructuring episodes have cost many thousands of jobs, resulted in structural unemployment and serious losses of revenues and income, and compromised the viability of urban neighbourhoods and communities.

In contrast to the fortunes of most staples-producing regions, Canada's city-regions have succeeded in securing new bundles of activity or economic "vocations," and have thus been able to attract (with varying degrees of success) new investment, business start-ups, and employment formation throughout a sequence of restructuring episodes. This sequence has included (1) growth in service industries, related in part to the expansion of services associated with growing urban populations (for example, retail, personal, and public services, including education and health services); (2) the subsequent expansion of intermediate or "producer" services, including legal, accounting, and consulting industries, which comprised the fastest-growing employment sectors among most advanced societies over the fourth quarter of the 20th century, reflecting *inter alia* the agglomeration advantages of cities over rural regions and smaller settlements; (3) the expansion of advanced-technology industries, closely associated with skilled labour pools and the presence of advanced research institutions, which tend to be situated in major urban (or suburban) centres; (4) the growth of the new economy, comprising "new media" and telecommunications industries, over the last decade; and (5) the rise of the "cultural economy of the city" identified by Allen Scott (2000) as an important new trajectory of urban development and encompassing what Richard Florida (2002) has described as a large, fast-growing, and culturally and politically significant urban "creative class." Some resource-dependent regions and communities have been able to attract a measure of these "growth sectors" over the past two decades, but have generally lacked the agglomeration economies, facilitating institutions, and specialized labour markets required to take full advantage of these opportunities.[12]

3. *Global processes of economic growth and change*

For staples industries and regions, the effects of globalization include both the integration of resource production within global (as opposed to national) commodity markets and a series of resource corporation mergers and acquisitions that have shifted the locus of control from regional or national centres to higher-order "world cities." Global commodity market integration tends to underscore the status of staples-producing regions as "price-takers" as opposed to price-leaders (Hayter and Barnes 1990), in many cases exerting downward pressures on commodity prices and profits, rendering sometimes precarious the viability of high-cost resource extraction operations in an era of relentless global competition.

City-regions in Canada also experience dislocation and destabilization accruing from engagement in global markets.[13] As Saskia Sassen (1991) has observed, globalization effects in cities can include social polarization, housing market inflation, and the exacerbation of an urban underclass problem. But metropolitan areas possess significant advantages over resource regions and communities when negotiating terms of engagement with global forces. These advantages include urban scale considerations, market concentration and industrial diversity, and city-region population expenditure thresholds and local capital (public, corporate, and household). This platform of metropolitan attributes and assets presents a measure of insulation from the destabilization of global processes and offers the potential for higher levels of endogenous economic development. As another point of contrast with staples regions, cities—especially larger metropolitan cities—can exercise a measure of choice when engaging with global markets and societies because of cities' recourse to significant powers and resources not available to smaller communities. Increasingly, Canada's metropolitan cities deploy these local powers and resources to foster engagement with international and global markets, cities, and societies, and, in the process, promote a greater measure of divergence from traditional regional resource regions and communities.

4. The emergence of transnational urban society

Allied to the concept of the global city, but in important respects representing a distinctive genre of urban-regional development, is the idea of the *transnational city* (or society). The conventional usage of the global city concept is ineluctably tied to corporate head offices, banking and finance, global networks and flows, and the international division of labour (although some more recent interpretations allow for a broader set of global roles and functions),[14] but *transnational urbanism* also connotes more diverse (and highly nuanced) social interdependencies and cultural relations. Key processes in the formation of transnational cities include international immigration, from an increasingly diverse range of foreign nations, societies, and cultures; the role of kinship in the establishment of linkages between cities; multiculturalism as an agency of multi-dimensional urban transformation (for example, in reconfiguring housing and labour markets, the built environment and cultural landscapes, civic participation and citizenship); the workings of ethnic and cultural non-governmental and community-based organizations (NGOs and CBOs) in assisting immigrant communities in job markets and in securing access to housing and services; the rapidly increasing representation of new immigrant community members in electoral processes and political representation; and the impact of international immigration on the shaping of new urban identities and imageries.

As is well known, these processes of transnational urbanism have deeply influenced the reshaping of Canada's urban communities, especially over the past two decades.[15] Of course, immigration also flows to smaller communities and resource-based towns, where immigrants contribute to local culture, society, and the economy; but overall the direction of immigrant settlement is powerfully linked to urban areas, and more especially to Canada's metropolitan cities. Among the chief impacts of transnational processes are injections of entrepreneurship, investment, and creativity into urban economies and labour markets, related in part to the idea of the multicultural city as a site of intercultural production and transmission, along with more problematic features. But the effects of transnationalism also include a powerful reinforcement of an *external reorientation* for many Canadian cities, as expressed in the proliferation of international linkages between ethnically defined communities and originating societies (and between immigrant and "host" communities within Canada), engaging immigrant cohorts described by Stoianovich (1994, 80) as "mobilized diasporas."[16] To some extent, these social and cultural relations, coupled with international tourism and travel, foreign direct investment (FDI), and other expressions of economic globalization, support a shift in urban imagery and social consciousness from long-established linkages with resource (or hinterland) regions toward a more comprehensive transnational affiliation. The "staples constituency" within Canada's cities therefore becomes ever weaker, relative to transnational and global cohorts, dislodging the historical sense of interdependency and connectivity that has at least in part characterized Canadian society.

5. The social inculcation of environmental values

Although an important global dimension is inherent to environmentalism, reflected in widespread concerns about (for example) the degradation of the Amazon rainforest and the encroachment of the Sahara Desert, and in the convening of momentous international conferences by the United Nations and other bodies, a very strong (and likely growing) Canadian constituency exists within the environmental movement. Canadians have been active in the establishment and development of Greenpeace (established in Vancouver in the 1960s), the Sierra Club, and other environmental associations, and this engagement is observed in national and regional political discourses, in the media, and in community dialogues. Recent polls place the support for the Green Party at about 5 percent nationally, and as high as 10 percent in British Columbia, where environmentalism is strongly rooted in decades of protest and a contemporary discourse of sustainable development. To a large extent, the strength of this environmental sensibility is associated not only with public "usage and experience" but also with the "imagined" connections of

Canadians to the iconic value of the boreal forests, coastal ecosystems, the Arctic as metaphor for the Canadian frontier, and the distinctive regional environments of the Prairies, the Great Lakes, the Canadian Shield, and the Maritimes.

Although the value structures among adherents of the environmental movement are both diverse and complex (and in some cases perhaps contradictory), a core social preference is for sharply reduced, tightly managed and regulated resource exploitation. In part, this preference may reflect the urban bias of environmentalists based in cities, where, as William Rees (2002) has suggested, a "disconnect" may exist between the constructed belief in a self-contained urban lifestyle and the reality of continuing dependency of city-dwellers on resources (water, food-stuffs, staple inputs to consumer goods and services) derived from the "regions." Significant environmental constituencies exist, of course, within resource regions and communities, but are likely to comprise a minority of the local population, particularly in cases where regional resource dependency ratios are high, although their influence in shaping progressive environmental policies cannot be discounted. We acknowledge the role of local environmentalists in the Tofino region of Vancouver Island and the commitment of First Nations communities in the protection of wilderness assets in British Columbia's Clayoquot Sound.

Broadly, though, attitudes concerning acceptable natural resource harvesting thresholds likely constitute a major fault line between communities within rural or wilderness regions and city-regions. For many city-dwellers, thinking about resource-based regions likely occurs in the context of either a symbolic connection to the imageries of Canada's wilderness areas or a selective experience of recreational visitations, not in an appreciation of the quotidian realities of making a living from the land and the resource base. The urban staples constituency of social groups directly engaged in the management or processing of resources has appreciably diminished, whereas the numbers of city-dwellers owning "country cottages" or second homes in high-amenity rural areas are rapidly increasing. Urban residents tend (when afforded the opportunity) to express a preference for policies that enhance the existence values of natural resources over more permissive harvesting regimes required to maintain the viability of resource-dependent communities.

6. Changing state policy priorities and discourses

Here we can discern critical interdependencies—conflicts as well as complements—among the state, markets, and society in the formation of a putative post-staples economy in Canada. A kind of reciprocal causality is at work in this process of generative change, as the multi-level state clearly functions as an "actor" in the restructuring of the economy, society, and polity; but the state is itself subject to reformation in the face of the processes cited in the preceding narrative: the rise of the metropolitan city, transnational urbanism, the growing influence of global processes, and the social diffusion of environmental attitudes. An exposition of the full range and complexities of changes in the post-staples state is beyond the scope of this essay (and these developments are addressed in subsequent chapters of this volume), but we can illustrate some of the principal new policy orientations as follows.

The first key shift in policy discourse and practice relates to assumptions underlying regional development policy at the federal level. From the generous (some would say profligate) policies of the Department of Regional Economic Expansion (DREE) and Department of Regional Industrial Expansion (DRIE) programs of the Trudeau era, which incorporated substantial subsidies for regional development and diversification for lagging regions,[17] the recent federal practice has embodied a more constrained vision in this sphere and a corresponding privileging of deficit control, production efficiency, and global competitiveness. The outcomes of the Trudeau-era programs were for the most part limited in achieving regional development goals and in enhancing socio-economic welfare in resource regions (both in terms of resources allocated and in comparison with the effects of direct transfers and taxation measures). But it is the shift in the underlying vision and priorities that underpins a more parsimonious attitude toward structural problems of regional disparity that is of cardinal relevance here. This more truncated sense of federal obligations to the "regions" is compounded by the erosion of federal powers and spending in key policy portfolios vis-à-vis the provincial order of government since the Mulroney governments of the 1980s.

Second, a shift occurred in assumptions concerning the development potential of principal industrial sectors. Here we can acknowledge (see Wellstead, chapter 2) a marked transition from a traditional view of staples as a lead sector of national development, buttressed by a Ricardian perspective emphasizing Canada's *comparative* advantage in raw resource endowments, to a more aggressively Schumpeterian *competitive* (that is, "induced") advantage model, with an advanced-industrial/technocratic bias. As Skogstad (chapter 4) notes, since the 1980s, changes in the international political economy and in domestic fiscal deficits and shifts in ideologies have led to a new model of competitiveness, in which market-oriented strategies that provide incentives to add value to raw commodities are "in vogue." Staples need to be acknowledged as essential production inputs, but a changing positioning of input criticality also needs to be considered: the value of "human" or man-made inputs (technology, human and social capital, amenity and cultural attributes) has markedly increased relative to raw natural resources.

Third, the regional (or industrial) policy agenda of the federal government (to the extent that it can be said that one exists) is clearly shifting to the problems and opportunities within Canadian *cities* and *city-regions*, not to those of Canada's resource and wilderness regions. This emerging regional policy sensibility is clearly linked to the metropolitanization phenomenon identified earlier in this essay, to the centrality of immigration and multiculturalism to the federal agenda (as well as to the electoral prospects of national parties), to the growing cultural and political power of cities and urban constituencies, and to the critical nexus between cities and new processes of industrial restructuring. Future federal policies are likely to be linked to individual cities as opposed to being articulated and delivered in the classic "national policy" manner of the Trudeau era. Cities will likely, however, be the prime beneficiaries of policy innovation and programmatic largesse, not the lagging resource regions in the periphery. Further, insofar as a vestige of the old Liberal industrial policy paradigm can be said to exist, the federal commitment appears to lie principally in supporting "lead" or propulsive, export-oriented multi-nationals, such as Bombardier and SNC Lavalin (whose Montreal base is likely not incidental to ongoing federal support), as opposed to supporting regional resource corporations.

CONCLUSION: NORMATIVE DIMENSIONS OF THE POST-STAPLES STATE

Over much of the 20th century, a robust staples economy supported a distinctive model of economic development in Canada. The balance of benefits and opportunities was almost always weighted in favour of the leading industrial metropolises, especially major central Canadian city-regions, but staples extraction supported a viable way of life and development culture within resource regions and constituent communities. Moreover, the clear chains of linkage and interdependency between the peripheral resource communities and the industrial cities of the national core provided a measure of "communal consciousness" in Canada, expressed in (among other things) a political commitment to regional development programs, in the interests of encouraging industrial diversification.

Given the relative abundance of natural resources in Canada and the future demand for staples associated with (for example) the unprecedented scale of industrialization in China and India, staples production will always occupy a higher place in national GDP and exports, relative to other advanced Organisation for Economic Co-operation and Development (OECD) nations.[18] But the capacity of staples to *lead* development in the Canada of the 21st century will be severely limited not only by the depletion (and even exhaustion) of key resource stocks but also by the job-shedding characteristic of advanced-technology resource industries striving to maintain competitive positions within global commodity markets, and by the increasing social and political hegemony of the larger metropolitan city-regions. The purpose of this essay has been to suggest that although many of the structural asymmetries of the core–periphery staples sector remain features of the Canadian economy, society, and polity, a new (or emergent) set of forces is sharply exacerbating the divergence of regional fortunes and is shaping the contours of a post-staples state and society.

The contemporary forces of change described in this essay underscore the likelihood of increasing regional divergence in a putatively post-staples Canadian society, characterized by a sharper divide in the socio-economic welfare of resource-dependent communities vis-à-vis urban society, a growing sense of social alienation and isolation, and a national policy and governance structure dominated increasingly by urban (and especially metropolitan) interests. These ascendant urban constituencies include not only the "new middle class" (after Ley 1996) of elite service industry managers and professionals, and a more recent cohort of new economy creative workers defined by synergies of culture and technology, but also the diverse populations of Canada's multicultural communities. Recent immigrants experience major (and likely increasing) problems (for example, in penetrating labour markets; see Travers 2005) and successes, but arguably enjoy higher levels of social status and political representation than the traditional staples constituencies of the periphery. From the viewpoint of the dominant city-regions, grounds may exist for a thesis that now positions resource workers and communities as the (exotic) "other" within Canadian society, subject to "outlier status" and marginalization within state political discourses, redefining social and cultural processes, and the narratives and focal points of the media.

Indeed, the primary (extractive) resource industries are increasingly viewed as outliers even within those areas of Canada beyond the large city-regions. Although stories of local–regional transition and diversification abound, they tend to encompass services and higher-value industries (see Skogstad, chapter 4); regional administration, health care, and higher education; and creative and new economy industries and occupations, not extractive industries per se, suggesting new processes of inter-regional divergence and a post-staples orientation for many of Canada's non-metropolitan areas (for an insightful discussion on opportunities for, and constraints upon, peripheral communities in the knowledge economy within Quebec and the Maritimes, see Polèse and Shearmur 2002).

Given the normative dimensions of a prospectively post-staples Canadian development trajectory, remedial interventions and measures should be actively investigated, although the scale and complexity of problems (including shifts in Canada's political economy and social identity) suggest that remedies will not be easily obtained. A detailed prescriptive treatment is beyond the scope of this essay, but perhaps a modest beginning would include, first, examining the experiences of similar jurisdictions, notably those of Australia (federal, state, and local), for what we might learn about common problems and responses (see, for example, O'Connor, Stimson, and Daly 2001); second, establishing a serious dialogue with resource communities to mutually explore models of transition and (re)development that might be both attractive and feasible; third, undertaking a review of contrasting provincial regional development strategies and models, taking advantage of progressive and innovative approaches, as in the case of the interesting new capacity-building program in Nova Scotia; and, finally, working with universities, NGOs, and other interested parties to develop advanced regional policy and community planning capacity within Canada's staples-producing regions *in situ*. The complexities and differentiation of the "staples region experience" will tend to militate both against generic policy templates characteristic of earlier periods of regional policy experimentation and against directing "solutions" from the seats of political power and economic privilege ensconced in the metropolitan archipelago of the Canadian south.

NOTES

1. The extraction of natural resources was, of course, also central to the daily life, industry, and cultures of the First Nations, but we are principally concerned here with the role of staples in the evolution of Canada's national economy.

2. I deploy the term *post-staples state* as a descriptor of significant change in Canada's development trajectory, in the spirit of Daniel Bell's (1973) social forecast of "post-industrial society" three decades ago. Neither of these concepts—Bell's post-industrial society or my notion of a post-staples state—is intended as an "absolute," as even episodes of quite fundamental and far-reaching industrial and socio-economic change necessarily encompass a sublation of conditions, both contemporary and historical, not a complete and total break with the past. Instead, these concepts represent ventures in capturing important new phases of economic change, together with the complex social, cultural, spatial, and political causalities and outcomes that comprise basic shifts in development modes.

3. For example, in British Columbia, because of the erosion of staples processing along the Fraser River and the associated decline of cohorts of resource processing workers (principally forestry and fisheries) and adjacent communities, production and social linkages between the Greater Vancouver "core" and the resource "periphery" have appreciably weakened (see Hutton 1997 for a more extensive discussion of this phenomenon).

4. For an illustration of the operations of core–periphery linkage systems in Quebec, see Polèse 1982.

5. As Peter Pearse (personal communication 2005) has observed, however, British Columbia is in some years a net importer of raw logs.

6. Some regional development models stress the essentially binary structure of metropolitan and hinterland development trajectories within a provincial core–periphery setting (see, for example, Davis and Hutton 1989). However, the increasing diversity of Canada's non-metropolitan communities (including processes of industrial diversification and the formation of new labour cohorts) suggested by this sample of communities in transition underscores the need to avoid essentializing development modes and prospects for areas beyond the large city-regions, in favour of a more nuanced appreciation of tendencies toward increasing industrial diversity and differentiation.

7. For a useful elucidation of the concept of "existence value" of resources in a staples economy setting, see Roessler and McDaniels (1994).

8. To the problems cited by Rayner and Howlett in the aquaculture industry, we could add increasing foreign ownership and control represented by multinational corporations, and conflicts with groups dependent on natural fisheries (commercial fisheries, sport fishing, First Nations) concerned about contamination from fish farm waste products and the intermingling of native Pacific salmon species with escaped farm (Atlantic) salmon.

9. A well-known illustration of the potential of community ingenuity in creating a post-staples development future is the case study of Chemainus, British Columbia, described in Barnes and Hayter (1992).

10. Within Canada's urban system, a clear hierarchy of influence and power exists, associated with specialization, competitive advantage, and urban scale. A national workshop on urban transformation in Canada, convened at the University of Toronto in December 2004, concluded that five major city-regions—the Greater Toronto Area, the Montreal city-region, Vancouver and the Lower Mainland, Ottawa–Gatineau, and the bipolar Calgary–Edmonton corridor—will constitute increasingly the dominant drivers of growth and change in the Canadian economy, society, and polity in the 21st century.

11. This phenomenon is replicated in some respects at the provincial level, as observed in the "structural conflicts" between provincial governments and the major city-regions (which constitute to some extent an alternative and competing power source), exemplified in the political struggles between Toronto and Queen's Park and between Montreal and the provincial government situated in Quebec City. In addition to the "structural" features of this relationship are dynamic features, influenced by the nature of political control in the provincial government and the quality of leadership and personality embodied in the premiership and mayoralty, each of which is subject to change over time.

12. That said, medium-size and smaller communities that have attracted culturally diverse and artistic migrants are becoming increasingly diverse in their socio-cultural composition and have, in many cases, succeeded in mobilizing both long-established creative talent and newcomers to promote arts and cultural activity. Creative industries and associations within these communities also access the Internet and other advanced telecommunications media to interact with distant colleagues, partners, and audiences. Timothy Wojan (2004) has written about the potential of creative industry development in rural areas, and William Beyers and David Lindahl (1996) of the University of Washington have conducted research on what they term "lone eagles" and "high fliers"—new economy exponents working in the more remote districts of Washington state.

13. As examples in the Canadian context, Montreal "lost" both its national primacy in corporate control and financial activity, and its historical "western gateway" role in the 1970s; and Vancouver has seen a steady stripping of its head office sector since the acceleration of globalization and deregulation of the 1980s, producing by 2005 a decidedly "post-corporate" downtown.

14. P.J. Taylor (2004) of the Global and World Cities research network in Loughborough University, England, has proposed a sectorally and functionally more diverse nomenclature for assessing rank-order of world cities, including a typology of social, cultural, political, and economic indices of global hierarchy and engagement.

15. For a sampling of the rich and diverse Canadian scholarship on the influence of immigration and multiculturalism on the remaking of Canada's cities, see the website of the Metropolis Project's Research on Immigration and Integration in the Metropolis (RIIM) network: http://riim.metropolis.net.

16. Stoianovich (1994, 80) describes a mobilized diaspora as "an ethnoreligious collectivity whose elite members are communication specialists … diasporas engage in international commerce as insurance against the political risks of privilege in a single polity."

17. In classic Canadian style, early DREE and DRIE programs focused on strategies for the most serious cases of regional deprivation and disparity, but over time (and with exigencies of political pressure) evolved to encompass most of the country beyond the largest and most successful city-regions. A similar experience has been observed in the case of the federal cities agenda, which initially was designed to address the special conditions (problems and opportunities) of the largest cities, but following relentless lobbying and advocacy now includes medium-size and even smaller urban communities.

18. In conducting an assessment of the merits of the competing schools of comparative advantage and dependency theory, Thomas Gunton (2003) suggests that given the importance of resource rents, staples can continue to play significant roles in regional development in Canada, although the escalating costs of resource extraction require a tighter scrutiny and management approach. The employment and community viability implications of a steadily shrinking resource sector workforce, however, cannot be avoided in any forecast of the broader development potential of staples extraction in this country.

REFERENCES

Agriculture and Agri-Food Canada. 2006. An overview of the Canadian agriculture and agri-food system. Online at http://www.agr.gc.ca/pol/pub/sys/pdf/sys_2006_e.pdf.

Barnes, T.J., and Hayter, R. 1992. "The little town that did": Flexible accumulation and community response in Chemainus, British Columbia. *Regional Studies* 26(7): 647–63.

Bell, D. 1973. *The coming of postindustrial society: A venture in social forecasting.* New York: Basic Books.

Beyers, W.B., and Lindahl, D.P. 1996. Lone eagles and high fliers in rural producer services. *Rural Development Perspectives* 11(3): 2–10.

Clement, W. 1975. Debates and directions: A political economy of resources. In *The New Canadian Political Economy*, eds. W. Clement and G. Williams, 36–53. Montreal and Kingston: McGill-Queen's University Press.

Coffey, W.J. 1994. *The evolution of Canada's metropolitan economies.* Montreal: Institute for Research on Public Policy.

Davis, H.C., and Hutton, T.A. 1989. The two economies of British Columbia. *BC Studies* 82(Summer): 3–15.

Florida, R. 2002. *The rise of the creative class: And how it's transforming work, leisure, and everyday life.* New York: Basic Books.

Gunton, T. 2003. Natural resources and regional development: An assessment of dependency and comparative advantage paradigms. *Economic Geography* 79(1): 67–94.

Hayter, R., and Barnes, T. 1990. Innis' staple theory, exports and recession: British Columbia, 1981–86. *Economic Geography* 66(2): 156–73.

Hutton, T.A. 1994. *Visions of a "post-staples" economy: Structural change and adjustment issues in British Columbia,* working paper PI #3. Vancouver: University of British Columbia Centre for Human Settlements.

Hutton, T.A. 1997. The Innisian core-periphery revisited: Vancouver's changing relationships with British Columbia's staple economy. *BC Studies* 113(Spring): 69–100.

Innis, H.A. 1933. *Problems of staple production in Canada.* Toronto: The Ryerson Press.

Ley, D.F. 1996. *The new middle class and the remaking of the central city.* Oxford: Oxford University Press Geographical and Environmental Studies.

Ley, D.F., and Hutton, T.A. 1987. Vancouver's corporate complex and producer services sector: Linkages and divergence within a provincial staples economy. *Regional Studies* 21(5): 413–24.

Mackintosh, W.A. 1964. *The economic background of dominion-provincial relations.* Toronto: McClelland & Stewart.

Naylor, R.T. 1972. The rise and fall of the third commercial empire of the St. Lawrence. In *Capitalism and the National Question in Canada,* ed. G. Teeple, 1–42. Toronto: University of Toronto Press.

O'Connor, K., Stimson, R., and Daly, M. 2001. *Australia's changing economic geography: A society dividing.* Melbourne: Oxford University Press.

Polèse, M. 1982. Regional demand for business services and inter-regional service flows in a small Canadian region. *Papers of the Regional Science Association* 50(1): 151–63.

Polèse, M., and Shearmur, R. (with Pierre-Marcel Desjardins and Marc Johnson). 2002. *The periphery in the knowledge economy: The spatial dynamics of the Canadian economy and the future of non-metropolitan regions in Québec and the Atlantic Provinces.* Montreal: INRS-Université du Québec.

Porter, M. 1990. *The competitive advantage of nations.* London: Macmillan.

Rees, W.E. 2002. Is humanity fatally successful? *Journal of Business Administration and Policy Analysis* 30–31(Annual 2002): 67–100.

Roessler, C.M., and McDaniels, T.L. 1994. *A taxonomy and elaboration of wilderness preservation values,* working paper PI #6. Vancouver: University of British Columbia Centre for Human Settlements.

Sassen, S. 1991. *The global city: New York, London, Tokyo.* Princeton, NJ: Princeton University Press.

Scott, A.J. 2000. *The cultural economy of cities.* Los Angeles: Sage.

Smith, M.P. 2001. *Transnational urbanism: Locating globalization.* Oxford: Blackwell.

Stoianovich, T. 1994. Cities, capital accumulation and the Ottoman Balkan command economy, 1500–1800. In *Cities and the Rise of States in Europe, A.D. 1000–1800,* eds. C. Tilly and W.P. Blockmans, 60–99. Boulder, CO: Westview Press.

Taylor, P.J. 2004. Leading world cities: Empirical evaluations of urban nodes in multiple networks. *Urban Studies* 42(9): 1593–1608.

Travers, J. 2005. Her story not today's story: Immigrants now have a more difficult time getting ahead. *Toronto Star,* August 6: F02.

Watkins, M.H. 1963. A staple theory of economic growth. *Canadian Journal of Economics and Political Science* 29(2): 141–58.

Wojan, T.R. 2004. Recasting the creative class to identify rural potential. Paper presented to the 51st annual North American meetings of the Regional Science Association International, Seattle, WA.

PART III

Consumption Industries: Agriculture and the Fisheries

CHAPTER 4

The Two Faces of Canadian Agriculture in a Post-Staples Economy

Grace Skogstad

INTRODUCTION

It has been a long time since wheat was "king." The grain that on its own was once so closely identified with prairie economic development now must share pride of place with many other agricultural commodities. More broadly, other resources and industries long ago eclipsed agriculture's importance to Canada's national and provincial economies.

The agriculture sector has been transformed, and contemporary Canadian agriculture now bears several trademarks of a mature staples sector. Commodity and food production is capital-intensive; technologically advanced; and concentrated in fewer, larger, and more specialized enterprises. Even while commodity producers occupy an essential position in the food supply system, most of the contribution of agriculture and food to Canada's gross domestic product (GDP) now comes from value-added activities beyond the farm gate. The agriculture and agri-food sector as a whole accounts for one in eight Canadian jobs, but three-quarters of these jobs are either upstream from the farm in the farm input supply sectors or, more often, downstream from the farm in the food manufacturing, retail, and distribution sectors. Exhibiting another feature of a mature staples economy, agriculture faces strong competitiveness pressures, including from countries with lower input costs.

Although these developments describe agriculture's transformation to a mature staples sector, other attributes of agriculture as a staple commodity persist and continue to make it an economically vulnerable sector. The sector as a whole relies on export markets to absorb almost half of its production, and the figure is far higher for some commodities (for example, grains, oilseeds, cattle, and hogs). This export dependence, combined with the chronic havoc wreaked by bad weather and disease, renders a large part of the sector as susceptible to boom-and-bust cycles today as it was a century ago. The effort of Canadian governments to secure export markets through North American regional and multilateral trade agreements has been only partly successful. The Canada–United States Free Trade Agreement, implemented in 1989, and its successor, the North American Free Trade Agreement, implemented in 1994, promoted Canadian trade and investment across the US and Mexican borders. However, the resulting integration of the Canadian and American agricultural and food sectors has simultaneously made the Canadian agri-food sector highly economically vulnerable when its access to the American market is disrupted.

Agricultural producers remain in what political economist Vernon Fowke (1957, 290) described in the mid-20th century as an inferior place in the pricing system. Farmers, who can be considered as thousands of individual commodity producers, compete with one another even while they purchase their supplies from and sell their commodities to parties who can avoid similar "rigours of competition" (ibid.). Continuing to undermine farmers' market power is the ongoing consolidation in the firms that supply the farmer with inputs of machinery, seeds, and fertilizer and in the food processing, manufacturing, and retail sectors. This inferior bargaining power is more pronounced for producers of commodities reliant upon export markets than for producers in the domestic-oriented, supply-managed poultry, dairy, and egg sectors. Although single-desk marketing agencies, such as the Canadian Wheat Board, and more particularly, national supply-management plans for dairy, egg, and poultry products, have helped to correct this competitive disability, producers nonetheless remain at the "wrong end of market power" (Harkin 2004, 8).

In its current state, agriculture and food production is Janus-faced. One face is worn by the many commodity producers whose productivity has increased but whose incomes in recent years have declined in real terms (Bowlby and Trant 2002; Agriculture and Agri-Food Canada 2006, 24, chart A3.6). The other face is borne by the value-added food processing and retail sectors, where firms enjoy, on average, higher rates of return on their equity than their non-food counterparts (Smith and Trant 2003; Agriculture and Agri-Food Canada 2006, 62, chart B3.15 for food processing and 50, chart B2.6 for retail sectors). The co-existence of these two faces—the one seemingly in chronic need of state support, the other more robust—invites examination of the political, ideological, and economic forces that have shaped the development of the agriculture and food sector over the past century and longer.

This chapter traces the evolution of agriculture from a staples sector to a mature staples sector in the post-staples Canadian economy. Public policies are deeply implicated in agriculture's restructuring to a mature staples sector, and, accordingly, the changing patterns of relations between state actors and the agri-food sector are addressed.

Four periods of structural transition and patterns of state–sector relationships are identified. The first period, the expansionist phase, extended from the late 19th century to the 1930s, when agricultural commodities were integral to the development of the Canadian economy and the political community. The second period, from the 1930s to the end of the Second World War, marked an interregnum when agriculture merited attention not simply because of its service to broader national goals but also because of recognition of the structural disadvantages faced by thousands of individual commodity producers in a market economy. The third period, from the end of the Second World War through to the early 1980s, witnessed significant structural and policy changes in the sector in a quest to make it more productive and profitable. The transition to a mature staples sector was supported by state intervention in agricultural markets and the introduction of a financial safety net for producers. In the current fourth phase, since the early 1980s, changes in the international political economy, domestic fiscal deficits, and ideological shifts have precipitated a new competitiveness model. Strategies that are more responsive to market signals and offer incentives to add value to raw commodities are in vogue.

The four periods are marked by distinct patterns of state–sector relationships. Except for a brief period in the early 1920s, when farmers engaged directly in electoral politics, organizations representing farmers have acted as important intermediaries. Their strategies, organizational cohesion, and influence have varied over time, but one constant in their capacity to prevail has been the ability of farm groups to forge alliances with provincial governments. Such coalitions have been facilitated by the significance of the production, processing, manufacture, and sale of agricultural commodities and food to several provincial political economies.

AGRICULTURE AS A DOMINANT STAPLE: LATE 19TH CENTURY TO 1930

From the late 19th century and well into the 20th century, agricultural commodities were closely identified with Canada's economic and political development, and none more so than wheat. The production and export of wheat was "the keystone" in the National Policy inaugurated in 1879 (Easterbrook and Aitken 1956, 476), which was designed to create Canadian jobs, investment, and economic prosperity. The National Policy included tariff protection for domestic manufacturing interests, initiatives to attract immigrants to western Canada, and the construction of a transcontinental railway to move people and central Canadian–manufactured goods into the prairie interior, and grain and flour out to ocean ports. The development of the prairie wheat economy tied these various policies together, and collectively they warded off American imperialist ambitions and promoted Canadian commercial and manufacturing interests (MacKintosh 1923; Easterbrook and Aitken 1956; Fowke 1957).

At the onset of the First World War, the contribution of the wheat economy to the nation-building goals of the National Policy was fully evident. An independent nation had been established in the northern part of the continent, and the prairies had been settled by immigrants. Wheat was Canada's number one export in 1910 and continued to hold that spot in 1930. Wheat and wheat flour exports accounted for more than a quarter of all Canada's exports in foreign markets in 1930, almost double the value of their closest rival, newsprint paper (Hart 2002, 96). Agriculture's contribution to the pursuit of commercial and nation-building goals led to state assistance, including government regulation of grain elevators and grain-handling and storage facilities, and regulated railway freight rates for the transport of grain and flour, as set "in perpetuity" by the 1897 Crowsnest Pass agreement.

From the early 20th century onward, farmers recognized their competitive inferiority in the price system and mobilized to take action. Farm organizations were transformed into farmers' parties and captured political office in Ontario (in 1919), Alberta (in 1921), and Manitoba (in 1922). Given that the government of Canada was much better positioned than the provinces to meet producers' needs for better terms of trade (owing to its legal authority over inter-provincial and export marketing), more important was the 1921 federal electoral success of the Progressive Party. Campaigning on a platform closely aligned with the Canadian Council of Agriculture, the Progressives became the second-largest political party in the House of Commons. The Progressives used their influence to have the Crowsnest Pass freight rates (which the government had suspended in 1918) reinstated in 1922 and made permanent in 1925.

DEPRESSION AND WAR AND THE NATIONAL INTEREST: 1930–1945

The Great Depression of the 1930s and the Second World War were interregnums during which the state's role in the sector increased but in the service of "national interest" goals. The farm population comprised a significant proportion of the total Canadian population, and the farm economy was nationally important. In 1930, one in three Canadians lived on farms. In 1941, more than one in four still did (Statistics Canada 2001). With some rare exceptions (notably between 1931 and 1933) exports of grains, and later oilseeds, livestock, and meats, contributed significantly to the country's positive balance of trade and payments, and their positive effects continued even after 1930, when these commodities were overtaken by mineral and forest resources as Canada's most significant exports (Hart 2002, 188). During the 1930s and 1940s, agriculture comprised, on average, 11 percent of Canada's gross domestic product (Urquhart and Buckley 1965).

Two important initiatives during this period reflected the logic of the preceding era, with agriculture receiving attention to the extent it contributed to broader national goals. One was the creation of the Canadian Wheat Board (CWB). It began first as a temporary agency (1919–1921) and was restored under farm pressure in 1935, when the farmer-owned wheat pools collapsed. The CWB was granted a monopoly to sell prairie farmers' wheat in 1943, not so much because farmers demanded it—they had for two decades—but because a single-desk marketing board would ensure sufficient supplies of grain to meet commitments to Britain and other allies. The CWB's monopoly was renewed and extended in the postwar period to fulfill additional commitments, also to wartime allies. The move enjoyed widespread support from opposition political parties, the Canadian Federation of Agriculture, the prairie wheat pools, and the three prairie provincial governments (Thompson 1996).

The second initiative was the federal government's provision of financial assistance to stabilize prices of 11 farm commodities, including grains, dairy, and meat products. This initiative was designed as much, if not more, to secure national interest objectives as to assist farmers. Although the price stabilization programs supported prices at levels farmers found unduly low, they encouraged the production needed to ensure food supplies for European allies and prevented domestic price inflation (Drummond, Anderson, and Kerr 1966).

STATE INTERVENTION AND RESTRUCTURING IN THE POSTWAR PERIOD

The three decades after the Second World War constitute a period of massive structural change in the agriculture sector. Between 1951 and 1967, capital investment in Canadian farming more than doubled (*Canadian agriculture in the seventies* 1970, 334). This large investment was made possible by government-subsidized credit, stemming from the Canadian government believing that larger and more mechanized farm units would increase efficiency, enhance agricultural productivity, and make the sector more competitive. Agrarian restructuring was also seen as a way to reduce the problem of farm poverty that plagued Canadian agriculture into the late 1960s (ibid., chapter 2). However, as the number of farms declined, the remaining farms expanded in size, and farm labour was replaced with machinery (see figures 4.1 and 4.2), a sharp gap developed between a small number of large "commercial" farms producing two-thirds of Canada's total agricultural

Figure 4.1   Canadians Living on Farms, 1931–2001

	1931	1941	1951	1961	1971	1981	1991	2001
% of Canadians living on farms	31.7	27.4	20.8	11.7	7.4	4.7	3.2	2.4
% change over decade	13.6	24.0	43.8	36.8	36.5	32.0	25.0	

Sources: Urquhart, M.C., and Buckley, K.A.H. 1965. *Historical statistics of Canada*. Toronto: Macmillan; Statistics Canada. 2001. Census of Canadian Agriculture. Ottawa: Queen's Printer.

Figure 4.2   Changes in Canadian Farm Structure, Selected Years

	1981	1986	1991	1996	2001
Total farms	318,361	293,089	280,043	276,548	246,923
Total hectares	65,888,916	67,825,757	67,753,700	68,054,956	67,502,447
Average hectares per farm	207	231	242	246	273

Source: Statistics Canada. 2002. Total area of farms, land tenure and land in crops, provinces. Online at http://www.statcan.ca/english/Pgdb/econ117a.htm.

commodities and a much larger number of small farms that were responsible for only about a third of the country's agricultural output.

This structural transformation was assisted and cushioned by an expansion of state assistance for agriculture. This increase in assistance was initiated by the Diefenbaker Conservatives (1957–1963), who scooped up prairie farmers' support in 1957, after the St. Laurent Liberals had alienated the region with their hardline stance against agricultural support (Smith 1981, 27–29). When the Liberals regained office, the farm lobby, mobilized and prepared to engage in militant protest, exploited its early minority government status (1963–1968) to extract measures to deal with a persistent cost–price squeeze in the sector. Besides subsidized capital, three additional policy programs were implemented. First, the price stabilization measures initiated in the 1940s were expanded to offer many more producers a backstop against fluctuations in their incomes stemming from commodity price volatility and climate-induced crop failures. Government financial transfers to farmers expanded threefold in the 15-year period from 1957–58 to 1972–73 (Berthelet 1985, 10) and increased further when a program to stabilize prairie grain prices was established in 1976. Second, governments searched out new export markets and entered into an international wheat agreement to stabilize wheat prices. And third, complementary federal and provincial legislation enabled national supply-management marketing schemes that established production quotas and commodity-pricing formulas for designated commodities. These plans established prices at a level that guaranteed most farmers a stable and profitable income. By the late 1970s, dairy, poultry, and egg producers—the bulk of whom farmed in central Canada—benefited from national marketing boards that regulated domestic supply and prices and protected domestic products from foreign imports. Their economic bargaining power contrasted dramatically with that of grain and oilseed producers who were located overwhelmingly in prairie Canada. For example, the stabilization programs for the grain and oilseed producers did not offer a similar degree of protection from the highs and lows of the international markets as did the policies in place for dairy, poultry, and egg producers.

These measures of state assistance were secured over the 1950s, 1960s, and 1970s, despite the organizational fragmentation of farmers. Farmers did not speak with one voice. Two national organizations, the Canadian Federation of Agriculture and the National Farmers' Union, competed to represent farmers on a national plane. They were flanked by organizations representing growers of specific commodities, not all of which were members of the Canadian Federation of Agriculture. This multiplicity of farm organizations undoubtedly dissipated the leadership and coherence of the farm lobby. However, this weakness was offset by the strong alliances that provincial farm federations and provincially significant commodity organizations forged with their provincial governments (Skogstad 1987).

STATE RETRENCHMENT, REGIONALIZATION, AND GLOBALIZATION IN THE 1980S AND 1990S

In the 1980s, developments in Canadian and international political economies destabilized state assistance and market intervention in Canadian agriculture and called for new strategies to increase productivity and competitiveness. Domestically, large and growing fiscal deficits and public debt made state transfers to producers vulnerable until the late 1990s. In the international arena, trade protectionism and an unstable international trading regime from the early 1980s through to the mid-1990s provided Canadian governments with strong incentives to support market-liberalizing trade agreements. Agri-food exports accounted for almost 50 percent of farm cash receipts (Agriculture Canada 1989, 15), grain exports had increased four to five times in value since the mid-1960s, and pork and beef exports were also growing in value. The portent and subsequent implementation of liberal trade agreements intensified pressures for an agri-food sector that could compete in both domestic and international markets. This new context of fiscal deficits and liberal trade agreements, provincial and federal governments agreed, necessitated a new "vision" of "a *more market-oriented agri-food industry* that aggressively pursues opportunities to grow and prosper … *a more self-reliant sector* that is able to earn a reasonable return from the market place" (Agriculture Canada 1989, 3).

One federal strategy to give life to this vision was the funding of research into new technologies, such as biotechnology, with the government encouraging their adoption by farmers (see Moore, chapter 5). To enhance their productivity and competitiveness, farmers were also encouraged to diversify into crops, including non-food uses for existing crops (ethanol, for example). In prairie Canada, diversification into cattle, hogs, and specialty crops reduced the dependence on grains and oilseeds. Even so, by 2002, the agriculture minister was forced to admit that the strategy had produced meagre results, at least in terms of encouraging farmers to embrace innovation, diversification, and value-added production (Vanclief 2002).

A second thrust of the vision to create a more competitive agri-food sector was to emphasize "value-added" activities beyond the farm gate, in the supply, processing, and retail chains, for example, and to remove policies and practices that hindered their growth. Indeed, to indicate its broader mandate, Agriculture Canada was renamed Agriculture and Agri-Food Canada in 1993. By the early 2000s, the emphasis on value-added activities had caused a substantial shift in the nature of agri-food exports. Whereas in the late 1980s, almost 75 percent of total agri-food exports were in the form of raw or partly processed cereals, oilseeds, and meat products (Agriculture Canada 1989, 27), by 2000, one-half of agri-food exports were "consumer-oriented" (Agriculture and Agri-Food Canada 2006, 13, chart A2.4).

The third and fourth strategies to reorient the sector in a more market-oriented and self-reliant direction were to enter into regional and multilateral liberalizing trade agreements and to restructure policies of state assistance policies. Each is now dealt with more fully.

Regional Market Integration and Dependence

The objective of Canadian negotiators in the 1989 Canada–US Free Trade Agreement (FTA), its successor North American Free Trade Agreement (NAFTA) in 1994, and the General Agreement on Tariffs and Trade (GATT), the predecessor to the World Trade Organization (WTO) in 1995, was a modest liberalization of trade in agriculture. Equally important were the goals of mutually agreed rules of trade that would replace the unilateral exercise of economic power, reduce cross-border barriers to trade and investment, and create effective procedures for the management of trade disputes.

With a few exceptions, the Canadian and American agriculture and food sectors have become integrated. The indicators of integration are the emergence of North American or multinational agri-food businesses, the coordination of prices of some important commodities, and trade interdependence (Hertel 2001). This integration owes much to NAFTA's elimination of most tariffs among Canada, the United States, and Mexico, and its provisions for cross-border investment opportunities.[1] By the mid-1990s, American investment in Canadian food processing had increased to account for three-fifths of total foreign direct investment (West and Vaughan 1995); by 2003, the American share had climbed to three-quarters of total foreign direct investment in Canadian food processing (Agriculture and Agri-Food Canada 2006, 26, chart A3.10). Significant portions of the Canadian meat-packing, flour-milling, oilseed-crushing, and grain-handling industries are now owned or controlled by US parent companies (Paddock, Destorel, and Short 2000, 6).

Two-way trade has surged. In 2003, agri-food exports to the United States accounted for 63 percent of total Canadian agricultural and agri-food export sales, up from 40 percent in 1990 (Agriculture and Agri-Food Canada 2006, 17, chart A2.14). The largest component of agricultural exports is high-value (consumer-ready) products, including processed fruits and vegetables, beef, and pork (Zahniser and Gehlhar 2001, 19).[2] The United States is Canada's major export destination for agri-food products and its major source of imports.

Not all Canadian agricultural commodities are dependent on the American market. The largest volumes of wheat and oilseeds continue to be sold in other countries, and these commodities are thus affected more by global developments and by issues in the multilateral trade regime (discussed in the next section). Canada successfully negotiated border protection for the "sensitive" dairy, egg, and poultry supply-managed sectors under NAFTA and the WTO, and these commodities are overwhelmingly sold in the domestic market. But north–south trade in some of Canada's most significant agricultural commodities—cattle and hogs being primary examples—occurs in a typically open market.

NAFTA has not, however, guaranteed secure access to the US market. It does not prohibit countries from using measures such as anti-dumping, countervailing, and safeguard duties to compensate domestic industries from "unfairly traded" imports. American use of such measures remains a permanent fixture of cross-border trade. Throughout the 1990s and into the 21st century, Canadian cattle, pork, hogs, sugar, wheat, and barley were all subject to American anti-dumping and/or countervailing actions, and some of these commodities more than once (Alston, Gray, and Sumner 2001; Cox, LeRoy, and Goddard 2001; Loyns, Young, and Carter 2001). Although Canadian governments have usually succeeded in having the duties withdrawn and in demonstrating that the allegations of unfair trading are unfounded, this seemingly endless trade harassment has cost Canada and the agriculture sector considerably in lost sales and legal fees.

The high dependence of many Canadian agricultural commodities on access to the US market is problematic, as Canadian cattle producers learned in graphic fashion following the discovery in May 2003 of a cow in Canada that was infected with BSE (bovine spongiform encephalopathy). The American market, accounting for about 80 percent of Canadian beef exports and nearly all cattle exports, was closed to Canadian cattle and beef imports. Between May 2003 and August 2005, when the American and most other export markets had reopened for most Canadian beef and cattle, losses to Canada were estimated to be $4 billion (LeRoy, Klein, and Klvacek 2006, 26).[3]

Integration into the Multilateral Trading Regime

As a medium-sized power with a small domestic market, Canada has been a long-standing supporter of multilateral trading agreements to reduce barriers to trade. Agriculture, however, had been largely exempt from GATT rules until the successful conclusion of the Uruguay Round of GATT (1986–1993), which negotiated both the Agreement on Agriculture and the transformation of GATT to the WTO. The subsequent implementation of the Agreement on Agriculture by the WTO in 1995 curbed a number of domestic agricultural policies. Existing export subsidies were required to be reduced in volume and value, and new export subsidies were prohibited. Import controls and licences needed to be converted to bound tariffs, and minimum access commitments for imports were established. The minimum import quotas and tariffs that replaced pre-1995 import control measures were set at levels that continued to afford Canadian supply-managed products a high—if not higher—level of protection from foreign competition (Schmitz, de Gorter, and Schmitz 1996). The Agreement on Agriculture also limited government expenditures on trade-distorting domestic support measures. The Dispute Settlement Understanding created new procedures to settle trade disputes by binding countries to the decisions of dispute settlement bodies and precluding the avoidance of their legal obligations under GATT/WTO.

The WTO has produced mixed results in terms of securing fairer terms of trade for export-oriented sectors. On the one hand, the WTO has been a bulwark against American attempts to undermine the Canadian Wheat Board, an institution that enhances the price-bargaining power of Canadian farmers in the international marketplace and treats individual farmers equitably in terms of their returns from that marketplace. In early 2004, the World Trade Organization found unwarranted an American complaint that the CWB operates in a non-commercial and discriminatory manner and unfairly restricts access by US farmers to the Canadian grain-handling and transportation system (World Trade Organization 2004). On the other hand, the WTO Agreement on Agriculture has failed to open markets and to curb government agricultural subsidies. The large subsidies that the United States and the European Union provide their farmers—much larger than those provided by Canadian governments—have a depressing effect on international grain and oilseed prices. At the same time, the prohibition on new export subsidies derailed a dairy export program that would have opened up new export markets for Canada's dairy sector (World Trade Organization 2002).

The launch of the Doha Development Round of WTO negotiations in 2000 presented both opportunities and costs to Canadian agriculture. As with the Uruguay Round negotiations, agriculture proved to be a stumbling block to successful resolution of the Doha Round. The negotiations were suspended in mid-2006 when the European Union refused to make further concessions on market access (lower tariffs on imports and/or larger volumes of low-tariff imports), and the

United States refused to agree to further cuts in its domestic subsidies for agriculture. Any gains Canadian grain farmers would reap from cuts in American farm subsidies were likely to be offset by the elimination of government financial guarantees for the operations of the Canadian Wheat Board and concessions to allow larger volumes of imports of supply-managed dairy and poultry products (Gray and Furtan 2005).

Redefining State Fiscal Obligations

Consistent with the vision of a more market-oriented and self-reliant agriculture, government financial transfers to the agriculture sector dropped during the 1990s. From 1986 to 1988, taxpayer and consumer transfers to Canadian farmers comprised 34 percent of farmers' gross receipts; by the 2000–2002 period, they accounted for only 19 percent (Organisation for Economic Co-operation and Development [OECD] 2003). Although transfers to agricultural producers have dropped in all OECD countries, the decline has been more dramatic in Canada than in OECD countries as a whole, the United States, and the European Union, and greater than required by the WTO Agreement on Agriculture. In addition, Canadian income support programs were reformed to make them more trade- and production-neutral and to require producers to share a greater proportion of their costs.

State fiscal retrenchment hit prairie grain and oilseed producers particularly hard. The 1995 Paul Martin budget curbed payments for income support and eliminated railway export freight subsidies.[4] Although prairie farmers received a one-time compensatory payment of $1.6 billion for the loss of railway freight subsidies, "the true value of the lost benefit was three to four times that amount" (Schmitz, Furtan, and Baylis 2002, 173). By the late 1990s, low international prices and climate-induced low yields, combined with rising fuel, machinery, fertilizer, and freight costs, resulted in historically low farm profits for grain and oilseed growers. Canadian governments came under pressure to treat Canadian farmers in a manner similar to their competitors in Europe and the United States. With their fiscal situations much improved, Ottawa and the provinces injected new monies—as much as $5 billion annually—into agriculture. Government efforts to require farmers to take more responsibility for managing their income risks—by accepting a bigger share of the costs of risk management programs—were also forestalled by continued low incomes in the grains and oilseeds sectors.

THE POLITICAL ORGANIZATION OF THE AGRI-FOOD SECTOR AND STATE–SECTOR RELATIONS

Over the past two decades, the composition of national and provincial agri-food policy communities has changed, and within them, the influence of farm organizations. Compared to earlier periods, the policy community is more pluralistic.

On a large array of issues, policy-making discussions now include representatives of non-producer groups, including processors, further processors, retailers, financial institutions, and export traders. Domestic and foreign consumers' heightened attention to food safety has also brought consumer representatives into policy-making forums. Environmentalists are also seeking a say in agricultural and food policy, particularly in some provincial agri-food policy communities, as the potentially damaging effects of agricultural production practices on the environment have become more politically salient. In this pluralistic arena, the influence of farm leaders now depends more than ever on their capacity to forge alliances with not just provincial governments but equally with other farm and non-farm organizations.

Simultaneously, the capacity of national farm organizations, such as the Canadian Federation of Agriculture (CFA), to represent the farm community has been handicapped by farmers' organizational fragmentation and internal divisions. These fissures are rooted in multiple and overlapping cleavages: between farmers whose surplus products depend upon export markets and those protected within the domestic market, between farmers who operate large commercial operations and those less profitable, and between farmers philosophically opposed to market-liberal reforms and those supportive of a market-oriented agriculture. By contrast, other components of the food sector beyond the farm gate—food processors, retailers, distributors, and suppliers of inputs—appear more united in their goals regarding the state's role in the sector.

Two patterns of state–sector relations are evident. One is a co-operative pattern in which representatives of the agri-food sector work closely with government officials and representatives of other agri-food interests on advisory committees. This pattern is typical of issues such as the design of farm income "safety nets" or risk management programs and in the formulation of Canadian external trade policy (Coleman and Skogstad 1995; Skogstad 1999). Since 1997, the CFA, commodity groups, and non-producer interests have been members of the National Safety Nets Advisory Committee. The CFA, which represents 80 percent of Canadian farmers, has the most members and chairs the committee. Although the committee is labelled "advisory," farm groups expect that the committee's advice will be followed and have been harsh in their criticism when it has not. With respect to international disputes over the provisions of regional and global trade agreements, such as those pertaining to dairy subsidies and the Canadian Wheat Board, commodity and farm organizations have been consulted closely on strategies to resolve these disputes and, where necessary, on how to bring domestic policies in line with international law (Skogstad 1999, 2002, 168–69).

These governing arrangements, in which state and non-state actors collectively determine the substance of public policies for the sector, tend to expose the conflicts and divergent interests within the Canadian farm community. Even so, the

CFA enjoyed considerable success into the 21st century in bridging these divisions, particularly those between its export-oriented and domestically oriented members, and had the ear of the federal government on trade policy. The CFA's influence during the Doha Development Round of WTO negotiations has been destabilized after the emergence of an alliance of export-oriented interests under the title of the Canadian Agri-Food Trade Alliance (CAFTA). Whereas the CFA has long advocated a "balanced trade policy" in which liberalization of export markets for the grains and oilseeds sector is accompanied by domestic protection for supply-managed poultry and dairy sectors, CAFTA is pressing the Canadian government to adopt a position of liberal trade across the board. CAFTA's members, which include producer organizations, processors, marketers, and exporters from Canada's major trade-reliant sectors, are said to account for almost 80 percent of Canada's agriculture and agri-food exports and more than half of Canada's farm cash receipts.

The second pattern of state–sector relations is more confrontational and occurs when the pattern of concertation described above breaks down. In this second mode, farm organizations resort to conventional lobbying through a broad coalition of support across farm groups, business organizations whose fate is closely tied to the well-being of the farm community, political parties, and provincial governments. When hog, grain, and oilseed producers found themselves in a severely depressed economic situation in the late 1990s and early 2000s, the farm lobby solicited the support of prairie premiers, federal opposition parties, members of Parliament and senators on parliamentary committees, and the rural caucus of the governing Liberal party. The lobbying effort showed the depth and non-partisan nature of political support for farm financial assistance and was ultimately successful.

These policy victories of farm organizations notwithstanding, considerable influence over agri-food policies has shifted to the non-producer components of the sector. Agri-businesses beyond the farm gate not only have more influence over agri-food policy-making, they also exercise considerable structural power vis-à-vis producers.

THE STRUCTURAL INFERIORITY OF STAPLES PRODUCERS IN A MATURE STAPLES SECTOR

An examination of the structure of the agri-food sector reveals consolidation of enterprises throughout the entire food supply chain and developments that undermine farmers' capacity to extract fair terms of trade in the marketplace as purchasers of supplies and sellers of foodstuffs.

Approximately 350,000 farmers operate 250,000 farms, and they currently comprise about 3 percent of the Canadian population (Agriculture and Agri-Food Canada 2006, 65, chart B4.3). Farms are larger than they were a decade ago, and food production has become increasingly consolidated in the farms with the largest sales (ibid., 66, chart B4.4, chart B4.5).[5] The one-third of Canada's farmers who operate farms with sales of $100,000 or more account for almost all production: 88 percent of all sales.[6]

The economic significance of primary agriculture (commodity production) has declined relative to the downstream, value-added activities of food processing, manufacturing, and retail sales. In 2003, primary-commodity producers accounted for 1.3 percent of gross domestic product (GDP), the food processing industry represented 2.1 percent, the food retail/wholesale sector contributed 2.5 percent, and the food service sector, 1.6 percent (ibid., 6, chart A1.1). In economic importance, food processing now surpasses primary (commodity) production in all provinces east of Manitoba. It is the third-largest manufacturing industry in Canada and the largest in seven provinces (ibid., 7, chart A1.3). Even so, retail, wholesale, and food services now account for a greater share of Canadian jobs and GDP than do food production and processing combined (ibid., 6, chart A1.1).

Consolidation continues in the farm input supply (machinery, seeds, fertilizer), food processing, and food (retail and wholesale) distribution sectors. In the input supply sector, three companies control three-fifths of nitrogen fertilizer production (International Federation of Agricultural Producers 2002, 4); three companies retail and distribute the bulk of oil, gasoline, and diesel fuel (Easter 2005); and three companies dominate farm machinery sales (ibid.). Significant decline has affected the market share of farmer-owned cooperatives in fertilizer, seed, and animal feed sales (Agriculture and Agri-Food Canada 2006, 90, chart B5.8).

In the downstream sector, fewer and larger enterprises participate in the processing (ibid., 49, charts B2.3 and B2.4), meat packing, and retail sectors (ibid., 59–60, charts B3.8 and B3.9). In the retail sector, the five largest food retailers account for 60 percent of national grocery sales (ibid., 49, chart B2.3). By 2003, takeovers in the western Canadian pork-processing sector had left a single Canadian firm (Maple Leaf Foods) with a 45 percent share in Canada's prepared meats sector (Maple Leaf moves show faith in pork 2003, 6). Before the 2003–2005 BSE-induced beef crisis, two companies controlled 37 percent of the capacity in the beef-packing sector, three-quarters of which is foreign-owned (Qualman and Wiebe 2002, 9). Chicken processing is now fairly concentrated: the five largest companies in terms of volume processed almost 60 percent of all chicken in 1999, and the 10 largest firms processed 80 percent (Agriculture and Agri-Food Canada 1999). Most provinces have only one processor; should it go out of business, chicken producers will as well. Flour milling is now dominated by two large American-owned firms that control about 75 percent of capacity (Agriculture and Agri-Food Canada 2003). In the dairy sector, the arrival of multinational firms, such as Danone, Unilever, and Parmalat, has engendered consolidation and takeovers. The market share of dairy co-operatives has been reduced to 50 percent from close to 70 percent in the 1990s (ibid.), and only one of the three major dairy processors (Agropur) is a co-operative.

Consolidation has also affected vertical integration of economic activity at more than one stage of the food supply chain. Seed companies, for example, have integrated into fertilizer production, and manufacturers of animal feed have entered into poultry and hog production. Many of these conglomerates/companies operate on a global scale. Canadian farmers, like their counterparts elsewhere, find themselves part of food supply chains that span national and even regional borders.

The foregoing developments—concentration of agri-food businesses and their vertical integration into more than one stage of food production—raise concern about the consequences for farmers' bargaining power over prices. Quagrainie et al. (2003, 397) suggest that the limited number of beef packers allowed them to exercise "a small but sustained amount of market power" in the Canadian finished cattle market from 1978 to 1997. Mergers that diminish the market power of farmer-owned co-operatives lead to a loss of farmers' ability to extract revenues further downstream. In the grain-handling (elevator) sector, four farmer-owned co-operatives have been replaced by one publicly traded co-operative (the Saskatchewan Wheat Pool).[7]

The dominance of a limited number of private processors in the supply-managed sectors jeopardizes the marketing boards that have augmented farmers' bargaining power. Private dairy processors have taken advantage of their market power to negotiate prices downward in western Canada (Doyon 2002, 507). Unlike dairy co-operatives that support supply-management principles of production and border controls, multinational corporations, such as Parmalat, do not (Goddard, Boxall, and Lerohl 2002). In the poultry sector, chicken processors remain supportive of supply management, but further processors, who use processed chicken as an input to their products and who face competition in the Canadian market from lower-cost imports, do not. Pricing concessions have been made to render Canadian food manufacturers who use dairy and poultry products as inputs—those who make pizzas and chicken pot pies, for example—competitive with their foreign counterparts. In the grain sector, the changes that have seen farmer-owned prairie wheat pools replaced by private grain companies and the publicly traded Saskatchewan Wheat Pool also eliminated important supporters of the export marketing monopoly of the Canadian Wheat Board.

CONCLUSION

Contemporary Canadian agriculture typifies the characteristics of a mature staples sector. It is technologically advanced, and capital has been substituted for labour. And yet, aside from supply-managed dairy, poultry, and egg producers, Canadian agriculture retains the dependence of a staples sector on external markets to absorb at least half its output. The uncertainty of international markets and weather-induced fluctuations in production leaves all farmers but those in the supply-managed sectors highly vulnerable to unstable incomes. The promise of international trade agreements, such as NAFTA and the WTO, to secure export markets remains unfulfilled.

Despite its "maturity," agricultural production too often looks like a sector in chronic crisis: "an endangered species" (Pratt 2000, 1). Farmers have increased their productivity but many have not reaped the benefits. Most farmers have witnessed sharp fluctuations and a decline in their real incomes over the past 30 years (Brinkman 2002; Agriculture and Agri-Food Canada 2006, 74, chart B4.20). This income decline is the result of input costs rising faster than market prices and of international aggregate supplies (grains and oilseeds, in particular) rising faster than aggregate demand. The most profitable segment of the sector is beyond the farm gate; the largest profits accrue to those who add to primary agricultural commodities. Indeed, operators of small farms, and increasingly those of larger operations, now find it necessary to have an off-farm job (Culver, Niekamp, and Zafiriou 2001, 521). Nearly 45 percent of all farm operators earned some portion of their income from off-farm work in 2000 (Agriculture and Agri-Food Canada 2006, 76, chart B4.24). The inability of farmers to earn incomes in the marketplace has required significant government transfers to the farm community to sustain it. Brinkman (2002, 400) reports that "net government transfers and rebates from 1985 to 2001 contributed the equivalent of 77% of all prairie net farm income."[8] The largest farms have been the biggest recipients of government program payments; the one-third responsible for 88 percent of gross farm receipts also received 80 percent of government payments in 2001 (Agriculture and Agri-Food Canada 2006, 79, chart B4.30).

The income crisis, the depopulation of rural Canada (Epp and Whitson 2001, xix–xx), and the aging of the farm population are all reasons to view agricultural producers as a beleaguered sector. In the early 21st century, the agriculture and food policy community, including provincial and federal governments, continues to search for the mixture of policies that will deliver profitability to the sector.

NOTES

1. Trade flows have also been affected by the low Canadian dollar relative to the US dollar and by the domestic public policies of the two countries. For example, the elimination of Canadian grain freight rate subsidies made the US market attractive for Canadian unprocessed grain and oilseed exports. Simultaneously, US grain export subsidies created a demand in the American market for Canadian grain by making it profitable for American producers to ship their grain overseas.

2. High-value processed products are distinguished from processed intermediates (live animals, animal feeds) and bulk commodities (grains, oilseeds).

3. After August 2005, Canadian live cattle over 30 months of age were still not admitted to the United States. These older animals were deemed to be more at risk for BSE than younger animals.

4. The government transfers to the railways were implemented in 1984, following the abolition of the statutory Crowsnest Pass freight rates.

5. Average farm size varies depending on the province. Grain farms in Saskatchewan tend to be the largest farms (see also Bowlby and Trant 2002, 8).

6. The small and medium-sized farms with sales between $10,000 and $99,000 account for 45 percent of all farms. The remaining 22 percent of farms are hobby firms; they account for 1 percent of production and are totally dependent on off-farm income (Agriculture and Agri-Food Canada 2006, 79, chart B4.30).

7. The Alberta and Manitoba wheat pools merged and were subsequently purchased by United Grain Growers to become Agricore United. The multinational grain company Archer Daniels Midland is a major shareholder in Agricore United.

8. These transfers brought the average farm family income up to that of non-farm families and resulted in an average net worth for farm households above that of non-farm households (Culver, Niekamp, Zafiriou 2001).

REFERENCES

Agriculture and Agri-Food Canada. 1999. *Snapshot of the Canadian chicken industry.* Ottawa: Agricultural Industry Services Directorate, Animal Industry Division (Poultry).

Agriculture and Agri-Food Canada. 2003. The Canadian cereal grain industry: Sub-sector profile. Online at http://www4.agr.gc.ca/AAFC-AAC/display-afficher.do?id =1171901319253&lang=e.

Agriculture and Agri-Food Canada. 2006. An overview of the Canadian agriculture and agri-food system. Online at http://www.agr.gc.ca/pol/pub/sys/pdf/sys_2006_e.pdf.

Agriculture Canada. 1989. *Growing together: A vision for Canada's agri-food industry.* Ottawa: Agriculture Canada.

Alston, J.M., Gray, R., and Sumner, D.A. 2001. Wheat disputes under NAFTA. In *Trade Liberalization Under NAFTA: Report Card on Agriculture,* eds. R.M.A. Loyns, K. Meilke, R.D. Knutson, and A. Yunez-Naude, 143–63. Guelph, ON: University of Guelph.

Berthelet, D. 1985. Agriculture Canada policy and expenditure patterns, 1868–1983. *Canadian Farm Economics,* 19(1): 5–15.

Bowlby, G., and Trant, M. 2002. Agricultural employment and productivity trends, observations and measurement methods. Presentation to the International Working Group on Agriculture, Paris, France. Online at http://www.oecd.org/dataoecd/34/23/2771249.pdf.

Brinkman, G.L. 2002. Report card for prairie agriculture. *Canadian Journal of Agricultural Economics* 50(4): 391–413.

Canadian agriculture in the seventies: Report of the federal task force on agriculture. 1970. Ottawa: Information Canada.

Coleman, W.D., and Skogstad, G. 1995. Neo-liberalism, policy networks, and policy change: Agricultural policy reform in Australia and Canada. *Australian Journal of Political Science* 30(2):242–63.

Cox, T.L., LeRoy, D.G., and Goddard, E.W. 2001. Dairy disputes in North America: A case study. In *Trade Liberalization Under NAFTA: Report Card on Agriculture*, eds. R.M.A. Loyns, K. Meilke, R.D. Knutson, and A. Yunez-Naude, 253–82. Guelph, ON: University of Guelph.

Culver, D., Niekamp, D., and Zafiriou, M. 2001. Canadian agricultural safety net programs and pressures for change. *Canadian Journal of Agricultural Economics* 49(4): 509–27.

Doyon, M. 2002. An overview of the evolution of agricultural cooperatives in Quebec. *Canadian Journal of Agricultural Economics* 50(4): 497–509.

Drummond, W.M., Anderson, W.J., and Kerr, T.C. 1966. *A review of agricultural policy in Canada.* Ottawa: Agricultural Economics Research Council of Canada.

Easter, W. 2005. Empowering Canadian farmers in the marketplace. Online at http://www.agr.gc.ca/farmincome_e.phtml.

Easterbrook, W.T., and Aitken, H.G.J. 1956. *Canadian economic history.* Toronto: University of Toronto Press.

Epp, R., and Whitson, D. 2001. Writing off rural communities? In *Writing off the Rural West: Globalization, Governments, and the Transformation of Rural Communities,* eds. R. Epp and D. Witson, xiii–xxv. Edmonton: Parkland Institute and University of Alberta Press.

Fowke, V.C. 1957. *The National Policy and the wheat economy.* Toronto: University of Toronto Press.

Goddard, E., Boxall, P., and Lerohl, M. 2002. Co-operatives and the commodity political agenda: A political economy approach. *Canadian Journal of Agricultural Economics* 50(4): 511–26.

Gray, R., and Furtan, W.H. 2005. What do the current WTO proposals mean to Canadian agriculture? Online at http://www.crerl.usask.ca/policy_wto_proposals.php.

Harkin, T. 2004. Economic concentration and structural change in the food and agriculture sector: Trends, consequences and policy options. Online at http://www.agribusinessaccountability.org/pdfs/300_Economic-Concentration-and-Structural-Change-in-Food-Ag-Sector.pdf.

Hart, M. 2002. *A trading nation.* Vancouver: University of British Columbia Press.

Hertel, T.W. 2001. A global perspective on regional integration in North America. In *Trade Liberalization Under NAFTA: Report Card on Agriculture*, eds. R.M.A. Loyns, K. Meilke, R.D. Knutson, and A. Yunez-Naude, 75–85. Guelph, ON: University of Guelph.

International Federation of Agricultural Producers. 2002. Sixth draft report on industrial concentration in the agri-food sector. Online at http://www.ifap.org/en/publications/documents/Concentration6thdraftrevE.pdf.

LeRoy, D., Klein, K.K., and Klvacek, T. 2006. *The losses in the beef sector in Canada from BSE*. Online at http://www.uoguelph.ca/~catprn/PDF/TPB-06-04-LeRoy.pdf.

Loyns, R.M.A., Young, L.M., and Carter, C.A. 2001. What have we learned from cattle/beef disputes? In *Trade Liberalization Under NAFTA: Report Card on Agriculture*, eds. R.M.A. Loyns, K. Meilke, R.D. Knutson, and A. Yunez-Naude, 175–207. Guelph, ON: University of Guelph.

Mackintosh, W.A. 1923. Economic factors in Canadian history. *The Canadian Historical Review* 4(1), 12–25.

Maple Leaf moves show faith in pork. 2003. *Western Producer*, October 2: 6.

Organisation for Economic Co-operation and Development (OECD). 2003. Agricultural policies in OECD countries: Monitoring and evaluation 2003—Highlights. Online at http://www.oecd.org/dataoecd/25/63/2956135.pdf.

Paddock, B., Destorel, J., and Short, C. 2000. Potential for further integration of agri-food markets in Canada and the US. Online at http://www.agr.gc.ca/pol/pub/integration/pdf/integration_e.pdf.

Pratt, S. 2000. Farmers an endangered species: Survey. *Western Producer*, September 21: 1.

Quagrainie, K., Unterschultz, J., Veeman, M., and Jeffrey, S. 2003. Testing for processor market power in the markets for cattle and hogs in Canada. *Canadian Journal of Agricultural Economics* 51(3): 397–411.

Qualman, D., and Wiebe, N. 2002. *The structural adjustment of Canadian agriculture*. Ottawa: Canadian Centre for Policy Alternatives.

Schmitz, A., de Gorter, H., and Schmitz, T.G. 1996. Consequences of tariffication. In *Regulation and Protection Under GATT*, eds. A. Schmitz, G. Coffin, and K.A. Rosaasen, 37–50. Boulder, CO: Westview Press.

Schmitz, A., Furtan, H., and Baylis, K. 2002. *Agricultural policy, agribusiness, and rent-seeking behaviour*. Toronto: University of Toronto Press.

Skogstad, G. 1987. *The politics of agricultural policy-making in Canada*. Toronto: University of Toronto Press.

Skogstad, G. 1999. Canadian agricultural trade policy: Continuity amidst change. In *Canada Among Nations: A Big League Player?* eds. F.O. Hampson, M. Hart, and M. Rudner, 73–90. Toronto: Oxford University Press.

Skogstad, G. 2002. International trade policy and Canadian federalism: A constructive tension? In *Canadian Federalism: Performance, Effectiveness, and Legitimacy*, eds. H. Bakvis and G. Skogstad, 159–77. Toronto: Oxford University Press.

Smith, D., and Trant, M. 2003. Performance in the food retailing sector of the agri-food chain. Online at http://www.agr.gc.ca/pol/pub/series-rpt-collect/pdf/retail-detail_e.pdf.

Smith, D.E. 1981. *The regional decline of a national party: Liberals on the prairies*. Toronto: University of Toronto Press.

Statistics Canada. 2001. Census of Canadian Agriculture. Ottawa: Queen's Printer.

Thompson, J.H. 1996. Farmers, governments and the Canadian Wheat Board: An historical perspective, 1919–1987. Statement submitted to the Federal Court of Canada, Trial Division, *Archibald et al. v. The Queen and the Canadian Wheat Board.*

Urquhart, M.C., and Buckley, K.A.H. 1965. *Historical statistics of Canada.* Toronto: Macmillan.

Vanclief, L. 2002. Proceedings of the Standing Senate Committee on Agriculture and Forestry, No. 32, February 19. Ottawa: Government of Canada.

West, D., and Vaughan, O. 1995. Multinational firms, investment and trade in Canada's food and beverage industry: Policy implications. Online at http://www.agr.gc.ca/pol/pub/multininvest/pdf/multininvest_e.pdf.

World Trade Organization. 2002. Canada—Measures affecting the importation of milk and the exportation of dairy products: Second recourse to Article 21.5 of the DSU by New Zealand and the United States. Available at http://www.wto.org/english/tratop_e/dispu_e/103_rw2_e.doc.

World Trade Organization. 2004. Canada—Measures relating to exports of wheat and treatment of imported grain: Reports of the panel. Available at http://www.wto.org/english/tratop_e/dispu_e/276_15_e.doc.

Zahniser, S., and Gehlhar, M.J. 2001. North American agricultural trade during 1975–98: A background paper on trade flows. In *Trade Liberalization Under NAFTA: Report Card on Agriculture*, eds. R.M.A. Loyns, K. Meilke, R.D. Knutson, and A. Yunez-Naude, 12–42. Guelph, ON: University of Guelph.

CHAPTER 5

The New Agriculture: Genetically Engineered Food in Canada*

Elizabeth Moore

INTRODUCTION

As Skogstad has described in chapter 4, agriculture in Canada is a mature staples industry. However, it also includes elements of a post-staples sector, notably the trend of an increasing technological component of basic foodstuffs. The growing reliance on technology in agricultural production and processing is evident in the mechanization of farm production, the growing sophistication of food inspection processes, and other developments of industrial farming, but has been most visible in the use of sophisticated gene-splicing to produce genetically engineered crops and livestock. The application of genetic engineering to agriculture remains controversial in the early years of the 21st century, however, rendering problematic a transition of agriculture from a staples industry to a post-staples industry

THE FIRST WAVE OF GENETICALLY ENGINEERED FOOD POLICY

Policy-making in Canada in response to the development and sale of genetically engineered (GE) food rests on a foundation of enthusiasm for technology in agriculture. In this aspect and others, the first wave of GE food policy, developed in the 1980s and 1990s, is consistent both with agriculture's current status as a mature staples sector and with long-standing policy legacies. As the 21st century unfolds, however, the evolution of the policy context for GE food creates potential for heightened post-staples sector pressures. Evidence also exists of the adoption of some post-staples strategies for industrial development. Looking toward the future, both the impact of GE technology on the broader agri-food sector and the policy response to this technology are important factors in determining whether and when agriculture becomes a post-staples sector.

The first wave of GE food policy in Canada was influenced strongly by contextual characteristics that conferred a mature staples status on the agri-food sector. Policy measures in the 1980s and 1990s consistent with a mature staples sector within a competitive state include government funding for technology development, the positioning of Saskatoon as an agri-food biotechnology centre, the launch of the Canadian Biotechnology Strategy, the federal biotechnology regulatory framework, and specific federal environmental and food safety measures regulating GE food (see Wellstead, chapter 2). As the foundation of a GE food policy, these policy measures promote technological solutions to economic problems, place a priority on competitiveness, acknowledge the export dependence of key commodities, and reflect the pressures exerted by environmental groups.

Although GE food policy sits comfortably within the mature staples context of the agri-food sector, some of the pressures and strategies associated with the transition to a post-staples sector are also present (see Hutton, chapter 3). In the 1980s and 1990s, GE food policy-making in Canada was more responsive to the concerns of rural staples communities and the agri-food industry than to urban communities, interpreting consumer concerns as a proxy for urban interests. However, pressure to alter GE food policy remains constant from Canadian and international non-governmental organizations skeptical of GE technology, and consumer resistance at home and abroad continues to complicate matters. Although GE food policy has always been influenced by factors outside Canada, the mix of external factors influencing GE food policy appears to be changing as consumer and environmental concerns become more prominent and influential in policy-making. In response, policy revision into the 21st century has been more reflective of consumer concerns, with an emphasis on increasing accountability and transparency. Emerging genetic engineering applications appear likely to heighten the post-staples pressures that are already visible. Whether agriculture remains a mature staples sector will be influenced by the impact of these new applications on the economic characteristics of the agri-food sector, consumer reaction to these applications, and the government's policy response.

GENETICALLY ENGINEERED FOOD POLICY IN CANADA: A MATURE STAPLES CONTEXT

The enthusiastic embrace of genetic engineering by Canadian policy-makers and much of the Canadian agri-food industry continues a long-standing practice of applying technology to agriculture in the hope of sustaining and increasing profitability. As expected in a mature staples sector, that technology has become more capital-intensive in recent decades. Genetic engineering is part of this capital-intensive trend and, in the private sector, is accompanied by significant dependence on intellectual property rights to attract and hold that capital investment. Genetic engineering incurs high costs and requires an extensive knowledge base. Its integration into Canadian agri-food research, for example, has encouraged policy change aimed at facilitating public–private research partnerships that can pool financial and technological resources.

GE food policy-making has also been framed by the larger context of the competitive state and the economic issues of the agricultural sector (see Skogstad, chapter 4), including competition from the rise of low-cost producers, such as Brazil. In fact, the emergence of GE agricultural applications coincided with the development of the new competitiveness model in Canada, both coming to prominence in the late 1980s. This model places a premium on securing international competitiveness to ensure economic growth. It embraces the concept of the knowledge economy in which GE technology is expected to play a central role (Abergel and Barrett 2002; Moore 2000) and promotes diversification from traditional economic activities that are perceived to be in decline. In the early 1980s, the federal government made genetic engineering a strategic priority within this new competitiveness model and heavily promoted its promise in many areas, including medical and agricultural applications.

Throughout the 1980s and 1990s, as the development of GE food crops for commercial use progressed, the Canadian federal government was pursuing technological, market-based, market-driven solutions to economic challenges, consistent with the competitiveness model. For example, within Agriculture and Agri-food Canada, agricultural research policy shifted toward a more market-driven approach in the late 1980s and early 1990s (E. Moore 2002). This approach encouraged investment in GE agri-food research efforts by giving plant biotechnology firms greater influence on the research agenda compared to public sector researchers and providing plant breeders' rights (PBR), a form of intellectual property rights. The focus on creating a competitive regulatory regime and selecting market-based instruments in GE food policy was also consistent with the desire to shift from policy instruments, such as subsidies, which were under fire as a result of the priorities placed on both deficit reduction and meeting trade regime obligations.

GE food policy has also been clearly designed with an eye on the international context. The first wave of policy development was influenced by the international economic issues of trade and foreign investment. Aligning key policy measures with international trading partners and competitors was considered essential, as was the development of a policy regime attractive to the multinational firms that dominated private-sector plant biotechnology. Also, the high degree of export dependence of some Canadian agri-food products arguably provided a stimulus for initial adoption of the technology (GE canola, for example), based on the belief that the use of biotechnology would contribute to competitiveness through better yields. Aligning policy decisions with both competitors and key import markets, particularly regulatory decisions, therefore, became a priority.

Environmental politics were also influential during the first wave of GE food policy development, ensuring a precedent-setting precautionary policy approach. The environmental effects of GE food have the potential to be both positive and negative. Genetic engineering is not a direct response to resource depletion, but offers potential solutions to the need to improve the economic viability of agriculture and reduce environmental degradation. However, GE food is also seen as contrary to the stewardship goals of the organic food industry and, due to the issue of contamination, a serious potential threat to the continued viability of the organic food industry if organic standards exclude or set very low thresholds for GE inputs. Several environmental groups are also concerned about risks to ecosystems.

JUMPING ON THE BANDWAGON: INVESTMENT IN GENETICALLY ENGINEERED FOOD TECHNOLOGY

Characteristics of a mature staples industry combined to create a favourable environment for public and private investment in GE food technology. In the late 1970s and early 1980s, speculation began to grow about the potential benefits of applying genetic engineering to agriculture. The impressive theoretical possibilities of genetic engineering fuelled excitement and controversy, with the concept that a trait in one organism could be isolated, then transferred to, and expressed in, another organism. The term *genetic engineering* is used in this chapter to refer to these recombinant DNA techniques. The term *biotechnology* is also used in this chapter, given its frequent use within the GE food policy community and for statistical purposes, although as a broader term, it can encompass other techniques resulting in genetic modification, such as mutagenesis.

The economic uncertainty that has historically been a pervasive aspect of crop production in Canada has heightened the appeal of new technologies that promise improved returns and competitive advantage. Into the 1980s, agricultural biotechnology appeared as a bright light on the horizon, as producers became preoccupied with falling land values and grain prices and with a global agricultural subsidy war (Science Council of Canada 1985). Both agriculture's long-standing embrace of technology and the immediate context of the 1980s help to explain the federal government's decision to facilitate the adoption of genetically engineered (GE) food crops. Globally, the first GE plant varieties were developed in the early 1980s, making them one of the earliest large-scale applications of biotechnology to the agri-food sector. As a result, this chapter focuses primarily on GE crops.

The federal government played a leading role in creating Canada's pioneering status in the commercial adoption of GE food crops by working on and funding their development and, later, by providing a regulatory framework designed to facilitate commercialization (Federal government agrees on new regulatory framework 1993). This proactive role was formalized through the 1983 National Biotechnology Strategy (NBS). Its goals included creating a robust research infrastructure to capture economic and social benefits. The NBS provided federal funding for public and private research on GE crops. The National Research Council (NRC) was given the mandate to act as lead federal agency on biotechnology research. Its Prairie Research Laboratory in Saskatoon was renamed the Plant Biotechnology Institute in 1983.

The integration of genetic engineering techniques into plant breeding programs was pursued in public agricultural research centres. In 1983, the total Canadian crop effort in crop biotechnology was estimated at 100 "person-years," including 50 permanent scientists, and more than 90 percent of this effort was based in the public sector (Canadian Agriculture Research Council [CARC] 1983). By 1998, an Agriculture and Agri-Food Canada (AAFC) official estimated that the department's research branch was allocating about 25 percent of crop research resources toward biotechnology-based projects, or about $25 million per year. In 2004–5, AAFC spent $67 million on biotechnology research, 24 percent of its total expenditures on research and development (Statistics Canada 2005).

By the mid-1990s, the combination of policy innovation in federal agricultural research and the lucrative potential of genetic engineering had prompted significant growth in private investment in GE crops. For example, in the breeding of new canola varieties, private varieties now outnumber public varieties. Private investment in biotechnology research and development in the Canadian agri-food sector was $36.8 million in 2000 (Statistics Canada 2003), marking notable growth but still much smaller than AAFC's effort.

Into the 21st century, the federal government's focus has shifted from biotechnology to genomics, the research foundation of genetic engineering. Genomics refers to the gathering and analyzing of genetic information, including genome characterization and sequencing (Dueck et al. 1999). Genome Canada, established by the federal government, has funded eight agricultural projects. In the 1999 federal budget, $55 million was provided for genomics research over three years, including $17 million for crop genomics in AAFC (canola, wheat, corn, soybeans) and $17 million for the National Research Council (NRC). One-third of the NRC funding was to be allocated to agricultural crops, focused on canola. However, although rapid progress is being made in sequencing genes, the time frame for understanding the functions of these genes is expected to be much longer. This significant public and private investment in GE food technology in Canada is most visible in the agri-biotechnology centre created in Saskatoon, which contributes to the viability and diversification of the city as a regional economic centre. For example, spending on agricultural genomics research in Saskatoon was estimated at $120 million in 2003 (AgWest Biotech 2003). Saskatoon hosts the world's largest research program in animal health genomics, at $27.5 million, and a large AAFC/NRC plant genomics project, at $21 million.

THE DUAL GOALS OF REGULATING GENETICALLY ENGINEERED FOOD

By the mid-1980s, the Canadian federal government was examining regulation of commercial applications of genetic engineering, with the hope of achieving both promotion of genetic engineering's promise and protection of the environment and human health from its potential risks. Environmental safety issues include concerns that GE plants could become "superweeds" or have other adverse impacts on biodiversity if, through gene escape, their traits are transferred to wild relatives (Barrett and Abergel 2000). In food safety, concerns focus on how genetic engineering might alter levels of allergens, toxins, or nutrients. For labelling, debate revolves around what consumers need to know about the origin of food ingredients compared to what they might like to know. Mandatory labelling of genetically engineered ingredients appears contradictory to current international trade rules and raises logistical issues, such as the lack of capacity to segregate and prevent contamination.

The federal government's visible financial and political commitment to genetic engineering indicated that commercialization of GE food would proceed. Thus, regulatory policy-making needed to provide an adequate level of protection from health and environmental risks, but ultimately could not jeopardize the perceived economic potential of GE food. It has been argued that biotechnology regulation in Canada was placed in the context of international competitiveness as early as 1980 (Kneen 1992, 171–72). The assurance of safety through regulation was intended to provide a solid basis for consumer acceptance and to facilitate international trade—a goal that would be achieved by a science-based foundation. Provinces have largely deferred to federal activity on regulation of GE food, although Quebec and Prince Edward Island have recently contemplated regulatory action.

In the first wave of regulatory policy-making, options were limited by the federal government's fundamental choices about appropriate goals and means, as expressed within the 1993 overarching regulatory framework for biotechnology. Regulation could not impede commercialization unduly: it must be science-based, it must rely on existing legal authorities, and it must be aligned with international developments. Both industry and government championed a regulatory framework that would provide a predictable regulatory climate and encourage domestic and foreign investment (Hollebone 1988).

By the late 1990s, the initial GE food regulatory regime was in place with its overarching framework, environmental safety and food safety assessments, and a labelling policy. For the first time in Canada, new plant varieties were potentially subject to environmental and food safety screenings. The regulatory regime placed clear boundaries around what was to be included within regulation and what was not. Acceptable goals and methods included human and environmental safety, a favourable development climate, national and international harmonization, a risk-based assessment, and an open consultative policy-making process. Outside the scope of regulation were ethical concerns beyond safety, using regulations as a tool to encourage GE food research toward securing public good benefits, such as food safety and sustainable agriculture, and distinguishing GE from non-GE products through regulatory treatment.

For environmental safety, the federal government created an environmental safety approval process. The focus of regulation is on novel traits, both those created by genetic engineering and those created by other means such as mutagenesis by use of chemicals or radiation. Health Canada developed a food safety assessment process, triggered when a new food product meets the definition of a novel food. Novel foods include food with no history of use as a food, food created by a process not used previously to produce food, and food produced with the use of genetic modification, including genetic engineering and mutagenesis. The definitions of novel traits and novel foods encompass GE crops and food but include other novel products as well. As with environmental release, the scope of regulation is not restricted to GE products. Labelling is required only when significant changes have occurred in nutritional levels or in potential allergenic or toxic effects. In 2004, a national standard for voluntary labelling was finalized.

Although biotechnology skeptics have consistently criticized the regulatory regime, it has in fact been precedent-setting in its precautionary approach. Regulatory development was pursued in a context in which the precautionary principle was becoming well-known. As novel products created through a novel technology, GE food crops were regulated on the basis of scientific speculation and comparison to conventional counterparts, as opposed to a response to evidence of negative impacts, consistent with a precautionary approach (Krimsky 1991, 182). Another important outcome of regulatory development was ensuring that regulation did not discriminate against genetic engineering, which was achieved by using the novelty of the product as a regulatory trigger, not the GE process through which it was produced. The regulatory response downplayed the novelty of the technology in terms of risks it might pose, contradicting the radical potential touted through the government's promotional efforts. This approach sidestepped the issue of scientific uncertainty regarding the risks of GE crops and provided relatively little opportunity for public input on non-science-based issues. This combination of a seemingly precautionary approach with a lack of scientific and democratic legitimacy provided a relatively unstable foundation for the post-staples challenges that grew in strength in the late 1990s.

THE SECOND WAVE OF GENETICALLY ENGINEERED FOOD POLICY: POST-STAPLES PRESSURES AND RESPONSES

In 1995, Canadian producers began widespread cultivation of GE food crops. Since then, the context for GE food policy has become more challenging. The environmental and food safety risks have become more concrete, fuelling biotechnology skeptics. Their criticism has focused on the lack of attention paid by policymakers to consumer choice, ethical issues, and the degree of scientific uncertainty underpinning the management of potential risks. Pressures external to Canada from consumers and public interest groups in key export markets continue. Further, confidence in the benefits of GE crops has weakened within some elements of the domestic agri-food industry. Since the late 1990s, the Canadian government has acted to bolster GE food policy, focusing on reinforcing the legitimacy of regulation by building capacity and increasing transparency. It renewed its biotechnology strategy and created a new advisory committee with a broad mandate, referred the scientific issues of GE food to a Royal Society of Canada expert panel, and increased regulatory resources within the federal government. Biotechnology skeptics, however, are far from content with what they view as relatively minor revisions and efforts.

In 1995, Canadian producers began to switch rapidly to GE crops from conventional varieties, especially in canola. Globally, GE cropland area has grown from 1.7 million hectares in 1996 to 102 million hectares in 2006 (James 2006), with most of this cultivation in a few crops across 22 countries. Four crops (soybeans, maize/corn, cotton, and canola) account for virtually the entire GE global cropland. The global market value of GE crops is projected to be US$6.15 billion by 2006, based on the sale price of seed and technology fees. Canada has the fourth-largest cropland area of GM crops worldwide, at 6.1 million hectares in 2006, in canola, corn, and soybeans. The United States ranks as the largest grower of GM crops globally, with 54.6 million hectares in 2006.

As GE food entered the marketplace, regulatory policy became the central focus of contestation. By mid-2007, Health Canada had completed food safety assessments for more than 100 novel foods, about two-thirds of which were produced through genetic engineering. During the same period, Agriculture and Agri-Food Canada (AAFC) and the Canadian Food Inspection Agency (CFIA) approved almost 60 plants with novel traits for environmental release. Public interest groups launched or increased campaigns to raise consumer awareness about potential risks (Leiss 2001). These groups have circulated environmental petitions to draw attention to GE food and related issues, including molecular farming, GE fish, and GE wheat.

The GE food regulatory regime has been challenged on its democratic and scientific legitimacy. The first wave of policy-making marginalized consumers and focused on a narrow set of concerns. Further, scientific uncertainty about the risks posed by GE food could not be easily dismissed. The regulatory regime's foundations are shaped by past practices of relying on exclusionary science-based authority. But during the 1980s and 1990s, the growing visibility of the precautionary principle encouraged an increased degree of skepticism about the certainty of science-based decision-making and contributed to demands for more democratic policy-making. Clearly, Canada's existing GE food regulatory system has not been a guarantee of market acceptance and consumer confidence, as initially intended.

The regulatory development process left many of the policy issues posed by genetic engineering outside of the scope of policy-making, raising the question of democratic legitimacy. The regulatory regime created in the 1990s was developed through relatively closed policy networks, enlarged occasionally through managed consultations. In 1993, a multi-departmental, multi-stakeholder workshop marked a departure from an initial focus of consulting largely within the industry and scientific and governmental circles (Agriculture and Agri-Food Canada, Health Canada, and Environment Canada 1993). However, this workshop and a subsequent workshop in 1994 on the technical aspects of labelling were criticized for their limited participant lists and circumscribed discussion. Policy networks around specific issues marginalized or excluded interests outside of government and industry. The lack of attention to consumer concerns was possible in part because public awareness in Canada of GE food was limited through much of the 1990s. Parliament played a minimal role in the discussion, with committees occasionally studying issues related to GE technology, often splitting down party lines on their recommendations (Canada, House of Commons, Standing Committee on Agriculture and Agri-Food 1998).

The lack of attention to possible consumer resistance in the first wave of GE food policy-making confirms the mature staples status of the agri-food sector. More recent policy efforts to respond to persistent consumer concerns suggest that urban constituencies may be growing in their influence on GE food policy. Urban consumers are likely to focus primarily on the risks and benefits of consuming GE food, and possibly the environmental risks, with minimal knowledge of their impact on the agri-food sector. Since the predominant traits in GE crops to date, notably herbicide tolerance, have offered no tangible benefits to consumers, not surprisingly, significant numbers are skeptical of consuming a new product that may cause risks. However, GE food policy is still primarily influenced by government and industry priorities; thus, the key consumer sovereignty measure of mandatory labelling has not been adopted. Instead, policy revision has been aimed more at facilitating public debate and shoring up risk assessment. An interesting side effect of the GE food debate is that consumer concern seems to be contributing to a trend of heightened urban interest in how food is produced, which in turn may serve to strengthen connections between urban and staples communities and reverse a long-standing detachment.

It is not clear whether Canada's new national voluntary standard for GE labelling, which took more than four years to develop, will satisfy consumer demand to have a choice of whether to buy these products. The multi-stakeholder standard development process, managed by the Canadian General Standards Board (CGSB), was boycotted by most of the consumer, environmental, and other public interest groups that support mandatory labelling. Polls suggest that Canadians' support for mandatory labelling remains high, and concern about genetic engineering grows as knowledge increases (Pratt 2003). A 2003 Consumers Association of Canada (CAC) poll by Decima found that 88 percent of those surveyed wanted mandatory labelling. The CAC, once supportive of voluntary labelling, has now become a proponent of mandatory labelling. In 2003, the CAC left the CGSB process, stating that the only way consumers can have assurance is through mandatory label rules. In particular, CAC was opposed to the intention a food product could have up to 5 percent GE content and still be labelled GE-free (Wilson 2003b).

To provide a vehicle for broader debate about GE food issues, the Canadian government created the Canadian Biotechnology Advisory Committee (CBAC) in 1999 to provide expert advice on all dimensions of biotechnology: ethical, social, economic, scientific, environmental, health, and regulatory. In 2002, the CBAC released a report on GE foods broadly supportive of the existing regulatory regime, but with many specific recommendations for improving accountability, communications, and transparency. The report suggests investment in evaluating and monitoring long-term health impacts and in improving information for consumers and urges more attention to social and ethical issues raised by genetic engineering, particularly the distribution of benefits and costs.

In 1999, in response to public debate over the risks of GE food, the federal government requested the Royal Society of Canada (RSC) create an expert scientific panel to study the scientific issues of GE foods. However, the RSC went beyond this mandate to examine issues such as the integrity of the risk assessment process. For example, it noted the institutionalized conflict of interest stemming from the government's dual role of promotion and protection (Royal Society of Canada 2001). The government's multi-departmental response to the RSC report came in the Action Plan of the Government of Canada, released in November 2001 (Health Canada et al. 2001). Periodic progress reports since then provide detailed descriptions of proposed and completed actions to respond to the RSC report, focusing on scientific assessment tools (substantial equivalence and precaution), transparency and increasing public confidence, human health impacts, and environmental safety.

Policy revision in the wake of the CBAC and RSC reports has included some efforts to broaden the policy network, but not consistently. For example, in May 2002, Health Canada and the CFIA held a technical consultation on regulations for novel foods, plants with novel traits, and livestock feeds from plants with novel traits. A broad range of interested parties was invited, but only two representatives from consumer and environmental groups attended. Other participants came from the agri-food industry, governments, and academic institutions. A Health Canada consultation in 2003 on novel food regulation was broader. Beyond technical questions, the consultation also raised issues of transparency and how best to involve the public and external experts. Health Canada's "biotechnology transparency pilot project" allows for public input on new submissions for approval on both scientific and non-scientific aspects and is exploring how to add external experts to the once-internal review process.

Prior to these reports, the 2000 federal budget provided $90 million to increase the capacity of government to respond to GE technology. This money has been used by the CFIA and Health Canada to hire new staff; to conduct research; and to develop and improve scientific assessment tools, such as those used for toxicological and allergenicity assessments and for whole food testing protocols. The CFIA contracted several short-term research projects on environmental and other issues and launched a long-term study of economic and environmental effects.

Despite these efforts by the Canadian government, biotechnology skeptics remain concerned about the use of public money for the promotion of genetic engineering. In November 2003, the Canadian Health Coalition stated that the Canadian government had spent more than $13 million since 1997 on communications to promote biotechnology, including $1.1 million on polling. The coalition argued this money should have been spent instead on testing and labelling GE foods (Aubrey 2003).

The CBAC is also a suspect organization for these skeptics because of its promotion of the development of genetic engineering applications. For example, in February 2004, the CBAC issued an "advisory memorandum" encouraging renewal of the regulatory regime, to ensure ongoing development and commercialization (Canadian Biotechnology Advisory Committee 2004). It warned (ibid., 3–4) that "delays in filling the gaps in the regulatory system threaten the research, development, and commercialization in Canada of socially beneficial biotechnology" and that Canada risks losing opportunities, as in the potential for plant molecular farming.

Both the transparency and scientific underpinnings of the GE food regulatory regime remain vulnerable to challenge. The exercise of the protection of "confidential business information" continues to limit public release of information such as location of field trials and details about novel products. The challenge of creating meaningful baselines for risk assessment of novel traits and novel foods appears immense. Recent studies, mostly on environmental issues, tend to support the concerns of both biotechnology proponents and skeptics rather than clarifying the issues. Researchers find evidence both to reduce and to amplify concerns about risks (Alexander 2003; O. Moore 2002), and little data are available on the environmental and health risks of GE fish and animals and of plant molecular farming.

At the international level, ongoing activities in multiple venues are likely to influence Canadian GE food policy in the future and may act as restraints on domestic policy-making. These activities include the Cartagena Protocol on Biosafety, regulatory harmonization initiatives by the Organisation for Economic Co-operation and Development (OECD), and efforts on labelling by Codex Alimentarius, a United Nations body.

The Cartagena Protocol on Biosafety, part of the United Nations Convention on Biological Diversity, came into force in September 2003, and 142 countries are parties to it. The goal of the protocol is to protect biodiversity from the risks of "living modified organisms" produced through genetic engineering. It creates the tool of "advanced informed agreement" to ensure importing countries are aware of the organisms they are importing. Canada has signed but not ratified the protocol, stating that it is awaiting clarification of key provisions. Negotiations took more than three years, and the protocol remains controversial, with concerns about its impact on trade.

The OECD continues its efforts, which began in the 1980s, to promote international regulatory harmonization through consensus and guidance documents that focus mainly on the scientific aspects of regulation. Finally, Codex has also been long involved in attempting to create guidelines for the labelling of GE food. These discussions continue to be bogged down by major divisions between countries that support mandatory or voluntary labelling on the basis of method of production in response to consumer interest, and those that feel that the method of production is irrelevant and disclosing this information is potentially a major trade barrier.

Beyond the pressures from environmental groups, consumers, and export markets, the domestic agri-food industry may be losing enthusiasm for GE food. An initially positive and sometimes enthusiastic embrace of GE technology in much of the Canadian agri-food sector has become tempered in some quarters. The food industry, for example, has found consumer concern about GE ingredients a significant headache. Further, GE technology has thus far failed to provide notable assistance in coping with the ongoing vulnerabilities of the agricultural sector, and producers in particular, to weather, disease, and economic challenges of globalized agricultural trade and industry consolidation. Some producers have become more skeptical, as they see the loss of export markets and the risks of contamination. For example, Canada's rapid adoption of GE canola varieties resulted in the loss, at least temporarily, of European markets. In 1994, Canadian exports to the European Union (EU) had reached $424 million, one-third of all canola exports that year. By 1998, Canadian exports to the EU had dropped to $2 million. In the late 1990s, the Canola Council of Canada lobbied the Canadian government to factor export market approvals into the criteria for approval for commercialization. Food processors and retailers also began to take a more defensive position on labelling policy, suggesting if mandatory labelling were adopted in Canada, they would stop using GE ingredients.

In fact, the application of genetic engineering technology still raises substantive socio-economic policy questions, which no broad public policy discussion in Canada has addressed. How might genetic engineering technology restructure economic relationships within the agricultural supply chain? What impact might there be on the family farm and the viability of the farm community? It remains unclear how genetic engineering will transform the economic structure of the agri-food industry, and where power will lie. For example, plant molecular farming has the potential to significantly alter Canadian farming through the development of GE plants that produce lucrative non-food crops, such as pharmaceuticals. However, molecular crop farming is still in its infancy and uncertainty surrounds the scale of development that will actually be achieved. In turn, the distribution of the benefits and costs of such change are difficult to predict. However, in the longer term, genetic engineering is a potential tool for Canada to shift from competing in bulk low-cost commodity markets to selling into premium, niche, value-added markets.

One key factor in the distribution of the costs and benefits of GE food technology lies in the use of intellectual property rights (IPRs) to set prices and to control access to the use of techniques and genetic material. For example, the commercialization of GE crops has contributed to changing relationships among producers, input suppliers, and processors. Contractual agreements, and sometimes vertical integration, are more common, as input suppliers seek to protect the intellectual property in their GE varieties through technology-use agreements and food processors become more interested in identity-preserved cultivation and handling systems, often to avoid GE varieties as much as to buy them. Pressure exists to strengthen IPRs in Canada for GE crops and other agricultural applications. Those opposed to strong IPRs believe they result in higher input costs for producers, oligopolistic control of the seed industry, and threats to genetic diversity. The issue of ownership, with the turn toward genomics research, presents huge economic and ethical issues. The potential of genomics raises issues about who will own and who will be able to access knowledge about the entire genetic makeup of any organism, be it human, animal, plant, insect, or micro-organism. How this question is settled will have a significant impact on the distribution of economic and technological power within the agri-food chain and the future of public research, which has greater potential to produce public goods.

CONCLUSION: THE ROAD AHEAD FOR GENETICALLY ENGINEERED FOOD POLICY IN CANADA

The examination of GE food policy-making in Canada provides solid evidence of the mature staples status of the agri-food sector, with policy generally more attuned to the needs of staples regions than to the urban, consumer, and environmental constituencies of the post-staples state. The government's enthusiasm for the potential economic and social benefits of biotechnology and genomics remains strong, but both immediate and longer-term policy challenges loom. New generations of products promise both greater benefits and greater costs and risks. For example, beyond the immediate issue of whether and when to commercialize GE wheat in Canada are the challenges of developing policy responses to molecular farming, GE fish, and GE animals. The impact of these newer applications, consumer and industry reactions, and the policy response to them will further demonstrate and influence whether GE food policy becomes more of a post-staples issue, possibly existing within a mature staples sector.

The most immediate issue is whether and when to allow GE wheat into widespread cultivation in Canada. Policy-makers have hesitated on this issue, illustrating that they find themselves on uncertain ground, as post-staples pressures mount. Monsanto has a GE herbicide-tolerant wheat ready for commercialization, but high Canadian dependence on export markets for wheat has caused hesitation regarding its adoption. GE wheat could cause significant economic harm if solid market acceptance is not in place ahead of time. The chief executive of Archer Daniels Midland, one of the largest food processors in the world, has cautioned Canada to think carefully about GE wheat, noting that the bottom line is consumer acceptance (Rampton 2004). The Canadian Wheat Board (CWB) has been one of the strongest voices urging the Canadian government to incorporate market impact and acceptance issues into its decision making. The CWB's recommended conditions for commercialization include widespread market acceptance, development of an effective segregation system, and a positive cost–benefit ratio throughout the wheat value chain, with particular emphasis on farmer income. In March 2004, the CWB announced that customers representing 87 percent of the wheat produced by western Canadian farmers required guarantees that the wheat had not been genetically engineered. In the wake of these concerns, Monsanto made a public commitment not to proceed with regulatory approvals and commercial sales until several of these issues were resolved. In 2004, Monsanto then decided to unilaterally suspend efforts to proceed with GE wheat until market conditions are more favourable.

Policy-makers are also grappling with the challenges of plant molecular farming (PMF)—the genetic engineering of plants to produce non-food products, such as pharmaceutical ingredients and industrial oils. Federal government–organized workshops in 2001 and 2004 highlighted some of the issues: the current inadequacy of segregation and containment systems to prevent contamination of food supplies by non-food products, the related risk of using food crops to produce non-food products (potato, corn, wheat, barley, canola, soybean, and flax have all been used as platforms for PMF), the implications of greater regulation of the use of land (the licensing of farms to produce pharmaceutical proteins, for example), the handling of contamination concerns, the use of human genes, the potential longer-term transformation of Canadian agriculture should PMF become a wide-scale production activity, and gaps in knowledge and science (detection methods, occupational exposure risks, handling of byproducts and waste, contamination pathways). The CFIA has held technical workshops and issued discussion papers and draft regulatory documents on the regulation of PMF (Canadian Food Inspection Agency 2004). Meanwhile, industry is complaining that government is being overly cautious and has been slow to approve field trials (Wilson 2003a).

Both GE wheat and plant molecular farming raise issues of potential conflict over the use of land and liability due to contamination concerns. To avoid contamination, significant new costs may be incurred related to segregation, tracing, and assurance. Some in the agri-food industry have argued that aiming for zero percent contamination is both impossible and impractical—instead, acceptable tolerance levels must be set. However, in molecular farming, zero percent contamination, especially for pharmaceutical products, may well be necessary. If GE wheat is released and its ability to contaminate proves similar to that of GE canola, researchers suggest that cleaning up herbicide-resistant volunteer wheat with chemicals could cost zero-till farmers $400 million a year (White 2003). The Plant Biotechnology Institute has spent $1 million over five years on research related to contamination.

A similar slow and cautious pace of regulatory development is occurring with GE fish and animals. Much current effort appears focused on gathering scientific data. Health Canada's 2003 interim policy on food from cloned animals (somatic cell nuclear transfer) states that these animals fall under the definition of novel foods and therefore a pre-market safety assessment will be required (Health Canada 2003). However, since insufficient data exist to guide safety assessment, developers have been asked to delay novel food notifications for such animals.

Beyond these specific applications, policy-makers continue to face the challenge of preserving and increasing the legitimacy of the GE food regulatory regime. Capacity and transparency issues have improved, but will they contribute to the democratic and scientific legitimacy of policy choices? Efforts have been made to increase the information available to the public and to provide for the input of both the public and external experts in the approval process. But it is not yet clear whether citizen concerns will be better reflected in revised approval guidelines.

The use of Parliament and its committees remains minimal, despite being venues where the options for capturing the social benefits of the technology could be debated. It will also take at least a few years to judge the success of the effort to meet consumer demands for choice in the marketplace through voluntary labelling instead of mandatory labelling.

There are calls for more radical change. Although some argue for total rejection of genetic engineering (Kneen 1999), others suggest concrete ways to improve policy-making. Leiss (2001) suggests the federal government stop promoting biotechnology, launch a large-scale long-term public risk dialogue, create a new biotechnology agency to provide oversight of the broader issues, and use independent expert panels more often. Those who have studied the use of risk analysis, the precautionary principle, and the involvement of citizens in environmental policy-making also have recommendations of relevance. These ideas include an "alternatives assessment" that focuses on avoiding or minimizing damage with a strong precautionary basis (O'Brien 2000) and providing participatory deliberative forums where the local knowledge of citizens can be used to make better policy (Fischer 2000).

But for the time being, radical change appears to be off the table. GE food policy continues to be driven primarily by economic concerns and the priorities of the agri-food industry. This outcome suggests that although the economic importance of the agri-food sector may have declined as a percentage of Canada's economy, politically this sector remains significant. This influence in turn likely contributed to the weakness in anticipating skepticism and resistance among domestic and international consumers. In the short term, some potential exists for a shift toward more consumer-responsive policy-making, if consumer resistance continues. However, such a shift seems unlikely to improve the weak bargaining position of producers in the economic agri-food supply chain, unless producers succeed in forging more direct producer–consumer links. And over the much longer term, GE technology may indeed be decisive in determining whether and when the sector makes a transition to a post-staples status. Most notably, if molecular farming becomes a significant activity, it may eventually dwarf traditional agri-food activity.

In some ways, Canada's significant public investment in agricultural biotechnology remains a largely unrewarded gamble. Public benefits from agricultural applications thus far appear minimal, considering the scale of public investment. Some producers may have increased their returns by using GE crops, but others have lost markets. Developers promise that new products, still in the pipeline, will bring much more obvious benefits to consumers, such as enhanced nutrition, and more important production traits, such as disease resistance and cold and drought tolerance. In the meantime, significant numbers of consumers in Canada and abroad actively avoid GE ingredients in their food. For biotechnology skeptics who remain fixed on questions of scientific uncertainty and sometimes question the fundamental utility and ethics of genetic engineering, persuading them to reduce or drop their opposition may take a massive shift in the cost–benefit equation. With much uncertainty ahead about who will benefit and how from GE food, and agricultural biotechnology more broadly, the polarization of public debate will likely continue for some time.

NOTE

*   The views expressed in this chapter do not necessarily reflect the view of Agriculture and Agri-Food Canada.

REFERENCES

Abergel, E., and Barrett, K. 2002. Putting the cart before the horse: A review of biotechnology policy in Canada. *Journal of Canadian Studies* 37(3): 135–61.

Agriculture and Agri-Food Canada, Health Canada, and Environment Canada. 1993. Workshop on regulating agricultural products of biotechnology. Ottawa, November 8–10.

AgWest Biotech. 2003. Saskatchewan: Canada's agricultural genomics powerhouse. Online at http://www.agwest.sk.ca/publications/docs/Genomics2003.pdf.

Alexander, D. 2003. Study throws GM crops in doubt. *Western Producer*, January 16: 20.

Aubrey, J. 2003. $13M polishes biotech image, critics charge. *Ottawa Citizen*, November 24: A5.

Barrett, K., and Abergel, E. 2000. Breeding familiarity: Environmental risk assessment for genetically-engineered crops in Canada. *Science and Public Policy* 27(1): 2–12.

Canada, House of Commons, Standing Committee on Agriculture and Agri-Food. 1998. Capturing the advantage: Agricultural biotechnology in the new millennium. Online at http://cmte.parl.gc.ca/cmte/CommitteePublication.aspx?COM=107&Lang=1&SourceId=36191.

Canadian Agriculture Research Council (CARC). 1983. *Biotechnology: Research and development for Canada's agriculture and food system.* Ottawa: CARC.

Canadian Biotechnology Advisory Committee. 2004. Completing the biotechnology regulatory frameworks. Online at http://cbac-cccb.ca/epic/site/cbac-cccb.nsf/vwapj/regulation_clean.pdf/$FILE/regulation_clean.pdf.

Canadian Food Inspection Agency. 2004. Executive summary: Technical workshop on the segregation and handling of potential commercial plant molecular farming products and by-products. Online at http://www.inspection.gc.ca/english/plaveg/bio/mf/segrege.shtml.

Dueck, J., Weller, W., Moore, S., and Scholes, G. 1999. Genomics in agriculture: A discussion paper. Online at http://www.carc-crac.ca/english/publications_documents/genomics.htm.

Federal government agrees on new regulatory framework for biotechnology. 1993. Online at http://www.inspection.gc.ca/english/sci/biotech/reg/fracade.shtml.

Fischer, F. 2000. *Citizens, experts, and the environment.* Durham, NC: Duke University Press.

Health Canada. 2003. Interim policy on foods from cloned animals. Online at http://www.hc-sc.gc.ca/fn-an/legislation/pol/pol-cloned_animal-clones_animaux_e.html.

Health Canada, the Canadian Food Inspection Agency, Environment Canada, Agriculture and Agri-Food Canada, and the Department of Fisheries and Oceans Canada. 2001. Action plan of the government of Canada in response to the Royal Society of Canada expert panel report. Online at http://www.hc-sc.gc.ca/sr-sr/alt_formats/hpfb-dgpsa/pdf/pubs/RSC_response-reponse_SRC_e.pdf.

Hollebone, J. 1988. An overview of the Canadian federal and agricultural regulatory frameworks for biotechnology. In *Proceedings of the Workshop on the Regulation of Agricultural Products of Biotechnology*, ed. I.L. Stevenson, 37–49. Ottawa: Canadian Agricultural Research Council.

James, C. 2006. ISAAA brief 35-2006: Executive Summary — Global status of commercialized biotech/GM crops: 2006. Online at http://www.isaaa.org/resources/publications/briefs/35/executivesummary/default.html.

Kneen, B. 1992. *The rape of canola.* Toronto: NC Press.

Kneen, B. 1999. *Farmageddon: Food and the culture of biotechnology.* Gabriola Island, BC: New Society Publishers.

Krimsky, S. 1991. *Biotechnics and society: The rise of industrial genetics.* New York: Praeger.

Leiss, W. 2001. *In the chamber of risks: Understanding risk controversies.* Montreal and Kingston: McGill-Queen's University Press.

Moore, E. 2000. Science, internationalization, and policy networks: Regulating genetically-engineered food crops in Canada and the United States, 1973–1998. Doctoral dissertation, University of Toronto.

Moore, E. 2002. The new direction of federal agricultural research in Canada: From public good to private gain? *Journal of Canadian Studies* 37(3): 112–34.

Moore, O. 2002. Plants with added antipest gene may beget superweeds, study says. *The Globe and Mail,* August 9: A6.

O'Brien, M. 2000. *Making better environmental decisions: An alternative to risk assessment.* Cambridge: MIT Press/Environmental Research Foundation.

Pratt, S. 2003. GM food worries grow in Canada. *Western Producer,* May 15: 15.

Rampton, R. 2004. Canada farmers should be wary of GM wheat: Andreas. Online at http://www.planetark.com/dailynewsstory.cfm/newsid/24624/story.htm.

Royal Society of Canada. 2001. Elements of precaution: Recommendations for the regulation of food biotechnology in Canada. Online at http://www.agbios.com/docroot/articles/2001035-A.pdf.

Science Council of Canada. 1985. *Seeds of renewal: Biotechnology and Canada's resource industries.* Ottawa: Science Council of Canada.

Statistics Canada. 2003. Biotechnology research and development (R&D) in Canadian industry, 2000. Online at http://www.statcan.ca/english/freepub/88-001-XIB/88-001-XIB2003004.pdf.

Statistics Canada. 2005. Biotechnology scientific activities in federal government departments and agencies, 2004–2005. Online at http://dsp-psd.pwgsc.gc.ca/Collection/Statcan/88-001-XIB/88-001-XIE2006002.pdf.

White, E. 2003. Researchers place dollar value on GM contamination. *Western Producer*, November 14: 4.

Wilson, B. 2003a. Biotech industry says gov't holding it back. *Western Producer*, October 16: 63.

Wilson, B. 2003b. Consumers walk away from GM label group. *Western Producer*, August 21: 54.

CHAPTER 6

The Canadian Fisheries Industry: Retrospect and Prospect

Gunhild Hoogensen

INTRODUCTION

> Five hundred years ago, the explorer John Cabot returned from the waters
> around what is now Newfoundland and reported that codfish ran so thick you
> could catch them by hanging wicker baskets over a ship's side. Cabot had dis-
> covered a resource that would change England forever, the basis of a maritime
> trade that would give that tiny island kingdom the wealth, skills and shipbuild-
> ing capacity which would transform it into a global empire. He had discovered
> the most fantastic fishing grounds the world had ever seen, waters so teeming
> with life that a vast swath of the new world was colonized just to harvest its
> seemingly limitless bounty. (Woodard 2001, 35)

The fishing industry is one of the oldest in Canada, having initiated trade primarily with Britain when Europeans first came to Canadian shores. Because fish were
one of the first bulk staples products exported from Canada, the fisheries have
played an important role in the development of Canada's economy. The Canadian
fisheries have been an increasing concern in recent years, however, not so much
for the contribution they now make to the Canadian economy (which is small)
but for the environmental and conservation costs that have been incurred within
the fisheries industry and its communities as exploitation of fish stocks using
mechanized harvesting techniques has pushed many fish stocks, not only cod, to
historically low levels. How to reverse these trends in a mature staples industry
and how to manage a sustainable fishery are increasing concerns and priorities not
only in Canada but also in international forums.[1] Although the impacts and costs

of fisheries' decline are felt domestically, fisheries management in the modern era has become much more of an international concern. Given the ability of harvesters from many countries to (over)exploit many species either in international waters or as they migrate through domestic oceans, various international forums and organizations increasingly provide the analyses that establish and illustrate the critical link among economic, environmental, cultural, political, and social values and variables in fisheries policy.

As Wellstead noted (see chapter 2), all natural resource sectors are subject to various notable influences, including trade liberalization, globalization, and trans-national organizations. Institutions such as the World Trade Organization (WTO), "the only global organization dealing with the rules of trade between nations" (World Trade Organization n.d.), hope to work in tandem with other non-governmental organizations (NGOs) and inter-governmental organizations (IGOs) in the interest of securing sustainable and economically successful fisheries. The ways in which these influences affect the fisheries depend on the nature of the governmental structures and regimes that govern the fisheries within each state, how the fisheries relate to these various institutions, and how natural resource sectors and governments relate to external institutions (for example, trade liberalization institutions, such as the World Trade Organization). These relationships change over time and are particularly relevant when examining the emergence of new economic sectors among the traditional sectors or the shifts from traditional staples economies to new post-staples economies. The relationship between these influences, particularly the trade liberalization pursued by the Ricardian state in this sector of economic activity, is the focus of this chapter.

THE FISHERIES AS STAPLES INDUSTRIES

As Wellstead and Hutton set out in their chapters (see Wellstead, chapter 2; Hutton, chapter 3), a staple is essentially a primary-sector "building block" in natural resource–based economies. It is a raw or unfinished commodity, such as timber or fish, which is sold on the market with little to no processing (Hessing and Howlett 1997). Staples economy theory, developed by Harold A. Innis, is based on the Canadian experience as a new settler society with a vast resource base. Proponents of this theory argue that the development of Canada's economy was strongly linked to its natural resources and driven by global demand for these resources or, more precisely, subject to the external pressures of global demand (ibid.; Laxer 1985). The pressures of external demand create a centre–periphery relationship, in which the external forces represent the metropole or centre that determines the development of, in this case, Canada's periphery economy.

A major international focus has always, therefore, been integral to staples theory (Laxer 1985); so much so that staples theory has sometimes been interpreted to take Canada "off the hook," regarding responsibility for its own economic development. Marchak (1985, 676) has argued "underdevelopment was due not to entrepreneurial weakness, cultural deficiencies, or lack of aggregate demand, but to the combination of control of internal surplus by a national bourgeoisie unconcerned with national industrial development, and the market demands and constraints imposed by Britain and, subsequently, the United States," demonstrating the way in which staples theory, in his view, can be applied to Canada.

As Gordon Laxer (1985) has argued, however, the development of the Canadian economy cannot be solely attributed to policy emanating from metropolitan countries. This approach echoes the view of Mel Watkins that "staple economies are often believed to be more at the mercy of destiny than they actually are" (Watkins 1967, 63, in Laxer 1985). That Canada has been heavily reliant on its natural resources is not a matter of dispute; the centre of this debate is who has controlled the development of this resource-based economy. Has Canadian internal policy been responsible for the creation of this staples state, or has it been the power of external forces or metropolitan countries, such as Britain and the United States? The dynamics between internal and external forces on the Canadian economy are particularly relevant when looking at the fisheries. Here, the relationships between Canadian and "metropolitan" policies come to the fore as international agreements concerning trade in general, and fisheries management specifically, represent the negotiated settlements between states regarding what they will trade and under what conditions.

This chapter highlights the developments in the Canadian fisheries, examining some of the problems experienced by the Canadian fishing industry and the effects on the Canadian fishing industry of trade liberalization and trade agreements, such as the North American Free Trade Agreement (NAFTA) and the WTO. The purpose of this chapter is to discuss where the Canadian fisheries stand in relation to the shifting of the Canadian economy from a staples economy to a post-staples economy and how this relationship is affected by external factors, such as international trade regimes and agreements.

THE STATUS OF THE CURRENT CANADIAN FISHERY

As Wellstead has discussed, Canada is arguably moving from a staples political economy to a post-staples political economy, at least insofar as a number of the dominant provinces, such as Quebec and Ontario, have left natural resources behind as fundamental features of their economic development (see Wellstead, chapter 2, figure 2.2). Even provinces such as British Columbia that have been traditionally labelled staples economies are demonstrating much more complex economies, in which manufacturing, particularly in electronics and communication, now far outstrips growth in the natural resource sectors (Hutton 1994). Nevertheless, the fisheries remain a feature of Canada's traditional staples base and a significant employer in many coastal communities, including the Atlantic, Pacific, and Arctic regions. Although fisheries harvests have declined, Canada's large extent of coastline and its location on key migration routes of critical food species, such as salmon and cod, ensure that it will have an active fisheries policy and will be a major player in international fisheries negotiations and accords.

As in the past (discussed in the following section), the leading export market for the Canadian fisheries today remains the United States, with the European Union (EU) coming in a distant second.[2] Other markets include non-EU European countries, Central and South America, Japan (whose export numbers are close behind those of the EU), Asia, and Africa. Figures 6.1 and 6.2 illustrate the developments of these markets over a seven-year period (2000 to 2006) and provide a glimpse into earlier developments during the 1990s (with statistics for 1990, 1995, and 1999).

The quantities of export commodities were high in 1990; exports to the EU were the highest in the 16 years between 1990 and 2006. The quantities of fisheries-based export commodities dropped significantly after the moratorium on cod in the early 1990s, after which both the US and EU quantities and value declined. However, both quantities and value (the value being also dependent on the price per kilogram) increased during the latter half of the 1990s and into the new millennium, although both increases were not based on the same species being fished over time.

Despite increases in groundfish quantities from 2000 to 2005, the cod fisheries continue to show a significant decline, whereas hake, flounder, and Greenland turbot show significant increases. Pelagic fish, those whose habitat is the open sea, such as Atlantic salmon, mackerel, and capelin, also saw increases in catch quantities, thereby increasing the overall value of the fisheries. The shrimp fisheries more than doubled in annual quantity over this same five-year period, with crab (including snow or queen crab and Dungeness crab) also exhibiting discernable increases (Fisheries and Oceans Canada 2006c). The summary of Canadian commercial catches shows that the quantities fished from 2000 to 2004 have increased each year (the value of the catches differs to some degree, though not radically, based on the market value of the fished products) (Fisheries and Oceans Canada 2006c, 2007). In other words, declining stocks have not significantly reduced the quantity fished and the value of the fisheries, because declining stocks are being replaced by other stocks.

Alternatives are also being sought—for example, through aquaculture. The increase in fish production since the mid-1980s has been enormous. Finfish (such as Atlantic, Chinook, and Coho salmons, and trout) and shellfish (such as clams, oysters, mussels, and scallops) are all a part of the aquaculture industry, which, in 1986, produced almost 10,500 tonnes of product; by 2004, it was almost 146,000

Figure 6.1   Imports of Selected Canadian Fishery Commodities[a] by the United States

Time period (January–December)	Quantity (in tonnes)	Total value (in Cdn $1,000)	Value per kilogram (in Cdn $)
2006	343,365	2,524,793	7.35
2005	363,245	2,663,239	7.33
2004	374,078	2,823,524	7.55
2003	375,320	3,007,872	8.01
2002	401,279	3,273,261	8.16
2001	368,526	3,065,753	8.32
2000	345,539	2,899,319	8.39
1999	338,524	2,583,531	7.63
1995	278,652	1,569,599	5.63
1990	362,366	1,411,079	3.89

[a] The selected commodities refer to seafish and freshwater fish (whole, dressed fresh, frozen, fillets, blocks); fish meat; smoked, salted, dried, pickled/cured, and canned fish; shellfish (fresh, frozen, and canned); fish livers and roes; shellfish meal; and fish oil (Fisheries and Oceans Canada 2006b).

Source: Fisheries and Oceans Canada. Various years. Domestic exports of selected commodities by major market and country quantity in tonnes, product weight/value in thousand Canadian dollars. Online at http://www.dfo-mpo.gc.ca/communic/statistics/trade/canadian_trade/export_data/index_e.htm.

Figure 6.2   Imports of Selected Canadian Fishery Commodities[a] by the European Union

Time period (January–December)	Quantity (in tonnes)	Total value (in Cdn $1,000)	Value per kilogram (in Cdn $)
2006	97,811	532,796	5.45
2005	79,207	459,055	5.80
2004	79,432	474,364	5.97
2003	70,649	455,983	6.45
2002	56,426	369,772	6.55
2001	59,255	366,169	6.18
2000	50,904	329,957	6.48
1999	57,432	361,686	6.30
1995	43,537	310,233	7.13
1990	99,095	509,846	5.15

[a] The selected commodities refer to seafish and freshwater fish (whole, dressed fresh, frozen, fillets, blocks); fish meat; smoked, salted, dried, pickled/cured, and canned fish; shellfish (fresh, frozen, and canned); fish livers and roes; shellfish meal; and fish oil (Fisheries and Oceans Canada 2006b).

Source: Fisheries and Oceans Canada. Various years. Domestic exports of selected commodities by major market and country quantity in tonnes, product weight/value in thousand Canadian dollars. Online at http://www.dfo-mpo.gc.ca/communic/statistics/trade/canadian_trade/export_data/index_e.htm.

tonnes (Fisheries and Oceans Canada 2005, 2006a). Aquaculture nevertheless still accounts for less than half of the total quantity of fish produced each year. Canada is still heavily dependent on wild freshwater and seafish in its fisheries. But for how long can this dependence be sustained? Is (over)fishing other stocks the answer? It seems to be the acceptable solution so far—but the solution does not appear to be mindful of the health of the oceans and its contents, on which the fisheries depend.

The current state of the global fisheries is tenuous. A recent article published in *Science* examines biodiversity loss due to various human impacts on the oceans, including exploitation, pollution, and habitat destruction (Worm et al. 2006). Global fisheries collapses have been increasing over time, with 29 percent of the fisheries considered collapsed as of 2003 (ibid.). Worm and his colleagues additionally claim that at the rate of eroding diversity, a total fisheries collapse can be expected by 2048 (ibid.). In species-rich ecosystems, the chances of species collapse are reduced, and the chances of species recovery are greater, in large part because of the diversity of product. In this respect, switching to other stocks can assist the overfished stocks to recover. Insofar as the authors of this article, who are not the first to articulate their view (see, for example, Pauly and Maclean 2003), have been able to demonstrate a crisis in our oceans, they offer solutions, suggesting that sustainable fisheries management, pollution control, the creation of marine reserves, and so forth (in other words, restraining overfishing) can assist in rebuilding biodiversity in the oceans ecosystems. To better comprehend what is needed, we need to understand some of the critical factors leading toward this impending fisheries collapse.

A HISTORY OF THE CANADIAN FISHERY: TRADE POLICY, STAPLES PRODUCTION, AND FISHERIES INDUSTRY DEVELOPMENT

The fisheries have experienced a myriad of trade relationships, including the truck and barter system (the exchange of commodities) and forms of exchange through the use of money or credit. The truck and barter system, in which fishers exchanged their fish directly for goods, usually at company stores, for a long time benefited the merchants who bought the fish: no money exchanged hands, and profit margins on traded goods in captive markets were very high. The fishers exchanged fish for foodstuffs and supplies from the merchant, but the merchant controlled the prices for both, ensuring that the fishers were constantly in their debt (Apostle et al. 1998; Innis 1935).

This system was kept in place by both the isolated nature of fisheries and the mercantile policies followed by leading colonial countries (notably Great Britain) that ensured merchant monopolies by prohibiting competing international players from entering colonial markets. Great Britain actively pursued a free trade agenda in the later 1800s, however, which was imposed upon its colonies. This free trade agenda, in conjunction with the policy toward the colonies that forced the likes of Canada to pursue broader trade possibilities (for example, with the United States), set Canada's course toward a predominantly, if not controversial and rocky, free trade direction, beginning with reciprocity.

The notion of reciprocity or free trade in British North America was intricately linked to the fisheries. Debates as to whether Canada should enter a reciprocity treaty with the United States in the 1850s centred, in part, on the interests of the fisheries. New Brunswick advocated reciprocity, for example, whereas other colonies, such as Nova Scotia, wished to pursue alternatives to reciprocity that would enhance fish monopolies (Innis 1935). Reciprocity entailed a reduction of tariffs between the co-operating nations, and although it was considered a measure of free trade between the contracting parties (a first step toward free trade for Canada and the United States), reciprocity did not mean free trade in and of itself since it raised differential duties against outside trading partners (Masters 1963). Although the system of trade was still mercantilistic, Canada was broadening its trade parameters and reaching out to new markets in the fisheries and other sectors. Although not consistent with a unilateral free trade approach, reciprocity featured aspects of a liberal free trade regime which, many hoped, would manifest itself into a broader free trade agreement in the future (Masters 1963).[3] In the meantime, however, the fisheries ensured that a reciprocity agreement would be signed. The threat of eliminating American fishing rights and privileges in Canadian waters was decisive in instituting a long-term relationship between the two neighbouring countries in relation to their successful and unsuccessful pursuits for freer trade.

After 1866, Canada's National Policy was to increase foreign (particularly US) capital in the creation of "branch plants," forcing even greater reliance on staple resources for export earnings (Clement et al. 1999). The fisheries were engaged in a "Fordist" program of industrialization as modern factories (canneries) using indigenous and imported labour began to flourish on both the Atlantic and Pacific coasts and on the Great Lakes and the large freshwater lakes in Canada's interior. As in other industries, "capital began to displace labour in importance and large-scale to succeed individual production" (Innis 1935, 282). The Fordist model demanded a stabilized supply of fish to canneries and therefore encouraged a constant and continuous flow of fish to market, replacing or augmenting previously seasonal fisheries with new or expanded ones. This demand, in turn, led to the development of greater and greater technological reliance, particularly in the development of mechanized steam- and oil-driven trawlers (Apostle et al. 1998).

This new large-scale, permanent, capital-intensive fishery required secure, permanent access to international markets; in 1911, Canada negotiated another free trade agreement with the United States, which covered a variety of natural resource products, including fish. Although the negotiating Canadian government lost the 1911 election and the treaty was never proclaimed, exports to the United States continued to rise as the US population had increased dramatically during the pre– and post–Second World War periods (Innis 1935).

In the 1930s, Canada was faced with protectionist pressures and punitive import tariffs in the United States and pursued a tariff-reduction direction with the United States, both multilaterally and bilaterally (Clement et al. 1999). Newfoundland, prior to its entry into Confederation in 1949, also attempted various measures to offset foreign control of its fisheries and its reliance on protected foreign markets. For example, the co-operative program developed in 1947 through the Newfoundland Associated Fish Exports Limited (NAFEL) complemented the work of the Newfoundland Fisheries Board in its attempt to control the export of salt fish (cod) through a monopoly or marketing co-operative.[4]

In the 1950s, the branch plant form of industrial organization, linking Canada to larger, foreign-owned companies (predominantly in the United States), took hold in Newfoundland, and in the Canadian fisheries industry overall.[5] The Canadian government encouraged Fordist development through private enterprise and focused on the expanding frozen (as opposed to salted) fish market. The government did not recognize any conflict with stabilizing supply, requiring extensive and continuous fishing with trawler technology. Although these fishing trawlers employed less than 10 percent of fishers, they could match and increase their current catches, as "there was room for expansion in the fisheries, as the potential of groundfish stocks was not fully utilized, and, in any case, Canadian fishermen took less than 7 percent of total codfish catches off the eastern shores" (Apostle et al. 1998, 76). The industrialization program employed by the Canadian government continuously called for "a longer fishing season and more fishing effort."

Ultimately Canada and the United States, Canada's largest trading partner, have to date engaged in seven fisheries agreements (see figure 6.3).

THE CONFLICT BETWEEN SUSTAINABILITY AND MARKET FORCES IN A MATURE STAPLES INDUSTRY

The supply–demand relationship, which was a continuing feature of Canada's staple fisheries industries, had particular significance in the overexploitation, or overfishing, of the mature fisheries industry in the last quarter of the 20th century.[6] Demand for fish continues to exceed supply, and thus the incentive to extract as much resource as possible—to overfish—does not cease. Overexploitation is further exacerbated by overcapacity in the harvesting sector—too many fishing boats chasing too few fish—which in turn was exacerbated by government subsidization of the fisheries industry in the 1950s and 1960s (Delgado et al. 2003). Subsidies (that is, the internal, national policies of fishing nations) have become

Figure 6.3   Canada–US Fishing Agreements

1. Agreement Between the UK and the USA Respecting the North Atlantic Fisheries (signed July 20, 1912; in force November 15, 1912). CUS 456.[a]

2. Convention for the Extension of Port Privileges to Halibut Fishing Vessels on the Pacific Coasts of the USA and Canada (signed March 24, 1950; in force July 13, 1950). CTS 1950/5.[b]

3. Convention on Great Lakes Fisheries (signed September 10, 1954; in force October 11, 1955). CTS 1955/19. Amended May 19, 1967. CTS 1967/10.

4. Convention for Preservation of the Halibut Fishery of the Northern Pacific Ocean and Bering Sea (signed March 2, 1953; in force October 28, 1953). CTS 1953/14. Amended March 29, 1979 and October 15, 1980. CTS 1979/27 and 1980/44.

5. Treaty on Pacific Coast Albacore Tuna Vessels and Port Privileges (signed May 26, 1981; in force July 29, 1981). CTS 1981/19.

6. Pacific Salmon Treaty (signed January 28, 1985; amended by Exchange of Notes May 5 and June 12, 1986; in force March 27, 1987). CTS 1985/7. Amended by Exchange of Notes October 18, 1989. CTS 1989/41. Exchange of Notes Constituting an Agreement Amending Annexes I and IV of the Treaty Concerning the Pacific Salmon, signed in Ottawa on January 28, 1985, as amended (with annexes) (signed and in force February 3, 1995). CTS 1995/39. Agreement on the Establishment of a Mediation Procedure Regarding the Pacific Salmon Treaty (signed and in force September 11, 1995). CTS 1995/13.

7. Agreement on Fisheries Enforcement (signed September 26, 1990; in force December 16, 1991). CTS 1991/36.

---

[a] Treaties and agreements from the period 1814 to 1925 are compiled in *Treaties and Agreements Affecting Canada in Force Between His Britannic Majesty and the United States of America*, known as the CUS series.

[b] Treaties and agreements after 1925 are compiled in the Canada Treaty Series (CTS).

Source: Canada, Department of Foreign Affairs and International Trade. 2001. *Treaties and agreements in force between Canada and the United States.* Ottawa: Department of Foreign Affairs and International Trade.

significant in international fisheries discussions: they are blamed in large part for the problems of overfishing and depleted stocks.

Subsidies are the response by government when it "enables producers of goods and services to avoid full payment for the factors of production and/or to behave differently in the marketplace than they would otherwise" (Schrank and Keithly 1999, 153). Subsidies are not necessarily evil in their own right; many exist for the purpose of promoting "the pre-eminent social goal of improving human safety" (ibid., 154). However, some subsidies no longer promote this goal, and some even detract from it, especially with regard to the fishing industry. Subsidization during earlier eras of undercapacity in harvesting technology may have served a greater social purpose, but it now contributes to overcapacity and to the destruction of the fish stocks, thereby reducing social, economic, and ecological security.[7] Most current proposals and actions attempt to promote fish stock recovery and to prevent further ecosystem damage. Both efforts, which are critical to a sustainable fishery, involve the elimination of all kinds of government subsidies to fishers and fish companies and the implementation of conservation policies, such as boat buy-backs, quotas, seasonal limits on catches, and outright fishing moratoriums.

Although Canada has managed to sustain, and even increase, its overall fish and seafood volumes, these volumes have been entirely dependent on new sources of product, not on the traditional stocks that previously defined the Canadian fisheries market. Cod stocks continue to be dangerously low, and the Pacific salmon stock, Coho in particular, are close behind cod if not surpassing it in terms of high risk of extinction. Overcapacity in the processing sector has placed undue pressure on the fish stocks, with the result that the government of Canada is pursuing initiatives to reorient the focus of the processing sector, including value-added secondary processing, aquaculture, and "rationalization" of the industry.

Pressure to export fish products continues to mount because Canada is the number one supplier of seafood to the US market, which is the world's second-largest importer of fish products in the world, after Japan (Wessells and Wallström 1994, 518). Dire though the Canadian fishing industry is, it remains the largest foreign supplier of seafood to the United States, accounting for 67 percent of total Canadian fish exports. The remaining 33 percent of fish exports are supplied to more than 100 countries around the world, including the countries of the European Union. There, the EU has opened its tariff quotas on cooked and peeled shrimp from Canada, allowing for even greater export potential. Canada imports some fish products, largely from the United States, most of which are turned around into value-added product and re-exported, primarily to the US market.

It may be misleading, however, to base an assessment of the overall situation of the fishery in this new era on financial or trade figures alone. New fish stocks replace the old exhausted ones, giving the impression of a financially healthy fisheries industry, although the industry is not, in fact, biologically sustainable. Thus, for example, the reports issued by the Organisation for Economic Co-operation and Development (OECD) in 2001 showed Canada's fisheries to be in financially good stead due to an increased focus on high-valued crustaceans, such as crab and lobster. The review (Organisation for Economic Co-operation and Development [OECD] 2001) acknowledged, however, the low volume of landings in most other species for the Canadian fishing industry as a whole in relation to historical levels (increased crustacean landings and an improvement in aquaculture secured Canada a record overall volume in 1999 of 1.1 million tonnes, or Cdn $1.9 billion in value). The report praised the Canadian government efforts to increase conservation through bilateral and multilateral fishing agreements, such as the Pacific Salmon Treaty and the International Plan of Action (IPOA) adopted by the UN Food and Agriculture Organization (FAO), but Canada nonetheless appears to be invigorating these efforts from a deficit position. Historically low levels of Canada's significant fish stocks, such as cod and salmon, make the conservation efforts appear to be too little too late, as the industry shifts its reliance to currently thriving stocks, such as crustaceans.

OVERFISHING, CONSERVATION EFFORTS, AND INTERNATIONAL AGREEMENTS IN THE MODERN ERA

In general, the Canadian fishing industry has been subject to market forces, with little government protection or substantial policy outside of trade agreements until government subsidies promoted overcapacity and overharvesting in the era following the Second World War. After 1975, however, new "buffering" strategies were employed in the interest of conserving fish resources through fisheries management strategies, which became increasingly relevant, but were recognized far too late for the cod fishery, as the fight against overfishing had already begun.

Trade agreements, and in some respects NAFTA, apply to the fisheries primarily with regard to the maintenance of international fisheries laws, such as the 200-mile extended economic zone, and in later agreements, conservation efforts.[8] Their impacts, both in earlier agreements as well as those more recent, have had a significant effect on the development of the fisheries industry. These agreements attempt to balance the needs of trade and economic security with the needs of conservation and environmental security. NAFTA and the WTO (and their predecessors, the 1989 Canada–United States Free Trade Agreement [FTA] and the General Agreement on Tariffs and Trade [GATT]) have had substantial impacts on the directions the fisheries have taken.[9] By 1998, the United States was receiving 83 percent of Canada's merchandise exports, including primary products (World Trade Organization 1998). Primary products still accounted for almost one-third of Canada's merchandise exports, illustrating yet again the heavy dependence on natural resources (ibid.). Due primarily to NAFTA, Canada's tariffs have almost entirely been eliminated for goods shipped between Canada and the United States. However, Canada has continued to impose high tariffs on other countries, particularly those in the developing world that would be considered to have a comparative advantage over Canada, especially in the area of food products (ibid.).

Due to Canada's very close relationship with the United States, fostered by FTA and NAFTA, some tension is developing with regard to Canada's additional commitments to other international treaty regimes. Because 90 percent of Canada's trade takes place within NAFTA, Canada's commitments are not global but regional, and many Canadian trade actions are motivated by conditions in the United States. As much as US trade policy dictates the moves of Canadian trade activities, regional trade agreements, such as FTA and NAFTA, rely on already established regulations in the GATT and the WTO.

The GATT article XX has often been used as the basis for decisions on conservation actions taken on behalf of either the Canadian or American fisheries. Although not specifically mentioning the environment, two sections of this article (General Agreement on Tariffs and Trade 1947, article XX) have been relevant to these decisions in the trade versus conservation arguments:

> Subject to the requirement that such measures are not applied in a manner which would constitute a means of arbitrary or unjustifiable discrimination between countries where the same conditions prevail, or a disguised restriction on international trade, nothing in this Agreement shall be construed to prevent the adoption or enforcement by any contracting party of measures: …
>
> (b) necessary to protect human, animal or plant life or health; …
>
> (g) relating to the conservation of exhaustible natural resources if such measures are made effective in conjunction with restrictions on domestic production or consumption.

Although article XX can be applied to fish products, these products are not specifically dealt with in the GATT, and were not addressed during the Uruguay Round Agreement on Agriculture. Although fish products have the highest share of international trade for food, they are treated as non-agricultural products and are considered in kind with industrial products (Ruckes 2000).

Under the GATT and the WTO, numerous cases have tried to justify the need to raise the barriers to trade on the basis of environmental concerns; however, the vast majority were ruled to be inapplicable and therefore the measures could not be maintained (Swenarchuk 2000). Alan Rugman, John Kirton, and Julie Soloway (1999) review a number of fisheries-related disputes between Canada and the United States to illustrate the impact of trade agreements upon the fisheries industry. For example, in 1979, Canada was subject to a US embargo preventing the export of tuna and tuna products from Canada. The GATT ruling concluded that although the US action could be understood as a measure of conservation of an exhaustible resource, it did not apply the same restrictions to domestic producers and therefore the US embargo was impermissible. Resource conservation was again raised in 1988, when Canada claimed it needed to restrict the export of unprocessed herring and sockeye salmon. In this case, GATT ruled against Canada under article XX, because the restriction was not applied to both foreign and domestic producers and therefore only penalized the United States. Shortly thereafter, Canadian fisheries authorities complied with the GATT ruling and lifted the restrictions on herring and sockeye salmon, but imposed a mandatory Canadian landing requirement on five species of salmon for the purpose of conservation, allowing for biological samples as each catch was landed. The United States complained, stating that forced Canadian landings restricted exports and forced fish to be processed in Canada because of the wait time before the fish could enter the United States. Because the FTA had recently been negotiated, the United States chose to mediate this dispute using the FTA (although the same regulations would apply because the FTA incorporated these provisions of the GATT). The Canadian measure was deemed illegal on two counts: first, that the restriction was not just a domestic measure but instead negatively affected and restricted trade with the United States, and second, that this restriction could not be construed as a conservation measure as "the panel concluded that this was not the case, since it was highly unlikely that Canada would have imposed the same requirements 'if its own nationals had to bear the actual costs of the measure'" (Rugman, Kirton, and Soloway 1999, 57). In 1990, it was Canada's turn to wage a complaint against US fisheries practices when the United States restricted lobster exports from Canada on the basis of size. This measure was instituted on the basis of conservation to allow US lobsters to mature to a greater size before being caught. Canada argued that this restriction discriminated against Canada since lobsters in the colder Canadian waters mature at a smaller size than those in US waters. The United States countered that lobsters were treated the same regardless of origin (domestic and foreign lobsters had to meet the same standards), and the FTA panel, split on the decision (3–2), upheld the US action, stating that it was "'primarily aimed' at the conservation of US lobsters" (ibid., 58).

Rugman, Kirton, and Soloway concluded:

One of the most striking findings is how the outcome of issues over environmental regulatory protectionism have benefited the United States and its firms. Of the 50 cases effectively resolved, the United States has won 29, Canada 8, and Mexico 7, while 8 have been resolved to the mutual benefit of two or three of the North American partners. Such a pattern, with the United States prevailing in 58 per cent of the cases, would appear to be a further testament to the realist presupposition that in this bargaining domain as in so many others, the United States with its overwhelmingly superior power, is bound to prevail. (Rugman, Kirton, and Soloway 1999, 229)

CONCLUSION: CANADIAN FISHERIES AS A DECLINING MATURE STAPLES INDUSTRY

Without question, Canadian domestic policy has had an influence on the development of the fisheries staple industry—from its National Policy to its subsidization of fishers and, more recently, its effort to conserve fish stocks. In this respect, Laxer (1985) is correct in allocating "blame" for the current dire status of the fisheries industry where it is, in part, due to the actions of the Canadian government itself. However, trade liberalization has played an enormous role on the development (if not the devastation) of the industry, ranging from the pressures exerted early on by the colonizing country of Britain to the current dependency upon the US market for fish exports.

In this respect, the Canadian government could have done much more by recognizing the severity of fish stock depletion and fostering a sustainable fisheries industry that could meet the needs of conservation and fisher communities. However, the Canadian fisheries have been exposed to a long-term, extensive process of liberalization since the decline of mercantilism in the fishing industry in the 1840s. Fisheries and free trade agreements, manifested currently through the FTA, NAFTA, and WTO, have institutionalized a mature staples industry and limit its ability to change. Fisheries management in Canada has largely reflected a mature staples view of increased and enhanced commodity production over most of the period of the fisheries history, only beginning to take a more scientific approach to fisheries management in the late 20th century, when it became obvious that the fisheries were in trouble due to rapidly declining stocks.

The present relationship between the Canadian fishing industry and community and trade liberalization as exemplified by the NAFTA and WTO reflects the antagonisms and contradictions apparent in a too late recognition that largely unfettered trade in the fishing sector leads to depleted stocks and threatened ecosystems. The Canadian government has turned to a more conservationist fisheries management practice, but must now fight for the right to do so within the confines of NAFTA and the WTO. The Canadian government, and the Department of Fisheries and Oceans (DFO) in particular, will likely defer to science not trade agreements to guide them in determining fisheries policy. However, science has been and continues to be imperfect in providing accurate measures of fish stocks and environmental conditions, making it clear that trade agreements play a greater role than DFO might want to acknowledge. Unless a DFO measure that has the appearance of limiting or restricting trade can be "scientifically" substantiated as a measure intended for conservation, the trade agreements entered into by Canada will prevail and curtail such "protective" measures. Some such measures are in fact disguised tactics (sometimes well disguised, sometimes less so) to protect domestic fishers and fisheries. As the examples of FTA and GATT rulings illustrate, under existing trade agreements, a panel needs to "judge" on the basis of impressions whether conservationism or protectionism dominates the nature of the measure taken, and in such rulings, panels tend to err on the side of the industry.

NOTES

1. These concerns and priorities are evidenced by the attention garnered at the March 2002 United Nations Environment Programme (UNEP) Workshop on the Impacts of Trade-Related Policies on Fisheries and Measures Required for their Sustainable Management, the November 2001 WTO Ministerial Conference held in Doha, the OECD Review of Fisheries published every two years, and the continuing efforts of the Food and Agriculture Organization (FAO) of the United Nations to bring fisheries issues to light.

2. Based on trade data from Fisheries and Oceans Canada, it is possible to argue that the category "other countries," comprising 58 nations from Africa, Asia, and the Pacific region, is Canada's second-largest "major market" as its export numbers sometimes exceed those of the EU. However, because the EU can be interpreted as a single unit, its significance outweighs that of the catch-all category of "other countries." See http://www.dfo-mpo.gc.ca/communic/statistics/trade/canadian_trade/export_data/xmkt06_e.htm.

3. Establishing a "most favoured nation" principle to be extended to other trading partners was one such hope.

4. The initiative failed in the 1950s, not long after its creation, in large part due to lack of "support in the political establishment" (Apostle et al. 1998, 75).

5. Newfoundland joined the Canadian Confederation in 1949. Therefore, in the 1950s, it was subject to Canadian political interests as opposed to only Newfoundland interests.

6. The US National Research Council defines overfishing as "fishing at an intensity great enough to reduce fish populations below the size at which they would provide the maximum long-term sustainable yield or great enough to prevent their returning to that size" (Pauly and MacLean 2003, 127n).

7. Perhaps one of the most controversial moves by the Canadian government in the fishing sector was the implementation of the Unemployment Insurance (UI) program in the fishing industry, which allowed fishers to collect stamps toward UI benefit entitlement. This program resulted in both reducing the fishing season (as fishers stopped as soon as they had enough stamps) and extending the salted fish production (as this work was counted toward the accumulation of stamps).

8. NAFTA does not specifically address the fisheries, and therefore is applicable only indirectly, in that the fisheries are an integral part of Canada's exports. According to the FAO, NAFTA does not pay any specific attention to fish and fish products, and additionally does not co-operate with the FAO on fisheries matters. As well, "at this time, there are no provisions in the GATT or NAFTA to equalize foreign access to coastal fishing" (Wathen 1996, 83). However, NAFTA cannot be ignored due to its pre-eminence in the Canada–US trade relationship. As noted by Christopher L. Delgado et al. (2003), institutional developments that apply to sectors outside of the fisheries nevertheless have great implications for the fisheries.

9. NAFTA, a trade agreement established among Canada, the United States, and Mexico, was implemented in 1994, integrating and expanding the 1989 FTA (Canada–United States Free Trade Agreement) with a new agreement with Mexico. NAFTA affirmed the rights and obligations all parties held to the General Agreement on Tariffs and Trade (GATT) by 1994, but stated that any inconsistency between other agreements and NAFTA would defer to NAFTA unless otherwise specified in NAFTA.

REFERENCES

Apostle, R., Barrett, G., Holm, P., Jentoft, S., Mazany, L., McCay, B., and Mikalsen, K.H. 1998. *Community, state, and market on the north Atlantic rim: Challenges to modernity in the fisheries.* Toronto: University of Toronto Press.

Canada, Department of Foreign Affairs and International Trade. 2001. *Treaties and agreements in force between Canada and the United States.* Ottawa: Department of Foreign Affairs and International Trade.

Clement, N.C., Vera, G.D., Gerber, J., Kerr, W.A., McFadyen, A.J., Zepeda, A.J., and Alacon, D. 1999. *North American economic integration: Theory and practice.* Northampton, MA: Edward Elgar.

Delgado, C.L., Wada, N., Rosegrant, M.W., Meijer, S., and Ahmed, M. 2003. *Fish to 2020: Supply and demand in changing global markets.* Washington, DC and Penang, Malaysia: International Food Policy Research Institute and WorldFish Center.

Fisheries and Oceans Canada. 2005. 1986 Canadian aquaculture production statistics (tonnes). Online at http://www.dfo-mpo.gc.ca/communic/statistics/aqua/aqua86_e.htm.

Fisheries and Oceans Canada. 2006a. 2004 Canadian aquaculture production statistics (tonnes). Online at http://www.dfo-mpo.gc.ca/communic/statistics/aqua/aqua04_e.htm.

Fisheries and Oceans Canada. 2006b. Domestic exports of selected commodities by species group and species quantity in tonnes, product weight/value in thousand Canadian dollars. Online at http://www.dfo-mpo.gc.ca/communic/statistics/trade/canadian_trade/export_data/xsps06_e.htm.

Fisheries and Oceans Canada. 2006c. Summary of Canadian commercial catches and values, 2000–2003. Online at http://www.dfo-mpo.gc.ca/communic/statistics/commercial/landings/sum0003_e.htm.

Fisheries and Oceans Canada. 2007. Summary of Canadian commercial catches and values, 2004–2005. Online at http://www.dfo-mpo.gc.ca/communic/statistics/commercial/landings/sum0407_e.htm.

Fisheries and Oceans Canada. Various years. Domestic exports of selected commodities by major market and country quantity in tonnes, product weight/value in thousand Canadian dollars. Online at http://www.dfo-mpo.gc.ca/communic/statistics/trade/canadian_trade/export_data/index_e.htm.

General Agreement on Tariffs and Trade. 1947. Article XX. Online at http://www.wto.org/english/docs_e/legal_e/gatt47_02_e.htm.

Hessing, M., and Howlett, M. 1997. *Canadian natural resource and environmental policy: Political economy and public policy.* Vancouver: University of British Columbia Press.

Hutton, T.A. 1994. *Visions of a "post-staples" economy: Structural change and adjustment issues in British Columbia,* working paper PI #3. Vancouver: University of British Columbia Centre for Human Settlements.

Innis, M.Q. 1935. *An economic history of Canada.* Toronto: The Ryerson Press.

Laxer, G. 1985. Foreign ownership and myths about Canadian development. *Canadian Review of Sociology and Anthropology* 22(3): 311–45.

Marchak, P. 1985. Canadian political economy. *Canadian Review of Sociology and Anthropology* 22(5): 673–709.

Masters, D.C. 1963. *The reciprocity treaty of 1854: Its history, its relation to British colonial and foreign policy and to the development of Canadian fiscal autonomy.* Toronto: McClelland & Stewart.

Organisation for Economic Co-operation and Development. 2001. Canada. In *Review of Fisheries in OECD Countries: Country Statistics 1998–1999,* 31–40. Paris: OECD.

Pauly, D., and Maclean, J. 2003. *In a perfect ocean: The state of fisheries and ecosystems in the North Atlantic Ocean.* Washington, DC: Island Press.

Ruckes, E. 2000. International trade in fishery products and the new global trading environment. Online at http://www.fao.org/docrep/003/x7353e/X7353e11.htm.

Rugman, A., Kirton, J., and Soloway, J. 1999. *Environmental regulations and corporate strategy: A NAFTA perspective.* Oxford: Oxford University Press.

Schrank, W.E., and Keithly, W.R., Jr. 1999. Thalassorama: The concept of subsidies. *Marine Resource Economics* 14(2): 151–64.

Swenarchuk, M. 2000. General agreement on trade in services: Negotiations concerning domestic regulations under GATS article VI (4). Online at http://www .healthyenvironmentforkids.ca/img_upload/f8e04c51a8e04041f6f7faa046b03a7c/ 397GATS.pdf.

Wathen, T.A. 1996. Trade policy: Clouds in the vision of sustainability. In *Building Sustainable Societies: A Blueprint for a Post-Industrial World,* ed. D.C. Pirages, 71–92. Armonk, NY: M.E. Sharpe.

Wessells, C.R., and Wallström, P. 1994. New dimensions in world fisheries: Implications for US and EC Trade in Seafood. In *Agricultural Trade Conflicts and GATT: New Dimensions in US–European Agricultural Trade Relations,* eds. G. Anania, C.A. Carter, and A.F. McCalla, 518–36. Boulder, CO: Westview Press.

Woodard, C. 2001. A run on the banks: How factory fishing decimated Newfoundland cod. *E Magazine* 12(2): 34–39.

World Trade Organization. n.d. What is the WTO? Online at http://www.wto.org/english/ thewto_e/whatis_e/whatis_e.htm.

World Trade Organization. 1998. Trade policy review: Canada—November 1998. Online at http://www.wto.org/english/tratop_e/tpr_e/tp98rev1_e.htm.

Worm, B., Barbier, E.B., Beaumont, N., Duffy, J.E., Folke, C., Halpern, B.S., Jackson, J.B.C., Lotze, H.K., Micheli, F., Palumbi, S.R., Sala, E., Selkoe, K.A., Stachowicz, J.J., and Watson, R. 2006. Impacts of biodiversity loss on ocean ecosystem services. *Science* 314(5800): 787–90.

CHAPTER 7

Caught in a Staples Vise: The Political Economy of Canadian Aquaculture

Jeremy Rayner and Michael Howlett

INTRODUCTION

Aquaculture, as Hoogensen notes in chapter 6, lies at the cusp of the mature staples fisheries sector, applying high-technology inputs in fisheries biology and agri-food production to such classic staples fisheries commodities as salmon, clams, oysters, mussels, trout, lobsters, and other species. As natural or "wild" stocks have declined, aquaculture has grown in its place, with many farmed fish and shellfish products now outnumbering their wild counterparts on store shelves and on consumers' tables.

Aquaculture in Canada is a small, rapidly growing, high-technology resource sector "caught in a staples vise." On the one hand, it is an archetypal case of a new "post-staples" resource industry, combining high-capital intensity and sophisticated technology to produce a new post-staples version of a classic staple resource—food fish (Hutton 1994). On the other hand, Canadian aquaculture perpetuates many of the same social and economic problems and issues that plagued traditional staples political economies: namely a hinterland location and heavy export reliance (Innis 1930, 1933). And, as is the case with most intensively farmed, technologically intensive foodstuffs (see Moore, chapter 5), aquaculture's rise and rivalry with the wild fishery is intense and conflict ridden, affected by the distrust and debate that surround contemporary aquacultural expansion. This chapter assesses these contradictory and sometimes conflicting developments in a resource industry situated for the most part in a very uneven transition toward a post-staples political economy.

The Consequences of Overly Optimistic Expansion

The Canadian aquaculture sector is composed of two basic industries that use very different techniques to produce different species of marine animals: the shellfish sector and the finfish sector. Shellfish volumes and values remain much smaller than their finfish equivalents at present, with finfish output accounting for about 75 percent of total volume and 90 percent of total Canadian production value in 2005 (Statistics Canada 2006). The Canadian finfish industry, until now based largely on Atlantic salmon (*Salmo salar*), has enjoyed phenomenal growth in output over the last two decades. Output in 2001 alone showed a 25 percent increase over 2000 levels, and reached 136,000 tonnes in 2002, declining gradually to 115,800 tonnes in 2005. Canadian shellfish production grew by 17 percent between 2000 and 2001, and continued to grow, albeit rather slowly, reaching 38,195 tonnes in 2005. After many years of rapid growth, the value of Canadian farmed-finfish sales also fell 3.3 percent between 2002 and 2003 to $643 million, before rebounding to 2002 levels in 2005, illustrating the continuing similarities between ostensibly post-staples and traditional staples industries dependent on foreign markets and subjected to boom-and-bust cycles as a result. Fluctuations in the US economy combined with overproduction and fierce competition between the two major salmon-producing countries, Chile and Norway, have continued to drive down world salmon prices. In the shellfish sector, where the species mix is more diverse and the associated environmental problems less severe, values have held up better and have led to increasing interest in the sector in recent years (PricewaterhouseCoopers 2002).

The very rapid growth of aquaculture volumes and values over the last decade is, of course, not unique to Canada (Burros 2005); here and in other countries, the growth of aquaculture is linked to declines in traditional "wild" or "capture" fisheries. As Hoogensen has detailed in chapter 6, the declines in many significant capture fisheries around the world, combined with increasing world demand for seafood products, has led to concerns about food security. To address this global food security issue, aquaculture has been widely promoted as an essential tool by governments and international agencies, such as the United Nations Food and Agriculture Organization (FAO) (Food and Agriculture Organization of the United Nations 2004). In 1997, the worldwide production volumes of farmed salmon surpassed those of the wild fishery. For two other finfish, cod and tuna, the development of new farmed species is also well advanced.

Rosy forecasts in this sector are common. Former Liberal federal fisheries minister Herb Dhaliwal, for example, predicted a Canadian industry worth $2 billion by the end of the decade (Canada, Senate, Standing Committee on Fisheries 2001). A widely quoted report by Coopers & Lybrand for the federal Western Economic Diversification (WED) program suggested that the value of British Columbia shellfish production alone could climb from $12 million to $100 million between 1997 and 2006 (Coopers & Lybrand 1997). The possibility of creating thousands of new jobs in post-staples resource industries and associated services, particularly in coastal communities hard hit by declines in other resource sectors, has helped persuade governments to lift moratoriums on new shellfish and finfish farm tenures and to launch policies such as the Shellfish Development Initiative (SDI) in British Columbia aimed at doubling areas under tenure over the next decade (British Columbia, Ministry of Agriculture and Lands 2001). In fact, the value of BC shellfish production appears to have peaked at around $20 million in 2003 and fell back to $18.7 million in 2005 (Statistics Canada 2006).

Emerging Problems with Aquacultural Development

As a result of declines in the wild fishery and the growing level of investment in finfish and shellfish aquaculture, Canadian aquaculture policy emerged in its modern form after 1984, when the federal government undertook a complex multi-level process of policy renewal after almost a century of benign neglect. Following an initial period during which the foundations for the new policy were laid through intergovernmental agreements, both the federal and provincial governments adopted numerous policies aimed at promoting the aquaculture industry.

Despite the optimism and the apparent convergence of government policy on promoting aquaculture development, including efforts to diversify into new species and new locations, progress in this post-staples sector has encountered a series of market and environmental problems that have restricted its expansion. The finfish industry, for example, remains dominated by the production of Atlantic salmon in a restricted number of locations in BC and New Brunswick. Although the value of farmed salmon output is now twice the landed value of the hard-pressed Pacific salmon fishery, by contrast, the total value of aquaculture output in Canada as a whole is still less than half the total landed value of Canadian capture fisheries ($580 million compared with $1.2 billion in 2003). Even in British Columbia, the total value of farmed salmon output is still dwarfed by the combined values of the capture fisheries for all species and by the lucrative, tourist-oriented, sport fishery (Marshall 2003). Consequently, the capture and sport fishery constituencies and their allies in the federal and provincial governments are formidable opponents when the interests of the wild fishery and the aquaculture industry come into conflict.

Thus, in addition to the weakness of international farmed-salmon prices and the shaky financial state of some of the world's largest fishing companies that have operations in Canada, Canadian aquaculture producers face significant scrutiny from a characteristically post-staples coalition of traditional fishers, First Nations, and environmentalists concerned about the impacts of the industry on the marine environment; on surviving stocks of wild fish; and on Aboriginal rights, title, and employment. Issues have been raised about every stage of the aquaculture production process, especially the use of wild fish stocks to make feed pellets for farmed fish; the impact of wastes, parasites, and diseases on local wild stocks; and the human health implications of therapeutant residues, colourants, and contaminants contained in the final food products.

The environmental coalition has adopted tactics familiar from other traditional staples resource areas, such as forestry (see Cashore et al., chapter 11), and those involving food production, such as struggles over genetically modified crops and food products (see Moore, chapter 5), to undermine consumer confidence and to promote enhanced government regulation and industry self-regulation. In particular, environmentalists have alleged collusion between industry and government to suppress unpleasant facts about the environmental impacts of finfish aquaculture. US consumers, for example, have been targeted with a slick "farmed and dangerous" campaign that has encouraged restaurant-goers to demand wild salmon, pressured some large US retailers to label farmed salmon as artificially coloured, and urged both consumers and retailers to express more general concerns about the negative publicity surrounding Canadian salmon farms (Coastal Alliance for Aquaculture Reform n.d.). More seriously still, in the critical American market, the US Congress has been successfully lobbied by the Alaskan salmon fishing industry and its allies to pass country of origin labelling (COOL) legislation that will enable the opponents of salmon farming to target Canadian imports.[1]

Although the shellfish aquaculture sector has, until recently, enjoyed less intense scrutiny from environmentalists, it has plenty of problems of its own. In BC, for example, more than halfway through the SDI, the value of farmed shellfish has barely reached a quarter of its 10-year target. Problems of poor intergovernmental coordination, premature tenure expansion announcements without adequate consultation with local communities, uncertainty surrounding unresolved First Nations' claims and their impact on the foreshore and coastal waters, declining water quality in traditional growing areas, lack of processing facilities and distribution networks for expanded production, and a host of other factors have surfaced (Howlett and Rayner 2004). In PEI, home to perhaps the most successful example of shellfish industry expansion in Canada, this growth has been marked by weakening mussel prices, allegations of dumping in US markets, and increasing conflicts with other users. In PEI, BC, and other provinces, shellfish aquaculture development now faces the same kind of serious legitimation problems that have bedevilled the finfish sector, threatening not only the future industry but also those operations already established (Hume 2003a, 2003b; Simpson 2003a, 2003b; Rud 2003; McInnes and LaVoie 2003).

A POST-STAPLES POLICY PROCESS?

The record of the Canadian aquaculture sector raises many questions about the principles of policy design adopted by policy-makers during the last two decades. Instead of responding appropriately to the challenges posed by post-staples development, policy-makers have simply reproduced a process typical of an earlier era of staples resource development (Howlett and Rayner 2004). In a mature staples economy, the resource allocation conflicts and environmental impacts surrounding the expansion of a new industry were largely managed through traditional instruments of regulation and subsidy. Development was often accepted as "an end in itself" and welcomed by local and metropolitan populations alike (Howlett 2001). In a post-staples economy, metropolitan populations become increasingly disconnected from resource-extraction activities, with the result that the development of metropolitan post-materialist values intensifies environmental conflicts (Hutton 1994). In a globalized marketplace, national and sub-national regulatory and subsidy policies are opened to international scrutiny, and environmentally sensitive and health-conscious consumers can be targeted by environmental activists in even the most distant export markets (Cashore, Auld, and Newsom 2003). The further up the value chain an industry moves—and thus, the further away from production of a traditional unprocessed or semiprocessed staple commodity—the more easily identifiable the product and the more intense the scrutiny.

The result is a more complex post-staples political economic environment requiring sophisticated policy-making that focuses on the use of policy instruments not only to promote industrial activity but also to legitimate the whole process, from the allocation of scarce coastal resources to the politics of food production and distribution (Randolph and Bauer 1999). However, as the discussion in the following section will show, instead of creating a system of "smart regulation" for the post-staples era, as Gunningham et al. have termed it (Gunningham, Grabosky, and Sinclair 1998), Canadian policy-makers have until recently pursued policies and policy processes more congruent with a mature staples trajectory—that is, a single-minded focus on industrial promotion—while leaving existing weak procedural instruments, notably industry-based advisory panels, in place. Although policy-makers are currently responding to the emerging crises in the sector with a plethora of consultations and other procedural devices, the requisite coordination is lacking, and these ill-considered consultations are themselves now engendering additional problems in the sector (Cook 2002; Wondelleck, Manring, and Cowfoot 1996; Suryanata and Umemoto 2003).

AQUACULTURE AS A PROBLEMATIC POST-STAPLES INDUSTRY

As the chapters by Wellstead (see chapter 2) and Hutton (see chapter 3) attest, the significance of having an economy based on the export of unfinished bulk resource commodities (or staples) lies not only in how these export commodities affect policy-making by creating continuing issues with resource location and availability but also in how populations in staples-dependent areas react to their continued vulnerability to international market conditions (Howlett 2003). The development of a staples-based economy, for example, often triggers government investments in areas such as transportation and communications infrastructure designed to extract and ship goods to markets efficiently, the provision of export subsidies and credits designed to facilitate trade, and regional development and other government expenditures designed to protect populations from price fluctuations caused by supply and demand conditions in international markets (Naylor 1972; Hodgetts 1973; Stone 1984; Whalley 1985; Hessing, Howlett, and Summerville 2005).

As Thomas Hutton observed (see Hutton, chapter 3), "mature, advanced" staple economies share several features that can be combined into a typical political economic "profile": (1) the substantial depletion of original resource endowments and consequent increasing pressure from environmental groups to inhibit traditional modes of resource extraction and stimulate development alternatives; (2) the increasing capital- and technology-intensiveness of resource extraction processes and the consequent decrease in employment in the staples sector; (3) the evolution of development from "pure" extraction to increased refining and secondary processing of resource commodities; and (4) the diversification of the economic structure with growth in non-staples-related areas, such as tourism and local administration and services (Hutton 1994).

Diversification of the local economy, in particular, creates important new political forces that see their interests as different from and sometimes in conflict with the old staples sector. Hence, although a mature staples political economy may still be characterized as "resource-dependent," the economy is, in fact, more diffused and diversified than in the past, and the politics of resource policy processes have changed accordingly. As Clapp (1998) and Hutton (1994) suggest, if this diffusion, diversification, and resource depletion continue, then an economy may make a further transition toward a post-staples state in which severe pressures on the critical resource sector coupled with the prospect of even more substantial contractions in the near future lead to an internal reconfiguration of growth and development. Typically, this transition to a post-staples economy involves a significant increase in metropolitan shares of population and employment; the emergence of regional economic centres; the subsequent decline of smaller resource-dependent communities; and the emergence of new resource industries, such as aquaculture, built on the rubble of depleted "classic" staples industries (in this case, the failed "wild" fishery).

In countries such as Canada, whose history has been strongly marked by the evolution of traditional staples industries, post-staples resource policy options are heavily constrained by policy legacies and path dependencies from the earlier era, notably the existence of towns and population centres, companies and industrial structures, labour skill sets and trade union organizations, and other remnants of bygone, or dwindling, classic staples activities. Resource industries do not disappear to be seamlessly replaced by an expanding service sector or "the new economy"; instead they assume new forms, layered with elements of older political economic regimes in an uneven process of transition that is, perhaps, even more complex and difficult than Hutton suggests (Rahnema and Howlett 2002).

In this light, Canadian aquaculture can be seen as a "problematic" post-staples resource industry strongly marked by governmental, corporate, and community attempts to make the transition to high-technology farmed fish from the failed or failing mature-staples fishery economy. In spite of its aura of high-tech novelty, though, Canadian aquaculture retains many of the features of its mature-staple predecessor. Both kinds of aquaculture are oriented to export, almost exclusively to the United States. In 2005, 89 percent of Canadian farmed salmon output was exported to the United States, which represented more than 90 percent of the Canadian export market, and total output closely tracks these exports (Statistics Canada 2006). The Canadian aquaculture sector also remains mired in the export of low-value-added bulk products.[2] With the Chilean industry spurred by its greater transportation costs to move ahead in value-added production, the "commodity market" in whole fish has been left to the Canadians and their favourable cost advantages vis-à-vis the US market.

The Finfish Sector

Aquaculture, like its wild fishery predecessor, is unevenly developed across the country. In the finfish sector, the industry has developed very rapidly but unevenly on both coasts. The leading finfish-producing province, British Columbia, is the fourth-largest producer of farmed salmon in the world; and the BC aquaculture industry has seen rapid consolidation, from 50 companies in 1989 to only 12 in 2002 (British Columbia, Ministry of Agriculture and Lands 2006). The capital for the transition has come largely from the Norwegian multinationals that have by-passed Vancouver and created a regional economic centre in Campbell River. The Norwegian interest in the BC industry is clearly motivated by the desire to locate production for the US market inside the North American Free Trade Agreement (NAFTA) and, as such, reproduces a feature of the old staples-related "branch plant" manufacturing economy. Nonetheless, some backward and forward linkages have developed in this sector. Feed and equipment are produced in Canada and exported to other jurisdictions, and investment in hatcheries is producing juveniles for growing out on the farms.[3] Significant resources are being deployed in researching scientific and technological solutions to problems faced by the industry, such as reducing the amount of fish protein in food pellets and breeding fish with increased resistance to the diseases and parasites found in intensive sea cage culture.

At the same time, the first payoff from this more capital-intensive aquaculture is, as usual, the reduction of labour inputs per unit of output. Despite the very rapid expansion of aquaculture output, aquaculture employment has grown much more slowly; some provincial industries, such as BC salmon farming, have recently seen almost no employment growth at all. As the Canadian Centre for Policy Alternatives noted, "BC's fish farm industry (including the vast majority of processing) was 60 times larger in 1999 than it was in 1984, but employment merely doubled over that period. During the 1990s, BC's industry tripled its production without any increase in employment" (Marshall 2003, 16). Like many classic staples industries, much of the work is part-time, seasonal, and relatively low-tech.

Similarly, although aquaculture is seen by the state as a valuable substitute for the declining capture fishery, this development has created a complex environmental discourse that is more challenging than Hutton's original picture of less environmentally destructive resource extraction in post-staples sectors. As we have noted, aquaculture is accused by environmentalists and fishers alike of contributing to the decline of wild fish stocks and the degradation of coastal ecosystems, and consequently does not function as an environmentally friendly substitute to allow the recovery of an overexploited traditional staple. Other elements of the overall post-staples political economy, notably recreation and tourism, add to the mix of interests and conflicts. Where coastal tourism, for example, is marketed as "a visit to a pristine environment," fish farms are identified as an alien intrusion.

And again, while a mature staples economy often pits urban populations with strongly developed post-materialist values against the inhabitants of resource hinterlands who perceive environmentalism as a threat to their livelihoods, the more complex post-staples landscape creates more complex politics as well. In particular, as the history of recent conflicts in the forestry sector has shown, the possibility exists of linking urban environmentalism with traditional resource users whose livelihoods are threatened by new resource developments (see Cashore et al., chapter 11). Aquaculture has created just such an opportunity, with opponents organizing around a core conception of "nature" that stigmatizes aquaculture as "artificial," "unnatural," and "dangerous." The paradoxical idea that escaped farmed fish are a kind of pollution flows directly from this conception of natural and unnatural activities (Mansfield 2004). As a result, it is no exaggeration to say that Canadian aquaculture is facing a legitimation crisis and not, as might be expected, a smooth and almost inevitable transition in political economic hegemonies.

The Shellfish Sector

Shellfish aquaculture is on a similar trajectory, with PEI as the most advanced province, which is even less far forward in the transition to an overall post-staples political economy than BC. Although the shellfish industry remains considerably smaller and less capital-intensive than its finfish counterpart, the beginnings of a consolidation are evident, as a smaller number of large companies engage in more intensive forms of cultivation.

Many of the complex post-staples alignments of interests found in the finfish sector can be observed here as well, it least in embryonic form. Shellfish farming, for example, is beginning to be accused of disrupting natural coastal ecosystems instead of reducing the resource pressures on them, with alleged negative impacts on migratory birds and their habitat leading the list of charges. Owners of waterfront properties are subject to visual and other social impacts, and conflicts arise with the increasingly important tourism and recreation industries. Leasing beaches and nearshore waters for shellfish production often results in excluding the use of the area by others, sometimes those engaged in traditional wild fisheries of shellfish species that are not being farmed, such as clams. Although shellfish aquaculture is often promoted as a source of employment and revenue for small coastal communities, especially First Nations, significant obstacles hinder the geographical dispersion of the industry, and people have a tendency to observe the characteristic post-staples "clustering" of successful enterprises to the exclusion of less-favoured locales. Certainly the model of New Zealand, the global leader in the farming of shellfish species, which is likely to be successful in Canada, suggests a framework of concentration and increasing intensity (Clancy 2002).

It is not surprising, then, that both finfish and shellfish aquacultures have proven to be contentious sites of political and policy struggle, existing at the cusp of the transition from a staples (wild fishery) to a post-staples (farmed fish) resource sector. This problematic positioning causes substantial regulatory challenges for governments, especially those dedicated to industrial promotion. In the following section, we focus on describing and then evaluating the existing mix of policy instruments used in the aquaculture sector in Canada, focusing on the less well-known shellfish sector but noting the unique problems of finfish aquaculture where relevant.

THE EXISTING CANADIAN AQUACULTURE REGULATORY FRAMEWORK

The Federal Situation

The Canadian approach to aquaculture, like the Canadian approach to most policy areas, is deeply affected by Canadian federalism. Aquaculture is not mentioned by name in the *Constitution Act, 1867* or in any subsequent constitution act or amendment. Federal involvement is based directly on constitutional jurisdiction over sea coasts and inland fisheries (s. 91(12)), over navigation and shipping (s. 91(10)), over Indians and land reserved for the Indians (s. 91(24)), and through the federal power to enter into international treaty obligations (s. 132). Indirectly, federal jurisdiction also derives from federal government activity in the area of environmental protection and from case law concerning the regulation of international and interprovincial trade.

Provincial involvement, on the other hand, is firmly based on constitutionally protected jurisdiction over property and civil rights within the province (s. 92(13)); over provincial Crown lands (including the foreshore) (s. 92(5)); over matters of a merely local or private nature within the province (s. 92(16)); over municipal institutions; and over the regulation of lands underlying freshwater lakes and rivers and of tidal areas within bays, inlets, and estuaries. Provincial jurisdiction also derives from existing provincial activity in the field of environmental protection and from case law supporting provincial rights to implement treaty obligations entered into by the federal government in areas of exclusive provincial jurisdiction. The *Constitution Act, 1867* recognizes a shared jurisdiction over agriculture (s. 95), which has not, as yet, proved significant for aquaculture policy.

Inevitably, the working out of the complex jurisdictional issues in the Canadian aquaculture industry has involved a sometimes rancorous series of negotiations punctuated by appeals to the courts. Wildsmith usefully summarizes the outcome as the founding of Canadian aquaculture policy on the basis of provincial rights that determine how property and resources are used within provinces, "hemmed in by" the federal power to enact legislation to protect wild fisheries and navigation and shipping (Wildsmith 1982). A series of early fisheries cases stemming from *The Queen v. Robertson* established that the federal power to legislate under section 91(12) of the Canadian constitution does not create any proprietary right with respect to a wild fishery and is confined to protection and conservation.

Some early attempts were made to reconcile the potential conflicts of regulatory authority over aquaculture by negotiated agreement, though no pattern is discernable.[4] In practice, the jurisdictional tangle that emerged in the sector proved to be a considerable obstacle to the sustainable development of the aquaculture industry. The industry complains about the added cost of regulatory overlap and duplication. The duplication of authority allows federal–provincial blame–avoidance strategies to contribute to a dangerous vacuum in addressing the pressing and potential social and environmental impacts of the industry.

When aquaculture entered its modern period of rapid expansion in the 1980s, the jurisdictional problem was approached within the prevailing model of intergovernmental federalism. The first ministers issued a statement of national goals and principles for aquaculture at their meeting in 1986, and this statement was followed by a series of memorandums of understanding (MOUs) between the provinces and Ottawa in attempts to provide the basis of a common working relationship between the two levels of government that could be tailored to the circumstances of each province. These MOUs superseded the previous patchwork of agreements and delineated agreed-upon areas of exclusive jurisdiction and areas for intergovernmental co-operation. Learned debate surrounded the legal status of the MOUs at the time (British Columbia, Ministry of Agriculture and Fisheries 1991, 19–21), and environmental organizations have periodically made noises about testing what they see as an unconstitutional delegation of powers from (environmentally friendly) federal to (industry-dominated) provincial governments in violation of the basic scheme of sections 91 and 92 of the *Constitution Act, 1867*; however, no cases have been filed to date.[5]

Two older pieces of classic "command-and-control" legislation, the *Fisheries Act* and the *Navigable Waters Protection Act* (NWPA), provide the opportunity for federal regulatory intervention. Depending on the nature of the process for inter-agency referrals developed in each province, section 35 of the *Fisheries Act* gives the federal Department of Fisheries and Oceans (DFO) significant ability to deny development or to require modification of proposals for new or amended leases and licences when the possibility exists of "harmful alteration, disruption, or destruction" (HADD) of fish habitat. At the operational level, some problems have been caused by the potential for some fish-farming practices to fall under section 36 of the *Fisheries Act*, "the deposition of deleterious substances into waters frequented by fish," and the regulatory regimes surrounding the capture and movement of seed stocks and the movement of new species, such as abalone. As is common in Canadian environmental regulation, both sections 35 and 36 of the *Fisheries Act* are written to allow extensive administrative discretion; the lack of transparency in the exercise of this discretion is often an issue.[6]

A different set of problems is posed by the provision of the NWPA that triggers an environmental assessment under the *Canadian Environmental Assessment Act* where a "work" may present a significant hazard to navigation. Whereas environmental assessment is potentially an important policy instrument that could allow for both public involvement and the adoption of a more holistic approach to assessing the environmental impacts of new resource development, it has not been used in this way for aquaculture. Involvement has been limited to the right to be notified and to express an opinion, whereas more complex environmental interactions have generally been ignored in developing assessments. Despite these restrictions, however, from the industry point of view, the ability of the DFO to cause delays in the approvals process has been a significant irritant, resulting in calls for a "single-window, one-stop-shopping" approach, in which assessments would be even more streamlined than at present. A critical tool for the potential re-legitimation of aquaculture activities has thus fallen into disfavour with all parties.

In the fashion of a mature staple state, the regulatory regime for aquaculture has also been complemented by the use of informational, expenditure, and organizational instruments (Office of the Commissioner for Aquaculture Development 2002): the development and continuing support of an aquaculture research capacity within the DFO and Canadian universities; a variety of federal tax incentives for farming and small business; the extension of farm credit facilities to fish farmers; and various targeted expenditures through the regional development agencies, currently the Atlantic Canada Opportunities Agency (ACOA) and, to a lesser extent, the Western Economic Diversification (WED) program. Nonetheless, supporters of aquaculture development have continued to look enviously at the substantial subsidies enjoyed by Canadian farmers, keeping alive the idea of using an agricultural model for aquaculture regulation. As the federal commissioner for aquaculture development has argued, although the resolution of the regulatory issues will provide some support to the industry, "the federal government should also analyze the appropriateness of other measures to ensure that aquaculture and other food sectors in Canada operate on a level playing field" (Office of the Commissioner for Aquaculture Development 2001, 20). He noted especially the various kinds of income support and stabilization programs, including crop insurance, enjoyed by terrestrial farmers but not (yet) by their marine counterparts.

Procedurally, various types of instruments have been used in this sector, many of which are also familiar in traditional staples sectors. At the intergovernmental level, coordination of aquaculture policy between the federal and provincial governments is handled by intergovernmental negotiation. To that end, after their discussion of aquaculture at the first ministers' conference in 1986, governments pursued aquaculture policy issues through the Canadian Council of Fisheries Ministers, later renamed the Canadian Council of Fisheries and Aquaculture Ministers (CCFAM). CCFAM was responsible for the negotiation of the Agreement on Interjurisdictional Cooperation with Respect to Fisheries and Aquaculture in 1999, and subsequently created the Aquaculture Task Group (ATG) to work on aquaculture policy–related issues (Vanderzwaag, Chao, and Covan 2003).

Among the network management projects recently completed by the ATG is the Canadian Action Plan for Aquaculture, which was envisaged as a mechanism that "would be a means of organizing information, linking activities, be cohesive and provide a measuring tool for achievement of objectives" (Canadian Council of Fisheries and Aquacultures Ministers 2001). The plan would set the broad pan-Canadian direction for consistent policy development, but would be implemented by each jurisdiction according to its specific circumstances. The development of a national industry organization, the Canadian Aquaculture Industry Alliance (CAIA), formed in 1995 and a member of the Alliance of Sector Councils, has been driven by, and has complemented, these efforts at network management on the government side.[7]

Information instruments have been used sparingly at the federal level; where they have been used, finfish aquaculture has been in the spotlight. Aquaculture was the object of an investigation by the Senate Standing Committee on Fisheries, which took submissions, held public hearings, and published a report in June 2001. The DFO had a similar consultative process before issuing its Aquaculture Policy Framework. Calls for a royal commission, directed largely at environmental issues arising from finfish aquaculture, have to date fallen on deaf ears.

The peculiarity of the regulatory framework at the federal level is clear. The main objective of post-1980 federal policy is undoubtedly the development of the industry; however, the principal regulatory instruments and the mandate of the lead agency supposedly charged with implementing the policy are both designed to protect the wild fisheries and other water users from negative impacts by aquaculturalists. Moreover, the means chosen—traditional command-and-control regulation—actually tends to exacerbate the conflicts between these different interests instead of providing a framework in which their conflicts could be resolved. Unfortunately, neither the mandate itself nor the peculiar nature of the instruments used to carry it out is the contingent outcome of policy choices that could easily be reversed. Both are based on the constitutional division of powers and reflect the limit of federal jurisdiction to what Wildsmith so aptly calls the "hemming in" of provincial jurisdiction over the property and resources used for aquaculture. This outcome of efforts to regulate post-staples industries in Canada is not uncommon and further exacerbates issues related to the layering of mature and post-staples resource sectors.

Provincial Developments

If the federal approach reflects the generally ambivalent attitudes of federal agencies and their clients toward aquaculture, the provincial picture is more clearly focused on promoting aquaculture development as a safe and legitimate activity in the coastal zone and as a promising replacement for traditional staples industries. However, although novel and more appropriate policy instruments have been tentatively experimented with, the provinces, like the federal government, have generally transferred the regulation and subsidy regimes that they inherited from other staples directly to aquaculture, compounding the legitimation problems of the industry and, paradoxically, hindering the very developments they are attempting to promote.

As noted above, the memorandums of understanding (MOUs) between the federal and provincial governments usually established provincial regulatory oversight for the operational aspects of aquaculture, including the siting of new farms and the mitigation of impacts, such as the stocking densities of sea cages; the escape of farmed fish from cages; and the "acceptable" levels of waste discharges, noise, odour, and other disagreeable side effects of farming. In all provinces, authorities began by adapting the traditional Canadian "licensing and permitting" regulatory regime to aquaculture. That is, use of the water column or the foreshore for aquaculture requires a licence from the province, the terms of which set legally allowable levels of otherwise impermissible discharges and protect the operator from prosecution.

The drawbacks of licensing and permitting regimes are well known. The actual levels of discharge are set by closed-door negotiation between the licensee and the province, the cumulative and interaction effects of different substances and multiple operations are usually ignored, and enforcement tends to be weak. Prosecutions, even in the rare instances when deemed in the public interest, are usually hampered by the Canadian judicial system's dislike of absolute liability offences and the consequent acceptability of due diligence defences (Boyd 2003).

As the situation in BC illustrates, although this approach, backed by loan guarantees and other subsidy programs, allowed for the rapid growth of the industry in the province that pioneered finfish farming, licensing and permitting did nothing to legitimate the aquaculture industry with either traditional coastal users or the urban populations who were expected to buy the product. By the mid-1990s, BC was faced with mounting evidence of poorly sited salmon farms, lax enforcement of regulations, concerns about the interaction of farmed fish with declining populations of wild fish, and conflicts between shellfish farmers and other users of the foreshore. The province, sensing the need for a break, announced a moratorium on the issuance of new aquaculture licences.

The immediate impact of the moratorium was to create a perverse incentive among existing operators to intensify the very practices that were at issue. During a period of favourable market conditions and with a moratorium on new provincial sites, both finfish and shellfish output grew strongly in the late 1990s. The growth was achieved not just by opening operations in other provinces but also by increasing stocking densities on BC fish farms and mechanizing shellfish operations, with easily foreseeable results in terms of increased environmental pressures. Opposition to aquaculture among the various and disparate constituencies solidified into an advocacy coalition bound together by a shared discourse that stressed the "unnatural" character of fish farming, dangerous to the natural environment and to human health alike. Thus, while the BC government used what it considered to be the breathing space created by the moratorium to commission a wide-ranging scientific study, the Salmon Aquaculture Review, the coalition of opponents was already one step ahead, ready to criticize the scope of the review, its science, and its recommendations (British Columbia, Environmental Assessment Office 1997). The coalition was well-organized enough to fund a parallel process, the Leggatt Inquiry (named for the retired BC Supreme Court justice who chaired it) to provide a forum for alternative evidence. Leggatt reached the predictable conclusion that salmon aquaculture as currently practised poses unacceptable risks to the marine environment and prejudices First Nations' rights and title on the coast (Leggatt 2001).

Nonetheless, the Salmon Aquaculture Review made a number of recommendations for regulatory reform that helped promote a general convergence on "smarter" regulation in BC and in the Atlantic provinces where finfish farming takes place. The reforms have focused on incorporating an improved "template" of management planning into licences, backed up by more stringent and transparent reporting requirements and by regulations if necessary. In other words, the emphasis is now on the progressive adoption of improved management practices that are expected to improve the perception of sound practices, not the outputs themselves. These improvements take place "in the shadow of hierarchy": the threat of regulatory enforcement (Scharpf 1997).

BC and Newfoundland and Labrador now require a best management practices plan with respect to escapes as a condition of licensing, backed up by legislated reporting requirements. New Brunswick has provincial guidelines for escape prevention practices that must be incorporated into management plans and a code of practice that addresses issues of net pen construction and maintenance. On siting, BC has identified and either moved or closed the worst sites (usually those where tidal scour was insufficient to stop wastes accumulating around the site) and, like Newfoundland and Labrador, Nova Scotia, and New Brunswick, now requires extensive baseline survey data for monitoring changes in the seabed caused by farm operations. Waste discharges are still controlled by licensing conditions in Newfoundland and Labrador and in Nova Scotia, but approached through best management practices plans and through monitoring against the baseline data in New Brunswick. In BC, the Salmon Aquaculture Review recommended that the province adopt New Brunswick's approach if it couldn't do better, but the government has opted for a lengthy process to develop its own standards. Thus, in spite of all the baseline data that is collected, BC currently has a standard only for hydrogen sulphide in sediments, which has predictably attracted the derision of aquaculture's opponents (Connell 2004).

Unfortunately, provincial progress toward the use of smarter procedural instruments has been much less evident. As even mature staples industries, such as forestry and mining, have discovered (see Thorpe and Sandberg, chapter 10; McAllister, chapter 8), intelligent public participation is critical, not just to deal with the increasingly complex interactions of different user groups in a crowded resource landscape but also to obtain that elusive social licence or "licence to operate" from environmentally sensitive, post-materialist, and largely urban populations (Yandle 2003; Cook 2002; Gunningham, Kagan, and Thornton 2002; Montpetit 2002). And, as noted above, obtaining social licence is even more pressing when the product is food. Here, the record of provincial governments and the aquaculture industry has been dismal. Aquaculture development was generally handled by traditional government and industry committees with a mandate only for expansion. Later, as conflicts with environmental and other user constituencies flared, management plans were opened to public consultation. However, as the forest industry learned 20 years ago, the public will generally not involve themselves in writing the footnotes to plans whose basic parameters have already been decided in policy and practice (Rayner 1996).

In its shellfish planning process, the BC government rediscovered that this kind of public involvement is only successful where currently low levels of development and conflict exist (ironically, precisely those areas where the industry finds it un-economic to operate); in high-intensity areas, these processes satisfied no one. More successful efforts in the finfish sector in the Atlantic provinces have addressed the criticism of token consultations by centring on community involvement in the award of new licences, especially the Nova Scotia Regional Aquaculture Development Advisory Committees (RADACs).[8]

Provincially, trends in the shellfish sector remain less clearly articulated. The environmental impacts of shellfish farming are generally less significant in terms of scale than sea cage finfish aquaculture, and policy development has generally focused on finding appropriate sites, speeding up the joint-approvals process with federal authorities, and providing loan guarantees and subsidy programs for farmers. In general, however, policy development lags behind the finfish sector and shows the same tendency for piecemeal and incremental adaptation of historical policies, with innovation tightly constrained by the inability to coordinate federal and provincial initiatives (Howlett and Rayner 2004).[9]

CONCLUSION: A POST-STAPLES INDUSTRY CAUGHT IN A "STAPLES TRAP"

Even after discounting some of the hyperbole surrounding industry growth fore-casts, farm-raised seafood is clearly becoming an increasingly important component of the Canadian resource economy, largely replacing the declining traditional wild-capture fishery in affected species. The combination of Canada's extensive coastline and its proximity to US consumers is an irresistible attraction to invest-ment in the industry, as the recent history of multinational involvement in BC salmon farming underlines. The development of farmed cod in the Atlantic provinces will be a key test of aquaculture's ability to drive a successful transition to a post-staples economy. However, as this overview has shown, Canada's current aquaculture implementation style, with its traditional staples mixture of regulation and subsidy overseen by industry advisory groups in a clientelistic relationship with pro-development provincial government agencies, is ill adapted to the challenges of steering aquaculture through the complexities of a post-staples political economy.

Compounding the problem are two significant policy legacies. The first is the constitutional division of powers and subsequent case law surrounding the juris-diction over fisheries, combined with the decision to treat aquaculture as a species of fishery, including the nomination of DFO as the lead federal agency.[10] The sec-ond policy legacy is the policy style inherited from the staples era. As in many other traditional staples sectors, the preferred substantive instrument in aquaculture policy has historically been regulation augmented, especially after 1984, by extensive use of another substantive instrument—financial incentives (Bohm and Russell 1985). Both legacies serve to pin aquaculture in a "staples vise," preventing its full emergence from a mature-staples past to a post-staples future.

NOTES

1. The power of this lobby was recently illustrated when the traditional bargaining between the US Congress and the administration over the final shape of the bill resulted in an indefinite delay in applying country of origin labelling (COOL) to agricultural products, but an immediate implementation for seafood (United States, Department of Agriculture, Agricultural Marketing Services 2007).

2. Both the finfish and shellfish industries remain heavily dependent on bulk production of a basic "unfinished" product. The Canadian aquaculture industry is well aware of the weakness of its position and continues to try to break out of this low-value "staples trap" through diversification into new products and new markets, but its success to date has obviously been limited. The salmon industry has made some efforts at moving up the value chain to sell fillets rather than gutted whole fish in recent years, with the result that sales of salmon fillets to the United States increased threefold in volume and nearly quadrupled in value between 1998 and 2003 (Statistics Canada 2006). However, both volumes and values of fillets have slipped since 2003; and by 2005, salmon fillets accounted for less than 20 percent of exports by volume (Statistics Canada 2006). Shellfish producers have had similar difficulties moving to such higher-value products as live oysters and ready-to-eat shellfish products such as clam- and mussel-based sauces.

3. The scope of the BC fishfeed industry (and the contents of fish food) was highlighted when Washington state fish farmers found their supplies delayed at the border by BSE (bovine spongiform encephalopathy) incidents (Canadian BSE report causes fish feed holdups 2003).

4. The 1912 oyster agreement between BC and the Dominion, for example, delegated the enforcement of federal regulations to the province. The 1936 Mollusc Agreement between Nova Scotia and the Dominion took the opposite tack, delegating the power to grant leases to the federal fisheries minister (Wildsmith 1982; Parisien 1972). Thus, some kind of working agreement appears to have been reached during the early years of aquaculture on the understanding that federal–provincial co-operation based on local production characteristics was essential if Canadian aquaculture was not to be strangled at birth.

5. Another key decision taken at the time, in 1984, was the designation by the federal government of the Department of Fisheries and Oceans (DFO) as the lead agency for aquaculture regulation. Although this move clarified the lines of responsibility in the federal government, it was not without its drawbacks. As critics of DFO's role in aquaculture development continue to complain, responsibility for aquaculture was placed within a ministry that had strong historical links with capture fisheries and long-established connections with fisheries clients on both coasts. Moreover, it effectively foreclosed an embryonic, but potentially very fruitful, debate about whether

aquaculture was more appropriately understood as a kind of farming, to which an agricultural rather than a fisheries model of regulation could be applied. The MOUs in most provinces give provincial agencies control over site selection; over lease or licence approval, including the terms and conditions attached to leases and licences; and over most operational aspects of fish farms. However, the DFO exerts a powerful influence over many of these decisions.

6. Both sections contain provisions for habitat to be harmed or deleterious substances to be discharged by regulation or by ministerial order (Canada, *Fisheries Act* 1985, ss. 35(2), 36(4),(5),(6)), creating the possibility for a classic "permitting" regime as has been proposed by the commissioner for aquaculture development: "By providing clear and transparent standards, regulations under section 36 could give confidence to stakeholders that environmental interactions are managed" (Office of the Commissioner for Aquaculture Development [OCAD] 2002, 23).The continuing lack of transparency in enforcement is at issue in a private prosecution being brought by a prominent member of the anti-aquaculture coalition, Dr. Alexandra Morton, alleging DFO's failure to enforce the relevant provisions of the *Fisheries Act*. A special prosecutor appointed by the BC government to consider the merits of the charge concluded that, although Morton's work is scientifically credible, a prosecution would be unlikely to result in a conviction, leaving both sides claiming victory (Palmer 2006).

7. These traditional Canadian tools of federal–provincial network management were accompanied by some relatively minor departmental reorganization at the federal level. Concerns about the capture-fishery culture within the DFO led to the creation of the Office of the Commissioner for Aquaculture Development (OCAD) reporting directly to the fisheries minister, intended to act as a "champion" for the development of the industry. The DFO also underwent a minor reorganization, creating an Office of Sustainable Aquaculture. Although the OCAD's mandate was extended by two years, it was eventually wound up in 2004. Some evidence of subsystem spillover, once again from agriculture, has resulted in the creation of the Canadian Food Inspection Agency, in response to public concerns about food safety, the cozy relationship between regulators and (terrestrial) farmers, and Agriculture Canada's involvement in the regulation of aquaculture food quality.

8. RADACs comprise representatives of the main local interests, which may include fishers, aquaculturists, recreational boaters, waterfront landowners, business operators, and local politicians—in short, people and groups affected by the installation of an aquaculture site. The result of the committee's advisory process is then passed on to the Nova Scotia minister of fisheries and aquaculture as a recommendation. The government hopes that most areas with significant potential for aquaculture development will form community RADACs. There are currently RADACs in all eight of Nova Scotia's regional fisheries territories. Areas not covered by a RADAC will have input through public hearing processes (Nova Scotia, Fisheries and Aquaculture 2007).

9. PEI, the leading shellfish-producing province, provides an intriguing exception to the general rule of provincial control over licensing and regulation: its MOU effectively streamlines these procedures by ceding provincial powers to the federal DFO. BC, by contrast, has struggled to find the new sites that would allow for the expansion

of its shellfish industry envisaged under the province's Shellfish Development Initiative, but has acted to protect the operations of existing sites by bringing shellfish aquaculture under the *Farm Practices (Right to Farm) Act.* A voluntary code of conduct developed by the industry sets out what are considered "normal farming practices," which now receive legal protection against upland owners who might complain about noise or odour. In addition to the Nova Scotia RADACs noted above, New Brunswick has some useful experience with community-led efforts to expand the range of possible sites for shellfish aquaculture by identifying sources of pollution and improving water quality.

10. As the federal commissioner on environment and sustainable development noted in 2004, three separate reports by federal and provincial auditors general pointed to federal–provincial coordination as the weak link in aquaculture policy: "All three audits identified gaps in co-ordination between the federal and provincial governments. Despite numerous committees, agreements, and protocols between the two provinces [BC and New Brunswick] and the federal government, problems still exist" (Office of the Auditor General of Canada 2004).

REFERENCES

Bohm, P., and Russell, C.S. 1985. Comparative analysis of alternative policy instruments. In *Handbook of Natural Resource and Energy Economics,* vol. I, eds. A.V. Kneese and J.L. Sweeney, 395–460. Dordrecht, Netherlands: Elsevier.

Boyd, D.R. 2003. *Unnatural law: Rethinking Canadian environmental law and policy.* Vancouver: University of British Columbia Press.

British Columbia, Environmental Assessment Office. 1997. *Salmon aquaculture review.* 5 vols. Victoria: Environmental Assessment Office.

British Columbia, Ministry of Agriculture and Fisheries. 1991. *Aquaculture legislation in British Columbia: A comparative legal analysis.* Aquaculture Industry Development Report 91-01. Victoria: Ministry of Agriculture and Fisheries.

British Columbia, Ministry of Agriculture and Lands. 2001. Shellfish development initiative. Online at http://www.agf.gov.bc.ca/fisheries/Shellfish/shellfish_dev.htm.

British Columbia, Ministry of Agriculture and Lands. 2006. Finfish agriculture: BC salmon aquaculture industry. Online at http://www.al.gov.bc.ca/fisheries/bcsalmon_aqua.htm.

Burros, M. 2005. Plan would expand ocean fish farming: Critics are concerned that draft has no environmental rules. *New York Times,* June 6: A17.

Canada, *Fisheries Act.* 1985. Online at http://www.canlii.org/ca/sta/f-14/whole.html.

Canada, Senate, Standing Committee on Fisheries. 2001. Aquaculture in Canada's Atlantic and Pacific regions. Online at http://www.parl.gc.ca/37/1/parlbus/commbus/senate/com-E/fish-e/rep-e/repintjun01-e.htm.

Canadian BSE report causes fish feed holdups. 2003. Online at www.intrafish.com.

Canadian Council of Fisheries and Aquacultures Ministers. 2001. Record of decision: CCFAM Aquaculture Task Group. Online at http://www.aquaculture.ca/English/CCFAM/CAIA_RecordsOf10.html.

Cashore, B., Auld, G., and Newsom, D. 2003. Forest certification (eco-labeling) programs and their policy-making authority: Explaining divergence among North American and European case studies. *Forest Policy and Economics* 5(3): 225–47.

Clancy, P. 2002. *New Zealand shellfish aquaculture: Politics and policy formation in a high growth sector.* PowerPoint presentation.

Clapp, R.A. 1998. The resource cycle in forestry and fishing. *Canadian Geographer* 42(2): 129–44.

Coastal Alliance for Aquaculture Reform. n.d. About CAAR: The Coastal Alliance for Aquaculture Reform. Online at http://www.farmedanddangerous.org/about/index.html.

Connell, S. 2004. Regulating salmon aquaculture in BC: A report card. Online at http://www.georgiastrait.org/BCFishFarmReportCard.pdf.

Cook, D. 2002. Consultation, for a change? Engaging users and communities in the policy process. *Social Policy and Administration* 36(5): 516–31.

Coopers & Lybrand. 1997. *Economic potential of the British Columbia aquaculture industry: Phase one—Shellfish.* Prepared for Western Economic Diversification Canada. Vancouver: Coopers & Lybrand.

Food and Agriculture Organization of the United Nations. 2004. The state of world fisheries and aquaculture (SOFIA). Online at http://www.fao.org/sof/sofia/index_en.htm.

Gunningham, N., Grabosky, P., and Sinclair, D. 1998. *Smart regulation: Designing environmental policy.* Oxford: Clarendon Press.

Gunningham, N., Kagan, R.A., and Thornton, D. 2002. Social licence and environmental protection: why businesses go beyond compliance. Online at http://www.lse.ac.uk/collections/CARR/pdf/Disspaper8.pdf.

Hessing, M., Howlett, M., and Summerville, T. 2005. *Canadian natural resource and environmental policy: Political economy and public policy.* Vancouver: University of British Columbia Press.

Hodgetts, J.E. 1973. *The Canadian public service.* Toronto: University of Toronto Press.

Howlett, M. 2001. Complex network management and the governance of the environment: Prospects for policy change and policy stability over the long term. In *Governing the Environment: Persistent Challenges, Uncertain Innovations,* ed. E. Parsons, 303–44. Toronto: University of Toronto Press.

Howlett, M. 2003. Canadian environmental policy and the natural resource sector: Paradoxical aspects of the transition to a post-staples political economy. In *The Integrity Gap: Canada's Environmental Policy and Institutions,* eds. E. Lee and A. Perl, 42–67. Vancouver: University of British Columbia Press.

Howlett, M., and Rayner, J. 2004. (Not so) "smart regulation"? Canadian shellfish aquaculture policy and the evolution of instrument choice for industrial development. *Marine Policy* 28(2): 171–84.

Hume, S. 2003a. "Lessons not learned" in Ireland: Sea trout supported a thriving business—until sea lice wiped them out. *Vancouver Sun,* February 22: A4.

Hume, S. 2003b. "We are going to stop these fish farms": Omega Salmon's hatchery at Ocean Falls has become a lightning rod for BC's growing Aboriginal rebellion. *Vancouver Sun*, March 1: A21.

Hutton, T.A. 1994. *Visions of a "post-staples" economy: Structural change and adjustment issues in British Columbia*, working paper PI #3. Vancouver: University of British Columbia Centre for Human Settlements.

Innis, H.A. 1930. *The fur trade in Canada: An introduction to Canadian economic history.* Toronto: University of Toronto Press.

Innis, H.A. 1933. *Problems of staple production in Canada.* Toronto: The Ryerson Press.

Leggatt, S. 2001. Clear choices, clean waters: The Leggatt inquiry into salmon farming in British Columbia. Online at http://www.davidsuzuki.org/files/Leggatt _reportfinal.pdf.

Mansfield, B. 2004. Organic views of nature: The debate over organic certification for aquatic animals. *Sociologica Ruralis* 44(2): 216–32.

Marshall, D. 2003. *Fishy business: The economics of salmon farming in BC.* Vancouver: Canadian Centre for Policy Alternatives.

McInnes, C., and LaVoie, J. 2003. Van Dongen embroiled in row over fish farm, papers show. *Vancouver Sun*, February 5: A3.

Montpetit, E. 2002. Policy networks, federal arrangements, and the development of environmental regulations: A comparison of the Canadian and American agricultural sectors. *Governance* 15(1): 1–20.

Naylor, R.T. 1972. The rise and fall of the third commercial empire of the St. Lawrence. In *Capitalism and the National Question in Canada*, ed. G. Teeple, 1–42. Toronto: University of Toronto Press.

Nova Scotia, Fisheries and Aquaculture. 2007. Regional Aquaculture Development Advisory Committees (RADACs): Background information. Online at http:// www.gov.ns.ca/fish/aquaculture/radac.

Office of the Auditor General of Canada. 2004. Report of the Commissioner of the Environment and Sustainable Development: Fisheries and Oceans Canada— Salmon Stocks, Habitat, and Aquaculture. Online at http://www.oag-bvg.gc.ca/ domino/reports.nsf/html/c20041005ce.html.

Office of the Commissioner for Aquaculture Development. 2001. Legislative and regulatory review of aquaculture in Canada. Online at http://www.dfo-mpo.gc.ca/ aquaculture/ref/legalreview_e.pdf.

Office of the Commissioner for Aquaculture Development. 2002. Review of federal programs in support of aquaculture development. Available online at http://www .dfo-mpo.gc.ca/aquaculture/ref/Study5_e.pdf.

Palmer, V. 2006. Stay of prosecution puts sea lice issue back into realm of politics. *Vancouver Sun* August 12. Online at http://www.friendsofwildsalmon.ca/news.

Parisien, R.W. 1972. *The Fisheries Act: Origins of federal delegation of administrative jurisdiction to the provinces.* Ottawa: Environment Canada.

PricewaterhouseCoopers. 2002. Net results: Northern aquaculture statistics 2001: The year in review. *Northern Aquaculture* 8(8).

Rahnema, S., and Howlett, M. 2002. Impediments to industrial policy: Overcoming path dependency in Canada's post staples transition. *Journal of Australian Political Economy* 49: 114–35.

Randolph, J., and Bauer, M. 1999. Improving environmental decision-making through collaborative methods. *Policy Studies Review* 16(3/4): 168–91.

Rayner, J. 1996. Implementing sustainability in west coast forests: CORE and FEMAT as experiments in process. *Journal of Canadian Studies* 31(1): 82–101.

Rud, J. 2003. Fish farm adviser an aquaculture supplier, NDP's MacPhail says. *Vancouver Sun*, February 13: A19.

Scharpf, F.W. 1997. *Games real actors play: Actor-centered institutionalism in policy research.* Boulder, CO: Westview Press.

Simpson, S. 2003a. Fishery officials license illegal catch. *Vancouver Sun*, February 7: D3.

Simpson, S. 2003b. Shellfish farms "disrupt" beaches. *Vancouver Sun*, January 10: F1.

Statistics Canada. 2006. *Aquaculture statistics 2005*, cat. 23-222-XIE. Ottawa: Statistics Canada.

Stone, F. 1984. *Canada, the GATT and the international trade system.* Montreal: Institute for Research on Public Policy.

Suryanata, K., and Umemoto, K.N. 2003. Tension at the nexus of the global and the local: Culture, property and marine aquaculture in Hawai'i. *Environment and Planning A* 35(2): 199–213.

United States, Department of Agriculture, Agricultural Marketing Services. 2007. 2002 farm bill provisions: Country of origin labeling. Online at http://www.ams.usda .gov/cool/.

Vanderzwaag, D., Chao, G., and Covan, M. 2003. Canadian aquaculture and the principles of sustainable development: Gauging the law and policy tides and charting a course. Paper presented at the AquaNet Law and Policy Workshop, Halifax.

Whalley, J. 1985. *Canadian trade policies and the world economy.* Toronto: University of Toronto Press.

Wildsmith, B.H. 1982. *Aquaculture: The legal framework.* Toronto: Emond Montgomery.

Wondelleck, J.M., Manring, N.J., and Cowfoot, J.E. 1996. Teetering at the top of the ladder: The experience of citizen group participants in alternative dispute resolution processes. *Sociological Perspectives* 39(2): 249–62.

Yandle, T. 2003. The challenge of building successful stakeholder organizations: New Zealand's experience in developing a fisheries co-management regime. *Marine Policy* 27(2): 179–92.

PART IV

Extraction Industries: Minerals and Forests

Shifting Foundations in a Mature Staples Industry: A History of Canadian Mineral Policy

Mary Louise McAllister*

INTRODUCTION

In the past few decades, the Canadian mineral policy arena has seen significant changes. Mining, long a staple of the Canadian political economy, a pillar of national policy, and a leading producer and exporter of minerals in the world, has been encountering new challenges. Political players have multiplied, economies have diversified, and policy issues have grown in complexity. These developments are of seismic proportions to members of the mineral industry worried about an increasingly uncertain and unpredictable investment and operating environment. As the 20th century drew to a close, new competitors in an increasingly open world market, such as those in Latin America, presented a serious challenge; they offered rich, readily accessible deposits, an inexpensive labour force, and welcoming governments anxious for the investment dollar to build their developing economies. The Canadian mineral industry was increasingly alert to the dangers of being labelled a "sunset industry." The tertiary sector had begun to elbow its way onto government agendas, capturing attention and offering intriguing new possibilities associated with a transition to a post-staples economy.

These changes are significant and affect all aspects of the mining and minerals industry. Mineworkers, the backbone of the Canadian mineral industry, have become increasingly concerned about the growing use of automation and robotics, which have been replacing jobs and requiring workers with new skill sets in applied science and computer operations. Labour organizations have had to develop strategies for dealing with a new phenomenon referred to as long-distance commuting in which workers are flown into remote mine operations for weekly or biweekly work shifts.

Meanwhile, non-governmental organizations, worried about the continuing and cumulative impact of mining, have had very different preoccupations. They dismiss the mineral industry's competitive concerns, observing that if the mineral wealth exists, exploration dollars and investment will follow. Canada's new diamond mines offer a case in point (see Fitzpatrick, chapter 9). Environmental and social organizations have argued that the primary industry continues to be supported by governments. They suggest that public commitments to sustainable development are often not realized in practice and represent very little in the way of meaningful change from older habits and routines.

Yet change is happening. In recent decades, notable adaptive strategies have taken place in governing institutional regimes and in industrial relations. References to corporate social responsibility, community partnerships, total cost assessment, and sustainable ecosystems are now part of the popular lexicon in industry and government documents. As Russell has observed, advocates of post-Fordist "new work relations" emphasize what they see as trends toward worker empowerment and democratization (Russell 1999, 167). Skeptics, however, argue that the results are anything but empowering for workers and communities. Moreover, they note that, despite efforts at mitigation and the introduction of remedial measures in various mines, little has occurred to lessen the overall adverse and cumulative global environmental impact of mining. Global and domestic economic and political imperatives continue to overshadow ecological, community, and other social considerations in this sector, as in many others.

Unquestionably, the Canadian mineral industry is finding itself operating within, and reacting to, an environment consistent with that of a mature, advanced staples economy, as discussed by Howlett and Brownsey (see chapter 1), Wellstead (see chapter 2), and Hutton (see chapter 3). Such an economy has been defined as one that is still primary resource–dependent but more diffused and diversified than in the past (Howlett 2003, 47). Nevertheless, the mineral industry remains an important element of Canadian economic activity, with all the associated social, industrial, environmental, and political implications.

PROMISING PROSPECTS: STAPLES AND THE NASCENT MINERAL INDUSTRY

They sailed upon her waterways and they walked the forests tall
And they built the mines, the mills and the factories for the good of us all …
For they looked in the future and what did they see
They saw an iron road running from sea to the sea

— "Canadian Railway Trilogy" (Lightfoot 1967)

From the eastern cod fisheries, to the forestry and fur trade, through to the prairies' agricultural wheat basket, and extending to the western gold-mining rushes, Canada's economy, society, and technological development have been firmly rooted in the staples-producing industries, as famously noted by economic historian, Harold A. Innis (1936). As Gordon Lightfoot's song "Canadian Railway Trilogy" (1967) illustrates, public interest has long been associated with resource development. The early developers and decision-makers saw the building of railways, industries, and the extraction of resources as an important part of the 19th century Canadian National Policy and the key to nation building.

Mining is one of the world's oldest professions and will likely continue to take place in some form as long as people need minerals—that is, indefinitely. Before European contact, Amerindians had developed economic networks with trade taking place throughout the extreme reaches of the North American continent. Minerals played an important role in trade extending back many thousand years BCE. Obsidian, copper, flint, and other minerals were used for tools or weapons (Dickason 1992, 78). After the Europeans arrived, early settlers used various minerals as building materials. Minerals are reported to have been exported as early as 1643, when coal was shipped from the east coast to England (Udd 2000, 1).

Coal mining played a large role in the formation and history of Canadian maritime culture and economy, with many communities rising and falling with the fortunes of the industry. In Nova Scotia, coal—discovered in Cape Breton Island in the late 1600s—was to become an important part of the provincial economy. In the 1800s, the production of coal in Pictou and Sydney increased from 21,000 tons in 1828 to 294,000 tons in 1858, making this region one of Canada's major coal producers (along with the western provinces), and provided power for the New England states, Quebec, and Ontario (Gray 1917).

Soon after the initiation of the coal industry, the mining of iron ore and gypsum began, followed by the discovery of gold in Quebec in the early 1800s. Numerous major mineral finds occurred between the mid-1880s and the turn of the century, including discoveries of gold in the West, which caused prospecting rushes to British Columbia and Yukon; asbestos in the Eastern Townships of Quebec; and huge copper-nickel deposits in the Sudbury Basin, during the building of the CPR Railway (Cranstone 2002, 10–11). After silver was discovered in Cobalt, Ontario, the area soon became one of the world's largest silver producers. Angus and Griffin note (1996, 20) that "by 1910 the money that had come out of Cobalt had dwarfed any other silver operation in North American history and had surpassed the money made in the Klondike rush … The infant steps of Canada's powerful mining industry were made in the narrow shafts of cobalt." The Canadian mineral industry was well launched.

The mineral industry did not achieve this success alone; it relied on the development of other primary industries and new technologies, supportive governments, and the labour of prospectors and mine workers. As Harold Innis (1936, 321) noted, railways built to open up agricultural areas led to the expansion of metal mining in northern Ontario and, later, on the prairies and in British Columbia.

With the construction of the railways to export commodities (an important component of Canada's National Policy), mining companies were able to ship their ore to market more efficiently (Udd 2000, 7).

In his well-known staples thesis, Harold Innis (1936) used the forces of production, such as capital, markets, and technology, to explain the evolution of Canadian resource development. Wallace Clement (1981, 19) added a class analysis in his specific application of this model to mining, suggesting that although the staples thesis emphasized the importance of the technology (in this case railways) to transport the raw resource to market, it is "equally important … to recognize that the ensuing 'technical division of labour' is infused with relations resulting from the 'social division of labour.'" Clement argued that, in the mining sector (and other industries), capital dominates labour, facilitated by technologies that shape the way in which work is organized. In the early years of Canadian mining history, the future pattern of mining and industrial relations took root. A dynamic tension between the mining industry and its workers continues to be played out in today's economy. Technology is still a pivotal tool with which mining development and productivity is achieved, although its form has led to different impacts on industrial relations.

At the turn of the 20th century, the rapid growth of the mineral industry generated a huge demand for labour. Companies were very powerful in terms of establishing and running mining camps, determining wages and living conditions, and organizing the social and political life of mines and mining communities. This latter activity extended to the organization of labour relations where, as Innis noted (1936, 323), mining companies were vehemently anti-union: "In 1906, the Nipissing Company discharged a miner from Montana for attempting to organize a union and leading mine operators decided not to employ union men." A major mine strike in 1907 was largely unsuccessful.

Nevertheless, the period was marked by the emergence of industrial labour unions as workers fought for better wages and working conditions, which were harsh even by the standards of the day. The early 1900s saw a number of large, violent strikes across Canada, and the military often stepped in to support property rights over those of the workers. Over the next several decades, ties first with the American trade union movement and later with the international movement became an important element of Canadian unionism, which would eventually include membership in the United Steelworkers of America and the International Union of Mine, Mill and Smelter Workers, among others.

In the early years, some government legislation did play a role in improving labour conditions. In Ontario, for example, the *Workmen's Compensation Act* came into effect in 1915, soon to be followed by Manitoba (in 1916) and British Columbia (in 1917). For the most part, however, governments invested in the promotion of the mineral industry. A major early step in this direction was the setting up of the Geological Survey of Canada (GSC) in 1842, to provide geological information to support the minerals exploration industry. The goal of undertaking a geological survey was closely associated with nation-building "based on the realization that the development of an industrial economy in Canada—an economy that could compete with those in Europe and the United States—would depend to a considerable extent on a viable mining industry" (Vodden 1992). Because primary resource ownership was originally assigned to the provinces under the Canadian constitution (with some exceptions), provincial governments have also actively promoted mineral development.[1] In Ontario, early government initiatives were primarily directed toward promoting the legal rights of prospectors and miners and offering exploration incentives. The first Bureau of Mines was established in 1891. The 1906 *Mines Act* was created to establish a stable, standardized legal environment that would encourage the establishment of mining. This act governed Ontario through much of the 20th century. As H.V. Nelles has observed (1974, 110), "promotion, embracing the improvement of access to resources, the extension of financial assistance wherever necessary, and the provision of information and technical education, was the public contribution to resource development."

Scientific management and business approaches to decision making heavily influenced the political culture of public and private organizations in the early 20th century. The mineral industry was no exception and prospered in this environment, garnering the attention of decision-makers and economic leaders alike and setting political agendas. The era was characterized by the discovery of numerous rich ore deposits. Sudbury's huge deposits, for example, ultimately led to the 1916 incorporation of the International Nickel Co. (Inco), which would shortly become the world's primary producer of nickel. In Toronto, the establishment of the head offices of mining companies led to the city becoming a leading international financial centre in mining.

EMBEDDED INTERESTS: ESTABLISHING THE STAPLES ECONOMY

The first 100 years of the federal government's approach to mining (from about 1880 to 1980) might be characterized as a "conventional" effort to promote mineral development as a classic staples industry (Clausen and McAllister 2001). Industrial policy was very much tied to building Canada's natural resources industries. In the first half of the 20th century, the federal government, actively involved in restructuring the economy, supported the growth of the mineral industry and other primary industries in numerous ways. Early mining departments were charged with the responsibility of promoting mining to serve the public interest (Canada,

Parliament 2006). During the mid-20th century, Canada's boom-and-bust economy, subject to the vagaries of the international marketplace and uncertain prices, motivated the federal government to support its export-oriented industries and resource regions through various policy and economic measures. Canadian industrial strategies were heavily linked to building up the resource industries. One notable promotional effort was John Diefenbaker's Road to Resources initiative. While he was prime minister from 1957 to 1963, Diefenbaker adopted a platform of opening up the North and northern resources for development, signalling a government actively involved in "staples-led" growth (Leslie 1987, 7).[2]

During the first half of the 20th century, Canada became a world leader in the production of many minerals. By the early 1980s, Canada was selling almost 80 percent of its mineral products to 100 countries (Wojciechowski and McAllister 1985, 21). The mineral industry was firmly embedded in the Canadian economy and society. The public interest was interpreted fairly narrowly, based on principles associated with liberal democracy, economic development, and private property rights. Decision making might be best characterized as a top-down approach in which the mineral industry and government were considered the key players in the mineral arena.

Throughout the century, labour unions struggled to achieve legitimacy under this regime. Part of the difficulty was trade unionism's own fragmentation: unionized workers were affiliated with different unions, such as the United Steelworkers, the United Auto Workers, the Canadian Union of Public Employees, and the Public Service Alliance. In addition, Clement notes (1981, 301) that unions have historically been trapped between two competing ends: "They are at one and the same time the most systematic and organized expression of [workers'] resistance and through the commitments they make to companies when they enter into collective agreements, a containment of many forms of workers' resistance."

For their part, government mining departments were expected to perform the dual role of promoting industrial development while regulating the activities of enterprises. Federal and provincial government promotion of the mineral industry included direct investment or equity participation in many mining corporations. Governments also provided millions of dollars in direct grants that funded geoscience, technology, marketing, and feasibility studies. Other assistance included infrastructure development, promotion of minerals in international trade meetings, and tax concessions. Although governments played the role of promoters of resource development, they also imposed corporate, income, and mining taxes and regulated the mineral industry through legislation and regulations governing land access and tenure, transportation, mineral investment, health and safety, and, increasingly, environmentally related concerns (McAllister and Schneider 1992). Federal and provincial mining departments saw their primary responsibility as fostering a stable investment environment while serving the public interest. In the late 1980s, the *Mineral and Metals Policy of the Government of Canada* laid out a number of objectives that were geared toward assisting the mineral industry, including regional economic development policies and improving access to international markets (Natural Resources Canada, Minerals and Metals Sector 2004).

A decade later, however, government approaches to resource development began to change; in mining, a new policy was introduced with a distinctly different tone and objectives. The government was now recognizing that the policies that had carried the mineral industry and Canada through more than a century of staples-led growth were out of step with the societal and political changes that had been taking place in Canadian political culture and economy. Most notably, the government had to respond to widely held concerns about environmental degradation and the demands of a diverse mineral policy community. By introducing the new policy, the federal minister of natural resources signalled a shift in the traditional position stating, "Turning the concept of sustainable development into practice will require stakeholders to question their old assumptions, and to examine minerals- and metals-related issues in light of the integration of economic, environmental and social objectives" (Natural Resources Canada, Minerals and Metals Sector 2004).

SHIFTING GROUND: COMPETING INTERESTS

In the closing years of the 20th century, the mineral industry faced a number of pressures that it saw as threatening its position as a valued component of the Canadian economy and society. These threats were not peculiar to the mineral industry; Canada's staples-based economy, used as the foundation for nation-building, was now being questioned both in terms of its continuing economic contributions and its environmental impacts.

By the 1980s and 1990s, the mineral sector shared characteristics noted by other authors in this volume with respect to mature industries in Canada. Specifically, public concerns were mounting about adverse ecological impacts of industrial activity; the economy was diversifying into other areas, most notably toward the tertiary sector, and population growth and employment were declining in the smaller resource communities. Significant international changes were also taking place, including the economic integration of markets, networks, and services (adapted after Hutton 1994, 1–2).

In the past quarter-century, such characteristics applied to Canada's mineral industry, which reacted in various ways to fluctuating economic cycles, new competition, uncertainty in land access for exploration, and the indifference of a primarily urban public frequently more concerned with the industry's environmental impacts than its economic contributions. A decline in the size and number of mining-dependent communities and lower levels of direct employment in mining operations contributed to the mineral industry's decreasing influence on public agendas.

COMPETITIVE PRESSURES ON THE RESOURCE INDUSTRY

Mining industry representatives (Canadian Mining Hall of Fame n.d.) state that the "object of any mining enterprise is to produce a product that someone wants to buy, at a price that can satisfy all the stakeholders. A modern mine in Canada often requires an investment of $200 million or more (large mines might cost $1 billion) before producing any income." These companies have a responsibility to their investors, lenders, and shareholders to generate a reasonable rate of return. A company must first make a number of expenditures: wages for labour, goods and services (which constitute about one-half of a mine's income), and taxes for government services. Money is also required for new exploration and development to ensure a continued supply of mineral reserves (ibid.). Government legislation and regulations monitor the mineral industry, govern access to land, provide guidelines for health and safety, and impose standards for environmental compliance, all of which affect the cost structure of mining operations.

Determining the economic viability of a mineral deposit is a complex process: each step must be factored into the estimated costs of bringing a mine into production. Uncertainties include the effect of international conditions of supply and demand on world prices, the changing investment and regulatory climate in the host jurisdiction, and, increasingly, the local reception of the community to mining activities. To survive unpredictable events, an industry must adapt. Such an occurrence hit the mineral industry when a recession in the early 1980s was followed by a subsequent recession in the early 1990s. The mineral industry responded with technological improvements to increase efficiency in the production of minerals.

Recently, the mineral industry received a boost with major developments in domestic mining, such as the rich nickel-copper-cobalt deposit in Voisey's Bay, Labrador, and the new diamond industry in northern Canada. Nevertheless, the overall rate of new discoveries has continued to decline, particularly top-tier discoveries (that is, large, mineral-rich, accessible, economic deposits). Moreover, existing reserves are becoming depleted. This situation continues to stimulate offshore exploration activities and to raise questions about domestic exploration potential (Gouveia, Rose, and Gingerich 2003, 9). Some argue that Canada is still one of the top targets for exploration dollars as long as world prices are strong and discoveries continue to maintain mineral reserves. Others, however, doubt this situation will continue to be the case (Cranstone 2002, 3).

ACCESS-TO-LAND ISSUES

Mineral exploration in Canada, which peaked in 1987 at more than $1 billion, fell by more than half by 1990. This decline could be attributed to many factors, including the growth of offshore competition. Mineral industry representatives, however, suggested that the decline was also a result of unfavourable government policies and public perceptions (Peeling 1998).

In the previous decade, environmental non-governmental organizations had been raising an alarm about the impact of resource development on wilderness areas, and governments were responding. Moreover, First Nations groups were gaining increasing legal recognition in the use, management, and ownership of lands claimed as traditional territories. Following the recommendations of the United Nations Brundtland commission, protected areas were designated, and a number of multi-stakeholder land use processes and commissions were launched. These actions signalled that governments were prepared to listen to a diversity of voices—including labour, environmental non-government organizations, and First Nations peoples—not only to the mineral industry and affected communities, as had been primarily the case in past years.

The 1991 British Columbia Commission on Resources and the Environment (CORE) was perhaps the most extensive of a number of large-scale public and stakeholder consultation exercises launched at that time. The CORE processes were initiated under the governing provincial New Democratic Party and led to the development of land-use planning strategies that assisted in the determination of where resource development could take place and under what conditions. In the protected areas, no exploration or development could take place.

During this era, one particular event, known as the Windy Craggy affair, turned into a flashpoint for the Canadian mineral industry. The mineral industry wanted to develop an enormous copper deposit (which included some cobalt, gold, and silver) in northwestern British Columbia. The proposed mine, however, was to be built at the confluence of the Tatshenshini and Alsek rivers, an area highly rated for its wilderness values. The environmental perspective prevailed, and the region was designated a World Heritage Site, protecting it from development. Although some may argue that the Windy Craggy situation was unique, many in the mineral industry believed it signalled that Canada was no longer open to mining.

A number of unresolved land claims also contributed to the air of uncertainty for the mineral industry. Because many years are required to bring a mine into production, investors are reluctant to put resources into a project when unresolved questions surround the ownership and the legal requirements governing the potential mine site. After the land claims are settled, the mineral industry must be able to negotiate effectively with First Nations peoples. Yet, the mineral industry's history of effective negotiation is spotty at best. As Jerry Asp (2004) discusses (see the following section), the mineral industry has a track record that would not always inspire trust in First Nations communities.

ADVERSE ENVIRONMENTAL AND SOCIAL IMPACTS OF MINING

Access to land and new investments in exploration require government support and public support. As noted earlier, at one time the mineral industry could count on both. Just as it was challenged on the international competitive front, however, the mineral industry has found itself facing barriers on the home front. As was the case with the Windy Craggy deposit, non-governmental environmental organizations and others were drawing public attention to the impact that resource development was having on the biophysical environment, important watersheds, and valued wilderness areas.

Economies and societies rely on natural resources (sometimes referred to as natural capital) for water, energy, primary materials, and habitable environments. The biophysical environment needs to be protected; on that point there is little debate. How that should happen, however, is a different question. Many members of the mineral industry, for example, have applied technological approaches to solve environmental concerns. They have, for example, modernized operating practices through environmental management systems, continual self-improvement, retrofitting, maximizing the ore body, minimizing waste, and taking lifecycle approaches to the management operations. The Canadian mineral industry has adopted these approaches to various degrees, believing that sustainability can be readily achieved within a global liberal-capitalist economy. Despite such efforts, however, some argue that technological fixes are not enough (see the following sections); they call instead for major institutional, industrial, and social restructuring that recognize the socio-ecological limits of the planet.

For its part, the mineral industry has continued to attempt to solve its problems in the traditional fashion through the application of technological improvements to increase efficiency and deal with the industry's environmental effects. The sector has been less sophisticated, however, at dealing with the political and social challenges that affect its long-term viability. Scientific advances in such areas as geophysics, robotics, and pollution abatement initiatives can take the industry only so far. As noted above, companies need access to land and a supportive regulatory and investment environment to undertake exploration activities and to mine deposits, circumstances that will not occur without government support.

Critics watching the mineral industry are ready to offer numerous examples of how the industry has failed to both comprehend and respond to the changing public agenda; examples range from the poor handling of international mining disasters, to failure to live up to national commitments, to inept negotiations with local communities or Indigenous peoples, to poorly handled industrial relations, and bad public relations with local property owners (MiningWatch Canada 2005; Russell 1999).

As a result of advances in the Internet and the increasing globalization of communications, non-governmental organizations at the local and national levels have developed connections throughout the world, spawning new organizations. The resources of the well-funded organizations have helped to support the causes of smaller associations. In Canada, the establishment of the Environmental Mining Council of British Columbia, formed in 1992 to promote environmentally sound mining policy and practices, was followed in 1999 by the launch of the national organization MiningWatch Canada. MiningWatch Canada focuses on the promotion of ecologically sound mineral practices and sustainable communities. The organization suggests that the mineral industry has acquired an unsustainable legacy in environmental costs in Canada and abroad:

> The very real legacy of mining includes an estimated twenty-seven thousand abandoned mines across Canada, billions of dollars of remediation liability for acid mine drainage contamination, extensive disruption of critical habitat areas, profound social impacts in many mining communities, and the boom and bust upheaval of local economies. The cost of Canadian mining operations in other parts of the world has been no less dramatic. (MiningWatch Canada 2005)

Although their figures may differ, governments acknowledge that these problems exist and must be addressed. For example, Natural Resources Canada notes that 10,000 abandoned mine sites have been identified (not to mention those that have not been uncovered) throughout Canada with liabilities associated with health, safety, and environmental concerns. One of the most serious concerns is that old tailings ponds containing mining wastes will fail, resulting in the poisoning of watersheds. Today, modern mining operations, governed by numerous environmental regulations and operations, are much improved. That said, the environmental and public safety concerns posed by contemporary mineral activities—in addition to the cumulative historical problems—leaves the industry open to public criticism. MiningWatch Canada is affiliated with numerous other organizations, including the Canadian Environmental Network, the Canadian Environmental Law Centre, and international organizations. The ability of these groups to pool resources, ideas, and initiatives makes them an influential alternative voice to the mineral industry when setting public agendas.

Canada's Aboriginal peoples have also become very influential members of the mineral policy community. This influence stems from the legal recognition of Indigenous peoples' rights in a variety of ways, including outright ownership in many mineral-rich regions of the country, and is both national and international in scope as Indigenous peoples' organizations around the world develop strategies to protect their interests. One member of the Canadian Aboriginal Minerals Association (CAMA), Jerry Asp (2004), raises some important issues related to the future of the mineral industry–Aboriginal peoples relations. If corporations wish to negotiate with First Nations people, he suggests, they would do well to handle their interactions differently. For example, Asp observes that abandoned mines have left an environmentally damaging legacy that continues to affect public perceptions of the mining industry today. Asp suggests that the industry is paying insufficient attention to this problem and needs to claim responsibility collectively.

Asp also notes the historical tendency of the industry to proclaim that it has a relatively small impact on the land, given that it does not occupy a large territory. Asp suggests that the mining industry should acknowledge its actual environmental impact. For example, members of the mining industry often proclaim that a mine takes up only a small "footprint" when it is in operation. Such a statement undermines the credibility of the industry and erodes any trust that it might have gained in public consultations and discussions. Asp, speaking from the perspective of First Nations peoples, comments on the mining industry's claims that it takes only a few acres of land to mine:

> It reminds me of the story of the railroad crossing the Great Plains of America. They told the First Nations that it was only two tracks and a whistle. They forgot to tell them about the people that the train will carry. You are forgetting to tell us about the related infrastructure that goes with your project. The road, the power transmission lines, etc. This opens up our country to anyone who owns a snow machine, or a four-wheeler. This is a real disruption to us. It has a major impact on our life … then all trust is gone … The mining company will have an uphill battle to get First Nations approval for their project. (Asp 2004, 3)

Given the well-documented adverse cumulative impacts of resource development activities on First Nations peoples, trust will be very difficult to achieve, particularly if the mining industry continues to attempt to minimize the very real, potential disruption of their activities.

On a local level, the activities of exploration companies can also erode public faith in the mineral industry. For example, old mining laws, devised at a time when mining exploration took place a long way from human settlement, continue to govern at a time when small property owners can be adversely affected by legislation that continues to support the concept of "free entry" for exploration (even on privately owned property).

THE DECLINE OF THE RESOURCE COMMUNITY

The problems facing the mining industry also affect rural Canada and vice versa. At the end of the 20th century, a number of Canada's 150 mining communities found themselves facing difficult economic times. Improvements in technology have led to the automation of mine operations, a decline in employment, and the development of long-distance commuting (also known as "fly-in" mining), whereby companies build housing for their workers as opposed to building permanent communities. Fly-in mining has its advantages, from both an ecological and economic point of view. Flying workers into a mine site eliminates all of the social, economic, and environmental costs associated with establishing isolated mining communities. It also weakens the ability of labour to form unions. A decline in the fortunes of resource-based towns and in levels of employment means that the mineral industry diminishes in importance on government agendas. Urban demands and employment concerns lead decision-makers away from the primary industries in search of answers to other pressing problems. Rural Canada and its industries are no longer able to command the large share of government attention that they once did.

Moreover, critics are increasingly questioning whether continuing to support investment in a staples-based economy is in the long-term interests of an economy and society, particularly when the investment is considered from a community perspective. The life of a mine is finite; therefore, communities need to think about what they will do when the ore reserves are depleted. Attempts to diversify the economy into tourism (hunting and fishing lodges), other types of resource production, or even retirement centres can be undermined by harsh weather conditions, isolated locations, and the residual effects of the mining activity: "Often, other resource-based economic activities such as farming, fishing and logging are damaged by the pollution from the mine and smelters, and these remote communities become dependent on power grids, chain shores and imported goods and services to supply their needs" (Kuyek and Coumans 2003, 13). Moreover, residents of the mining communities are accustomed to the high wages associated with mining, and any economic activity that existed before the mine development has usually been replaced or is insufficient to replace the needs of a resource-dependent economy (ibid.).

With the exception of a few regions that have successfully diversified, Sudbury being the most notable case, sustaining a mining town over the long term requires the fortuitous confluence of many supportive variables. Unless significant government support and private investment are directed toward clusters of regions that have demonstrated a potential for diversification and are located along major transportation routes, many isolated mining towns face economic decline or closure as soon as a mine shuts down.

By the end of the 1990s, the mineral industry was entering increasingly unfamiliar territory as it was confronted with a complex array of new challenges, ranging in scope from the global to the local. Similar to other primary industries subject to recent global economic changes, the new challenges included international competition, restricted access to land, a diversifying economy competing with the traditional resource sector for government attention and resources, widespread public concerns about the environmental impact of mining, new influential actors questioning the role of the mineral industry in setting government agendas, and a decline in ore reserves and mining communities.

Dealing with complex systems requires new policy approaches to understanding and managing human interactions with biophysical systems (McCarthy 2003). In the mining sector, resource managers, labour representatives, government decision-makers, and community leaders are now trying to develop strategies to deal with the inevitable complexity and uncertainty that accompanies contemporary resource and environmental policy-making. Institutional techniques for bringing together groups, interests, and concerns to address resource complexity include multi-stakeholder consultations, co-management, integrated resource management, and institutional interplay at vertical or cross-scale linkages (Berkes 2003). These new systems perspectives have been influencing the mining industry policy environment in a number of ways and to varying degrees. Public and private decision-makers in the mineral sector have had many different responses.

RISING TO THE CHALLENGE? RESPONSES TO CHANGE

Those working in the mineral industry and public officials in government departments of mines have traditionally been educated in such fields as geology, engineering, and finance. None of these disciplines adequately equips people with the tools required to operate within a complex systems paradigm mentioned in the previous section. The mining industry has, however, once again responded to competitive challenges in the ways it knows best, primarily through technical innovation. For many years, the mining industry has been investing heavily in research to mitigate its adverse environmental impacts (such as acid rock drainage, considered to be mining's most devastating environmental impact), develop recycling programs to recover metals, and adopt integrated environmental management systems.

The mineral industry is also aware that it needs to work more effectively with other groups affected by mineral activities. To that end, from the 1990s onward, the mineral industry initiated a number of multi-stakeholder approaches to mining development, with varying degrees of commitment from companies and mining associations. One of the most notable of these initiatives was the national Whitehorse Mining Initiative (WMI), an extensive attempt by the mineral industry and government to foster a broader consensus about how mining should proceed in the future (McAllister and Alexander 1997). The spirit of the accord can be summed us as follows: "Our vision is of a socially, economically, and environmentally sustainable, and prosperous mining industry, underpinned by social and community consensus" (Whitehorse Mining Initiative Leadership Council 1994, 7).

More recently, consultative efforts have extended to international efforts, such as a three-year Global Mining Initiative (GMI) created by international mining companies (including Canadian corporations) in preparation for the World Summit on Sustainable Development in Johannesburg in 2002. The GMI provided funding for the Mining, Minerals and Sustainable Development (MMSD) project, which was billed as an "independent two-year process ... with the objective of understanding how to maximize the contribution of the mining and minerals sector to sustainable development at the global, national, regional and local levels" (International Institute for Environment and Development 2004).[3]

Nevertheless, efforts such as the WMI and the MMSD project do indicate a recognition by governments and the mining industry that they need to develop effective consultation processes, distribute the economic benefits from mining more widely, and mitigate the environmental impacts. The question remains: do these changes indicate a significant shift toward a new approach to staples development?

Seismic Shifts or Minor Tremors in the Status Quo?

In the past few decades, questions have been raised about whether the mineral industry could be classified as a sunset industry, with Canada moving into a post-staples, knowledge-based economy. As the Sudbury example suggests, an economy can diversify, based on its resource-based strengths. The mineral industry, much like other enterprises in Canada, has adapted to competitive challenges with many technological innovations contributing to a so-called knowledge economy. An examination of its production values suggests that its economic contributions remain very strong and Canada continues to be a world leader in mineral exports and exploration (Natural Resources Canada, Minerals and Metals Sector 2001). Canada exports 80 percent of its mineral production, which accounts for 13 percent of the country's total export earnings. Canada is the base for more mining companies than any other country in the world, and its largest city, Toronto, is touted as the mine-financing capital of the world (Ontario, Ministry of Northern Development and Mines 2004).

The total value of all mineral commodities mined in Canada in 2005 reached $26.4 billion. Of that amount, nickel accounts for 13.3 percent, gold and potash about 9 percent, diamonds for 8.6 percent, and copper 8.4 percent. Ontario leads production (accounting for 27.4 percent of Canada's total production), followed by British Columbia (at 18.5 percent), Saskatchewan (at 15.5 percent), Quebec (at 13.7 percent), and the Northwest Territories (at 6.5 percent) (McMullen and Birchfield 2007, 1.5). The inclusion of smelting and mining of domestic and importing ores, concentrates and recycling, and the oil sands bitumen production raises the figure to $60 billion (Birchfield 2006, 1). The mineral industry includes mining, smelting, and refining; the production of primary steel; the semi-fabrication of metals and nonmetals; and the fabrication of metals. It accounts for 3.9 percent of Canada's gross domestic product (McMullen and Birchfield 2007, 1.4).

Recently, mergers and acquisitions are taking place at an unprecedented rate, with many events of a "seismic" nature taking place. To cite just two examples, in late 2006, Canadian nickel company giant Inco was acquired by the Brazilian Companhia Vale do Rio Doce (CVRD); and Falconbridge Inc. was acquired by the Swiss company Xstrada. Globalization was cited as one of the reasons for these mergers and acquisitions: it has become economically necessary for operations to take place at a scale sufficiently large and diversified to respond to customers who are also operating on a global scale (Humphries 2006).

With respect to the overall economy, Michael Howlett suggests (2003, 58) that Canada has diversified by experiencing growth in the tertiary sector, industrial expansion in regional centres, significant growth of metropolitan regions, and decline in resource-based communities. Howlett poses two possibilities. The first is that Canada will remain "stuck in a mature staples trap" and will continue "to reinforce existing economic policy measures promoting increased resource extraction" (ibid., 59). The second would see the diversification of the economy, based on the traditional primary industries with value-added products, including environmentally related services (ibid.). With respect to the mineral industry, we are seeing elements of both trends developing.

Many examples can be found both of government policies that continue to subsidize industry and of supportive policies that continue to promote primary resource extraction. For example, the Canadian mineral exploration sector led the world in exploration expenditures in 2002 and 2003. One singularly important reason for these high expenditures is that the mineral industry received the benefits of a national flow-through share program, also referred to as "super flow-through." These tax incentives were enhanced by provincial tax incentives in British Columbia, Saskatchewan, Manitoba, Ontario, and Quebec (Natural Resources Canada, Minerals and Metals Sector 2007). These kinds of incentives signal that governments are continuing to actively promote policy measures in order to reinforce the economic position of extractive industries. This reality runs counter to a post-staples argument that suggests post-industrial economies often have a competitive advantage over staples-dependent economies. These "new" economies are competitive, some have argued, because the government uses taxation incentives and regulatory measures to develop goods and services that do not rely as much on the costly production of raw materials and substantial energy inputs (Dale 2001). Clearly, the current Canadian taxation and regulatory environment continues to promote staples-based development.

In Canada, we are also seeing developments that reflect Howlett's second, more optimistic, alternative suggested above; that is, the Canadian economy will continue to diversify supported by its traditional resource industries. Recent Natural Resources Canada documents identifying diversification and shifts in the industry suggest that the industry is undergoing structural changes. Economic diversification of the mineral industry has been growing in terms of downstream, value-added processes. Employment in mining itself has declined, in part because of the substitution of labour through technological developments, but employment is growing in other areas, such as materials handling, specifically recycling, which is becoming an important source of metals in many regions (Natural Resources Canada, Minerals and Metals Sector 2001, 9).

Canadians are large investors in exploration. In 2005, of the 1,431 companies that planned to spend $6 billion in worldwide mineral exploration (in 103 countries), almost 890 of them (62 percent) were based in Canada (Lemieux 2006, 1). International investment, in turn, generates a demand for Canadian mining equipment, services, and expertise—all of which contribute to the secondary and tertiary economic sectors. Promising trends are evident in Canada's ability to diversify: Canadian innovations in the mineral industry and its global leadership in the production of minerals, research, and development and in environmental technologies. The most notable example of these developments is Sudbury, which has diversified its economic base to mining-related spin-off businesses associated with equipment, robotics, and technology.

The shift to a knowledge economy has not diverted attention from the mineral industry. In fact, this industry, along with other economic enterprises, has been both using information technology to foster productivity and creating value-added goods and services. The federal government has been encouraging this direction, suggesting that investment in products that rely on mineral production, such as fuel cells, batteries, sensors, and lightweight and structural materials, will provide new opportunities for the mineral industry (Natural Resources Canada, Minerals and Metals Sector 2001, 16). Continuing public concerns about the ongoing adverse biophysical and socio-economic impacts of Canadian mining operations in Canada and around the world are fuelled by reports of the failure of tailings dams contaminating watersheds, displaced communities and workers, and unwanted resource development. One commentator has this to say about the new post-Fordist environment:

> About the empowerment of workers, households, and communities, it is not. About the creation of more participative, skilled labour processes, it is, at best, tangential. Rather, the emerging economy is, first and foremost, about doing more with less and for less … Thus, despite local variations, downsizing, the expansion of work areas, and the addition of new tasks to old jobs were the real trademarks of the changes that were besetting the mining industries. (Russell 1999, 199)

That said, in Canada, we are seeing some pockets of change in the way traditional resource activities are carried out. In some areas, institutional and individual learning is taking place in new consultative forums as people bring a diverse suite of resource values to the negotiating table. In such forums, positions must be justified on the basis of their contribution to the broader public interests, which now include ecological and community sustainability.

One analyst, Robert Gibson, suggests that evidence shows that changes may be taking place in the mineral development process—changes that distribute wealth and proceed in a more economically and ecologically sustainable manner. The example Gibson offers is that of the Voisey's Bay mine development, a huge nickel-copper-cobalt deposit in Labrador, owned by a subsidiary of nickel giant Inco Ltd. (now CVRD Inco Ltd.). In June 2002, the Aboriginal peoples in the area, the Innu and the Inuit, agreed to the ratification of an agreement to open the mine following an environmental assessment process and negotiations with the major stakeholders, which included affected communities, governments, and the mining industry.

Gibson suggests (2002) that the agreements were remarkable given the vast difference in cultures, priorities, and interests involved and the fact that the agreement was able to encompass and integrate biophysical and socio-economic considerations. He notes that the reasons for success, at least up until this point of the development, can be attributed to the substantial power given to the Indigenous people in the decision-making processes; the fact that all the main players had an important level of influence; and that the planning and assessment processes called for an integrated lifecycle approach to ecological, socio-cultural, and economic aspects of the project. Notably, the agreements emphasized long-term benefits and requirements that the evaluative and decision-making process be continuing and adaptive through the life of the project. Although this situation was a single case, decision-making processes are frequently built on previous experiences and lessons learned. The Voisey's Bay case sets some standards for a new approach to mineral development that others might follow.

CONCLUSIONS: NEW FRONTIERS

Processes and agreements of the kind undertaken in the Voisey's Bay case indicate that mining can continue to take place in a new political arena—one that recognizes a diversity of interests. The status quo need not prevail, and in fact it is unlikely to do so, given the new sets of players now participating in the decision-making arenas. A new generation of policy-makers has grown up with environmental considerations as part of its educational curriculum. The comparatively recent recognition of the rights of Aboriginal peoples to make decisions with respect to their territories has also altered the dynamics of the game. Government departments now temper their promotional mineral-related activities by acknowledging the need to ensure adequate environmental protection measures are in place and that attention is paid to the socio-economic health of affected communities (Natural Resources Canada, Minerals and Metals Sector 2007).

A precautionary note is needed, however, with respect to the prevailing drive for mineral development: it is based on the same profit motive that has always driven capitalist development. Moreover, the predominant method for dealing with competitive and other challenges has remained technological, as opposed to social or environmental, innovation. Numerous changes may take place on a variety of levels. At this most fundamental level, however, industrial relations, community relations, and new managerial paradigms will all be informed by the choices made by the mineral industry to develop a mine, introduce a measure of "workplace democracy," or adopt other voluntary initiatives. As Russell has noted (1999, 16), in the case of industrial relations and work reorganization, "changes would be at the margins to jobs that had been essentially predesigned to meet corporate requirements."

An examination of the mineral industry appears to support Howlett's analysis (2003) that Canada is experiencing uneven economic development. Given concerns about depleting ore reserves, changing public values about resource development, and growing global competitiveness, Canada's long-term economic and ecological health will depend on its ability to diversify into other value-added enterprises. Although Canada remains a world leader in the production and export of minerals, the economy shows signs of beginning to diversify into other areas, albeit using the primary sector as the basis for the production of new goods and services.

On a final note, or perhaps as a caveat to the above statement, although the Canadian mineral industry is an old one, staples production always appears to have new frontiers. Today, in addition to the more typical exploration targets, engineers are discussing the possibilities of using new technologies to pursue deep-mining techniques to extend the life of existing ore bodies, or even to mine deep-sea deposits or asteroids (Scoble et al. 2001). The development of the nascent diamond industry in the Canadian North has continued to fuel exploration interest. In 1998, the first diamond mine, the Ekati mine, began production in the Northwest Territories. As Patricia Fitzpatrick discusses in the next chapter, however, the old approach to staples-led economic development will no longer suffice in the complex policy environment of the 21st century.

NOTES

* The author would like to thank Patricia Fitzpatrick for her intelligent and helpful observations during drafts of this article and providing very useful sources. Thanks also to Michael Howlett and Keith Brownsey for facilitating this chapter and project.

1. Exceptions include the Canadian northern territories, where authority over mining has been devolving from the federal government to the territorial and First Nations governments, and other areas of Canada, where some comprehensive agreements have been settled with First Nations (see Brownsey, chapter 12).

2. Although Diefenbaker's initiative has been criticized as being to some degree ineffective (Leslie 1987, 7), it highlights governmental preoccupation with the importance of the resource sector to Canada during that era.

3. However, one representative from a Peruvian non-governmental organization observed that "The MMSD, however much good work has gone into it, is still an attempt to set an agenda from the top down, to limit the debate, and to define who the legitimate actors or stakeholders are. The role of NGOs [non-governmental organizations] is to support processes that are built from below, to construct a new social agenda, and to support communities' struggles to recuperate their economic, social, and cultural rights" (International Institute for Environment and Development 2004).

REFERENCES

Angus, C., and Griffin, B. 1996. *We lived a life and then some.* Toronto: Between the Lines.

Asp, J. 2004. Mining and Aboriginal relationships in Canada. Paper presented to the Prospectors and Developers Association of Canada 2004 international convention, March 7–10. Online at http://pdac.ca/pdac/publications/papers/2004/techprgm -asp.pdf.

Berkes, F. 2003. Can cross-scale linkages increase the resilience of social-ecological systems? Paper presented at the Regional Center for Social Science and Sustainable Development (RCSD) International Conference, Chiang Mai, Thailand.

Birchfield, G. 2006. Year in review: Canadian overview. In *Canadian Minerals Yearbook 2005.* Online at http://www.nrcan.gc.ca/ms/cmy/2005revu/con_e.htm.

Canada, Parliament. 2006. History of departments: 1867 to date. Online at http://www2 .parl.gc.ca/Parlinfo/Legacy/pages/DepHist.asp?Language=E.

Canadian Mining Hall of Fame. n.d. The Canadian mining industry. Online at http:// www.halloffame.mining.ca/halloffame/english/industry.html.

Clausen, S., and McAllister, M.L. 2001. An integrated approach to mineral policy. *Journal of Environmental Planning and Management* 44(2): 227–44.

Clement, W. 1981. *Hardrock mining: Industrial relations and technological changes at Inco.* Toronto: McClelland & Stewart.

Cranstone, D.A. 2002. *A history of mining and mineral exploration in Canada and outlook for the future.* Ottawa: Natural Resources Canada, Public Works, and Government Services Canada.

Dale, A. 2001. *At the edge: Sustainable development in the 21st century.* Vancouver: University of British Columbia Press.

Dickason, O.P. 1992. *Canada's First Nations: A history of founding peoples from earliest times.* Toronto: McClelland & Stewart.

Gibson, R. 2002. Power, sustainability and adaptation: Environmental conflict resolution leading to the agreements to proceed with the Voisey's Bay nickel mine. Paper presented at Towards Adaptive Environmental Conflict Resolution: Lessons from Canada and Chile, a conference co-sponsored by The Liu Centre for the Study of

Global Issues, the Faculty of Agricultural Sciences, the University of British Columbia; the Canadian International Development Agency; the Centre for Environmental Research and Planning (CIPMA), Chile; and the generous support of the International Development Research Centre (IDRC), Vancouver, BC.

Gouveia, J., Rose, P., and Gingerich, J. 2003. The prospector myth: Coming to terms with risk management in minerals development. Paper presented to the Prospectors and Developers Association of Canada 2003 international convention, March 9–12. Online at http://www.pdac.ca/pdac/publications/papers/2003/Gingerich-Risk.pdf.

Gray, F.W. 1917. *The coal fields and coal industry of eastern Canada: A general survey and description*. Ottawa: Department of Mines.

Howlett, M. 2003. Canadian environmental policy and the natural resource sector: Paradoxical aspects of the transition to a post-staples political economy. In *The Integrity Gap: Canada's Environmental Policy and Institutions*, eds. E. Lee and A. Perl, 42–67. Vancouver: University of British Columbia Press.

Humphries, D. 2006. Industry consolidation and integration: Implications for the base metals sector. Paper presented to the GFMS Precious and Base Metals Seminar, London, September 14. Online at http://www.nornik.ru/_upload/presentation/ Humphreys-GFMS.pdf.

Hutton, T.A. 1994. *Visions of a "post-staples" economy: Structural change and adjustment issues in British Columbia*, working paper PI #3. Vancouver: University of British Columbia Centre for Human Settlements.

Innis, H.A. 1936. *Settlement and the mining frontier*. Toronto: Macmillan.

International Institute for Environment and Development. 2004. The Mining, Minerals and Sustainable Development (MMSD) Project. Online at http://www.iied.org/ mmsd/what_is_mmsd.html.

Kuyek, J., and Coumans, C. 2003. *No rock unturned: Revitalizing the economies of mining dependent communities*. Ottawa: MiningWatch Canada.

Lemieux, A. 2006. Canada's Global Mining Presence. In *Canadian Minerals Yearbook 2005*. Online at http://www.nrcan.gc.ca/ms/cmy/2005CMY_e.htm.

Leslie, P. 1987. *Federal state, national economy*. Toronto: University of Toronto Press.

Lightfoot, G. 1967. Canadian railway trilogy. In *The Way I Feel*, track 11. Los Angeles: United Artists Records.

McAllister, M.L., and Alexander, C.J. 1997. *A stake in the future: Redefining the Canadian mineral industry*. Vancouver: University of British Columbia Press.

McAllister, M.L., and Schneider, T.F. 1992. *Mineral policy update 1985-89*. Kingston: Centre for Resource Studies, Queen's University.

McCarthy, D.D.P. 2003. Post-normal governance: An emerging counter-proposal. *Environments* 31(1): 78–92.

McMullen, M., and Birchfield G. 2007. General review. In *Canadian Minerals Yearbook 2005*. Online at http://www.nrcan.gc.ca/ms/cmy/2005CMY_e.htm.

MiningWatch Canada. 2005. The need for MiningWatch Canada. Online at http://www .miningwatch.ca/index.php?/About/Need_for_MWC.

Natural Resources Canada, Minerals and Metals Sector. 2001. *Focus 2006: Vision for 2001–2006.* Ottawa: Minister of Public Works and Government Services Canada.

Natural Resources Canada, Minerals and Metals Sector. 2004. *The minerals and metals policy of the Government of Canada.* Ottawa: Minister of Public Works and Government Services Canada. Online at http://www.nrcan.gc.ca/mms/policy/policy_e.htm.

Natural Resources Canada, Minerals and Metals Sector. 2007. Mining specific tax provisions: Investment tax credit for exploration in Canada. Online at http://www.nrcan.gc.ca/miningtax/d_inv_2d2_taxcredit2000.htm.

Nelles, H.V. 1974. *The politics of development: Forests, mines and hydro-electric power in Ontario, 1849–1941.* Toronto: Macmillan.

Ontario, Ministry of Northern Development and Mines. 2004. *Ontario, the future of mining … explore the opportunities.* Online at http://www.mndm.gov.on.ca/mndm/mines/ims/investment/publications/profile/profile.pdf.

Peeling, G.R. 1998. Canada and the challenge of attracting investment in mining. Online at http://www.mining.ca/www/media_lib/MAC_Documents/Speeches/English/london.pdf.

Russell, B., 1999. *More with less: Work reorganization in the Canadian mineral industry.* Toronto: University of Toronto Press.

Scoble, M., Archibald, J., Hassani, F., Frimpong, S., Hadjigeoriou, J., Singh, P., Yemenidjian, N., Corthesy, R., Bawden, W., and Stevens, R. 2001. The Canadian Mining Education Council: An initiative to network Canada's mining schools. Paper presented at the Canadian Conference on Engineering Education, University of Victoria, Victoria, BC.

Udd, J.E. 2000. *A century of achievement: The development of Canada's minerals industries.* Montreal: Canadian Institute of Mining and Metallurgy and Petroleum.

Vodden, C. 1992. No stone unturned: The first 150 years of the Geological Survey of Canada. Online at http://gsc.nrcan.gc.ca/hist/150_e.php.

Whitehorse Mining Initiative Leadership Council. 1994. *Whitehorse Mining Initiative Leadership Council Accord.* Ottawa: Mining Association for Canada and Natural Resources Canada.

Wojciechowski, M.J., and McAllister, M.L. 1985. *Mineral policy update 1984.* Kingston: Centre for Resource Studies, Queen's University.

CHAPTER 9

A New Staples Industry? Complexity, Governance, and Canada's Diamond Mines

Patricia J. Fitzpatrick

INTRODUCTION

The discovery of diamond indicator minerals in the Slave geological province in the Northwest Territories (NWT) began a staking and development rush that, in a little more than a decade, led to Canada becoming one of the world's largest producers of diamonds. The first two diamond mines were constructed in the late 1990s, the first by Broken Hills Proprietary (BHP) Diamonds Inc. (later renamed BHP Billiton Diamonds Inc.) and the second by Diavik Diamond Mines Inc. (DDMI). The impacts of these developments introduced a new dynamic into the northern political economy. Moreover, as Mary Louise McAllister discussed in the previous chapter, if the mineral industry wished to produce new mines in the current era, it needed to operate within a completely different political and social environment from what had traditionally been the case. Unlike in previous eras when the mineral industry could count on government and public support, the case of Canadian diamond mining illustrates the complexity of new mineral development processes in an era marked by environmental concerns and the entrance of new actors, such as Aboriginal groups, into the mineral policy process.

Diamond mining in Canada has become a lucrative business, with each diamond afforded a price based on its size, clarity, and colour. In 2001, the average price per carat of Canadian diamonds was $228, making it the third-highest world price (Santarossa 2003). By 2003, Canada had become the world's third-largest producer of diamonds. The economic impact of this industry has been significant. In the six-year period prior to full production of the first diamond mines, the annual increase of the gross domestic product (GDP) of the Northwest Territories was just below half the national average. Between 1999 and 2004, the period in which BHP and DDMI entered full production, this figure "rose at an annual average rate of almost 13%. This was three times the average annual rate of growth of 4.2% in the rest of Canada" (Byrd 2006, 6). Beyond the positive effect on the GDP, diamond development is associated with significant favourable trends related to manufacturing, employment, and services within the territory.

An examination of the development and operation of both projects illustrates how mineral policy institutions have evolved to reflect the dynamics of new power relations in Canada's North. Governance of the diamond mining industry in the Northwest Territories is influenced by rapid industrial development within the context of evolving environmental assessment (EA) processes and changing relations with First Nations—all of which have come about in a broader political economic era often referred to as a "new" staples state.

THE NORTHWEST TERRITORIES POLICY COMMUNITY

Natural resource development is an important component of the economy of Canada's three northern territories: Yukon, NWT, and Nunavut (Conference Board of Canada 2002). Although the modern-historical economy of the NWT originally relied on the fur trade, the economic base has shifted to other forms of resource development. Non-renewable-staples resource industries, including mineral and oil and gas development, are among the strongest economic-generating activities in the NWT. For example, in 2001, non-renewable-resource development contributed $585 million, or 24 percent, to the NWT's GDP. In addition to these activities, renewable-resource industries (including hydro-power generation), tourism, and traditional economic activities play modest roles in the wage economy.

The continued (and growing) contribution of mining to overall wealth generation in the territory offers evidence that staples, particularly minerals and oil and gas, remain an important component of the economy. As noted by the NWT Department of Renewable Resources (2003), "the economy of the NWT is inextricably linked to mining." This trend shows little sign of changing, as new mineral discoveries (diamonds) and oil and gas exploration (see Brownsey, chapter 12) have contributed to recent growth in GDP. As such, "non-renewable resources will continue to be the focus of economic activity in the Territory in the years to come" (Conference Board of Canada 2002, viii).

The mineral policy community in the NWT and Nunavut (NU)[1] reflects a unique set of constituents with diverse values and needs. These territories include roughly 37 percent of Canada's land mass, encompassing a large ecological environment of taiga and tundra. In terms of population, the NWT and NU are home to less than 0.2 percent of Canada's people and comprise numerous Aboriginal cultures. The federal government, territorial governments, non-governmental organizations (NGOs), and specific project proponents serve as advocates for other northern interests, thereby resulting in an increasingly complex set of interactions between actors and institutions and very different developmental dynamics from what has historically been the case in northern staples economies.

Aboriginal Organizations

As discussed elsewhere (see Booth and Skelton 2004), Aboriginal communities share a unique relationship with the land and water. This relationship and the relatively high proportion of Aboriginal people in the territories merit particular consideration regarding the relative power of these policy actors with respect to natural resource management. Since the early 1970s, legislation, treaties, and legal challenges have served to clarify (and strengthen) the rights of Aboriginal people over the land and resources within their traditional land.

In terms of legislation, section 35 of the 1982 Canadian constitution establishes that Aboriginal people have treaty rights and, therefore, access to resources. Drawing on this section, the judicial system has been employed as recourse when Aboriginal rights have not been respected. Recent Supreme Court of Canada decisions reaffirm this special relationship with the land (for example, *R. v. Sparrow* 1990; *Delgamuukw v. British Columbia* 1997). Although infringement of these rights is possible on the basis of compelling and substantive legislative purposes, to do so, the Crown must demonstrate "Aboriginal participation in resource development, consultation and in restricted circumstances, consent, and fair compensation" (Usher 2003, 378). Given this judicial mandate, Aboriginal organizations have experienced an ever-increasing role in resource development.

Historical treaties and modern-day land claims settlements are designed to address the Aboriginal title to land areas. Of particular interest to this discussion is how land claims agreements address natural resource management. The early 1990s saw the settlement of three land claims agreements within the geographic boundaries of what was then the NWT. Each of these agreements and subsequent agreements provide for a system of land, water, and environmental management inclusive of representation by delegates of the affected claims block. These management boards, consisting of tripartite membership (federal, territorial, and Aboriginal appointments) have, in fact, strong Aboriginal representation. Despite structural shortcomings,[2] White (2002, 97) believes that the boards represent introductory efforts at power-sharing and cross-cultural governance: "The all but universally held view is that the claims boards do represent important instruments of Aboriginal influence over important land, environment and wildlife decisions."

Beyond the management of natural resources, land claims agreements contribute to additional factors that influence development in the North. Initial cash settlements for the surrender of traditional lands, for example, can foster economic development (Saku 2002), and agreements provide opportunities for revenue-sharing when wealth is generated on traditional lands, which occurs through the sharing of royalties and the negotiation of impact and benefit agreements (IBAs) between the proponent and the affected organization(s), as discussed later in this chapter (Booth and Skelton 2004). These provisions increase the economic capacity of Aboriginal organizations to become engaged in secondary and tertiary industries associated with the development.

Despite these changes that ensure Aboriginal organizations are no longer at the margins of resource management issues, a long list of issues of power and control remain unresolved (Usher 2003) regarding Aboriginal title, nationhood, and access to and management of land and resources. Furthermore, as noted by Poelzer (2002), each Aboriginal organization has its own context—its own localized approach and resources—regarding specific environmental issues. Multiple and different Aboriginal policy actors come to the negotiating table with unique agendas.

Notwithstanding these cautionary notes, the reaffirmation of treaty rights, the progressive settlement of outstanding land claims, and changing dynamics related to natural resource management have significantly increased the relative power of Aboriginal organizations over resources in their traditional land. This power shift has influenced patterns of northern governance and, inevitably, its political economy.

Territorial Government

Formal institutional government in the territories is complex. Clancy (2001, 45) details the history of governance in the NWT from 1940, when the territories "remained a federal colony, still awaiting representative and responsible government" to the present. Since 1940, federal authority has devolved to the territorial governments. To date, the territorial governments have acquired control of some of the powers of provincial governments with two notable exceptions: full participation in constitutional reform, and control of Crown land (and the financial resources associated with Crown land) (Dickerson 1992). Although the federal government has committed to further devolution of powers to manage land and natural resources, this commitment remains unfulfilled (Canadian Institute of Resources Law 1997). This evolving relationship between the federal and territorial governments affects the relative power of each level of government and has the potential to affect the interaction of the two levels of government in issues concerning Crown lands, including diamond development.

Beyond the federal–territorial rapport, the 1990s saw the development and implementation of the Nunavut Final Agreement, which created the distinct territory of Nunavut. The increasing role of Aboriginal people in natural resource management, as provided through the settlement of outstanding claims, affects the governance of these issues. Negotiations surrounding the changing legal regimes and relationships required by the territorial division occurred during early diamond development. As such, another layer of complexity influenced the development of Canada's diamond mines.

Non-Governmental Organizations

An NGO is a label for multiple types of organizations whose sole common attribute is that they are not government (Martens 2003). In the broadest sense, NGOs include industry and business associations, research and teaching organizations, labour unions, media, and other interest groups. For the purpose of this discussion, we will focus on two categories: interest groups (specifically environmental NGOs) and business and industry organizations.

As with Aboriginal organizations, many environmental NGOs occupy a specific niche and use unique political approaches (Wilson 2002). Some environmental NGOs are active in environmental management issues in the NWT, including the Canadian Arctic Resources Committee, Ecology North, the Canadian Nature Federation, World Wildlife Fund Canada, and the Canadian Parks and Wilderness Society. However, although both mature- and post-staples political economies are characterized by an increasing role of environmental NGOs in policy development, the relative influence of these groups on staples development processes is difficult to evaluate. Harrison (1996) observes that environmental NGOs have played a role in shaping government policy. Furthermore, Greer-Wooten (1994, 282) notes that NGOs are "widely regarded by industry opinion leaders as representing legitimate public interests, staffed by knowledgeable persons," and provide a greater role in decision making, particularly through positions on advisory boards. However, Wilson (1992) suggests that environmental NGOs operate only in the peripheral zones of the environmental management communities. Although he later revised this position (Wilson 2002, 62), nonetheless, these broad and seemingly contrary assessments suggest that the relative power of environmental NGOs merits consideration on a case-by-case basis.

Differing in their mandate from environmental NGOs, business and industry associations represent industry and private-sector interests. Among the business and industry associations that are active in both the northern policy community and northern resource management are the NWT and NU Chamber of Mines and the Yellowknife Chamber of Commerce. Like environmental NGOs, however, the relative power of these policy actors requires consideration on a case-by-case basis.

Proponents

Proponents serve as the fourth category of policy actors involved in the mineral industry. Although linked with business and industry associations, because proponents represent private-sector interests, these policy actors are unique in their financial interest in specific resource projects. As such, it is important to consider the degree to which proponents have power, relative to the institutions that govern their investment.

THE FIRST DIAMOND DEVELOPMENT IN THE NORTH: THE BHP PROCESS

The 1989 discovery of diamond-indicator minerals (garnets and chrome diopsides) by explorationists Charles Fipke and Stu Blusson began a staking and diamond-development rush in the NWT (Hoos and Williams 1999). Diamonds are found in kimberlite pipes, also known as volcanic intrusions, found in the Slave geological province. The BHP Diamonds Inc. claim block is located near Lac de Gras, at the headwaters of the Coppermine River.

The closest community of Gameti, a Tlicho village, is more than 150 kilometres away, and the city of Yellowknife is more than 300 kilometres from the site. This area, however, was historically subject to extensive and overlapping land use by the ancestors of numerous groups of claimants. The site is in the traditional land use and settlement territories of the Tlicho, the Akaitcho Territory Dene (including the Lutsel K'e Dene First Nation and the Yellowknives Dene First Nation), and the North Slave Métis Alliance (Ritter 2001). The site is also in the traditional land use area of the Kitikmeot Inuit Association. In addition to historical use of this land, modern-day residents of the NWT and NU continue to rely on caribou and other wildlife that live in or migrate through the area. Drinking water for residents of Kugluktuk originates in this watershed. Thus, policy actors' interests were established not only through proximity to the project and historical land claims but also by use of resources originating or migrating through the project site.

The environmental assessment (EA) of the BHP NWT diamond project[3] occurred between January 1994 and August 1996. This project was subject to a panel review under the terms of the first federal EA process, *The Environmental Assessment and Review Panel Guidelines Order* (1984). A four-person panel, whose expertise includes NWT Aboriginal peoples, geology, resource issues, and environmental issues, evaluated the proponent's impact statement, weighed evidence related to potential impacts, and recommended to the minister of the environment that the project be allowed to proceed, subject to 29 recommendations regarding the project and related issues.

New institutions, specifically the West Kitikmeot/Slave Study Society, created in anticipation of this development, illustrate how the mineral industry was faced with a new political approach to resource development.

The West Kitikmeot/Slave Study Society

Concurrent with the announcement of the panel members for the first diamond mine was notice of a research program centred on the Slave geological province.

Recognizing the likelihood of increased mineral exploration and the potential for development, the West Kitikmeot/Slave Study (WKSS) Society was formed to oversee a research program directed at providing baseline information to be used in resource management in this region. The objectives of this society addressed multiple agendas, including the collection of traditional and scientific knowledge, development of cross-cultural research linkages, and implementation of community-research training opportunities. Over the course of five years, 19 projects were funded by WKSS Society, covering a range of issues.

The program was governed by a management board consisting of representatives appointed by various policy actors, including the Dogrib Treaty 11 Council, the Lutsel K'e/Yellowknives Dene First Nations, Inuit organizations, Nunavut co-management organizations, Métis Nation NWT, industry and business associations (through the NWT and NU Chamber of Mines), environmental organizations (representing the Canadian Arctic Resources Committee, Ecology North, World Wildlife Fund Canada, and the Canadian Nature Federation), the government of the NWT, and the government of Canada. The management board was "responsible for managing Study resources, making decisions on the design and conduct of research, ensuring that the interests and policies of the Partners are respected, public involvement, and directing the operations of the Study Office" (West Kitikmeot/Slave Study Society 2005). The board had decision-making authority over the projects it would fund, subject to the availability of financial resources.

The WKSS was an innovative research program, ensuring that those with historical and current interest in the area under study were actively involved in furthering the research agenda. However, because of the timing of the program, research from the WKSS was not available for the EA of the BHP NWT diamonds project. Beyond this effort to improve baseline research of the development region, however, the implementation of the EA process with an active public involvement program allowed the policy actors a role in the mining development.

Community Capacity and Public Participation in the BHP Review Process

Although an analysis of the public participation program completed as part of the BHP panel review is outside the scope of this chapter, two factors merit discussion: participant assistance and opportunity for public comment. Participant assistance involves the provision of funding to the interested public to facilitate participation in large-scale EAs. This money can finance research and administrative expenses related to participation in the assessment. Participants of the BHP EA received funding totalling $255,000 to engage in discussions surrounding the scope of the EA ($105,000 to 14 groups) and to review the impact statement ($150,000 to 12 groups) (Couch 2002). Applications for funding were reviewed by a committee of experts selected by the Canadian Environmental Assessment Agency, which is the standard process for participant funding. Although the specific policy actors were not involved in determining resource allocation (which would be a conflict of interest), funding increased the capacity of each organization to participate.

Keeping with the tradition of public engagement promoted during the 1974 Mackenzie Valley Pipeline Inquiry (known familiarly as the Berger Inquiry), meetings were organized in communities that could potentially be affected. The public reviewed the guidelines for the impact statement through scoping meetings (held in eight communities) and written submissions. The public review of the impact statement included written submissions and hearings held in 9 communities over an 18-day period. During the assessment, the panel received more than 125 written submissions and listened to more than 410 verbal presentations by various participants (Canadian Institute of Resources Law 1997). These participants included representative organizations of each of the policy actors discussed above.

As with public participation in other EA processes (see, for example, Fitzpatrick and Sinclair 2003), concerns arose regarding the level of funding, the timing of resource disbursement, and the timing of the public consultation. The Canadian Institute of Resources Law (1997) noted that although participation was inclusive of affected interests, a greater balance should have been sought between imposing deadlines and allowing for time in the process to proceed, and providing adequate financial resources for participants through the assessment and regulatory process. O'Reilly (1998) takes this point further, concluding that "few if any of the participants came away from the EA with any satisfaction including the proponent."

Despite this negative perception on the part of some participants, activities surrounding the BHP EA have been identified in the mining industry as setting a high standard for community engagement in project development. In a recent survey of 38 mining executives, representing 70 percent of the mining industries listed on the Toronto Stock Exchange, Annadale (2000) noted that mining companies were driven to exploring a more interactive approach to EAs because of the BHP experience. This interactive approach to mine development, featuring input from all policy actors, is a marked departure from the historical staples-development era discussed by McAllister (see chapter 8). Beyond this input, however, different policy actors are also playing a role in the institutions governing mineral development.

The Implications of the Superadded Agreements

Numerous authors, including Valiante (2002), Hessing and Howlett (1997), and Harrison (1996), have detailed how provinces and federal governments share constitutional authority over natural resource management. One impact of this shared jurisdiction, which has led to overlapping legislative responsibilities, is that during the course of an EA, recommendations are made in areas for which the responsible authority has limited or no constitutional authority to enforce. The responsible authorities, which must issue permits, leases, and licences regarding the project, are in a difficult position: they are expected to ensure these issues are implemented by the proponent, despite having limited or no regulatory authority to do so. In other words, these were commitments that either could not "be formalized in legal or regulatory requirements or that were better suited to a more flexible approach" (Canadian Institute of Resources Law 1997, 23).

To resolve this issue, following the acceptance of the EA to address how monitoring should be undertaken in the context of these superadded responsibilities, two agreements were negotiated: the environmental agreement and the socio-economic agreement. Four organizations negotiated the BHP environmental agreement: the proponent, the federal government, the territorial government, and the Aboriginal organizations. Aboriginal organizations were not signatories to the agreement, but were included in the process through the implementation protocol attached to the agreement. Neither environmental NGOs nor business and industry NGOs were involved in negotiating or implementing this institution.

Although environmental agreements were used to "superadd" responsibilities in the past, the scope and public nature of the BHP environmental agreement were unprecedented (Canadian Institute of Resources Law 1997): "The Environmental Agreement was seen as a tool to ensure BHP lived up to the many promises it made both in its EIS [environmental impact statement] and verbally during the hearings before the panel. The Agreement was also viewed as a way to demonstrate an integrated and innovative approach to monitoring and environmental management of the project's effects" (O'Reilly 1998). The environmental agreement covered a range of issues, including the development of environmental management programs, reporting requirements, closure, and reclamation plans; the provision of security deposits to act as remedies for potential infringements on the agreements; and the establishment of an independent environmental monitoring agency (discussed in the next section).

The socio-economic agreement was negotiated between the proponent and the government of the NWT. The federal government, Aboriginal organizations, and the NGOs were not involved. "The principal purposes of the Socio-Economic Agreement are to maximize the economic benefits of the BHP project to residents of the NWT and to minimize its negative social impacts" (Canadian Institute of Resources Law 1997, 23). The agreement covered a range of issues, including training commitments, health and social services programs and monitoring, and local business development initiatives. In terms of employment, a number of commitments established in the agreement ensure that northern residents, including Aboriginal people, have opportunities to profit from this staples development. The agreement includes hiring targets for northern residents and Aboriginal people during both the construction and operational phases of the mine (see figure 9.1). Furthermore, the company committed to specific targets for local business supply. However,

Figure 9.1   Northern and Aboriginal Employment Targets (as Identified in the Socio-Economic Agreement) and Actuals at Ekati™

Phase	Target		Actual	
	Northern residents	Aboriginal residents (as a percentage of northern residents)	Northern residents	Aboriginal residents (as a percentage of northern residents)
Construction...........	33%	44%	N/A	N/A
Early operation.........	62%	50%	75%	39%
Late operation..........	72%	50%	N/A	N/A

Sources: Santarossa, B. 2003. *Diamonds: Adding lustre to the Canadian economy.* Catalogue no. 11-621-MIE. Ottawa: Statistics Canada; and Northwest Territories, Resources, Wildlife and Economic Development, and BHP Diamonds Inc. 1996. Socio-economic agreement: BHP diamonds project. Online at http://www.iti.gov.nt.ca/industrial_benefit/pdf/bhp_sea.pdf.

as this agreement does not include discussion of penalties for non-compliance, it is primarily a contract outlining co-operation between the signatories (Canadian Institute of Resources Law 1997).

In addition to proponent–government agreements, impact and benefit agreements (IBAs) were negotiated between BHP and the affected Aboriginal communities. These bilateral agreements address the specific impacts of development on Aboriginal people. Although specific agreements are confidential, Ritter (2001) notes they "cover such things as job opportunities, training, and preferential hiring programs; financial transfer payments, royalties and equity participation; new business development and contractual arrangements; and compensation for declines in harvests of wildlife and fish." Although these agreements are requirements of some of the settled land claims, IBAs were not required in the BHP case (Canadian Institute of Resources Law 1997). However, the minister of Indian affairs required the illustration of "significant progress" in negotiations prior to the approval of the company's leases and licenses.[4]

The superadded agreements negotiated around the BHP NWT diamonds project provide specific requirements for the company to address environmental and social impacts associated with the development, with efforts made to mitigate negative impacts. These requirements are indicative of the new political approach to staples development. One subset of the environmental agreement, the BHP Independent Environmental Monitoring Agency (IEMA), merits specific discussion.

The BHP Diamonds Inc. Independent Environmental Monitoring Agency

As indicated in the previous section, one of the requirements of the environmental agreement was the formation of the Independent Environmental Monitoring Agency (IEMA). This agency consists of a seven-member board of directors: four appointed by Aboriginal organizations and three appointed jointly by BHP and the federal and territorial governments, in consultation with Aboriginal organizations. NGOs are not represented on the IEMA. As per the panel recommendation, the IEMA reports on company monitoring and compliance by the company to commitments related to the environment; thus, "although the name of the Agency might imply that monitoring is directly carried out, the real function of the Agency is as more of an oversight or audit mechanism" (O'Reilly 1998). The agency does not have decision-making authority; IEMA reviews documentation and makes recommendations to the appropriate responsible authority.

The Canadian Institute of Resources Law (1997) has argued that although the IEMA is a positive step, horizontal linkages need to be strengthened between the agency and broader initiatives, such as those of the WKSS. IEMA is charged to "participate as an intervenor in regulatory and other legal processes respecting environmental matters" (Canada, Indian Affairs and Northern Development; Northwest Territories, Resources, Wildlife and Economic Development; and BHP Diamonds Inc. 1997, article IV.2(d)), as a project-specific monitoring agency, these matters must relate to the BHP NWT diamonds project. Despite this criticism, the development of an independent agency charged with monitoring the impacts of a project is an important tool for balancing system components.

Institutions involved in the governance of the BHP NWT diamonds project are indicative of the "new" staples economy, one that responds to a diverse group of policy actors and forces. This new economy includes consideration of the longitudinal environmental, social, and economic implications of mineral development. The strengths of the BHP case were replicated in the consultation initiatives designed for the DDMI EA.

THE DIAVIK DIAMOND MINES INC. (DDMI) PROJECT: A COMPREHENSIVE STUDY

The Diavik Diamond Mine Inc. (DDMI) project is also located at the headwaters of the Coppermine River, in and around Lac de Gras. When DDMI submitted its applications for required leases and licences, and thereby triggered an EA, the federal review process was governed by the newer *Canadian Environmental Assessment Act* (CEAA [1992]). As stipulated in this process, the DDMI project also triggered a comprehensive study review. This assessment required consideration of the purpose of, the need for, and the alternatives to the project, in addition to its environmental effects.

Consistent with the legislative requirements, the federal departments involved in issuing leases, licences, and permits for the project—in this case the Department of Indian Affairs and Northern Development (Indian and Northern Affairs Canada [INAC]), the Department of Fisheries and Oceans (DFO), and Natural Resources

Canada (NRCan)—facilitated the assessment. As the lead responsible authority for the EA, INAC coordinated the assessment and maintained the public registry. Despite these changes, many of the institutions involved in governance of the DDMI had their origins in the BHP NWT diamonds project.

As with the BHP NWT diamonds project, many different policy actors were involved in the mining development. The approach taken in the DDMI case, however, allowed key policy actors a more active role in the EA.

Community Capacity and Public Participation in the Diavik Diamond Mines Inc. (DDMI) Environmental Assessment

An EA steering committee was struck in response to the desire of Aboriginal organizations to be actively engaged in the assessment process. This committee included representatives of Aboriginal organizations, the responsible authorities, and the government of the NWT. Neither NGOs nor the proponent was represented on the steering committee. Although not all organizations provided a seat on this committee chose to participate, all representative groups were provided with key documentation related to both the steering committee and the assessment process.

Although the steering committee did not have decision-making authority, it served as "an advisory body reporting to the RA [Responsible Authority] Caucus on all matters relating to the comprehensive study review process for the Diavik Diamonds Project" (Canada, Indian Affairs and Northern Development; Department of Fisheries and Oceans; and Natural Resources Canada 1999, Appendix B). Meeting on a monthly basis, this committee advised the responsible authorities on how to address outstanding issues, including how to manage the public consultation process.

This role in facilitating the assessment process did not preempt participation in the EA, and organizations involved in the steering committee joined the EA public consultation program. Public involvement was encouraged during the formal EA process through written submissions and three types of gatherings held in various communities: community and information meetings, technical meetings, and public technical sessions. Community and information meetings allowed opportunities for the affected communities to ask questions about the impact statement. These meetings were arranged primarily between the proponent and Aboriginal organizations, with contributions by INAC. Technical meetings focused on key issues of interest to stakeholders. These meetings were held in different communities and included evening sessions for members of the general public to ask questions and engage in discussion with experts. Public technical sessions, held between September 1998 and March 1999, provided government an opportunity to report on findings and to address public questions posed through the course of the review. Each of the technical-session formats was advised by the steering committee. Following the completion of the comprehensive study report, the

Canadian Environmental Assessment Agency facilitated a one-month public review of the report, consistent with the terms of the *Canadian Environmental Assessment Act* (CEAA).

Money was offered to different policy actors interested in participating in the assessment process, although this payment was not required by the legislation. Aboriginal organizations and NGOs received funds to participate in the assessment process.[5] Similar to the funding process used for the BHP NWT diamonds project, applications were evaluated on a case-by-case. basis. In this situation, however, INAC (not an independent committee appointed by the Canadian Environmental Assessment Agency) reviewed the applications; NGOs (again) did not contribute to decision-making regarding funding disbursement.

The EA of the DDMI project greatly expanded opportunities for the public to be engaged in the assessment process; however, concerns were expressed about this consultation strategy. As noted by the Mackenzie Valley Environmental Impact Review Board (MVEIRB) (1999, 13), the adaptive approach taken by the responsible authorities and the steering committee resulted in a process that "fell short of public expectations for an independent assessment that provided a clear and consistent process for public involvement." To support this assertion, the MVEIRB observed that although the steering committee included Aboriginal organizations in the assessment design, the institution served in an advisory (not a management) role. Second, concerns arose regarding the adjustment of the assessment schedule to include workshops. These changes, although designed to address public concern, may have confused the process. Finally, the board questioned the timing of the assessment process, suggesting that the need of the proponent may have unduly influenced the timing of the release of the comprehensive study report.

Again, despite these shortcomings, the inclusion of Aboriginal organizations in the committee designing the EA process increased the relative power of these policy actors in governing mineral development. These shifting dynamics continued through the negotiation of superadded agreements associated with the project.

Superadded Agreements: New Players

Environmental and socio-economic agreements addressed the superadded duties associated with the DDMI EA. As with the BHP environmental agreement, issues addressed through this institutional framework included the development of environmental management programs, reporting requirements, closure and reclamation plans, the provision of security deposits to act as remedies for potential infringements on the agreements, and the establishment of an environmental monitoring advisory board (discussed in the following section). In addition, the agreement compels DDMI to participate in the development of a regional cumulative-effects assessment and management framework (discussed later in this chapter). The socio-economic agreement covered a range of issues, including employment and training commitments, health and social services programs and monitoring, local business development initiatives, and formation of the Diavik Projects Community Group Advisory Board (discussed in the next section). Again, the socio-economic agreement ensured that northern residents, including Aboriginal people, had opportunities to profit from the development. The agreement also included hiring targets (see figure 9.2) and local business supply targets to increase the economic return of the development to northern residents.

A salient difference between these two institutional frameworks was the role of Aboriginal organizations. Unlike the BHP environmental agreement, Aboriginal organizations could become a party to the socio-economic agreement. The initial agreement was signed in October 1999, and all five potential Aboriginal organizations became signatories by the end of 2001 (Eggleston 2002). NGOs, however, were not involved.

Finally, DDMI also negotiated impact and benefit agreements (IBAs), termed "participation agreements," with various communities. The structure and timing of these negotiations were similar to those experienced with the BHP NWT diamonds project; 18 months lapsed between the final regulatory approval for the project and the signing of the last IBA. As noted by the MVEIRB, the (continued) separate negotiations for three types of superadded agreements (the environmental agreement, the socio-economic agreement, and the IBAs) created a gap in understanding how impacts could be mitigated and monitored. Although the EA considers potential impacts, mitigation measures, and monitoring programs, if the monitoring programs are created through agreements signed 18 months after the assessment, the content cannot be considered through the assessment.

The Advisory Board

The environmental agreement included provision for the formation of the Environmental Monitoring Advisory Board (EMAB). This board is the second independent monitoring agency assembled in conjunction with diamond development in the North. The EMAB includes one representative for each of the Dogrib Treaty 11 Council, the Yellowknives Dene First Nation, the Lutsel K'e Dene First Nation, the Kitikmeot Inuit Association, the North Slave Métis Alliance, the government of the NWT, the government of Canada, and DDMI, for a total of eight members. Again, NGOs are not represented on the board, although the agreement includes a provision to expand the EMAB, should all parties agree.

In addition to monitoring both company reports and compliance with commitments, the EMAB has the added function of ensuring communication among parties to the agreement (Canada, Indian Affairs and Northern Development et al. 2000, section 14.1). This agreement also includes more direct requirements for public participation. Whereas the BHP IEMA is directed to facilitate participation to achieve its purpose, the advisory board is also required to *create opportunities* for community and public participation (section 1.1(e)).

Figure 9.2   Northern and Aboriginal Employment Targets (as Identified in the Socio-Economic Agreement) and Actuals at DDMI

	Target		Actual	
Phase	Northern residents	Aboriginal residents (as a percentage of northern residents)	Northern residents	Aboriginal residents (as a percentage of northern residents)
Construction..........	40%	Unspecified	N/A	N/A
Early operation.........	66%	40%	73%	37%
Late operation..........	100%	40%	N/A	N/A

Sources: Santarossa, B. 2003. *Diamonds: Adding lustre to the Canadian economy.* Catalogue no. 11-621-MIE. Ottawa: Statistics Canada; Diavik Diamond Mines Inc., and Northwest Territories, Department of Resources, Wildlife and Economic Development. 1999. Diavik diamonds project: Socio-economic monitoring agreement. Online at http://www.diavik.ca/PDF/socioeconomic.pdf.

The Diavik Projects Community Group Advisory Board reflects the structure of the previous monitoring institutions, but also addresses the issue of socio-economic monitoring. This board is community based in its representation: the government of the NWT (two members), DDMI (two members), the Dogrib Treaty 11 communities (four members), the Yellowknives Dene Band (two members), the Lutsel K'e Dene First Nation (one member) the North Slave Métis Alliance (one member) and the Kitikmeot Inuit Association (one member). The federal government and NGOs do not have seats on the board.

The Community Group Advisory Board provides an advisory function in its monitoring of employment, training, the business opportunity strategy, and the Employee and Family Assistance Program implemented by DDMI, among others (section 2.1.2(c)). Representatives on this board also act as a liaison and communications link between their respective communities and the board; as such, instead of acting as independent watchdogs, the representatives serve as advocates for their respective constituents. The agreement also requires the board to implement opportunities for public participation. The Community Group Advisory Board expands consideration of social impacts of development beyond the original EA; this innovation further illustrates the changes in the social and political reality of the "new" staples economy.

The Cumulative Effects Assessment and Management Strategy

The comprehensive study also recommended that DDMI participate on the Cumulative Effects Assessment and Management (CEAM) Strategy steering committee, which includes representatives of Aboriginal organizations, industry, co-management boards, federal and territorial governments, and environmental NGOs. The steering committee is charged with creating a plan to "facilitate the protection of ecological integrity, the building of sustainable communities (including social and economic dimensions), and responsible economic development within a sound environmental management framework" (Northwest Territories Cumulative Effects Assessment & Management Strategy and Framework 2002). To achieve this goal, the strategy blueprint addresses such areas as land use planning, baseline studies, and research that built on the WKSS, decision-support research, engagement in project-specific assessment (as it relates to cumulative impacts), and information management. The committee serves an advisory function, with decision making resting with the federal departments and other organizations, including co-management boards, which have mandates related to cumulative effects assessment and management.

The commitment to cumulative-effects assessment marks a new effort in government policy to expand consideration of environmental impacts to a regional level; the inclusion of policy actors in facilitating this commitment illustrates an effort to consider the complex biophysical and social environment in the North.

OTHER DIAMOND DEVELOPMENTS IN THE NORTH: THE DEBEERS PROJECT

Since the completion of the DDMI project in 1999, numerous changes have occurred in the governance institutions. The implementation of the *Mackenzie Valley Resource Management Act* (MVRMA) and the assessment of the third diamond mine under the terms of that act have influenced the cross-scale linkages among institutions governing diamond development (see Armitage 2005a, 2005b). For the most part, the MVRMA replaces the jurisdiction of the CEAA and provides a different vehicle for land and water management boards in the NWT. MVEIRB now facilitates EA in the Mackenzie Valley, which includes the NWT portion of the Slave geological province. This public review board has a minimum of seven members: one-half nominated by Aboriginal organizations and one-half nominated by government. NGOs are not involved in the nomination process. Although the federal government funds the board, the board is independent from both government and the Aboriginal organizations that nominate members.

The third diamond project was assessed under the terms of the MVRMA (see Ellis 2005; Fitzpatrick, Sinclair, and Mitchell 2007). The Debeers Canada Mining Inc. Snap Lake development project involved the construction and operation of a diamond mine 220 kilometres northeast of Yellowknife, at the headwater of the Lockhart River drainage system. The EA was completed on October 10, 2003. A detailed comparison of the assessment requirements and process is outside the scope of this paper; however, similar environmental and socio-economic agreements were negotiated as with the BHP and DDMI processes. Noting the increasing number of institutions governing development in the Slave geological province, concern is increasing about a fragmented approach to resource development. Interest is also increasing in the intersection between EA and the superadded agreements outlined above. Results suggest that superadded agreements are a means of addressing areas not adequately addressed through EA, including ensuring Aboriginal participation, follow-up, and the distribution of local benefits (Galbraith, Bradshaw, and Rutherford 2007; O'Faircheallaigh 2006). Preliminary discussions suggest there is increasing support for a regional monitoring agency. This regional agency would include monitoring of project-specific activities, and cumulative impacts.

CONCLUSION

Mining, by definition, is a staples-based sector. Recognizing both the finite nature of mineral development and the policy issues associated with a staples-based economy, policy actors in the mining industry are adopting innovative practices to address cumulative impacts of development and to mitigate negative structural economic issues that mark a staples-based economy. These innovations—including fly-in, fly-out operations with northern and Aboriginal hiring targets, requirements to undertake primary processing in the North, and attempts to develop "value-added" economic activities—mark the development of a "new" staples economy. To respond to these changing dynamics, institutions governing mineral development are attempting to provide a foundation for balancing the social-ecological environment with political and economic realities. These institutions strengthen the capacity for balancing system components, including economic diversification, prior to the depletion of resource endowments and economic competition from lower-cost staples regions.

As illustrated through the review of the BHP NWT diamonds project and the DDMI project, the new diamond economy of the North developed in a very different political and economic environment from the environment traditionally associated with mining as discussed by McAllister (see chapter 8). At the turn of the 20th century, governments took an active role in promoting mining as a nation-building tool, unconcerned with maintaining biophysical integrity of valued ecosystems, the presence of NGOs raising concerns about the impacts of resource development, or the place of Aboriginal peoples at the decision-making table. Moreover, activities did not take place under the glare of international media attention. All these factors were in place as a new kind of staples economy was developing at the turn of the 21st century. Resource development in the North necessitated the incorporation of a group of policy actors with agendas, needs, and requirements qualitatively different from those of the traditional resource developers and producers. Governments required a more flexible and inclusive regulatory approach, but because of the results of this process, the governance of resources in the NWT is now very complex. Mines are governed through a variety of old and new institutions, with input from different policy actors.

A discussion of such institutions as the West Kitikmeot/Slave Study Society and the Environmental Monitoring Advisory Board reveals an emerging picture of a new approach to the northern staples-based economy, one that is striving for responsible economic development within a sound environmental framework. The new diamond projects are proceeding in a way that is qualitatively different from historical practices that have governed staples development in the mineral sector. The very existence of the EA, which, in addition to economic factors, requires consideration of the biophysical and socio-economic impacts of a proposed development, is a tangible illustration that Canada operates in a "new" staples economy—one that attempts to manage pressure on the resource sector, minimize adverse impacts, and balance the economic benefits of development on a spatial and temporal basis.

NOTES

1. On April 1, 1999, the Northwest Territories and Nunavut became separate territories, as per the Nunavut Final Agreement.

2. Two concerns associated with these boards are that representatives are to serve as individuals, not as representatives of appointing organizations, and that boards serve an advisory function, not a decision-making function.

3. The mine is now called the Ekati™ Diamond Mine.

4. Concerns regarding types of arrangements relate primarily to the process surrounding the negotiation of IBAs. Ritter (2001) notes that federal guidance is needed in terms of the issues the agreement should cover, the implications of these bilateral agreements on the public interest, and the timing of IBA negotiations. For example, although "significant" progress in negotiation was a requirement of project approval, more than two years passed before BHP signed the final IBA. Furthermore, since agreements are signed with one group at a time, potential exists that a "divide and conquer" strategy will be adopted.

5. Although a coalition of northern environmental NGOs (Canadian Arctic Resources Council, Ecology North, and the Canadian Parks and Wilderness Society) were offered funding to participate in the assessment, they declined the resources as being inadequate. Funding was later provided to the Canadian Parks and Wilderness Society, and the Status of Women Council of the Northwest Territories.

REFERENCES

Annadale, D. 2000. Mining company approaches to environmental approvals regulation: A survey of senior environmental managers in Canadian firms. *Resources Policy* 26(1): 51–59.

Armitage, D.R. 2005a. Collaborative environmental assessment in the Northwest Territories, Canada. *Environmental Impact Assessment Review* 25(3): 239–58.

Armitage, D.R. 2005b. Environmental impact assessment in Canada's Northwest Territories: Integration, collaboration and the Mackenzie Valley Resource Management Act. In *Environmental Impact Assessment: Practice and Participation*, ed. K. Hanna, 185–211. Toronto: Oxford University Press.

Booth, A.L., and Skelton, N.W. 2004. First Nations access and rights to resources. In *Resource and Environmental Management in Canada: Addressing Conflict and Uncertainty*, ed. B. Mitchell, 80–103. Toronto: Oxford University Press.

Byrd, C. 2006. *Diamonds: Still shining brightly for Canada's north.* Catalogue no. 65-507-MIE. Ottawa: Statistics Canada.

Canada, Indian Affairs and Northern Development; Department of Fisheries and Oceans; and Natural Resources Canada. 1999. *Diavik diamonds project comprehensive study.* Yellowknife: Department of Indian Affairs and Northern Development.

Canada, Indian Affairs and Northern Development; Northwest Territories, Resources, Wildlife and Economic Development; and BHP Diamonds Inc. 1997. Environmental agreement. Online at http://www.monitoringagency.net/Portals/0/pdf/key_documents/BHP%20Environmental%20Agreement1997.pdf.

Canada, Indian Affairs and Northern Development; Northwest Territories, Resources, Wildlife and Economic Development; Diavik Diamond Mines Inc.; Dogrib Treaty 11 Council; Lutsel K'E Dene Band; Yellowknives Dene First Nation; North Slave Métis Alliance; and Kitikmeot Inuit Association. 2000. Environmental agreement. Online at http://www.diavik.ca/PDF/DiavikEnvironmentalAgreement.pdf.

Canadian Institute of Resources Law. 1997. *Independent review of the BHP diamond mine process.* Hull, QC: Mineral Resources Directorate, Department of Indian Affairs and Northern Development.

Clancy, P. 2001. The Northwest Territories: Old and new class politics on the northern frontier. In *The Provincial State in Canada: Politics in the Provinces and Territories*, eds. K. Brownsey and M. Howlett, 335–68. Peterborough, ON: Broadview Press.

Conference Board of Canada. 2002. *Setting the pace for development: An economic outlook report for the Northwest Territories.* Yellowknife: Department of Resources, Wildlife and Economic Development.

Couch, W. 2002. Strategic resolution of policy, environmental and socio-economic impacts in Canadian Arctic diamond mining: BHP's NWT diamond project. *Impact Assessment and Project Appraisal* 20(4): 265–78.

Delgamuukw v. British Columbia, [1997] 3 SCR 1010.

Diavik Diamond Mines Inc., and Northwest Territories, Department of Resources, Wildlife and Economic Development. 1999. Diavik diamonds project: Socio-economic monitoring agreement. Online at http://www.diavik.ca/PDF/socioeconomic.pdf.

Dickerson, M.O. 1992. *Whose north? Political change, political development, and self-government in the Northwest Territories.* Vancouver: University of British Columbia Press.

Eggleston, P. 2002. Gaining Aboriginal community support for a new mine development and making a contribution to sustainable development. Paper presented at the Energy and Resources Law Conference, Edinburgh, Scotland.

Ellis, S.C. 2005. Meaningful consideration? A review of traditional knowledge in environmental decision making. *Arctic* 58(1): 66–77.

Fitzpatrick, P., and Sinclair, A.J. 2003. Learning through public involvement in environmental assessment hearings. *Journal of Environmental Management* 67(2): 161–74.

Fitzpatrick, P., Sinclair A.J., and Mitchell, B. 2007. Deliberative democracy in Canada's North? The Mackenzie Resource Management Act. Manuscript submitted for publication.

Galbraith, L., Bradshaw, B., and Rutherford, M.B. 2007. Towards a new supraregulatory approach to environmental assessment in Northern Canada. *Impact Assessment and Project Appraisal* 25(1): 27–41.

Greer-Wootten, B. 1994. The politics of interest groups in environmental decision-making. In *Public Issues: A Geographical Perspective*, eds. J. Andrey and J.G. Nelson, 271–93. Waterloo, ON: Department of Geography, University of Waterloo.

Harrison, K. 1996. *Passing the buck: Federalism and Canadian environmental policy.* Vancouver: University of British Columbia Press.

Hessing, M., and Howlett, M. 1997. *Canadian natural resource and environmental policy: Political economy and public policy.* Vancouver: University of British Columbia Press.

Hoos, R.A.W., and Williams, W.S. 1999. Environmental management at BHP's Ekati diamond mine in the Western Arctic. Paper presented at the Proceedings of the International Symposium on Mining in the Arctic.

Mackenzie Valley Environmental Impact Review Board. 1999. *Views on the Diavik Diamonds Project comprehensive study report.* Yellowknife: Mackenzie Valley Environmental Impact Review Board.

Martens, K. 2003. Examining the (non-) status of NGOs in international law. *Indiana Journal of Global Legal Studies* 10(2): 1–24.

Northwest Territories Cumulative Effects Assessment & Management (CEAM) Strategy and Framework. 2002. CEAM vision, purpose and principles. Online at http://www.ceamf.ca/01_who/01_purpose.htm.

Northwest Territories, Department of Renewable Resources. 2003. *Minerals, oil and gas: Minerals and metals, history of exploration and development.* Online at http://www.iti.gov.nt.ca/mog/minerals/mins_history.htm.

Northwest Territories, Resources, Wildlife and Economic Development, and BHP Diamonds Inc. 1996. Socio-economic agreement: BHP diamonds project. Online at http://www.iti.gov.nt.ca/industrial_benefit/pdf/bhp_sea.pdf.

O'Faircheallaigh, C. 2006. *Environmental agreements in Canada: Aboriginal participation, EIA follow-up and environmental management of major projects.* Calgary: Canadian Institute of Resources Law.

O'Reilly, K. 1998. *The BHP Independent Environmental Monitoring Agency as a management tool.* Online at http://www.carc.org/rndtable/vbpanels.html.

Poelzer, G. 2002. Aboriginal peoples and environmental policy in Canada: No longer at the margins. In *Canadian Environmental Policy: Contexts and Cases*, eds. D.L. VanNijnatten and R. Boardman, 87–106. Toronto: Oxford University Press.

Ritter, A. 2001. Canada: From fly-in, fly-out to mining metropolis. In *Large Mines and the Community: Socioeconomic and Environmental Effects in Latin America, Canada and Spain*, eds. G. McMahon and F. Remy, 223–61. Washington, DC: The World Bank.

Saku, J.C. 2002. Modern land claim agreements and northern Canadian Aboriginal communities. *World Development* 30(1): 141–51.

Santarossa, B. 2003. *Diamonds: Adding lustre to the Canadian economy*. Catalogue no. 11-621-MIE. Ottawa: Statistics Canada.

Sparrow, R. v., [1990] 1 SCR 1075.

Usher, P.J. 2003. Environment, race and nation reconsidered: Reflections on Aboriginal land claims in Canada. *Canadian Geographer* 47(4): 365–82.

Valiante, M. 2002. Legal foundations of Canadian environmental policy: Underlining our values in a shifting landscape. In *Canadian Environmental Policy: Context and Cases*, eds. D. VanNijnatten and R. Boardman, 3–24. Toronto: Oxford University Press.

West Kitikmeot/Slave Study Society. 2005. Renewed mandate and terms of reference, January 31, 2005. Online at http://www.wkss.nt.ca/HTML/03_Terms/03_index.htm.

White, G. 2002. Treaty federalism in northern Canada: Aboriginal–government land claims boards. *Publius* 32(3): 89–114.

Wilson, J. 1992. Green lobbies. In *Canadian Environmental Policy: Ecosystems, Politics and Process*, ed. Robert Boardman, 109–25. Toronto: Oxford University Press.

Wilson, J. 2002. Continuity and change in the Canadian environmental movement: Assessing the effects of institutionalization. In *Canadian Environmental Policy: Context and Cases*, eds. D.L. VanNijnatten and R. Boardman, 46–65. Toronto: Oxford University Press.

CHAPTER 10

Knotty Tales: Forest Policy Narratives in an Era of Transition

Jocelyn Thorpe and L. Anders Sandberg*

INTRODUCTION

The forest sector plays an important role in Canadian political economy, which is not surprising, given that almost half of Canada's land mass (more than 400 million hectares) comprises forests and other wooded land. Canada exports more forest products than any other country in the world; it is the number one world producer of newsprint and the number two producer of softwood lumber and wood pulp. The United States is the biggest market for Canadian forest products, followed by the European Union, Japan, and China. In 2005, the total value of Canadian forest-product exports was $41.9 billion, with forest industries in British Columbia, Quebec, and Ontario claiming the largest proportion. Also in 2005, the forest industry in Canada contributed 2.9 percent to the gross domestic product (GDP) and $31.9 billion to the trade balance and employed 339,900 people in direct jobs (Canadian Forest Service, Natural Resources Canada [NRC] 2006).

Despite the significant place of the forest sector in Canada, especially for the more than 300 communities across the nation that depend on this sector for at least half of their income, the forest industry is in decline. With few exceptions, the export of forest products has dropped since 2000, and along with it, the contribution of forest product exports to Canada's trade surplus has also fallen (Canadian Forest Service, NRC 2006). In addition, wood supply is in decline. Whereas the Canadian Forest Service, Natural Resources Canada (2006), basing its estimate on annual harvest levels and annual allowable cuts, contends that wood supply remained stable between 1994 and 2004, other commentators disagree (Howlett and Rayner 2001; Marchak, Aycock, and Herbert 1999). The province of Quebec recently took steps toward rectifying its wood supply crisis by reducing its annual allowable cut by 20 percent. Employment in the forest industry has also diminished, with

22,200 fewer people working in the forest sector in 2005 than in 2004. This drop in employment is due in part to the closure of many mills since 2003 (Canadian Forest Service, NRC 2006).

Political economists have typically understood the forest sector as part of the Canadian staples economy: early European settlers used forests for fuel, farming, and construction purposes, and industry began later to cut raw timber and manufacture pulp and paper for export (Howlett and Rayner 2001, 25–26). According to the staples narrative, introduced by William Mackintosh (see essay collection published in 1974 [1967]) and elaborated by Harold Innis (1930), in order to settle the land and extract its resources (including forest products), colonists and settlers built an entire society and economy "organized around the labour force, technological regime, legal order, and financial system needed to serve the ends of resource extraction" (Luke 2003, 95). Building upon Innis's work, a nationalist political economy school has criticized the domination of the Canadian resource economy by foreign capital, markets, and technology, and has advocated a "made-in-Canada" industrial strategy. Studies on the forest sector have been especially prominent in probing the contingencies, specificities, and possibilities of building a forest policy that is more socially equitable, more oriented toward value-added products, and more integrated into the national economy.

Recently, however, many observers in the political economy and policy community tradition have noted a shift from an "*extractive* to an *attractive* model of development" (Luke 2003, 92, emphasis ours) within the forest sector, or what Hutton (see chapter 3, 39) calls the "staples in decline" syndrome. Although he concedes that the staples-in-decline syndrome can be overstated, Hutton maintains that we may be "at the advent of a post-staples state, in which resource extraction is increasingly seen by policy-makers and the broader public as a *residual* of the national economic structure, a vestige of a historical development path that sustained many Canadian regions and communities" (ibid., 47). In order to evaluate the extent to which Hutton's observations ring true, this chapter grapples with divergent methods of approaching and analyzing forestry. This mode of inquiry allows us room not only to evaluate historical and contemporary forestry concerns but also to explore how specific concerns have come to be understood as central *through* the approaches employed to analyze the sector. For example, political economy perspectives typically concentrate on European settlers' impact on an "unexploited frontier" and the subsequent development of a resource-extractive, export-oriented economy. Concerns stemming from this approach often centre on how to create a forest sector that is domestically owned and controlled and integrated through backward and forward linkages into a national economy. Peripheral to this narrative is First Nations' presence in and claim to forest land, as well as their often violent removal from the land upon which the Canadian forest sector is built (Willems-Braun 1997).

In contrast, accounts that centre on the colonial encounter often focus on First Nations communities' particular relationships with and claims to the land and understand European immigration and policy-making as influencing, disrupting, and shaping, but never completely severing, relationships between First Nations and the land. Concerns based on this approach usually focus on the importance of First Nations self-government and access to land (see, for example, G.R. Alfred 1995; T. Alfred, 1999; Monture-Angus 1995, 1999) in contemporary forestry policy.[1]

In the first section of this chapter, we rely on a political economy perspective to review the history of Canadian forest policy. Then, using the contemporary examples of the softwood lumber dispute, forests as carbon sinks, and forests as parks, we argue that although some indications point to a shift from a staples to a post-staples forest economy, a high degree of continuity also exists. In the second part of the chapter, we identify narratives that extend beyond the political economics of the situation, and we question, re-examine, redefine, and reformulate the very terms and assumptions upon which forest sector analysis has traditionally rested. In conclusion, we discuss the implications of this analysis for Canadian forest policy and the potential for change that emerges from action inspired by the identified stories.

THE STAPLES-TO-POST-STAPLES NARRATIVE IN THE CANADIAN FOREST SECTOR

The staples story typically begins by discussing how early settlers cut or burned down forests in order to clear land for homes, crops, and livestock and to obtain wood for fuel and building purposes. The forests are here first considered impediments to settlement and "civilization" in the new colony, but quickly become sources of income through extraction (Drushka 2003, 27). By 1763, both France and Britain had secured royal reserves of timber in eastern Canada. The purpose of such early forest policies was to serve the interests of imperial powers in attaining naval timbers for masts and shipbuilding (ibid., 20, 23). Britain became dependent on Canadian timber after US independence and especially during Napoleon's blockade of the Baltic (Lower 1973; Mackay 1985). Commentators often point out that early emphasis on the export of forest products, as opposed to the manufacturing of forest products within Canada, served to stimulate the industrial capacity of Britain and France while simultaneously foreclosing the emergence of a manufacturing base in the colony (see Beyers and Sandberg 1998, 100).

Confederation in 1867 is seen as having occurred to facilitate the further development of a national staples economy. It provided the central organization and the guarantees for funds to build railways and canals to transport large and heavy lumber across long distances. The *Constitution Act, 1867* granted the provinces ownership, legislative authority, and therefore definite jurisdiction over forest land

(Nelles 1974; Beyers and Sandberg 1998, 101). Commentators view government ownership of forest land and the development of an economy based on staples export as crucial to the emergence of the Canadian forest sector and often highlight the resulting mutually beneficial relationship established between government and industry (Beyers and Sandberg 1998; Howlett and Rayner 2001). As provincial governments started to implement various tenure and licensing policies, they generated considerable revenues by allowing industry to remove trees from Crown lands (Howlett and Rayner 2001, 25–26). This system is seen to have worked well for both parties, as industry could access trees while avoiding the costs of land ownership, and governments could create jobs and use forest-generated income for measures popular with the electorate (ibid., 33).

Provincial governments' claiming of the income generated from forests has been viewed as placing them in the contradictory position of both regulating and profiting from industrial forest practices (ibid., 43). This position provides a strong bargaining position for corporate interests (ibid., 33) and has served to undermine provincial governments' autonomy (Beyers and Sandberg 1998, 102). Closed policy networks, which have emerged in the sector as a result of this situation, have allowed forest policy to be decided by the state and the forest industry, with provincial governments favouring large forest companies that hold long-term leases (Beyers and Sandberg 1998, 102, 103; Pratt and Urquhart 1994; Sandberg 1992).

Staples narratives usually emphasize the role mechanization played in the development of the Canadian forest sector (Drushka 2003; Rajala 1998; Swift 1983); for example, the effect of the introduction of steam-powered machinery, chain saws, mechanical wheeled skidders, and harvesting machines in speeding up the pace of logging (Drushka 2003, 33; Swift 1983, 133–34). As clear-cut logging became increasingly common, entire watersheds were progressively emptied of trees (Drushka 2003, 34).

Despite the early establishment of forestry schools and the emergence of scientifically trained forestry professionals (Nelles 1974; Gillis and Roach 1986; Judd 1993; Sandberg 1999), several forest inventories conducted in the 1930s revealed that many forests had been seriously depleted (Drushka 2003, 42). Short-run profit, not preservation, was the driving force behind scientific forestry, and conservationist measures were confined to fire suppression and the creation of timber reserves (Beyers and Sandberg 1998, 103). After 1947, sustained yield—the principle that tree fibre removed from the forest each year should equal the amount of fibre added through tree growth—came into effect. In the 1970s and 1980s, foresters embraced integrated and multiple-use resource management that aims to manage forests concurrently for a number of values, including timber, recreation, and animal habitat. Ecosystem management emerged in the 1980s and 1990s, with the goal of sustaining the ecosystem as opposed to managing timber health (Howlett and Rayner 2001, 46–47).

Authors in the political economy tradition (Drushka 2003, 59; Lawson, Levy, and Sandberg 2001, 292) have often pointed out that Canadian conservationist measures have resulted in the exacerbation of the wood supply crisis, not relief from it: both the volume of timber and the area of forest cut down increased throughout the 20th century. Critics (Lawson, Levy, and Sandberg 2001, 293) discuss how measurements of a "sustainable" extraction rate can be manipulated heavily to favour industry's economic imperatives and how sustained yield's encouragement to eliminate older stands first allowed companies to persist in their preference for cutting previously uncut forests instead of forcing them to revamp their logging practices. Canada's staples-based economy, with its previously established commitment to providing foreign markets with a large supply of raw material, is argued to be partially responsible for allowing forest management to be particularly open to economic dominance of forest companies (Beyers and Sandberg 1998, 103).

Since the 1960s, however, many groups and individuals, displeased with the way the forest sector favoured timber interests to the exclusion of alternative forest values, mobilized to affect forest policy. These groups included First Nations, who challenged the unjust policies and practices that left them increasingly isolated from lands over which they had claim (Willems-Braun 1997, 99). Also involved, with goals for the forest that differed widely from one another, were conservation groups: hunting, fishing, and outdoor recreation groups; tourism and fishing operators; and small-bush operators for whom tenure and licensing systems are difficult to obtain (Howlett and Rayner 2001, 43–44). Preservationist environmental groups succeeded in having more lands designated as parks (Lawson, Levy, and Sandberg 2001, 294–96). The mass support garnered for anti-logging protests, such as the ones in Clayoquot Sound, British Columbia, and in Temagami, Ontario, revealed the growing strength of the environmental movement in contending with Canada's dominant forestry model.

The Canadian forest industry now faces not only a declining resource base and a number of challenges from First Nations and from environmental groups (Howlett and Rayner 2001, 51) but also increasing competition from industries in rival countries that are able to produce and export timber less expensively than Canadian firms (Marchak 1995). To aggravate the situation, and despite increased production, the forest sector has experienced serious job loss (Howlett and Rayner 2001, 37), and forestry dependent communities have consequently suffered (Baldwin 2000, 30).

Paradoxically, such conflicts over the fate of Canada's forests have transformed these areas into international tourist destinations, allowing attractive development strategies that enable communities to remain viable (Luke 2003, 97–98). For example, tourism at Clayoquot Sound did not take off until the early 1980s, when the international media turned its gaze on the environmental struggle to "save" the last of this forest (Luke 2003, 96). Clayoquot Sound thus became a tourist destination not only because of its beauty but also because of the perception that its beauty might at any time disappear (Braun 2002). By the mid-1980s, several tour operators, in response to the growing number of visitors, had started to provide ecotourism packages, including whale-watching, kayaking, and hot springs tours.

QUESTIONING THE STAPLES-TO-POST-STAPLES TRANSITION

To what extent has the Canadian forest sector, as suggested by a political economy analysis, experienced a staples-to-post-staples transition? We contend that many contemporary trends reveal the staples extraction model continues to exert a strong influence on the Canadian forest political economy. This model is evidenced in the continued revenue associated with the forest resource and trade sector (Global Forest Watch 2000), but it is perhaps most obvious in the increasing grip of the market on all things forest-related. Neo-liberal policies in government have cut the funding of forest and natural resource departments and, in effect, reduced their capacities to develop and enforce forest regulations. Forest management and monitoring have been delegated to the forest companies, which now more or less police themselves. Another ingredient of this phenomenon, as suggested by Ben Cashore et al. (see chapter 11) is the increase in certification of environmentally and sustainably produced wood products that involves industry-wide initiatives and input from environmental organizations (Clancy and Sandberg 1997). But the trend extends further and in subtler ways. In the following sections, we review several recent developments in the forestry sector—the softwood lumber dispute, forest carbon sequestration, and preserved areas—and show how these issues challenge some aspects of, but in many ways continue to support, the staples model.

The Softwood Lumber Dispute

The softwood lumber dispute focuses on the US forest industry's claims that Canadian lumber exports are unfairly subsidized through the Canadian Crown land lease system. According to the US industry, some provincial governments set artificially low harvesting or stumpage fees on forests cut on Crown lands, thus providing an unfair competitive advantage to Canadian lumber producers exporting to the US market. From the Canadian perspective, by contrast, the stumpage rates are not considered low, but are an integral tool to attract forest-industry investment to remote regions in Canada. This strategy has allowed the forest industry to remain competitive in international markets where it faces severe transportation cost disadvantages. In the see-saw battle that has ensued, various American, North American Free Trade Association, and World Trade Organization trade tribunals have consistently ruled in Canada's favour. In April 2006, Canada and the United States reached a framework agreement outlining terms of a settlement to this dispute. However, a considerable number of politicians and industry partners remain skeptical about the fairness of the deal (Canadian Forest Service, NRC 2006).

Apart from trade considerations, environmental issues have also been connected with the softwood lumber dispute. In recent years, Canadian environmental, labour, and First Nations groups have supported the US position, maintaining that low stumpage rates are related to job loss and environmental degradation. They argue that the provision of a steady supply of cheap raw materials to industry prevents the growth of labour-intensive, higher-value-added products and promotes practices such as clear-cutting over alternatives such as selective logging (Hayter 2003, 716; Peters 2002). These groups have called for forest policies that ensure full market value for the forest resource; resist calls for compensation by industry if stumpage prices rise; strengthen export bans on raw logs; implement environmental protection; and recognize Aboriginal title. Yet these aspects of the softwood lumber dispute have had a very low profile in the Canadian public debate, which persistently calls for "free trade" in lumber products while retaining low stumpage rates.

In some cases, even those prominently opposed to the forest practices of the industry have come to this position. Former Ontario NDP premier Bob Rae, when in opposition, was arrested for protesting the cutting of old-growth red and white pine in Temagami in the early 1990s. By 2001, however, he represented a coalition of Canadian lumber producers promoting the intercontinental free trade of lumber products (Free trade Bob 2001). Also supporting both the Canadian forest-industry lobby and free trade in lumber products are prominent figures in the labour and environmental fields, such as Jack Munro, once president of the International Woodworkers of America, and Patrick Moore, founder of Greenpeace.

The story of the softwood lumber dispute is routinely told as an economic story and characterized in the public, political, and academic discourse as a competition between Canada and the United States. Conventional magazines and newspapers, as expressed in the Virtual News Index, contain scant references to the environmental aspects of the dispute while focusing on the trade gains or losses of Canada (The softwood-lumber dispute 2003). In the academic literature, a nationalist narrative remains prominent in which the softwood lumber dispute is referred to as "an unanticipated and undesirable outcome [read fewer exports] for the lumber industry" (Hayter 1992, 153). The coverage repeats the nature of similar trade disputes in the past in which the United States is portrayed as the bully and Canada as the hapless victim (Parenteau and Sandberg 1995; Sandberg and Parenteau 1997), whereas the truth is more complex and subtle.

Forests as Carbon Sinks

Our second example concerns the forest's role in carbon sequestration. Carbon sequestration, or the "carbon sink" concept, operates on the principle that forests are capable of holding or "sequestering" greenhouse gases and therefore play an important role in the global efforts to deal with climate change. The Kyoto Protocol of 1997, the first global initiative to deal with carbon emissions, focused primarily on the reduction of such emissions through conservation measures.

The United States introduced the carbon sink concept at a United Nations Conference in The Hague in 2000, arguing that afforestation efforts as well as existing forests should be part of the overall calculation when determining the emission quotas for individual countries. This concept is based on dubious science showing that tree plantations are better carbon sinks than old-growth forests, which allows for the proposition that clearing old-growth forests and replanting them will result in carbon reductions (Scott 2001a, 2001b). The European Union countries were outraged by the proposal, labelling it "a farce" and a means to escape previous commitments to carbon emission reductions. In the United States and Canada, however, the idea of forests as carbon sinks became conveniently incorporated into a staples model, in which new forest plantations were put forth as important ingredients in calculating those countries' contributions toward the reduction of carbon emissions under the Kyoto Protocol.

In 2001, the United States withdrew from the Kyoto Protocol entirely (Reguly 2007), and Canada recently followed suit. Although the Liberal government ratified the agreement in 2002, this government was defeated in 2006. The following year, the Conservative government announced that Canada could not meet its targets under the protocol without hurting the economy. According to Environment Minister John Baird, "We will not spin the wheel so hard as to put the Canadian economy in the ditch to deliver [the] environmental plan asked for in *some* quarters" (An overdue dose of eco-realism 2007, A20, emphasis ours). Thus, a staples economy apparently continues to take precedent over environmental concerns, even in this time of climate change and public interest in environmental issues.

Parks Versus Staples?

Canada has always been economically dependent on the export of natural resources; however, it appears to be moving away from its resource-extractive economy with the decision to set aside areas for preservation, including as provincial and national parks across the nation. Yet a closer inspection leaves a different impression. First, only a very small percentage of land has actually been set aside for protection, less than 8 percent across the nation (Global Forest Watch 2000, 11). Although the decision to protect 13 percent of forest land on Vancouver Island is considered a major environmental accomplishment, 87 percent of forest land remains open to industrial forestry. Similarly, provincial and national parks occupy only a small percentage of protected lands in Canada.

Although national parks now have a mandate to ensure the ecological integrity of each park (Parks Canada 2007), provincial parks do not share this mandate and continue to allow resource extraction to take place within park boundaries (Bella 1987, 2). Since neither industry nor provincial governments want to have exploitable resources locked up in parks, both generally prefer the opening of provincial parks over national parks (ibid.). Also, in deciding locations for national parks, governments have attempted to ensure that resources have either already been exhausted within the proposed park boundaries or remain outside the proposed boundaries (ibid., 38). National parks continue to be encroached upon by development and resource-extractive activities that sometimes involve intensive resource use directly adjacent to park borders (Sandilands 2000, 137).

Although seemingly contrary, a productivist bias is also evident in the non-extractive uses of parks. Not only do high volumes of tourist traffic and their corresponding roads and recreational services place ecological stress on parks (Hermer 2002; Sandilands 2000) but also parks in Canada have always been motivated at least as much by profit as preservation (Bella 1987). For example, Banff National Park was opened in 1885 for the explicit purpose of drawing wealthy travellers to enjoy scenic vistas while spending money on fine dining and accommodations (Stefanick 2001, 159). Bella (1987, ix) argues that although logging exploits the timber resource, parks exploit another natural resource—scenery. Although M'Gonigle (2003, 131) cautions us not to think that the industry of viewing forests is as ecologically destructive of forests as the industry of chopping them down, these seemingly opposing activities may have some important similarities. As Braun (2002) argues, by remaking forests into the image of the timber commodity, the forestry industry abstracts forests from their cultural and ecological surrounds. Similarly, by valuing forests for their scenery or "viewscapes," attractive industries, such as (eco)tourism, create nature as *visually*, as opposed to ecologically, important (Braun 2002, 143, 146).

STAPLES BY AND FOR MORE PEOPLE? FROM EXTRACTIVE TO ATTRACTIVE FOREST INDUSTRIES

As argued by Williams (1992), Canadian resource policy suffers from an "environmental blind spot" that is a function of Canada's continued dependence both on resource industries that pollute and on international markets. Canadian timber companies remain vulnerable to the export markets of the United States, Europe, and Southeast Asia, and to the international demand for staple products and the requests of international customers of forest products. As a result, innovative industrial development and environmental protection or preservation remain difficult to achieve.

Although this narrative of the forest sector as a mature staples industry is the one most often told in Canada, it is not necessarily *the* story about forestry in

Canada. In this section, we review various other interpretations of the situation of the Canadian forest sector that both add to and challenge the dominant political economy narrative. One important alternative to envision Canadian forest development is by concentrating on labour instead of trade and by tracing the means by which forest labour has been controlled and displaced over time. Labour and social historians, such as Ian Radforth (1987) and Richard Rajala (1998), focus specifically on how mechanization affected forest labour. Although mechanization of the forest sector was a boon to industry because it allowed access to new forest land and enabled trees to be cut down more quickly, these authors show how workers suffered from mechanization. They demonstrate that pre-industrial logging practices, such as oxen- or horse-powered logging, required a great deal of skill and knowledge on the part of wage workers and contract labour, particularly those in charge of driving the animal teams. Consequently, employers depended heavily on this labour, which resulted in a high degree of labour control over the workplace. Radforth (1986, 1987) argues that the introduction of machinery in northern Ontario offered a way for employers to overcome the independence, skills, and militancy of bush workers and, after the Second World War, the scarcity of such workers. Rajala (1998) similarly contends that mechanization in British Columbia was an attempt to make the "working forest" operate like a factory, where employers would seize relatively more power and workers would receive relatively less. Other authors (M'Gonigle and Parfit 1994; Mercure 1996; Howlett and Rayner 2001) show how technological innovations continue to affect forest workers negatively, for example through creating huge mills and machines that process more wood with fewer workers, thus substantially lowering employment and union membership in the forest sector.

Other historians challenge the assumption that it was entirely workers of European descent who participated in Canadian forestry (McManus 1999). Knight (1978, 118) and Van Wyck (1979) show that many First Nations people laboured in the forest industry in British Columbia and Ontario in the very earliest days of logging. Some bands prospered early from trading timber with Europeans; others performed wage work as loggers and mill employees and sometimes made independent contracts with the lumber industry to cut sawlogs or railway ties (Van Wyck 1979, 78–87). Such studies reveal that Aboriginal people were not only present within the forest industry but were also essential to the emergence of the industry. These studies disrupt both the common assumption that the lives of First Nations people were and remain peripheral to the development of Canadian society and the popular stereotype that Aboriginal people are somehow inherently ecological beings opposed to extractive industry (see also Furniss 1999; Perry 2001). Indeed, Aboriginal people remain very active in the forest industry, and some narratives emphasize their struggle for benefits associated with the current industrial regime of employment, revenue, and timber (Westman 2005). Many recent discussions about First Nations involvement in the forest sector focus on "joint business ventures" between industry and various First Nations (Hayter 2000, 339). These partnerships allow corporations access to timber on Aboriginal reserves and secure resources for corporations at a time when corporate access is increasingly threatened by First Nations land-claim and treaty-making processes (Hayter 2003, 723). These partnerships are often touted as "win–win" situations for industry because "it's increasingly becoming a marketplace expectation that businesses demonstrate good corporate citizenship" (Kimble 2003, 2) and for First Nations because "they've been able to provide employment opportunities for their people" (Company [Weyerhauser Canada] develops solid partnership 1998, 12). Partnerships have also been criticized for potentially lessening the chances for more radical changes by taking attention away from land-claim issues (Lawson, Levy, and Sandberg 2001, 301).

Along similar lines, various authors show that immigrants of colour, and not only white Europeans, built the forest sector. Although colonial officials believed that Canada should become a white settler nation, or a "Britain of the North" (Berger 1966, 4), this racist desire often conflicted with Canada's growing demand for labour needed to build the nation (Mackey 1999; Perry 2001). Indeed, since the Canadian government had difficulty attracting enough British and European migrants, it allowed immigration from China, India, and Japan. In the context of attempting to build a white settler colony, however, racial hierarchies of citizenship emerged, and Asian migrants were considered temporary workers, not potential citizens, a bias that was reflected in the regulated entry of Asian men according to labour market needs and a differential residency and citizenship status (Dua 1999a, 244). Attempts to restrict entry to Asian women through a series of changing regulations designed to prevent the permanent settlement of Asian men lasted until 1947 (Dua 1999a, 245; Dua 1999b).

Some commentators show how such racial hierarchies of citizenship directly affected the forest sector. Adachi (1976, 27), for example, discusses how Japanese labourers at sawmills in British Columbia worked in the early 1900s for lower pay than white workers. In 1922, British Columbia "passed a resolution asking the federal government to … empower the province to make laws prohibiting 'Asiatics' from acquiring proprietary interests in … timber lands … and other industries as well as employment in them" (ibid., 140). In 1934, the Board of Industrial Relations in British Columbia developed a minimum wage system for the province's sawmill industry. This system also allowed for up to 25 percent of the total number of employees to be paid less than the minimum wage, an allowance created so that employers could hire low-paid Asian workers (Li 1988, 45). This research shows that immigrants who differed from the "British norms of racial, cultural, and political acceptability" (Abele and Stasiulis 1989, 241) were less fortunate in the forest sector than were white male workers, thus revealing racial hierarchies in the labour force that contributed to the profitability of the forest industry. Indeed, as Li points out, white workers and capitalists directly benefited from racist labour policies: because Asian workers were paid less, white workers were paid more, and profit margins remained high (Li 1988, 45).

Although most political economy approaches to the forest sector focus on the activities of European men, some studies reveal the critical role played by women. Scholars argue that even during periods of mostly male migration to Canada, women, though undervalued and unpaid or underpaid, have always performed essential labour, for example, as household workers or cooks in logging camps (Abele and Stasiulis 1989; Marchak 1983; Reed 2003). In a recent study, Reed (2003) explores the lives and perceptions of women who support industrial forestry in British Columbia, demonstrating how the socially and historically constructed notion of "working forest" history as a story of white working*man*'s culture (Dunk 1991) has dramatically shaped women's experiences in forest communities. Reed (2003, 37) highlights how, despite most jobs in the forest sector being currently unstable due in part to restructuring and job loss, women who work in the forest industry frequently have jobs that are more economically marginalized than men's jobs (see also Hayter 2000, 266). Perhaps more revealing, however, is the difficulty women face in obtaining steady, well-paying jobs in forestry towns. Women are more than three times as likely than men to enter into a service occupation, whereas men are more than six times as likely than women to be employed in primary industries (Reed 2003, 88). As one of Reed's interviewees, who works four part-time jobs, states, "a woman in this area cannot get a full-time, forty-hour-a-week job that pays properly to support a family ... women are still making seven-fifty an hour" (quoted in Reed 2003, 93).

Abele and Stasiulis (1989, 242) argue that the Canadian staples economy cannot be sufficiently comprehended without attending to the ways in which hierarchies of gender, race, and ethnicity led to the exploitation of some groups more than others (see also Adachi 1976; Li 1988), and therefore to "significant conflicts, contradictions, and hierarchies in the structuring of the Canadian working class" (Abele and Stasiulis 1989, 260). Although, as previously discussed, the racial composition of Canada never matched the colonial intention to inhabit the nation with white Europeans, Abele and Stasiulis (1989) show how power operated to shape a system of forest governance whereby white male subjects comprised the decision-making elite. Racial and gender hierarchies continue to shape the forest sector today (Reed 2003).

Earlier we suggested that though some signs indicate a shift from large-scale industrial forestry, much evidence supports Canada's continued dependence on the export of the timber staple. Here we examine the staples-to-post-staples transition in a different light. Recalling that environmental pressure to save forests is closely tied with an increase in attractive industries, the insight of some authors that those privileged in terms of class (that is, those who can afford to visit pristine sites of attractive development) are the ones who have usually benefited from environmental initiatives will not come as a surprise (Stefanick 2001; Lawson, Levy, and Sandberg 2001; Bella 1987). Luke (2003, 97) complicates the extractive-to-attractive discourse by arguing that attractive development strategies have been historically tied to locations where no other alternative to extractive or manufacturing industry exists, and job opportunities can only be provided "if these attractions can be made alluring enough by aggressive mass-media promotions." Further, employment in attractive industries is often low-paid, non-union service work, most often performed by women and people of colour (ibid., 98). His study makes clear the consequences of viewing this form of capitalist development as innocent. As Sandilands (2003, 153) elaborates, constructing a good attractive capitalism against a bad extractive capitalism may serve to marginalize forestry workers while failing to inquire into the consumptive practices of (eco)tourists. Injustices associated with attractive development are also masked—for example, job insecurity and unlivable wages.

The representation of attractive capitalism as inherently beneficial also has the potential to allow an extremely commodified notion of nature—the image commodity—to pass as "true" nature, thereby foreclosing discussions about the kinds of human–nature interactions that should be fostered (Cronon 1995, 81). Thus, although attractive industry may provide some alternative employment opportunities for suffering communities in resource towns and may engender some positive ecological outcomes, attractive industry is not the solution, either economically or environmentally, that it is sometimes represented to be.

CONCLUSION: BEYOND THE STAPLES-TO-POST-STAPLES TRANSITION IN THE CANADIAN FOREST SECTOR

Innis's early studies, and more recent political economy analyses, allow us to comprehend how Canada's position as a European colony led to the country's historical and contemporary situation as an exporter of staples products. More recent accounts demonstrate the essential roles played by various actors not generally featured in the political economy tradition, thereby providing a more nuanced reading of the history of the Canadian forest sector. Juxtaposing these two forms of analysis allows us to rethink forest policy analysis and to move beyond the "staples-to-post-staples" political economy debate.

The stories told by post-colonial and feminist authors force us to examine some "uncomfortable facts about Canada" (Abele and Stasiulis 1989, 242), including the ways in which the marginalization of First Nations peoples both preceded and has been inscribed into forest policy, and how various groups of immigrants have been incorporated differently into Canadian political economy. These stories also reveal that changes within the forest sector (for example, through increased environmental concern and attractive industry), although perhaps indicating a shift from environmentally destructive resource extraction, do not necessarily signify a move toward social and environmental justice.

For First Nations, justice may require a thorough exploration and recapture of traditional governance structures and dynamics based on oral and spiritual foundations that emphasize sharing, nurturing, and promoting place-based interpersonal, interspecies, and intergenerational responsibilities. These ideas may be congruent with some of the ideas of ecoforestry and bioregionalism, such as the notion that place-centredness, ecological integrity, and social equity ought to be the point of departure in any forest endeavour (Drengson and Taylor 1998). A move toward these ideas suggests that we must re-examine the dominant view of nature as commodity that has informed the construction of forests both as resources to be extracted and as viewscapes to be commodified. In sum, these alternative approaches call upon those interested in social and environmental justice to explore the ways in which colonialism, capitalism, and a neo-liberal economy have fundamentally shaped the forest sector in Canada and to attempt to think about forests and forest policy in dramatically new ways.

A very unfortunate but plausible conclusion that can be drawn from this account is that most progressive attempts at reforming Canadian forest policy, be they oriented toward extractive or attractive goals, are hopelessly compromised. The federal and provincial governments' fight for access to the American market for lumber through the pursuit of a "fair" softwood lumber agreement and the prominence of this debate in the public sphere continue to chain the Canadian forest industry to the role of a staple supplier of crude material and to the neglect of environmental concerns. The invention of the carbon sink concept in the context of the climate change debate allowed Canada to divert attention from reducing carbon emissions to lobbying hard for having its forests, and better still its forest plantations, count toward meeting its Kyoto targets. Now Canada has gone so far as to give up on these targets entirely. Parks and preserved areas, we conclude, form a limited strategy to protect forests. Many of these areas are confined to marginal locations, others are compromised by their commercialization, and both constitute part of a mind trick that suggests forest preservation is all about setting aside a small percentage of protected forests while vigorously exploiting the rest.

We have also explored the historical and contemporary work that recognizes the role of marginal and dissenting groups within the forest sector. These studies are surely important in relating and celebrating the often untold stories of contributions and challenges posed by allegedly marginal (although, in fact, central) actors in the Canadian forest sector. We caution, though, that such stories may lead to affirmative action policies that assist such groups in becoming integrated into the very social forest structure that marginalized them in the first place. The last set of analyses provides, we suggest, the lens with the widest implications for forest policy: we question the very categories that are used to define the forest industry and preservation sectors and the social relationships that go along with them. This approach involves critically examining the notion of forests as "resources" and "commodities" and the notion of a market economy with the private property rights and profit incentives that comprise it.

Criticisms of the staples and the staples-to-post-staples transition ideas are strategically important because of the way in which these categories and definitions shape our thinking about policy alternatives and future political economic trajectories. If forest reforms in First Nations, for example, result in just the same forest-industry activities and social divisions as in the current society, they fail to represent substantial change from the status quo. In the end, the path ahead needs to be determined by communities themselves, with critical analyses and self-reflection forming important ingredients for taking short-term strategic action while at the same time working for long-term fundamental change.

NOTES

*   The authors would like very much to thank Michael Howlett and Keith Brownsey for all their hard work and for their dedication to this project. Thanks also to the anonymous reviewers for their comments that helped to improve an earlier draft.

1. These two stories emphasize different kinds of concerns that involve different policy implications. Many scholars (Braun 2002; Haraway 1989; King 2003; Jacobs 1996; McLeod 2000; Said 1993) argue that storytelling practices cannot be separated from political and economic practices; they therefore recognize the importance of attending not only to stories themselves, but also to how and by whom the stories are told.

REFERENCES

Abele, F., and Stasiulis, D. 1989. Canada as a "white settler colony": What about Natives and immigrants? In *The New Canadian Political Economy*, eds. W. Clement and G. Williams, 240–77. Montreal and Kingston: McGill-Queen's University Press.

Adachi, K. 1976. *The enemy that never was: A history of the Japanese Canadians.* Toronto: McClelland & Stewart.

Alfred, G.R. 1995. *Heeding the voices of our ancestors: Kahnawake Mohawk politics and the rise of Native nationalism.* Oxford and New York: Oxford University Press.

Alfred, T. 1999. *Peace, power, righteousness: An indigenous manifesto.* Oxford and New York: Oxford University Press.

Baldwin, A. 2000. Post-Fordism and ecological modernization: A case of the Canadian pulp and paper industry. Unpublished master's major paper, Faculty of Environmental Studies, York University, Toronto.

Bella, L. 1987. *Parks for profit*. Montreal: Harvest House.

Berger, C. 1966. The true north strong and free. In *Nationalism in Canada*, ed. P. Russell, 3–26. Toronto: McGraw-Hill.

Beyers, J.M., and Sandberg, L.A. 1998. Canadian federal forest policy: Present initiatives and historical constraints. In *Sustainability: The Challenge—People, Power, and the Environment*, eds. L.A. Sandberg and S. Sörlin, 99–107. Montreal, New York, and London: Black Rose Books.

Braun, B. 2002. *The intemperate rainforest: Nature, culture, and power on Canada's west coast*. Minneapolis: University of Minnesota Press.

Canadian Forest Service, Natural Resources Canada. 2006. *The state of Canada's forests 2005–2006: Forest industry competitiveness*. Online at http://cfs.nrcan.gc.ca/sof/latest_e.html.

Clancy, P., and Sandberg, L.A. 1997. Formulating standards for sustainable forest management in Canada. *Business Strategy and the Environment* 6(4): 206–17.

Company (Weyerhauser Canada) develops solid partnership with First Nations in Saskatchewan: Forestry resources provide economic opportunities. 1998. *First Perspective* 7(9): 12.

Cronon, W. 1995. The trouble with wilderness; Or, getting back to the wrong nature. In *Uncommon Ground: Toward Reinventing Nature*, ed. W. Cronon, 69–90. New York: W.W. Norton.

Drengson, A., and Taylor D., eds. 1998. *Ecoforestry: The art and science of sustainable forest use*. Gabriola Island, BC: New Society.

Drushka, K. 2003. *Canada's forests: A history*. Forest history issues series. Montreal and Kingston: McGill-Queen's University Press.

Dua, E. 1999a. Beyond diversity: Exploring the ways in which the discourse of race has shaped the institution of the nuclear family. In *Scratching the Surface: Canadian Anti-Racist Feminist Thought*, eds. E. Dua and A. Robertson, 237–59. Toronto: Women's Press.

Dua, E. 1999b. Racializing imperial Canada: Indian women and the making of ethnic communities. In *Gender, Sexuality and Colonial Modernities*, ed. A. Burton, 119–33. London and New York: Routledge.

Dunk, T. 1991. *It's a working man's town: Male working-class culture in northwestern Ontario*. Montreal and Kingston: McGill-Queen's University Press.

Free trade Bob. 2001. *Waterloo Region Record*, March 12: A06.

Furniss, E. 1999. *The burden of history: Colonialism and the frontier myth in a rural Canadian community*. Vancouver: University of British Columbia Press.

Gillis, R.P., and Roach, T. 1986. *Lost initiatives: Canada's forest industries, forest policy and forest conservation*. New York: Greenwood Press.

Global Forest Watch. 2000. *Canada's forests at a crossroads: An assessment in the year 2000*. Washington, DC: World Resources Institute.

Haraway, D.J. 1989. *Primate visions: Gender, race, and nation in the world of modern science*. New York: Routledge.

Hayter, R. 1992. International trade relations and regional industrial adjustment: The implications of the 1982–86 Canadian–US softwood lumber dispute for British Columbia. *Environment and Planning A* 24(1): 153–70.

Hayter, R. 2000. *Flexible crossroads: The restructuring of British Columbia's forest economy.* Vancouver: University of British Columbia Press.

Hayter, R. 2003. The war in the woods: Post-Fordist restructuring, globalization, and the contested remapping of British Columbia's forest economy. *Annals of the Association of American Geographers* 93(3): 706–29.

Hermer, J. 2002. *Regulating Eden: The nature of order in North American parks.* Toronto: University of Toronto Press.

Howlett, M., and Rayner, J. 2001. The business and government nexus: Principal elements and dynamics of the Canadian forest policy regime. In *Canadian Forest Policy: Adapting to Change*, ed. M. Howlett, 23–62. Toronto: University of Toronto Press.

Innis, H.A. 1930. *The fur trade in Canada: An introduction to Canadian economic history.* Toronto: University of Toronto Press.

Jacobs, J.M. 1996. *Edge of empire: Postcolonialism and the city.* London: Routledge.

Judd, R. 1993. Policy and ecology in forest history. *Acadiensis* 23(1): 188–93.

Kimble, R. 2003. Certification process valued by participants. *Windspeaker* 21(2): 2, 4.

King, T. 2003. *The truth about stories: A Native narrative.* Toronto: House of Anansi Press.

Knight, R. 1978. *Indians at work: An informal history of Native Indian labour in British Columbia, 1858–1930.* Vancouver: New Star Books.

Lawson, J., Levy, M., and Sandberg, L.A. 2001. Perpetual revenues and the delights of the primitive: Change, continuity, and forest policy regimes in Ontario. In *Canadian Forest Policy: Adapting to Change*, ed. M. Howlett, 279–315. Toronto: University of Toronto Press.

Li, P.S. 1988. *The Chinese in Canada.* Toronto: Oxford University Press.

Lower, A.R.M. 1973. *Great Britain's woodyard: British America and the timber trade, 1763–1867.* Montreal and Kingston: McGill-Queen's University Press.

Luke, T.W. 2003. On the political economy of Clayoquot Sound: The uneasy transition from extractive to attractive models of development. In *A Political Space: Reading the Global Through Clayoquot Sound*, eds. W. Magnusson and K. Shaw, 91–112. Minneapolis: University of Minnesota Press.

Mackay, D. 1985. *Heritage lost: The crisis in Canada's forests.* Toronto: Macmillan.

Mackey, E. 1999. *The house of difference: Cultural politics and national identity in Canada.* London: Routledge.

Mackintosh, W.A. 1974 [1967]. *Approaches to Canadian history: Essays by W.A. Mackintosh.* Toronto: University of Toronto Press.

Marchak, P. 1983. *Green gold: The forest industry in British Columbia.* Vancouver: University of British Columbia Press.

Marchak, P. 1995. *Logging the globe.* Montreal and Kingston: McGill-Queen's University Press.

Marchak, P., Aycock, S., and Herbert, D. 1999. *Falldown: Forest policy in British Columbia*. Vancouver: David Suzuki Foundation and Ecotrust Canada.

McLeod, J. 2000. *Beginning postcolonialism*. Manchester: Manchester University Press.

McManus, P. 1999. Histories of forestry: Ideas, networks and silences. *Environment and History* 5(2): 185–208.

Mercure, D. 1996. *Le travail déraciné: L'impartition flexible dans la dynamique sociale des entreprises forestières au Quebec*. Montreal: Boreal Press.

M'Gonigle, M. 2003. Somewhere between center and territory: Exploring a nodal site in the struggle against vertical authority and horizontal flows. In *A Political Space: Reading the Global Through Clayoquot Sound*, eds. W. Magnusson and K. Shaw, 121–37. Minneapolis: University of Minnesota Press.

M'Gonigle, M., and Parfit, B. 1994. *Forestopia: A practical guide to the new forest economy*. Madeira Park, BC: Harbour Publishing.

Monture-Angus, P. 1995. *Thunder in my soul: A Mohawk woman speaks*. Halifax: Fernwood.

Monture-Angus, P. 1999. *Journeying forward: Dreaming First Nations' independence*. Halifax: Fernwood.

Nelles, H.V. 1974. *The politics of development: Forests, mines and hydro-electric power in Ontario, 1849–1941*. Toronto: Macmillan.

An overdue dose of eco-realism. 2007. *The Globe and Mail*, April 26: A20.

Parenteau, W., and Sandberg, L.A. 1995. Conservation and the gospel of economic nationalism: The Canadian pulpwood question in Nova Scotia and New Brunswick, 1919–1933. *Environmental History Review* 19(2): 55–83.

Parks Canada. 2007. Parks Canada mandate. Online at http://www.pc.gc.ca/agen/index_E.asp.

Perry, A. 2001. *On the edge of empire: Gender, race, and the making of British Columbia, 1849–1871*. Toronto: University of Toronto Press.

Peters, S. 2002. Lumber stance "devastating," politicians told firms defended at workers' expense, coalition charges. *Toronto Star*, May 15: E03.

Pratt, L., and Urquhart, I. 1994. *The last great forest: Japanese multinationals and Alberta's northern forests*. Edmonton: NeWest Press.

Radforth, I. 1986. Logging pulpwood in northern Ontario. In *On the Job: Confronting the Labour Process in Canada*, eds. C. Heron and R. Storey, 245–80. Montreal and Kingston: McGill-Queen's University Press.

Radforth, I. 1987. *Bushworkers and bosses: Logging in northern Ontario, 1900–1980*. Toronto: University of Toronto Press.

Rajala, R. 1998. *Clearcutting the Pacific rain forest: Production, science, and regulation*. Vancouver: University of British Columbia Press.

Reed, M. 2003. *Taking stands: Gender and the sustainability of rural communities*. Vancouver: University of British Columbia Press.

Reguly, E. 2007. Canada poised to tip balance in "clash of wills" over emissions. *The Globe and Mail*, June 4: A4.

Said, E. 1993. *Culture and imperialism*. New York: Vintage Press.

Sandberg, L.A., ed. 1992. *Trouble in the woods: Forest policy and conflict in Nova Scotia and New Brunswick*. Fredericton, NB: Acadiensis Press.

Sandberg, L.A. 1999. Skogshistoria i USA och Kanada (Forest history in the United States and Canada). In *Skogshistorisk Forskning i Europa och Nord Amerika: Vad är skogshistoria, hur har den skrivits och varför?* (*Forest History Research in Europe and North America: What Is Forest History, How Has It Been Written and Why?*), ed. R. Pettersson, 291–322. Stockholm: Royal Swedish Academy of Agriculture and Forestry. Online at http://www.kslab.ksla.se/Eng.htm.

Sandberg, L.A., and Parenteau, W. 1997. From weapons to symbols of privilege: The role of cartoons in the pulpwood export embargo debate in Nova Scotia, 1925–1933. *Acadiensis* 26(2): 31–58.

Sandilands, C. 2000. Ecological integrity and national narrative: Cleaning up Canada's national parks. *Canadian Women's Studies* 20(2): 137–42.

Sandilands, C. 2003. Between the local and the global: Clayoquot Sound and simulacral politics. In *A Political Space: Reading the Global Through Clayoquot Sound*, eds. W. Magnusson and K. Shaw, 139–68. Minneapolis: University of Minnesota Press.

Scott, D.N. 2001a. Looking for loopholes. *Alternatives Journal* 27(4): 22–29.

Scott, D.N. 2001b. Carbon sinks and the preservation of old-growth forests under the Kyoto Protocol. *Journal of Environmental Law and Practice* 10(2): 105–45.

The softwood-lumber dispute: A simple lesson in economics. 2003. *The Economist*, February 1: 34.

Stefanick, L. 2001. Environmentalism and environmental actors in the Canadian forest sector. In *Canadian Forest Policy: Adapting to Change*, ed. M. Howlett, 157–71. Toronto: University of Toronto Press.

Swift, J. 1983. *Cut and run: The assault on Canada's forests*. Toronto: Between the Lines.

Van Wyck, S.M. 1979. The fruits of their labour: Native Indian involvement in the Canadian wage economy—A regional case study of the Upper Ottawa Valley, 1850–1930. Unpublished master's thesis, Department of Anthropology, University of Toronto.

Westman, C.N. 2005. Tutelage, development and legitimacy: A brief critique of Canada's Indian reserve forest management regime. *Canadian Journal of Native Studies* 25(1): 207–14.

Willems-Braun, B. 1997. Colonial vestiges: Representing forest landscapes on Canada's west coast. In *Troubles in the Rainforest: British Columbia's Forest Economy in Transition*, eds. T.J. Barnes and R. Hayter, 99–127. Victoria: Western Geographical Press.

Williams, G. 1992. Greening the new Canadian political economy. *Studies in Political Economy* 37(Spring): 5–30.

CHAPTER 11

The Future of Non-State Authority in Canadian Staples Industries: Assessing the Emergence of Forest Certification

Benjamin Cashore, Graeme Auld, James Lawson, and Deanna Newsom*

INTRODUCTION

Virtually all of the literature on Canada as a "staples state" has focused on two related topics: the impact of a historically staples-based economy on the development of Canada's political and economic structure, function, and policy outcomes; and, based on these historical influences, the ability and capacity of state officials to veer Canada off this "hinterland" pathway by facilitating a more diversified Canadian economy less dependent on the US "metropole." These focuses are important; however, in the 1990s, new questions were raised for students of the staples state with the dramatic arrival of non-state, market-driven (NSMD) governance systems that focus largely on regulating staples-extracting sectors, such as forestry, fisheries, and mining.

First, what impact do non-state forms of governance have on the ability of state officials to promote the development of a post-staples state? Second, can non-state forms of governance address policy problems (such as environmental and social regulations governing resource exploitation) in ways that a staples and/or a post-staples state have proven unable? Third, and arguably most importantly, ought scholarship on the staples (and especially the post-staples) state (see

Wellstead, chapter 2) confront the underlying assumption that power and authority have a state-based territorial logic? The answer to this last question deserves careful reflection—because NSMD governance systems, which are united by transnational supply chains, do not conform to traditional state-centred territorial boundaries.

This chapter addresses these questions by carefully exploring, in the Canadian forest sector, the development of "forest certification," the most advanced case of NSMD governance globally. We focus the bulk of our empirical analysis on British Columbia and the Canadian Maritimes, two regions where debates and interest over forest certification occurred relatively early. We reflect, in the conclusion, on the very different evolution of support for forest certification in other regions in Canada and on the broader lessons for NSMD uptake in general.

EMERGENCE OF FOREST CERTIFICATION AND ITS TWO CONCEPTIONS OF NON-STATE GOVERNANCE

Six key features distinguish NSMD governance from other forms of public and private authority (Cashore 2002; Cashore, Auld, and Newsom 2004; Bernstein and Cashore 2007). The most important feature of NSMD governance is *the lack of state sovereignty used to enforce compliance*. In its place, a private organization develops rules designed to achieve pre-established objectives (sustainable forestry, in the case of forest certification). A second feature of NSMD governance is its institutions constitute governing arenas in which adaptation, inclusion, and learning occur over time and across a wide range of stakeholders. A third is that these systems govern the "social domain" (Ruggie 2004), requiring profit-maximizing firms to undertake costly reforms that they otherwise would not pursue. The fourth is that the various stakeholders, including environmental groups, companies, and landowners, make their own evaluations about whether to grant authority to these new systems. These evaluations are affected or empowered by the fifth key feature of NSMD governance: authority is granted through the market's supply chain. The sixth feature of NSMD governance is the existence of verification procedures designed to ensure the regulated entity actually meets the stated standards. Verification provides the validation necessary for the certification program to achieve legitimacy, because certified products are then demanded and consumed along the market's supply chain. This final feature distinguishes NSMD systems from many forms of corporate social responsibility initiatives that require limited or no outside monitoring (Gunningham, Grabosky, and Sinclair 1998, chapter 4).

A number of key trends have coalesced to produce increasing interest in NSMD governance systems generally and within forestry specifically. The first trend can be traced to the increasing attention placed on a country's foreign markets in an effort to influence domestic policy (Risse-Kappen 1995; Keck and Sikkink 1998), a process Bernstein and Cashore (2000) refer to as "internationalization." Market-based campaigns often deemed these internationalization processes more efficient and effective than attempting to influence domestic business-dominated policy networks directly. The second trend is the increasing interest in the use of voluntary and market mechanisms (Harrison 1999; Tollefson 1998; Prakash 1999; Gun-ningham, Grabosky, and Sinclair 1998; Webb 2002). At the international level, Bernstein (2002) has noted that a norm complex of "liberal environmentalism" has come to permeate international environmental governance, in which propos-als based on traditional command-and-control, "business-versus-environment" approaches rarely make it to the policy agenda (Esty and Geradin 1998). A third trend can be traced to the beginning in the 1980s, when environmental groups and the general public became increasingly concerned about tropical forest de-struction. Boycotts were launched, and a number of forest product retailers, such as B&Q in the United Kingdom, IKEA in Sweden, and The Home Depot in the United States, paid increasing attention to understanding better the *sources* of their fibre and whether their products were harvested in an environmentally friendly manner. The final trend favouring an interest in NSMD environmental gover-nance in the forest sector can be traced to the failure of the 1992 Earth Summit to sign a global forest convention (Humphreys 1996), with the result that little alter-native exists to voluntary regulation in this sector.

Two Conceptions of Forest Certification

In 1992, transnational environmental groups took the lead in creating certification institutions. In the case of forestry, the World Wide Fund for Nature (WWF)[1] spear-headed a coalition of socially concerned environmental groups that joined with select retailers, governmental officials, and a handful of forest company officials to create the international Forest Stewardship Council (FSC). Officially formed in 1993, the FSC turned to the market for rule-making authority, by offering forest landowners and forest companies that practise "sustainable forestry" (in accordance with FSC policies) an environmental stamp of approval through its certification process, thus expanding the traditional "stick" approach of a boycott campaign with the offering of a "carrot."

The FSC created nine principles (later expanded to 10) and more detailed criteria that are performance-based and broad in scope and address tenure and resource use rights, community relations, Indigenous peoples, workers' rights, environmen-tal impact, management plans, monitoring and conservation of old-growth for-ests, and plantation management (Moffatt 1998, 44; Forest Stewardship Council 1999b). The FSC program also mandated the creation of national or regional working groups to develop more specific standards based on the broad principles and criteria.

The FSC program is based on a conception of NSMD governance that sees private-sector certification programs as pushing for more stringent sustainable forest management (SFM) standards, including the requirement for upward environmental and social protection in their actual practices. Perhaps more important than the rules themselves is the "tripartite" FSC conception of governance. A three-chamber format of environmental, social, and economic actors has emerged, with each chamber enjoying equal voting rights. At the international level, each chamber is itself divided equally between North and South representation (Domask 2003).[2]

Much controversy and criticism has been generated by the lumping together in one chamber of the economic interests (that is, companies and non-industrial forest owners) that must implement SFM rules, alongside companies further along the supply chain who might demand FSC products. This contentious situation has negatively affected forest owners' evaluations of the FSC (Sasser 2002; Rametsteiner 1999) and encouraged the development of "FSC alternative" certification programs offered in all countries in North America and Europe where the FSC has been active. In the United States, the American Forest and Paper Association created the Sustainable Forestry Initiative (SFI) certification program. In Canada, the Canadian Standards Association (CSA) program was initiated by the Canadian Sustainable Forestry Certification Coalition, a group of 23 industry associations from across Canada (Lapointe 1998). And in Europe, following the Swedish and Finnish experiences with FSC-style forest certification, an "umbrella" Pan European Forest Certification (PEFC) system (renamed the Programme for the Endorsement of Forest Certification in 2003) was created in 1999 by European landowner associations that felt especially excluded from the FSC processes.

These FSC-competitor programs initially operated under a different conception of NSMD governance from that of the FSC. These alternative programs are grounded in the belief that business interests ought to strongly shape rule-making, with other non-governmental and governmental organizations acting in advisory and consultative capacities. Underlying these programs is a strongly held view that incongruence exists between the quality of current forest practices and civil society's perception of these practices. Under the SFI, CSA, and PEFC conceptions, certification is, in part, a communication tool that allows companies and landowners to better educate civil society (Clapp 1998; Cutler, Haufler, and Porter 1999). These two alternative conceptions of certification are set out in figure 11.1.

EMERGENCE AND SUPPORT FOR FOREST CERTIFICATION IN CANADA

The FSC conception of forest certification first entered the Canadian forest policy community as an idea in the mid-1990s, following the FSC's founding meeting in Toronto in 1993. A national FSC office was officially established in 1996. In addition

Figure 11.1   Conceptions of Forest Sector Non-State, Market-Driven Certification Governance Systems

	Conception one	Conception two
Participants in rule-making	Environmental and social interests and business interests	Business-led
Substantive rules	Non-discretionary	Discretionary–flexible
Procedural rules	Used to facilitate implementation of substantive rules	An end in themselves (based on the belief that procedural rules by themselves will result in decreased environmental impact)
Policy scope	Broad (includes rules on labour and Indigenous rights and wide-ranging environmental impacts)	Narrower (forestry management rules and continual improvement)

Sources: Cashore, B. 2002. Legitimacy and the privatization of environmental governance: How non-state market-driven (NSMD) governance systems gain rule-making authority. *Governance* 15(4): 503–29; Cashore, B., Auld, G., and Newsom, D. 2004. *Governing through markets: Forest certification and the emergence of non-state authority*. New Haven, CT: Yale University Press.

to social, environmental, and economic chambers, a fourth "Aboriginal" chamber was created for national board deliberations and for regional standards-setting processes (Forest Stewardship Council 1999a). However, some time would pass before the FSC idea attracted significant attention in Canada. Instead, industry turned to the second conception of certification, with the Canadian Pulp and Paper Association (CPPA, renamed the Forest Products Association of Canada in 2001) taking a leadership role in creating the Canadian Sustainable Forestry Certification Coalition.[3] The mandate of the latter organization was to create an internationally recognized, third-party certification system for Canadian forest companies. Ultimately, the CPPA approached the Canadian Standards Association, which operates under the rules and discipline of the National Standards System, about creating a CSA forest certification standard (see figure 11.2).

The Canadian Council of Forest Ministers, the Canadian Forest Service, Industry Canada, and most Canadian forest companies gave early support to the CSA certification process, viewing it as a more legitimate alternative to the FSC, which, they hoped, would be adequate to maintain market access (Elliott 1999). Most major environmental groups, along with other social organizations,[4] boycotted the CSA process (Gale and Burda 1997), arguing that the CSA was an effort to reduce the stricter environmental regulations offered by the FSC (von Mirbach 1997), and that the CSA would permit, among other things, continued clear-cutting (Curtis 1995) and the application of chemical pesticides (Greenpeace Canada, Greenpeace International, and Greenpeace San Francisco 1997, 25).

Figure 11.2   Comparison of the Forest Stewardship Council and Its Competitor Programs in Canada, as of 2007

General features	Forest Stewardship Council (FSC)	Sustainable Forestry Initiative (SFI)[a]	Canadian Standards Association (CSA)
Sponsor	Forest Stewardship Council	Original—American Forest and Paper Association Current—Sustainable Forestry Board	Canadian Standards Association
Primary scope	Worldwide	United States and Canada	Canada
Year forestry standard established	1993	1995	1996
Standard development	Committees of stakeholders with public input	SFI board with public input	CSA multi-interest technical committee, including broad stakeholder involvement
Types of standards: performance-based or systems-based[b]	Performance emphasis	Combination	Combination
Chain of custody[c]	Yes	Yes	Yes
Eco-label[d]	Yes	Yes	Yes
Website link	www.fscus.org www.fsc.org	www.aboutsfi.org	http://www.csa-international.org/certification/forestry/

[a] The Sustainable Forestry Initiative (SFI) includes two components: a declaration of key sustainable forestry principles that all members of the American Forest & Paper Association (AF&PA) are required to affirm their commitment to; and a set of detailed standards to which members of the AF&PA and non-members can choose to have their operations certified as being in accordance with. Our review focuses on the certification component of the SFI program.

[b] Performance-based standards refer to programs that focus primarily on the creation of mandatory, on-the-ground rules governing forest management, whereas systems-based standards refer to the development of more flexible and often non-mandatory procedures to address environmental concerns.

[c] Chain of custody refers to the tracking of wood from certified forests along the supply chain to the individual consumer.

[d] An eco-label is used in the supply chain to inform institutional consumers that a specific product is derived from a certified source.

Sources: Cashore, B., Auld, G., and Newsom, D. 2004. *Governing through markets: Forest certification and the emergence of non-state authority*. New Haven, CT: Yale University Press; Hansen, E., Fletcher, R., Cashore, G., and McDermott, C. 2006. *Forest certification in North America*. Corvallis, OR: Oregon State University Extension Service.

FSC supporters responded to these intense efforts to promote a certification alternative with aggressive market-focused strategies targeting European purchasers of Canadian forest products. Drawing on previously successful boycott campaigns, environmental groups were now returning to the same companies to offer them a carrot (public recognition that they were supporting sustainable forest management) alongside their usual stick (the threat of a boycott if they did not comply). Most of these efforts were focused on Germany and the United Kingdom and were promoted by the British Broadcasting Corporation's magazine publishing division; the British home retailer B&Q; and key German companies, such as publisher Springer-Verlag and paper producer Haindl.[5]

In addition to the targeting of individual companies, the World Wide Fund for Nature (WWF) also helped establish "buyers groups" where "environmentally and socially aware" businesses would be recognized by the WWF as supporting environmentally sensitive harvesting practices. The first example was the creation of the WWF 95 group, later renamed the "95 plus group," established in anticipation of the FSC in 1991. By 1997, FSC buyers groups existed in Germany, Belgium, Austria, Switzerland, and the Netherlands (Hansen and Juslin 1999).

As we show in the next section, support from Canadian forest companies has mirrored a pendulum of sorts—with strong and unified support for the CSA dissipating as key companies, including J.D. Irving in the Maritimes (Lawson and Cashore 2001) and six of the top nine industrial companies in BC (Cashore, Auld, and Newsom 2004, chapter 3), direct some serious attention to the FSC. Following standards-setting processes in both regions, however, much of this support, in turn, evaporated, leaving the CSA and SFI as the preferred programs of most companies. However, revealing its highly dynamic processes, the FSC enjoyed a sort of revival in 2004, as industry giant Tembec was joined by Domtar in promoting FSC certification on its forest lands, most of which are located away from the historical battle zones of their competitors in BC and the Maritimes.

THE POLITICS OF FOREST CERTIFICATION: THE BC AND MARITIME CASES

Forest Certification in British Columbia

The British Columbia case is significant because it became a key battleground in which industry and environmental groups pursued their efforts to define and address sustainable forestry regulation through NSMD governance. However, such attention was not preordained or expected; certification was originally deemed of little value among members of the BC forest policy community. The first group to champion forest certification in BC was the Silva Forest Foundation, an organization that fundamentally challenged traditional industrial forestry approaches to forest harvesting and emphasized community-based, smaller-scale, and lower-impact "eco-forestry" harvesting (Gale and Burda 1997).

In these early days, forest certification efforts were poorly funded, receiving little in-kind support from domestic and international environmental groups and no support from US philanthropic foundations that had been the lifeblood of the province's environmental movement. Most environmental groups at this time were focusing mainly on public forest policy in BC, including the effectiveness of the provincial Forest Practices Code (Sierra Legal Defence Fund 1996), which came into effect on June 15, 1995 (British Columbia, Ministry of Forests 1995). However, high-profile environmental organizations, such as Greenpeace, did recognize the value of the FSC, offering its support to the fledgling program in the hopes that such a move might apply further pressure on the BC government and forest companies to reform their forest management practices and policies (Greenpeace n.d.). The idea that BC companies might actually be able to meet FSC's high standards was deemed unlikely.

The initial support and direction of the FSC reinforced the view within most forest companies that if certification were to occur it ought to be through the CSA process (Paget and Morton 1999). The hope was that the CSA program would assure international customers that Canada was working toward sustainability in its forests without having to adhere to the stricter standards promoted by the FSC.[6] Environmental groups, such as Friends of the Earth, Greenpeace, and the Rainforest Action Network, stepped up their media campaigns to criticize BC forest practices and, following what they perceived to be a weakening of BC's Forest Practices Code, began to directly relate their demands that Canadian companies undertake steps toward FSC certification (Paget and Morton 1999; Hansen and Juslin 1999).

By the mid-1990s, the mood within BC forest policy deliberations was one of continued conflict. Environmental groups remained dissatisfied with the provincial government's forest policy initiatives and were unwilling to offer support to the CSA program. They continued pressing international buyers of wood from BC's large vertically integrated firms in the hope that BC companies would modify their forest management practices. However, the FSC principle nine—which addresses the management of high-conservation-value forests—continued to pose problems to BC forest companies that might otherwise have been willing to consider the FSC.

In September 1998, with neither side willing to back down, market efforts expanded through the creation of the Global Forest and Trade Network (GFTN), which was designed to coordinate the activities of the national buyers groups around the world (World Wildlife Fund for Nature 1999). In the United States, the Certified Forest Products Council (CFPC) was launched officially in 1998, merging the former US buyers group with the Good Wood Alliance (ibid.). This development was significant for the BC forest companies, which together sent approximately 73 percent of their softwood products to the US market (Council of Forest Industries 2001). Seeing an important window, market campaigners, led by the San Francisco–based Rainforest Action Network, decided to target much of their efforts on the US do-it-yourself giant, The Home Depot.[7]

The market-based campaigns were further facilitated by focusing on the most vulnerable firms (Stanbury 2000), of which Western Forest Products (WFP), operating on the central coast, was a key target. Initial successes forced BC companies to re-evaluate their previous forest certification choices. For example, the British Broadcasting Corporation, after being informed by Greenpeace UK that some of its products bought from German suppliers (publishers) might be coming from the central coast's Great Bear Rainforest, asked for verification from the German suppliers, who subsequently decided to suspend their contract with WFP.[8]

Faced with intense scrutiny, Western Forest Products became the first company in BC to announce its application for FSC certification (Hayward 1998; Hogben 1998). One industry official called this application a "breaking of ranks" from the previous industry support for only the CSA.[9] And just a week later, MacMillan Bloedel also "broke ranks," announcing its intention to pursue FSC certification (Alden 1998; Tice 1998) and its withdrawal from membership in the Forest Alliance (Hamilton 1998).

These early commitments were undertaken before any changes had been made to the FSC's principle nine, but on the belief, or hope, that after BC standards were developed, the existing practices would suffice. As WFP's chief forester, Bill Dumont, was quoted as saying, "We do not expect in any way to have to make significant changes in our operations" (Hogben 1998, F2).

Two important caveats are in order to describe this period. First, companies in BC were clearly hedging their bets—they had not given up on the CSA approach and could easily turn to support the CSA alone if the market pressure ended. Second, CPPA efforts to support the CSA in European markets had not in any way abated. Still, European buyers continued to view the CSA as unable to satisfy their own certification requirements, including the lack of an international profile. The CSA responded to the latter criticism by joining, and having its approach formally recognized by, the PEFC program. The CSA also addressed its credibility issue by launching a new Forest Products Marking Program, which introduced a chain-of-custody system and a product label (Canadian Standards Association 2001).

By the end of 2001 the FSC in BC was in the rather enviable position of working to maintain key forest company support, as opposed to its previous preoccupation with striving to achieve it. Forest companies were working within the FSC to make it more hospitable to their profit-maximizing goals, whereas environmental groups pressed to keep the standard as high as possible. Despite this rosy picture painted for FSC supporters in BC, the year 2002 would witness what some observers had predicted—increased acrimony between industry and environmental groups over the final draft of the regional standards and a signal from industry actors that their support of the FSC might be short-lived. Produced in the summer of 2001, the final draft standards were crafted by an eight-person technical standards team and were then revised by the working group's steering committee after having been subject to widespread public comment. By a 7–1 margin with Bill Bourgeois (Spalding 2002), the sole industrial forestry representative, voicing his opposition, the committee voted to send the standards to FSC Canada for approval.

These actions led the FSC international office to scramble to put its British Columbia egg back together again. If FSC Canada accepted the standards, it risked losing support from industry in one of the places in the global North that had been most hospitable to FSC-style certification. It also risked sending signals to other potential industry supporters to be very careful before offering support to the FSC.

This conundrum came at a time when the CSA had been given new life. In 2001 the CPPA recreated itself as the Forest Products Association of Canada, hired a new director, moved to the nation's capital, and immediately began to set a path of "rapprochement" with WWF and the Global Forest and Trade Network. Faced with this competition, in January 2003, the FSC proposed a compromise solution for the BC case in which standards would be approved, but subject to revisiting a number of the most controversial rules and to involving forest companies directly in such revisions. Indeed, the FSC report went out of its way to note that a number of the BC standards went "significantly beyond the requirements of the FSC P&C [Principles and Criteria]" (Forest Stewardship Council 2002, 5). In a direct rebuke to the BC regional standards-setting process for moving ahead without industry support, the report asserted that such high standards would require a "higher than normal degree of agreement" (ibid.).

Forest Certification in the Maritimes

In contrast to the situation in BC, forest certification gained support in the Canadian Maritimes among environmental groups who had focused their efforts on domestic-centred processes, with limited efforts or abilities expended in using European markets to influence forest company evaluations. Environmental groups in this region had developed long-standing critiques of industrial forest practices in the Maritimes, particularly regarding the use of biocides (herbicides and pesticides) and the maintenance of naturally functioning ecosystems. However, although the environmental groups had claimed some success in limiting such chemical agents, notably in parts of Nova Scotia, they also perceived limited overall success in influencing the forestry regulations and practices they had criticized. As a result, environmental groups saw the FSC as a new, more hospitable arena in which to both force change and seek redress over their long-standing industrial forestry critiques. They were joined by some small-woodlot owners and Aboriginal groups that were attempting to gain increased access to the forest resource. (The many regional associations representing the region's small woodlot owners were divided over the benefits of certification, but despite their role in supplying industrial operators, leadership of several of these regional bodies had developed a long-standing critique of industrial forestry practices [Lord 2000; Guptill 2000; May 1998; Sandberg 1992].)

However, the Maritimes process *also* involved industrial participation from one of the region's most dominant industrial forest companies, the domestically owned J.D. Irving, Limited (Irving).[10] Irving officials saw the FSC standards as an opportunity to demonstrate to the world and to the marketplace that Irving was indeed practising responsible forestry. In fact, Irving was quite proactive in its support of the FSC, having been in contact with Scientific Certification Systems (SCS) about third-party certification of its practices. A business relationship between Irving and The Home Depot also figured in this period of discussion and reflection, even before the giant retailer committed itself in 1999 to FSC-style certification. Largely owing to its proactive approach, which straddled the Canadian Maritimes and the US northeast, Irving had decided to proceed with FSC certification before a regional standards process had been developed, relying instead on provisional rules developed by its FSC-endorsed auditor, SCS.

These different starting points among the stakeholders meant that although non-industrial stakeholders saw the FSC primarily as a way of offsetting perceived industrial influence over public policy development in forestry matters, Irving saw support of the FSC as a way to have its conception of industrial forestry recognized as environmentally appropriate, including what it asserted to be the responsible use of biocides in intensive forest management.

These two very different conceptions about the role of the FSC explain the ultimate clash during the FSC regional standards-setting process. With limited initial direction[11] from FSC International and FSC Canada regarding how the process itself ought to be structured, the initial regional approach did not immediately adhere to the international "three-chamber" format or to the "four-chamber" format that would later come to be a requirement of Canadian FSC standards-setting processes. Instead, the April 1996 stakeholders' meeting in Truro, Nova Scotia (known within FSC circles as "Truro I"), decided on a nine-group structure, of which only one member came from large industry. Two representatives from each group formed the Technical Standards Writing Committee to draft regional standards and refer them back to a second large meeting.

Although participants agreed to follow a consensus approach, the exact meaning of this resolve remained unclear when it came time to address the key public policy controversies of the preceding two decades. On one side, Irving felt isolated from the non-industrial interests; on the other side, environmental groups and their supporters felt, similarly, that Irving was being intransigent. Over more than two years, the Technical Standards Writing Committee met monthly for two- to three-day sessions. Step by step, the least controversial aspects of the draft standards were developed and refined, but the most important controversies that had dominated the public policy-making processes were not resolved. Public consultation meetings were held in August and November 1997 and again in May 1998: the initial turnouts seemed to indicate considerable interest from the general forest-policy community, including economic interests. On June 23, 1998, a second review meeting was held (known as "Truro II"). Fewer industrial interests attended this meeting, while the industry, championed by J.D. Irving, felt increased frustration at its lack of influence.

The FSC Maritime Regional Steering Committee then met to reconsider its standards, with environmental groups and their allies announcing that a consensus had now been reached among all participants on biocides (sections 6.6.1 and 10.7.2), exotics (section 6.9.2), and conversions (section 10.1.1) (Duinker 1999, 47). Although debates long continued between the two sides about whether a fleeting consensus had indeed been achieved at this meeting (Boetekess, Moore, and Weber 2000, 29–30), the next day, Irving's chief forester, Blake Brundson, made it clear that he, and by implication Irving, could not support the standards.

At this point, J.D. Irving faced a dilemma. It had just earned a precedent-setting industrial certification at its Black Brook site under the Scientific Certification Standards. The choice of Black Brook as the lead site for certification was significant. It had been known for years for its intensive industrial forest management, in which the use of biocides and the conversion of logged sites to single-species stands were key components. Irving faced two choices: adhere to the new, stricter FSC regional standards to maintain its FSC certification, or launch a final attempt to convince FSC Canada and FSC International that its current practices should be FSC-certified. Deeming the draft standards so costly to its operations that the costs of adherence would outweigh any economic and social-licence benefits, Irving reasoned that its only chance to stick with the FSC lay in attempting the latter route. Such a strategy would not be easy. Shocked by FSC approval of the Black Brook site, the Sierra Club of Canada immediately appealed, reasoning that FSC certification of the site would entrench FSC acceptance of the very forest practices against which it and other environmentalists had spent decades campaigning.

This time, Irving's efforts to seek redress at the Canadian FSC national level failed, mirroring dynamics similar to those in the BC case. With strong dissent from Tembec, the lone industrial representative at the FSC national level, the majority of board members voted to pass the draft standards to FSC International for consideration and approval, while requesting advice from FSC International on the controversial biocides standards (Boetekess, Moore, and Weber 2000, 4).

Irving simultaneously appealed to FSC International to have the FSC Canada approval overturned, registering formal complaints about the Maritimes process (Boetekess, Moore, and Weber 2000, 4; Duinker 1999, 49). As with the BC situation, the FSC International officials knew they faced a conundrum: how to maintain one of their biggest industrial supporters in the Canadian Maritimes and the US northeast without alienating some of their most committed environmental and social stakeholders.

The FSC International attempted to strike a delicate balance in two ways: it provided conditional approval for the standards in January 1999, but it also required the Canadian office to address Irving's appeal. Preconditions for the approval included requirements that (1) standards would have to be "harmonized" with the standards of other FSC regions; and (2) a number of specific procedural requirements in the standards, including those for biocide use, would have to be re-examined (Synnott 1999). The FSC International executive director was to assess the results in three months' time. According to FSC International, any biocide standards that remained different from FSC standards elsewhere would have to be supported by "significant agreement by all relevant stakeholder groups" (Synnott 1999, 1) and even then, such standards would be reviewed after two years. In the background of this requirement was Irving's simultaneous participation in the FSC's US northeast process, which had generated less controversial standards in these subject areas. Conflict now arose within the Maritimes about whether "significant agreement" could be met *without* specific support from industry, because the other economic representative involved with the FSC Maritimes, the owner of a small private woodlot, had tended to resist the initiative. Whereas a number of revisions were made to the draft standards, efforts to gain industrial support for the final standards ultimately failed, owing largely to continuing disagreements about the use of biocides. Faced with essentially the same dilemma in September 1999 that it had repeatedly faced during the spring and summer, the FSC regional process did not find any new solution to the fundamental structural and policy issues. Meanwhile, the FSC national office's dispute resolution process, for the most part, ruled against Irving's appeal.

Recognizing that this ruling could be the last straw for Irving and would likely undermine general efforts to obtain industrial support for the FSC, FSC International officials undertook three strategic overtures. First, they initiated reforms to representation and decision-making requirements in the region that they believed would strike a new balance in future power relationships among participating stakeholders (Synnott 1999; Boetekess, Moore, and Weber 2000, 39; Duinker 1999, 1, 49). Second, they commissioned a leading forest academic from the region, Peter Duinker, to report on whether the Maritimes Regional Steering Committee had reached the level of agreement FSC International had required of it, notably on the biocides issue. (Duinker [1999, 51–52] reported in November that, given Irving's dissent, the committee had not reached agreement.) Third, the FSC International officials proposed that on the most controversial issue—the use of biocides—companies would have to make a clear commitment to phase out biocides, but they would *not be required to meet an explicit time frame*. Within the tight constraints that now limited its actions, FSC International was clearly trying to show its best face to industry in general and to Irving in particular. Its denial of the Sierra Club's appeal of the Black Brook certification—on the grounds that key appeal documents had been filed late—coincided with these efforts, and was also seen by some as an attempt to accommodate industrial concerns.

The efforts at compromise pleased no one. On December 29, 1999, nine days after the FSC International endorsed the regional standards, Irving publicly broke with the FSC Maritimes process, returning its Black Brook certification and characterizing the Maritimes Regional Steering Committee as unrepresentative and biased (Brunsdon 1999; Canadian Broadcasting Corporation 1999). Observers initially wrote of a crisis with implications for the FSC well beyond the Maritimes region, though subsequent assessments were less alarmed (Boetekess, Moore, and Weber 2000, 57). The international leadership of the FSC moved rapidly in January to investigate events to that point, to renegotiate controversial elements of the standards, and to reorganize its Maritimes section (Johansson and Synnott 2000).

Although many FSC supporters in the Maritimes continue to seek a reconciliation with Irving, the relationship appears to have been permanently damaged. Irving has remained disconnected from the FSC Maritimes process, and despite FSC overtures toward it, Irving ultimately withdrew its support for the FSC in the US northeast, which operated under more flexible rules (Cashore and Lawson 2003). More recently, the Canadian Maritimes Standards have undergone major revisions, in part to ensure that standards addressed the situation of both large- and small-scale operators (Forest Stewardship Council 2007b).

CONCLUSIONS: NON-STATE GOVERNANCE

Wellstead's analysis (see chapter 2, under the heading "Defining the Staples State") revealed that traditional "minimal," "emergent," "Keynesian," and "competitive" categories of the staples-state literature have been confronted by a new era of post-staples state policy analyses denoted by a decline of state sovereignty (Jessop 2002). However, significant conceptual problems continue to exist within this literature because it has yet to analyze NSMD governance as an arena of authority *outside* of existing state-centred approaches. Whether certification systems are ultimately subsumed by some form of traditional public policy or become enduring features of NSMD governance that could replace or compete with traditional state authority is one of the most critical questions facing students of a post-staples state and policy development. This chapter has contributed to such a study by carefully reviewing the key features that constitute NSMD governance and discussing whether and how NSMD systems might come to gain widespread support among societal interests and the industrial staples extractors they seek to regulate.

Our review of the British Columbia and Maritimes experiences with certification reveals strong interest in the structure and form of NSMD governance, but uncertainty on the part of industry about whether adhering to the FSC principles—the main advantage of which was the support that would be engendered from most domestic and transnational environmental groups—would, for the same reasons, impose costs, both in terms of the level of behavioural change and the uncertainty that accompanies industry's relatively limited influence over the policy-making process. Strikingly, as industrial companies in these regions came to feel marginalized by the FSC process, they did not abandon the idea of NSMD at all, but turned to alternative programs.

Where the competition between the FSC and its competitors will head is far from preordained. In recognition of its members' ambivalence about which certification program to join, and their nearly unanimous support for NSMD governance, the Forest Products Association of Canada (FPAC) announced in 2003 that its members would be required to undergo independent third-party certification of their forestry operations by 2006, leaving open to individual companies whether they supported the FSC, the CSA, or the SFI (FPAC certification requirement applauded 2002).

Because FPAC granted its members the option to choose their certification program, and FSC strategists increasingly recognized that its standards ought to be consistent with a positive cost–benefit analysis, in regions outside of BC and the Maritimes, FSC standards development processes, and firms' support of them, have taken different directions from the trends noted above. For example, in 2003, eastern Canadian giant Domtar decided to join Tembec in pursuing FSC certification (Auld 2006; Canada NewsWire 2003), giving new life to support for the FSC in Canada. As part of its efforts to engage environmental groups, including the innovative Boreal Accord (Canadian Boreal Initiative 2003), Domtar made the strategic choice that the goodwill and market-access issues associated with FSC certification made its support worthwhile. And with environmental groups and other FSC supporters "learning" from the BC and Maritimes experiences, all parties seem intent on finding a negotiated solution to FSC boreal forest standards.

Illustrative of FSC standards-setting processes representing commercial interests to a greater degree than had been perceived in BC and the Maritimes, Alberta forestry giant Alberta-Pacific stunned forestry circles by becoming FSC-certified in 2005 (Alberta-Pacific 2005). The large-scale FSC certifications also paved the way for meeting market demands in the United States, where environmental activists, such as ForestEthics, launched successful campaigns to have Limited Brands (which produces millions of catalogues through operation of its retail brand Victoria's Secret) agree to use FSC-certified paper.

As a result of these trends, the Canadian forest sector contained, as of October 2007, more than 18.5 million hectares of FSC-certified forests, representing 20 percent of the FSC global total and more certified forest land than any other country

(Forest Stewardship Council 2007a). And reflecting the increasingly global dimensions over the emergence of NSMD, the two key North American certification programs, the CSA and the SFI, each announced in 2005 that they had been formally recognized by the PEFC—a crucial step in entrenching forest-industry and forest-owner association efforts to create a credible global alternative to the FSC.

Given these trends, what is the future of NSMD governance as an entrenched system of private authority that simultaneously enjoys support from firms and addresses global forest degradation? The answer, we suspect, rests, in part, on where the environmental activists view forest certification's biggest impact (Cashore et al. 2007). For example, do supporters see the FSC as primarily useful for influencing a country's domestic forestry debates; or more important for its indirect effects, as a lever to improve forest practices elsewhere? That is, it matters very much in the early days of NSMD "institutionalization" (Bernstein and Cashore 2007) whether certification is used as a baseline for improving forest practices in some of the most critically sensitive, yet under-regulated forests, such as in the tropics, or as a gold standard that few firms operating anywhere would actually be able to meet. In the former case we would expect, and as is consistent with the empirical record in Canada, that those firms that are relatively highly regulated will support FSC certification, in the hopes that their endorsement might pressure their less regulated competitors to improve their forestry practices. In the latter case we would expect FSC certification to remain in a "niche" phase, with widespread support occurring through industry-initiated alternative programs.

For students of the Canadian staples state, then, understanding where certification is headed is imperative, as is a familiarity with the potential effects of NSMD in regulating extractive industries. Clearly, from the above review, for NSMD systems to gain support, the market benefits must be evaluated as higher than the increased costs of compliance. Thus, in the short run, NSMD systems cannot require standards that impose higher costs than the economic benefits—otherwise these systems risk placing forest companies at a competitive disadvantage. However, in the long run, the more that NSMD systems gain support and recognition and become "accepted" practices by all or most firms, the more these governance systems will be able to develop more holistic and comprehensive requirements, which would render them an essential component of the very mature or post-staples state.

NOTES

* This paper draws on a more detailed analysis in Governing Through Markets: Forest Certification and the Emergence of Non-State Authority (Cashore, Auld, and Newsom 2004). Much of the research for this project originated from a wide range of personal interviews in Europe and North America. For brevity, we limit direct citations to these research interviews. We are grateful to Steven Bernstein, whose collaborative work on a related project has greatly improved our analysis.

1. Known as World Wildlife Fund in Canada and the United States.

2. Originally the FSC created two chambers: one with social and environmental interests that was given 70 percent of the voting weight, and an economic chamber with 30 percent of the votes. Currently, three equal chambers among these groups have one-third of the votes each. Each chamber is further divided equally between the North and the South. Two objectives prompted this institutional design. The first objective was to prevent business dominance in policy-making processes, justified in the belief that limiting business influence would facilitate the development of relatively stringent standards and facilitate on-the-ground implementation. The second was to ensure that the North does not dominate at the expense of the South—a strong criticism of the failed efforts at the Rio Earth Summit to achieving a binding global forest convention (Domask 2003; Meidinger 1997, 2000).

3. BC members of the coalition included the BC Pulp and Paper Association, the Council of Forest Industries, and the Interior Lumber Manufacturers' Association (Canadian Sustainable Forestry Certification Coalition 2000).

4. This group included, among others, the Confederation of Canadian Unions; the Pulp, Paper and Woodworkers of Canada Union; the Union of BC Indian Chiefs; the Canadian Environmental Law Association; and Greenpeace Canada.

5. From personal interviews with senior officials of Haindl, Augsburg, Germany, May 4, 2001.

6. At this time, federal and provincial agencies offered funding and technical support to assist in correcting what they asserted to be "misinformation" distributed by environmental groups about BC forest companies (Greenpeace Canada, Greenpeace International, and Greenpeace San Francisco 1997, 20–25; British Columbia, Ministry of Forests 1998). Reflecting their trade-oriented mission, Canadian embassy officials in Europe played a key role, setting up meetings where local buyers were invited to presentations by executives from BC forest companies and government officials. From a personal interview with an official at the Canadian High Commission, London, England, April 25, 2001.

7. These developments occurred alongside the parallel market campaign led by Greenpeace to force logging companies to stop harvesting in BC's central coast region. The central coast campaign focused on MacMillan Bloedel (now Weyerhaeuser), Western Forest Products (WFP), and International Forest Products International (Interfor), which were all suffering economically owing to their reliance on the collapsed Asian markets and their inability to move more products into the US market owing to the Canada–US Softwood Lumber Agreement (SLA) quota system,

which rendered FSC European market strategies even more effective on BC companies than they might otherwise have been.

8. From a personal interview with a senior official, British Broadcasting Corporation Magazine, London, England, July 3, 2001.

9. From personal interviews with a senior official, Forest Alliance of British Columbia, Vancouver, Canada, September 19, 2000, and with a senior official, British Columbia Council of Forest Industries, Vancouver, Canada, September 1, 2000.

10. In addition to Irving, GPI*Atlantic* and BA Fraser Lumber Ltd. had expressed early interest in the FSC standards network.

11. FSC Canada's central office was still in its organizational stages during most of the initial Maritimes drafting process.

REFERENCES

Alberta-Pacific. 2005. *Alberta-Pacific awarded Forest Stewardship Council certification* (news release). Online at http://www.alpac.ca/index.cfm?id=newsreleases.

Alden, E. 1998. MacMillan Bloedel bows to the pressure from Greenpeace: The company is to stop clear-cut logging in British Columbia. *Financial Times*, June 19: 28.

Auld, G. 2006. Choosing how to be green: An examination of Domtar Inc.'s approach to forest certification. *Journal of Strategic Management Education* 3: 37–92.

Bernstein, S. 2002. *The compromise of liberal environmentalism*. New York: Columbia University Press.

Bernstein, S., and Cashore, B. 2000. Globalization, four paths of internationalization and domestic policy change: The case of eco-forestry in British Columbia, Canada. *Canadian Journal of Political Science* 33(1): 67–99.

Bernstein, S., and Cashore, B. 2007. Can non-state global governance be legitimate? An analytical framework. *Regulation & Governance* 4(1): 347–71.

Boetekess, G., Moore, K., and Weber, G. 2000. Forest stewardship standards for the Maritime forest region, Commission of Enquiry: Final Report. Oaxaca, Mexico: FSC-International.

British Columbia, Ministry of Forests. 1995. BC's Forest Practices Code: A living process—1995. Online at http://www.for.gov.bc.ca/tasb/legsregs/fpc/pubs/alivingprocess/process.htm.

British Columbia, Ministry of Forests. 1998. Inaccurate environmental ad hurts B.C. communities (news release). Online at http://www.for.gov.bc.ca/pscripts/pab/newsrel/mofnews.asp?refnum=1998%3A094&searchtext=.

Brunsdon, B. 1999. Chief forester responds to FSC approval of Maritime regional standards (news release, December 29). Online at http://jdirving.com/Index.asp?Site_Id=1&Page_Id=316.

Canada NewsWire. 2003. Domtar-WWF-Canada partnership leads to groundbreaking FSC certification effort. *Canada NewsWire Ltd.*, November 14.

Canadian Boreal Initiative. 2003. *The boreal forest at risk: A progress report*. Ottawa: Canadian Boreal Initiative.

Canadian Broadcasting Corporation. 1999. Irving opts out of green plan. Online at http://www.cbc.ca/news/story/1999/12/29/nb_mh_green_122899.html.

Canadian Standards Association (CSA). 2001. CSA International launches forest product marking program. Toronto: CSA.

Canadian Sustainable Forestry Certification Coalition. 2000. Canadian Forest Management Certification status report: Company info. *Bulletin: Sustainable Forestry* 6(1): 4.

Cashore, B. 2002. Legitimacy and the privatization of environmental governance: How non-state market-driven (NSMD) governance systems gain rule-making authority. *Governance* 15(4): 503–29.

Cashore, B., Auld, G., Bernstein, S., and McDermott, C. 2007. Can non-state governance "ratchet up" global environmental standards? Lessons from the forest sector. *Review of European Community and International Environmental Law* 16(2): 158–72.

Cashore, B., Auld, G., and Newsom, D. 2004. *Governing through markets: Forest certification and the emergence of non-state authority.* New Haven, CT: Yale University Press.

Cashore, B., and Lawson, L. 2003. Private policy networks and sustainable forestry policy: Comparing forest certification experiences in the US northeast and the Canadian Maritimes. *Canadian American Public Policy,* Series No. 53. Orono, ME: Canadian–American Center, University of Maine.

Clapp, J. 1998. The privatization of global environmental governance: ISO 14000 and the developing world. *Environmental Governance* 4(3): 295–316.

Council of Forest Industries. 2001. *Fact book 2000.* Online at http://www.cofi.org/library_and_resources/statistics/factbooks/factbook2000.htm.

Curtis, M. 1995. Battle rages over arbiter of wood product labeling. *Victoria Times Colonist,* October 19: B4.

Cutler, C., Haufler, V., and Porter, T. 1999. Private authority and international affairs. In *Private Authority and International Affairs,* eds. C. Cutler, V. Haufler, and T. Porter, 3–28. New York: State University of New York Press.

Domask, J. 2003. From boycotts to partnership: NGOs, the private sector, and the world's forests. In *Globalization and NGOs: Transforming Business, Governments, and Society,* eds. J.P. Doh and H. Teegen, 157–86. New York: Praeger.

Duinker, P. 1999. *What is "significant agreement" in the context of FSC preconditions?* Halifax: Forest Stewardship Council.

Elliott, C. 1999. Forest certification: Analysis from a policy network perspective. Doctoral thesis, Département de génie rural, Ecole Polytechnique Fédérale de Lausanne, Lausanne, Switzerland.

Esty, D.C., and Geradin, D. 1998. Environmental protection and international competitiveness: A conceptual framework. *Journal of World Trade* 32(3): 5–46.

Forest Stewardship Council. 1999a. Forest Stewardship Council regional certification standard for British Columbia. Nelson, BC: Forest Stewardship Council.

Forest Stewardship Council. 1999b. FSC principles and criteria: Forest Stewardship Council. Nelson, BC: Forest Stewardship Council.

Forest Stewardship Council. 2002. *Staff report on BC standards.* Toronto: Forest Stewardship Council, Canada.

Forest Stewardship Council. 2007a. FSC certified forests. Online at http://www.fsc.org/keepout/en/content_areas/92/1/files/2007_10_08_FSC_Certified_Forests.pdf.

Forest Stewardship Council. 2007b. Maritime standard revision process. Online at http://www.fsccanada.org/maritimerevision.htm.

FPAC certification requirement applauded. 2002. *The Hill Times,* May 6.

Gale, F., and Burda, C. 1997. The pitfalls and potential of eco-certification as a market incentive for sustainable forest management. In *The Wealth of Forests: Markets, Regulation and Sustainable Forestry,* ed. C. Tollefson, 414–41. Vancouver: University of British Columbia Press.

Greenpeace. n.d. Just did it! The Vernon model of ecologically responsible forestry: Canada's first eco-certified forest—Clearcut-free? Vancouver: Greenpeace.

Greenpeace Canada, Greenpeace International, and Greenpeace San Francisco. 1997. *Broken promises: The truth about what's happening to British Columbia's forests.* Vancouver: Greenpeace Canada, Greenpeace International, Greenpeace San Francisco.

Gunningham, N., Grabosky, P., and Sinclair, D., eds. 1998. *Smart regulation: Designing environmental policy.* Oxford: Clarendon Press.

Guptill, M. 2000. The theory and practice of field forestry. In *Against the Grain: Foresters and Politics in Nova Scotia,* eds. L.A. Sandberg and P. Clancy, 240–70. Vancouver: University of British Columbia Press.

Hamilton, G. 1998. MacBlo decides to abandon pro-logging forest alliance. *Vancouver Sun,* August 18.

Hansen, E., Fletcher, R., Cashore, G., and McDermott, C. 2006. *Forest certification in North America.* Corvallis, OR: Oregon State University Extension Service.

Hansen, E., and Juslin, H. 1999. *Geneva timber and forest discussion papers: The status of forest certification in the ECE region.* New York and Geneva: United Nations Economic Commission for Europe and Food and Agriculture Organization of the United Nations.

Harrison, K. 1999. Racing to the top or the bottom? Industry resistance to eco-labelling of paper products in three jurisdictions. *Environmental Politics* 8(4): 110–36.

Hayward, J. 1998. Certifying industrial forestry in BC: European market drives big timber to the FSC. *Understory* 8(4): 1, 6–9.

Hogben, D. 1998. Western seeks certification to satisfy European buyers. *Vancouver Sun,* June 5: F2.

Humphreys, D. 1996. NGOs and regime theory: The case of forest conservation. *Journal of Commonwealth and Comparative Politics* 23(1): 90–115.

Jessop, B. 2002. *The future of the capitalist state.* Cambridge, UK: Blackwell.

Johansson, O., and Synnott, T. 2000. Statement on the FSC endorsement of the Maritime regional standards, Canada. Online at http://www.fscus.org/news/?article=256.

Keck, M.E., and Sikkink, K. 1998. *Activists beyond borders: Advocacy networks in international politics.* Ithaca, NY: Cornell University Press.

Lapointe, G. 1998. Sustainable forest management certification: The Canadian programme. *The Forestry Chronicle* 74(2): 227–30.

Lawson, J., and Cashore, B. 2001. Firm choices on sustainable forestry forest certification: The case of JD Irving Lumber Company. In *Forest Policy for Private Forestry*, eds. B.C.L. Teeter and D. Zhang, 245–58. Wallingford, UK: CABI.

Lord, R. 2000. Forestry and landowner organizations. In *Against the Grain: Foresters and Politics in Nova Scotia*, eds. L.A. Sandberg and P. Clancy, 201–39. Vancouver: University of British Columbia Press.

May, E. 1998. *At the cutting edge: The crisis in Canada's forests*, 78–110. Toronto: Key Porter Books.

Meidinger, E.E. 1997. Look who's making the rules: International environmental standard setting by non-governmental organizations. *Human Ecology Review* 4(1): 52–54.

Meidinger, E.E. 2000. *Incorporating environmental certification systems in North American legal systems.* Buffalo: University of Buffalo.

Moffat, A.C. 1998. *Forest certification: An examination of the compatibility of the Canadian Standards Association and Forest Stewardship Council systems in the Maritime region.* Halifax: MES, Environmental Studies, Dalhousie University.

Paget, G., and Morton, B. 1999. Forest certification and "radical" forest stewardship in British Columbia, Canada: The influence of corporate environmental procurement. Paper presented at Greening of Industry Network Conference, Kenan-Flagler Business School, University of North Carolina, Chapel Hill.

Prakash, A. 1999. A new-institutional perspective on ISO 14000 and responsible care. *Business Strategy and the Environment* 8(6): 322–35.

Rametsteiner, E. 1999. The attitude of European consumers toward forests and forestry. *Unasylva* 50(196): 42–48.

Risse-Kappen, T., ed. 1995. *Bringing transnational relations back in: Non-state actors, domestic structures and international institutions.* Cambridge: Cambridge University Press.

Ruggie, J.G. 2004. Reconstituting the global public domain: Issues, actors, and practices. *European Journal of International Relations* 10(4): 499–531.

Sandberg, L.A., ed. 1992. *Trouble in the woods: Forest policy and social conflict in Nova Scotia and New Brunswick.* Fredericton, NB: Acadiensis Press.

Sasser, E.N. 2002. The certification solution: NGO promotion of private, voluntary self-regulation. Paper read at 74th annual meeting of the Canadian Political Science Association, May 29–31, Toronto.

Sierra Legal Defence Fund. 1996. *British Columbia's clear cut code: Changing the way we manage our forests? Tough enforcement.* Vancouver: Sierra Legal Defence Fund.

Spalding, S. 2002. An assessment of the utility, usability and cost implications associated with the Forest Stewardship Council Regional Certification Standards for British Columbia (Draft 3 April 22, 2002) when applied to large-scale forestry operations.

In *For Bill Bourgeois, FSC-BC Steering Committee, In cooperation with Canfor (IFS), Tembec, Weyerhaeuser (Timberline)*. Vancouver.

Stanbury, W.T. 2000. *Environmental groups and the international conflict over the forest of British Columbia, 1990 to 2000*. Vancouver: Simon Fraser University–University of British Columbia Centre for the Study of Government and Business.

Synnott, T. 1999. Letter to James Drescher and Marcelo Levy. Subject: Maritime standards (December 20). In *Certification Standards for Best Forestry Practices in the Maritime Forest Region: Canadian Maritime Regional Initiative of the Canadian FSC Working Group*, appendix IV. n.p.: FSC Working Group.

Tice, C. 1998. MacMillan Bloedel to end clearcutting. *National Home Center News* 24(13): 17.

Tollefson, C., ed. 1998. *The wealth of forests: Markets, regulation, and sustainable forestry*, 2 vols. Vancouver: University of British Columbia Press.

von Mirbach, M. 1997. Demanding good wood. *Alternatives Journal* 23(3): 10–17.

Webb, K, ed. 2002. *Voluntary codes: Private governance, the public interest and innovation*. Ottawa: Carleton University Research Unit Innovation, Science and the Environment.

World Wildlife Fund for Nature. 1999. *WWF's global forests and trade initiative*. Washington, DC: World Wildlife Fund United States.

PART V

Transmission Industries: Oil & Gas and Water

CHAPTER 12

The New Oil Order: The Staples Paradigm and the Canadian Upstream Oil and Gas Industry

Keith Brownsey

INTRODUCTION

It is the best of times for the Canadian upstream oil and gas industry. As natural gas and crude oil prices have risen, the upstream petroleum industry—the exploration and production companies—has seen its profits and stock value increase dramatically (Polczer 2007). Domestic exploration is at unprecedented levels, and investment in conventional and non-conventional oil and gas production has reached new heights.

The issues facing the oil patch, however, have changed dramatically from earlier years. Far from concerns about industrial expansion and transportation of ever-larger amounts of energy to foreign markets which characterized the heyday of the industry, new debates focus on the impact of the Kyoto Protocol, demands for greater environmental controls, overseas competition, market access, and increasing fiscal scrutiny, augmented by concerns over skilled labour shortages, Aboriginal land claims, regulatory reform, and growing consumer unrest with high fuel costs. This new agenda indicates the start if not the completion of a shift in the Canadian oil and gas sector—a transition that can be described as development from a staples industry to a mature staples industry, and perhaps even some aspects of a post-staples industry.

Although the current problems facing the oil patch are significant, they reflect an industry that has matured and found its place within an advanced industrial economy. No sudden break signalled the end of the traditional staples model of development that characterized the post–Second World War evolution of Canada's petroleum sector. Instead, the transition has taken decades, beginning with the realization in the 1960s that Canada and especially the western sedimentary basin contained a finite amount of conventional crude oil and natural gas reserves. This realization has culminated in a technologically advanced, capital-intensive industry with secure and expanding markets.

THE CANADIAN OIL PATCH: FROM CONVENTIONAL TO UNCONVENTIONAL SOURCES OF ENERGY

Canadian oil production in 2006 amounted to 2.6 million barrels per day (mbl/d) or 3.8 percent of the world's total petroleum production. Of this total, approximately 1.4 mbl/d was in conventional oil and 1.2 mbl/d was in non-conventional production from the oil sands. Sixty-eight percent of production is located in Alberta. Over the last several years, the production of conventional crude has declined by about 5 percent. As the production of conventional crude oil has decreased, non-conventional production has increased. The western sedimentary basin has the largest oil sands resources in the world. An estimated 174 billion barrels (bbl) of crude are recoverable from the oil sands with today's technology, with estimates of 315 bbl of potential resources.

Located in Alberta and Saskatchewan, oil production from raw bitumen—the oil sands and heavy oil—exceeded conventional oil production for the first time in 2001. Taking these non-conventional sources into account, Canadian reserves compare very favourably with Saudi Arabian reserves, estimated at 261.1 bbl (Alberta Energy and Utilities Board 2004, 50–51). At the end of 2006, only 2 percent of established crude bitumen reserves had been produced.[1]

Since the mid-1970s, Canada's conventional reserves of crude oil have continued to decline. With reserves estimated at an ultimate potential of 19.7 bbl and annual production of 1.4 mbl/d in 2000, at current rates of production Alberta's supplies of conventional crude will run out sometime around 2060. But as the demand for oil increases in the next decade, Alberta's conventional reserves are likely to deplete long before this date. Although conventional oil production will continue to decline, the provincial energy regulatory agency, the Alberta Energy and Utilities Board (EUB) estimates that production of bitumen will triple by 2011. This figure would then account for as much as 75 percent of Alberta's total oil supply.

Approximately $85 billion of investment has been announced for the oil sands since 1996. This investment is expected to double the current production of oil in Alberta and Saskatchewan. Moreover, at the current rate of depletion of 1.2 mbl/d, approximately 400 years of production remain in the tar sands. The future of the western sedimentary basin's oil and gas industry rests with the production of oil from bitumen reserves (Alberta Energy and Utilities Board 2004, 50–51). Although this amount is significant for domestic and North American production, the total ultimate reserves of heavy oil and the tar sands would extend current world consumption patterns less than a decade beyond the current estimates.

Natural gas reserves in Alberta are estimated at 40 trillion cubic feet (tcf) of marketable reserves. New drilling has not replaced natural gas production since 1982, and in 2003 production outstripped additions by about 4 percent (Alberta Energy and Utilities Board 2004, 52). Natural gas reserve estimates do not include coalbed methane, which, according to the Alberta Energy and Utilities Board, has the potential to add significantly to Canada's reserves. If this projection is correct, gas supply could be revised upward by a considerable amount.

The price of a barrel of oil in Alberta (and Canada) is determined in the global market and is measured in US dollars at the benchmark West Texas Intermediate (WTI) price level. Oil prices rose to more than US$85 per barrel in 2007. At these price levels, the oil and gas industry has an enormous impact on Alberta's economy. In 2006–7, the oil patch generated $12.3 billion in royalties, leases, and other taxes for the province, which was 32 percent of total provincial revenues. Approximately 275,000 individuals are directly and indirectly employed in the Alberta petroleum industry—about 20 percent of the provincial workforce. The Alberta oil and gas industry also contributes to Canada's trade surplus—especially with the United States (Canadian Association of Petroleum Producers 2004; Alberta Energy 2007, 13).[2]

Canada-wide, about 230,000 additional jobs have been created in both service-sector and manufacturing employment to provide goods and services for the industry. Although exports of petroleum products—mainly to the United States—are partly offset by crude oil imports into the eastern provinces, Canada still produces more oil and gas than it consumes. About 1.7 million barrels of crude oil per day, worth nearly $39 billion annually, were exported to the United States—most of it from Alberta. In 2006, natural gas production averaged 17.1 billion cubic feet per day (bcf/d) and generated about $27.5 billion in annual export revenues (Canada, National Energy Board 2007). Again, most natural gas exports originate in Alberta.

Supply projections indicate that total Canadian conventional crude oil reserves will be substantially depleted by 2025. Non-conventional reserves, the Atlantic offshore area, and the North are now the focus of energy planning in Canada (for the latter two, see Clancy, chapter 13). Although Canada's conventional reserves of oil and natural gas in the western sedimentary basin are in decline and are expected to be depleted within 40 years, extraction of the reserves of heavy oil and the tar sands will allow the oil patch to maintain and expand current levels of production, investment, and employment. Since 1994, light crude production has increased in British Columbia and Saskatchewan, remained constant in Manitoba, and declined by approximately 4 percent a year in Alberta. Because Alberta accounts for 75 percent of total production of light crude, the combined effect on the western sedimentary basin has been a decrease in production of about 3 percent each year.

The other major reserves of oil and gas include the Northern Frontier, the Scotian Shelf, and the East Coast Frontier. The Northern Frontier includes the Mackenzie Delta/Beaufort Sea area and the Arctic Islands. Estimates for natural gas in the Mackenzie Delta/Beaufort Sea area are 9 tcf of discovered resources, 55 tcf of undiscovered potential in natural gas, and 161 million cubic metres of oil reserves. The Arctic islands and other areas are estimated to contain 15 tcf of discovered and an estimated 90 tcf of undiscovered resources of natural gas and 65 million cubic metres of oil reserves. The Scotian Shelf (Sable Island) has estimated reserves of 3 tcf and discovered reserves of 2 tcf of natural gas and 11 million cubic metres of oil reserves. The East Coast Frontier of the Grand Banks and Labrador contain 9 tcf of natural gas and 251 million cubic metres in oil reserves (Canada, National Energy Board 1999, 62–64).

THE EVOLUTION OF THE CANADIAN OIL AND GAS INDUSTRY

Although currently largely based in Alberta, the oil and gas industry likes to think of itself as being national in scope. The theme of the Canadian Association of Petroleum Producers (CAPP) 2002 Annual General Meeting was "The Canadian Industry." Three premiers attended the annual general meeting and dinner: Stephen Kakfwi of the Northwest Territories, Gordon Campbell of British Columbia, and Ralph Klein of Alberta. A fourth premier, John Hamm of Nova Scotia, sent a video message. Each speaker described the oil and gas industry in Canada-wide terms. Nevertheless, the fact that the CAPP meeting was held in Calgary indicates the importance of Calgary and Alberta to the oil and gas industry in Canada. Despite an increase in production in the east coast offshore area and in Saskatchewan, British Columbia, and the North, Alberta still dominates the industry.

The history of Canada's oil and gas industry reveals a struggle between competing levels of government for control of the provincial petroleum industry. Under section 109 of the *Constitution Act, 1867*, the provinces have jurisdictional authority over natural resources. But the constitution also assigns jurisdiction over interprovincial and international trade and other powers to the federal government, and Ottawa has used its authority to play a significant role in the oil patch. The best-known example of federal involvement in the oil and gas sector was the 1980 National Energy Program. Although Ottawa continued to play a significant role in the oil patch through its regulatory agency, the National Energy Board, deregulation in the mid-1980s diminished its presence in the oil patch. However, the September 2002 announcement by Liberal Prime Minister Jean Chrétien that the Kyoto Protocol would be ratified and implemented signalled a renewed federal presence in the Canadian petroleum industry. Ottawa's efforts to re-regulate the oil and gas industry through an international environmental treaty caused a federal–provincial debate over jurisdiction of natural resources and the federal government's international treaty obligations. This time, however, Ottawa pursued a type of negotiative horizontal environmental regulation as opposed to the more traditional "command and control" economic regulation. Although the effects of this type of rule-making authority remain uncertain, federal–provincial conflict has continued (Doern 1999, 82–97).

The history of the industry can be divided into four different phases: the semi-colonial period, 1867–1930; the era of multinational domination, 1930–1969; the withdrawal of the multinationals and the Canadianization of the industry, 1969–1985; and the current era in the evolution of Canada's oil and natural gas industry beginning with the switch to non-conventional oil recovery, the rise of natural gas as the dominant segment of the industry, and the Canada–US Free Trade Agreement, which guaranteed a reliable market for Canada's oil and natural gas. The re-entry of the federal government into the provincial oil and gas industry through the Kyoto Protocol challenged the free-market continentalism that had dominated the Canadian oil patch since the mid-1980s and signalled the beginning of a new phase of environmental regulation in the industry.

Several other studies of the oil and gas industry have examined the history of Canada's oil and gas sector in terms of its evolution but always with criteria from outside the industry. For example, several assessments of Alberta's oil and gas sector have looked at the industry through the perspective of federal–provincial relations (Richards and Pratt 1979; Doern and Toner 1985), whereas others have viewed the industry as a battle between competing elites for control of the industry or as an appendage to the federal energy regulatory regime (Stevenson 1989). No study has examined the industry as a distinct political–economic entity that both influences and is influenced by indigenous and exogenous factors in the near traditional pattern of staples production inherent in the evolution of many primary industries in Canada.

The Colonial Period

In 1850, the first registered oil company in North America was established in Woodstock, Ontario. Earth oil, as petroleum was then called, was used as an illuminant. By the 1870s, approximately 18 refineries were operating in Ontario. With the rise of the internal combustion engine and the decision of the Royal Navy to switch from coal to oil, the demand for petroleum in Canada increased dramatically. In the early 20th century, Canada relied on imported oil for more than 90 percent of its needs. This dependency on imported oil led to a number of discoveries, such as Turner Valley southwest of Calgary in 1914 and Norman Wells in the Northwest Territories in 1920. However, the high cost and engineering difficulties of bringing oil and natural gas from the Canadian West and North to market encouraged Canadian petroleum companies to rely on imports.

The early days of Canada's petroleum industry were characterized by federal control and neglect. Under section 109 of the *Constitution Act, 1867*, provincial governments were given control over natural resources, but between 1869, when Canada assumed control of the Hudson Bay lands in the prairie west and 1930—25 years after the creation of Alberta and Saskatchewan and the formalization of Manitoba's provincial boundaries—the federal government retained control over natural resources in the Prairie provinces. The introduction of the *Dominion Lands Act* in 1872 provided the legal framework for federal control of natural resources in the Northwest Territories and in the provinces of Alberta, Saskatchewan, and Manitoba after 1905 (Breen 1993, chapter 1). After years of lobbying and protest over this semi-colonial status, the three Prairie provinces were given control over their natural resources in 1930.

The Era of Multinational Domination

The rapid depletion of oil and gas reserves continued after jurisdiction over natural resources was transferred to the Prairie provinces in 1930. In an attempt to curb the rapacious depletion of known reserves, the United Farmers of Alberta government established the Turner Valley Conservation Board in 1932. Because of fierce opposition from local producers, the Turner Valley Board was disbanded within months. When the Turner Valley Royalties No. 1 well struck oil in 1936, it became the largest oil field in the British Commonwealth. Finally, in 1938, at the instigation of Imperial Oil and other major producers, the Social Credit government of William Aberhart created the Oil and Gas Conservation Board to regulate the industry. Modelled after conservation commissions in Oklahoma and Texas, and in keeping with the radical agrarian ideology of the early Social Credit government, the board was an attempt to end the competition between Imperial Oil and the small local producers. Each side recognized that some form of regulation was necessary if the life of the field was to be expanded and recovery rates and profits were to be maximized (Breen 1993, 125; Richards and Pratt 1979, 55–58).

After Aberhart's death in 1943, his successor, Ernest Manning, encouraged multinational companies to develop Alberta's petroleum reserves as quickly as possible. At its peak during the Second World War, the Turner Valley well produced 30,000 barrels of oil per day. The secure and plentiful supply of gasoline from the field attracted the Commonwealth air crews to train in the Calgary area during the Second World War.

In the postwar period, however, the Turner Valley area was in decline, and the future of Alberta's petroleum sector looked bleak. No new finds of commercial value had been discovered in several years, and Imperial Oil, the Canadian subsidiary of Standard Oil of New Jersey, had decided to discontinue its exploration program in the western sedimentary basin. Then, on February 13, 1947, the Leduc No. 1 well was hit. Combined with the establishment of the Oil and Gas Conservation Board, the Leduc well created the conditions for the entry of multinational petroleum companies—mainly but not exclusively American corporations—into Alberta. For the next 20 years, the Social Credit government actively encouraged the development of Alberta's oil and gas reserves through the multinationals at the expense of smaller Canadian firms.

The production side of Alberta's oil and gas industry in the 1950s and 1960s was dominated by four large, vertically integrated, multinational oil and gas companies: Shell, Imperial/Exxon, Gulf, and Texaco. These Canadian "sisters" were referred to as the "big four" and dominated the Canadian oil market, while also holding significant interests in the natural gas sector.

In the early 1950s, Canadian oil and gas producers were lobbying the federal government to protect them from low-priced foreign imports. The Diefenbaker government appointed Henry Borden to examine Canada's energy situation. The Borden Inquiry discovered a conflict between the multinational oil companies and local producers. The Canadian subsidiaries of the big four were the biggest producers of Canadian oil and gas, but they had little interest in shipping Alberta crude to central and eastern Canada. Through their multinational parents, the big four provided their refineries in the Montreal area with cheap imported oil because there was very little incentive to sell expensive Alberta oil to consumers in Ontario and Quebec.

But Alberta producers wanted secure markets. Because various restrictions kept them out of the United States, their only options were central and eastern Canada. The local companies wanted a more efficient pipeline than the existing interprovincial line to Ontario, and they wanted a tariff on imported oil. The Alberta producers received a compromise. The federal government erected an oil barrier at the Ottawa Valley line. Markets west of the line were reserved for Alberta oil, and those markets east of the Ottawa River would continue to rely on inexpensive imported oil and gas. This National Oil Policy was introduced in 1960, at the same time as the Organization of Petroleum Exporting Countries (OPEC) was established to prevent the large, integrated multinationals from driving oil and gas prices any lower in major producing states, mainly in the Middle East (Foster 1979, 27–31).

By the mid-1950s, Alberta's reserves of natural gas had been determined to be sufficient to supply markets on the west coast and in central Canada. Three major pipelines were constructed during this period to ship these reserves to market. The largest was Trans Canada Pipelines (TCPL). Created by the federal government in the late 1950s, TCPL was designed to bring Alberta gas to markets in central Canada. Although subsidized and partially constructed by the federal government, TCPL was a privately held corporation. Incorporation of TCPL indicated an interest by the federal government in Alberta's stock of natural gas and oil and represented the first major federal incursion into the oil patch since the federal government had ceded control over natural resources to the Prairie provinces in 1930.

The Alberta Gas Trunk Line (AGTL) was the second major pipeline, incorporated by the province in 1954 to act as a common carrier for natural gas. Its purpose was to stabilize the price of natural gas and reassure consumers. Voting shares in the new provincial enterprise were distributed among Alberta's utilities, gas processors, export interests, and the government, whereas non-voting shares were made available to Alberta residents. Although the AGTL was funded by the province, control was vested in the hands of the natural gas processors and the utilities. Whereas the public–private partnership reflected Ernest Manning's aversion to Crown corporations and his faith in the private sector, it allowed the province a window into the industry and an advantage over the federal government's renewed interest in Alberta's petroleum reserves (Breen 1993, 403–7; Bregha 1979).

The third major pipeline built in the 1950s was Frank McMahon's Westcoast Transmission. Designed to transport natural gas to the Pacific coast of British Columbia and eventually to US markets, this project met with federal, provincial, and American resistance (Breen 1993, 391). Despite numerous regulatory and political obstacles, however, approval was given for the scheme in November 1955.

By the late 1960s, conventional reserves were declining. The big four transnational oil companies were looking to areas outside the province for new reserves. With the enormous find of Prudhoe Bay on the Alaskan north slope in 1968, many in the oil patch believed Canada's oil and gas future would be found in the Arctic region—the area of the Mackenzie Delta, the Beaufort Sea, and the Arctic Islands. As a consequence, wildcat drilling in Alberta—exploration away from known reserves—dropped by 40 percent between 1969 and 1971. In the same period, Alberta's share of exploration dropped from three-quarters of the Canadian total to just more than half. By the early 1970s, the big four had come to the conclusion that no more large deposits of oil or gas—what the industry calls elephants—were to be found in Alberta. Their focus was now on the frontier areas of the Arctic and overseas.

The Nationalization of Oil and Gas

In the late 1960s and early 1970s, a number of circumstances combined to alter the structure of Canada's oil and gas industry. After the big four had decided to abandon their explorations in Alberta in favour of other locations, the exploration side of the industry was left to the smaller multinationals and to a number of emerging Canadian-owned companies. Although Canadian companies had always been active in the Alberta industry, their numbers and size had been small. As the 1960s ended, 98 percent of the provincial oil and gas industry was foreign-controlled, mainly by American interests. This situation was the result of several factors. First, the foreign firms had the capital and the expertise to develop the oil and gas reserves found in Canada. Second, the Alberta Social Credit government actively encouraged foreign multinationals. Not only did Manning believe that the multinationals provided the easiest and quickest way to develop the province's petroleum reserves, but a residual populist resentment continued against central Canada within the ruling Social Credit Party. As a result, Manning discouraged Canadian corporations based in Ontario and Quebec while encouraging foreign-owned capital to invest. The result had been a domination of the industry by a few large multinational oil and gas companies. Little room was left for small Canadian firms to get a start in the industry—that is, until the multinationals began to pull back their operations in the 1960s.

Two Alberta-based oil and gas companies came to prominence in the late 1960s and early 1970s. Alberta Gas Trunk Line and Dome were the flagship Canadian oil and gas companies of an emerging domestic industry. They reflected a shift in policies both at the provincial and federal levels that emphasized security of supplies of oil and gas and a Canadian-controlled industry—traditional concerns of a staples industry. As a private–public corporation created by the province, AGTL increased its role in the pipeline business and became an active participant in the exploration and production side of the oil and gas industry. Dome, which began as a small start-up dependent on the majors for its survival, played a significant role in frontier exploration and in conventional oil and gas production in Alberta. Because of Dome's interest in the Beaufort Sea, its agenda complemented the federal government's efforts to increase domestic supplies of oil and gas while increasing Canadian control of the industry.

In August 1971, the Progressive Conservatives, led by Peter Lougheed, defeated the 36-year-old Social Credit government. One of the reasons for the Social Credit defeat was concern that Alberta was not receiving its fair share of oil and gas revenues. The Social Credit governments of Ernest Manning and his successor Harry Strom had allowed the multinationals to exploit reserves as quickly as possible for a minimum return to the government in royalties and taxes. Manning saw his role as providing a stable political environment for the foreign-based industry. Lougheed, on the other hand, had a different attitude to big oil. He understood that the interests of the multinationals did not necessarily coincide with those of the province. Although he was willing to offer incentives to smaller Canadian companies, he did not advocate a policy of rapid depletion of conventional reserves by the large foreign-based oil and gas companies. Lougheed's campaign focused on the problem of what to do when the oil and gas ran out—when Alberta entered a post-staples state (Foster 1979, 38–41). After negotiating a royalty increase on oil and price increases for natural gas, Lougheed asserted Alberta's position as the centre of Canada's petroleum industry.

In 1972, the federal government began to exhibit a new interest in western Canadian petroleum. The price of a barrel of oil increased from US$3.00 to US$3.40 that year. This price rise was enough to startle the federal Liberal government of Pierre Trudeau. With world prices for oil and natural gas increasing, the federal government realized that it could keep down the price of Alberta crude much more easily than it could keep down the cost of imported oil from South America and the Middle East. However, the oil- and gas-producing provinces, led by Alberta, resisted any incursion by the federal government into what they argued was exclusive provincial jurisdiction over natural resources.

The debate between the Alberta and federal governments over energy pricing shifted suddenly in October 1973, when an OPEC oil embargo was called in response to Western support for Israel in the Yom Kippur War. Several oil-producing Arab states cut off shipments of crude oil to the West. Suddenly the price of a barrel of crude oil shot up from approximately US$3 per barrel to more than US$12 per barrel. The oil shock of 1973 sent the multinationals scrambling to find secure supplies of crude and natural gas. One obvious location was Alberta. The price jump in oil was an incentive for the renewal of interest by the multinationals in the western sedimentary basin.

In 1974, the federal government, seeking a better window on the oil and gas sector, and inspired by Canadian nationalists, created a state-owned oil company, Petro-Canada (PetroCan). Petro-Canada was resented by both oil patch veterans and the oil-producing provinces. With a self-image of rugged individualism and ferocious commitment to a free-market ideology, the oil patch veterans resented any state incursion as an unnecessary impediment to their God-given right to drill, produce, and market oil and natural gas (House 1980). Embarrassed by the minister of natural resources, Joe Greene, who, in the House of Commons in June 1971, had stated that Canada had a 923-year supply of oil and a 392-year supply of gas (Foster 1979, 51), and caught by surprise by the OPEC embargo in October 1973, the federal government believed it necessary to create a national oil and gas company that would promote a variety of national goals. These goals included increased domestic ownership of the industry, development of reserves not located in the western provinces (that is, the promotion of the lands under federal jurisdiction in the North and offshore), better information about the petroleum industry, security of supply, decreased dependence on the large multinational oil corporations (especially the big four), and increased revenues flowing to the federal treasury from the oil and gas sector (Fossum 1997). Although these goals were very similar to those of state-owned corporations in other countries, they were controversial in Canada (Fjell 2000).

The new federal oil and gas policy was resented by the Alberta government. Lougheed had committed his government to economic diversification through increased petroleum revenues. Any attempt to decrease these revenues or interfere in any way with Alberta's efforts to create a viable post–oil and gas economy were strongly resented. The ensuing struggle over which level of government would set policy direction for the oil patch resulted in a lack of coherence. Instead of working toward maximization of revenues and recovery and planning for a post-oil economy, the federal government and the governments of the oil- and gas-producing provinces were in a continuous conflict over the control of the industry (Fossum 1997, 10).

A second oil shock came with the 1979 Iranian Revolution. Although the overthrow of the Shah of Iran was widely welcomed by the Iranian people, the revolution was soon overtaken by Islamist fundamentalists, whose hatred of the West was profound. The Iranian revolutionaries simply stopped oil exports to the West. After the seizure of the United States embassy and the taking of American hostages by state-sponsored protestors in Tehran in 1979, the United States imposed economic sanctions, froze Iranian assets in the United States, and prohibited the import of Iranian oil into the United States. Oil and gas prices increased dramatically, rising from just less than US$20 a barrel to US$40 a barrel. Petroleum prices were expected to go much higher.

The response of the federal government was to increase state involvement in the provision of energy. As part of the National Energy Program (NEP), the federal government offered incentives for drilling in the Canada lands (the Arctic and the offshore areas under federal jurisdiction), increased export taxes on oil and gas, and offered a variety of "off-oil" measures in an effort to conserve domestic oil and gas reserves while decreasing dependence on foreign energy supplies. Although a number of domestic companies benefited from the federal initiatives, the NEP was strongly resented by the oil patch and the oil-producing provinces.

After a series of negotiations between the oil- and gas-producing provinces and the federal government, an agreement was reached concerning pricing and taxation. And, in 1982, Alberta and the other oil- and gas-producing provinces were able to secure an amendment to the existing constitutional division of powers that strengthened provincial control over natural resources. But the constitutional amendments and negotiations with the federal government maintained the basic structure of the NEP.

During the NEP, exploration and drilling in the Northwest Territories and the Atlantic offshore area met with some success. Natural gas was discovered in the Beaufort Sea and in the Arctic islands; however, high development costs and the distance from markets combined with concerns over Aboriginal land claims and the effect of development on the indigenous population have delayed exploitation of the northern reserves.

With the approval of the federal government, oil exploration in the Atlantic offshore area had begun with the first deep well off Prince Edward Island in 1943. Mobil was given a licence to drill off Sable Island in 1959 and began seismic testing in 1960. Natural gas and oil were found in the Nova Scotia offshore area in the 1970s. These finds included the Panuke-Cohasset fields, which were put into production in 1992, and the Sable Island natural gas field, which came into production in 1999. In the late 1970s and early 1980s, oil was discovered in two Newfoundland offshore areas: in 1979 in the Hibernia field and in 1984 in the Terra Nova field. Hibernia began producing large volumes of oil in 1997, and Terra Nova started producing commercial quantities of oil in 2000. The Atlantic offshore area has estimated reserves of 159,634 million cubic metres of crude oil and 67,083 million cubic metres of natural gas (Canadian Association of Petroleum Producers 2000).

During the 1970s and 1980s, the Trudeau government faced pressure to transfer the offshore areas to the provinces. Ottawa compromised by offering to pool revenues until the provinces no longer qualified for equalization payments. In 1982, Nova Scotia agreed to this arrangement. Newfoundland held out for better terms and challenged the federal offshore jurisdiction in court. References were made to both the Newfoundland Court of Appeal and the Supreme Court. The Supreme Court ruled that Newfoundland had no right to exploit the offshore resources or to make laws affecting those resources.

The Era of Benign Neglect

Two events in the mid-1980s greatly affected the Canadian oil and gas industry. First, the election of a federal Progressive Conservative government in September 1984, under the leadership of Brian Mulroney, altered the political situation. With a strong western and Atlantic contingent in the caucus and cabinet, the new Mulroney government was sympathetic to the demands of the western and Atlantic oil- and gas-producing provinces to dismantle the NEP and to allow some provincial control over the offshore resources to Newfoundland and Nova Scotia. After years of negotiations between the federal government and the Atlantic provinces, the Mulroney government in Ottawa signed the Atlantic Accord with the east coast provinces in 1985. The Atlantic Accord allowed Newfoundland and the Maritime provinces responsibility in developing their offshore oil and gas resources and a share in the revenues. Although the federal government retained ownership of the offshore resources, it reached an agreement with Newfoundland in 1985 over Hibernia and other offshore fields. The Canada–Newfoundland Offshore Petroleum Board was established in 1988 to administer the Hibernia and Terra Nova fields, and the Nova Scotia–Canada Offshore Petroleum Board was created at the same time to regulate the Nova Scotia offshore resources.[3]

The signing of the Western Accord with the western provinces in April 1985 dismantled the National Energy Program; however, the end of the NEP failed to revive the Canadian oil and gas industry. World energy prices collapsed in 1986. Oil sold for approximately US$12 per barrel, and natural gas fell to US$1 per million cubic feet (mcf). In the Alberta oil patch, thousands of workers were laid off, northern frontier exploration was halted, and the development of the Atlantic offshore was curtailed. The federal government's response to the decline in oil and gas prices was one of benign neglect. Provincial revenues shrank, and Alberta faced a series of budget deficits and rising unemployment in the oil and gas industry as thousands of workers were dismissed. Investment in Alberta's oil and gas industry had come to a halt.

In addition to the Western Accord, the Foreign Investment Review Agency (FIRA)—a product of the 1972–1974 Trudeau government's efforts to protect domestic industry from foreign control—was dismantled by the Mulroney government, and Canada was declared "open for business." The questions of Canada's ownership and its maintaining security of the supply were no longer concerns of federal energy policy—oil and natural gas were to be treated as any other commodity. Ottawa now relied on low prices and the market to supply Canadian demand for oil and gas. With the signing of the Canada–US Free Trade Agreement (FTA) in 1988 and its implementation in 1989, restrictions were placed on state intervention in the oil and gas sector. Simply put, under the terms of the FTA, Canada could no longer give preference to Canadians. US markets and businesses were to be treated the same as domestic consumers and companies. The subsidized price and other benefits given to Canadian producers and consumers through the NEP ended. This arrangement fit the ideological predisposition of both the Mulroney government in Ottawa and the oil- and gas-producing provinces. The election of the Liberal party in 1993 did little to change the federal government's oil and natural gas policy. One of the first acts of the new government was the ratification of the North American Free Trade Agreement (NAFTA) in late 1993. NAFTA further restricted the ability of the federal and provincial governments to determine pricing and secure the supply of oil and gas for domestic markets.

The oil and gas industry in Canada was now almost completely integrated into the North American market. Although provincial royalty exemptions and tax expenditures continued to subsidize the oil patch, the period following the Canada–US Free Trade Agreement and NAFTA saw the end of attempts to insulate Canadian consumers from high oil and gas prices. Federal government price controls had been removed from oil pricing, and provincial efforts to use revenues from the industry to diversify the economy had come to an end. Always subject to the boom-and-bust cycle, the oil- and gas-producing provinces and territories were now even more dependent on international markets. When prices for oil and gas rose, the provincial and territorial economies surged; when prices declined, oil and gas companies cut back on exploration and production, with provincial and territorial revenues following the downward trend. In Alberta, for example, the government continued the policy of royalty holidays and various tax expenditures to encourage further exploration and production, especially in the oil sands. Also designed to encourage exploration and production, the royalty structure in the Atlantic offshore was very generous to the various petroleum companies. Exploration activity in the Mackenzie Delta and the Beaufort Sea resumed in the late 1990s, with the result that extensive geophysical and well-drilling programs have been in place since 2000. As well, exploration and production activities began in 2001 in the southern Northwest Territories near Fort Laird. The economic feasibility of these northern projects was assured by an expanding pipeline system in northern Alberta and a projected shortage of natural gas in the North American markets.[4]

The New National Energy Program and the Kyoto Protocol

This scenario of a classic mature staples industry expanding to support increases in demand in international markets changed in December 1997, when the government of Canada signed the Kyoto Protocol on atmospheric greenhouse gas (GHG) emissions. The Kyoto Protocol mandates the reduction of greenhouse gas emissions to below-1990 levels. GHGs are primarily carbon dioxide emissions (CO_2), methane, and nitrous oxide. Caused by the burning of carbon-based fuels, such as oil, natural gas, and coal, these emissions are agreed to be a major contributor to global warming.

Ratified in late 2002, the Kyoto Protocol bound Canada to a 6 percent reduction of 1990 emissions between 2008 and 2012. The protocol "stipulates that progress in achieving this reduction commitment will be measured through the use of a set of internationally agreed-to emissions and removals inventory methodologies and reporting guidelines" (Olsen et al. 2002, iii). Canada's implementation strategy was released in 2003 (Government of Canada 2003).

Through the Alberta, Newfoundland and Labrador, and Nova Scotia governments and several industry organizations, the Canadian oil and gas industry expressed its dislike of the agreement.[5] In September 2002, the Alberta government launched a $1.5 million advertising campaign designed to weaken public support for the agreement. Polling data indicated that the apocalyptic provincial advertising—with its warning that thousands of jobs could be lost and living standards could be lowered—was successful. A majority of Albertans soon opposed the ratification and implementation of the Kyoto Protocol (Chase and Mahoney 2002, 1).

The oil- and gas-producing provinces, various industry groups, and the federal government had all indicated that the Kyoto Protocol could not be implemented in its present form. Moreover, the US administration of George W. Bush had stated it would not ratify or implement the protocol. Any effort to require Canadian industry to reduce greenhouse gas emissions without the active participation of the United States would place Canada at a comparative economic disadvantage with its largest trading partner. The domestic oil and gas industry believed it would suffer a disproportionate burden of the Kyoto Protocol effort to reduce greenhouse gases (GHGs) and Alberta was particularly concerned with the protocol's possible effects. Although Alberta's conventional production of oil and natural gas would be affected by the implementation of the protocol, the non-conventional oil reserves found in the tar sands and in heavy oil would suffer the greatest blow. The costs associated with reducing GHGs would fall disproportionately on the non-conventional supplies of oil, raising recovery costs by as much as US$6 per barrel. Because Middle Eastern oil averaged a recovery cost of $6 per barrel, the costs of the Kyoto Protocol would decrease profits and discourage investment in the oil sands. In Alberta's oil patch, comparisons with the widely unpopular National Energy Program of 1980 abounded.

A few months before Prime Minister Jean Chrétien's announcement in Johannesburg that Canada would ratify the Kyoto Protocol, the situation in Canada's oil and gas sector had been very different. In May 2001, the Bush administration had released its National Energy Policy. The policy—written by the National Energy Policy Advisory Group and chaired by Dick Cheney, who was both the American vice-president and a former chief executive officer of Halliburton Corp. (one of the largest oil and gas field service firms in the world)—called for secure supplies of oil and gas for the United States through such mechanisms as enhanced recovery, increasing domestic supplies, and global alliances (US, National Energy Policy Development Group 2001). Canada's deregulated energy sector had become the largest energy trading partner of the United States and its leading supplier of natural gas, oil, and electricity. In 2000, Canada supplied 14 percent of US energy needs through an integrated network of pipelines and electricity lines. Canadian energy supplies—especially natural gas and oil—were not described as a foreign source of energy but as part of the US domestic supply. American recognition of Canada's importance as a source of energy was seen as part of the evolution of an integrated North American energy sector.

Although major oil- and gas-producing provinces, such as Alberta, were quite content with the pre–Kyoto Protocol status quo and would have liked it to return, the federal government under the Liberals persisted in other measures designed to give it an increased influence over Canadian energy policy in the new post–Kyoto Protocol world. One such initiative was the North American Energy Working Group (NAEWG), a government-to-government body established to enhance the functioning of the North American energy market. Formation of the group was announced in 2001 by President Bush, Prime Minister Chrétien, and Mexico's President Vicente Fox.

When the NAEWG was announced, however, Alberta called an emergency meeting of all provincial ministers of energy. In response to these perceived federal incursions into provincial energy jurisdiction, the western provincial and territorial energy ministers established the Western Energy Alliance. The inaugural meeting was held on February 18, 2005, in Calgary. Announced at the Western Premiers' Conference in July 2004, the Western Energy Alliance was mandated to "promote the west as a secure and sustainable supplier to Canadians and North Americans"

(Alberta Energy 2005, 1). Along with efforts to raise awareness of western Canada as a safe and secure supplier of energy and to pursue harmonization of energy regulation, the Western Energy Alliance would, according to the February 18 news release, communicate "with their Federal counterpart regarding a commitment to meaningful provincial and territorial participation in international energy discussions and negotiations" (Alberta Energy 2005, 1).

Another bilateral agreement—the Canada–China Energy Working Group—was announced by the prime minister of Canada, Paul Martin, and the premier of China on January 20, 2005, in Beijing. The announcement, from a provincial perspective, signalled a continuing willingness on the part of the federal government to meddle in Canadian oil and gas production and trade. Two major Chinese oil and gas companies, Sinopec and PetroChina (both state corporations), have expressed interest in investing in the Canadian oil and gas industry. The consequences of Chinese investment in Canadian oil and gas could have serious effects on the Canada–United States relationship if the Americans view the Chinese interest in Canadian energy as a threat to their security.

The ratification of the Kyoto Protocol and the formation of the North American Energy Working Group and the Canada–China Energy Working Group signalled a re-entry by the federal government into the oil and gas industry. Unlike the 1980 National Energy Program, however, Ottawa was not seeking to "Canadianize" the industry, to secure oil and gas for domestic consumption and industrial advantage, or even to share in the profits generated by the oil patch. Instead, Ottawa was responding to various internal and external pressures for the mitigation of GHGs, trade relations, and a world demand for Canada's petroleum resources.

The industry reaction to these initiatives was mixed. The large exploration and production companies were capable of dealing with mandatory GHG reduction through technological innovation and already available practices (several of the larger companies, such as Royal Dutch/Shell and BP, were already "Kyoto-compliant" in their operations). These companies were also prepared to increase production in the oil sands to meet increasing demand for petroleum resources. But the small Canadian producers—those with production of less than 1,000 barrels of oil equivalent (boe) per day—did not have the knowledge, technology, or fiscal capability of meeting either the Kyoto Protocol requirements or the criteria for trade with China. Because the small producers were not capable of procuring the enormous financial resources necessary for oil sands exploration and production and because of the depletion of conventional stocks of crude oil and natural gas, many small producers have invested in sour gas and methane projects—both of which are highly regulated, socially controversial, and expensive. As a result, small producers, through the Small Explorers and Producers Association of Canada—a 400-plus-member lobby association—have turned to the provincial governments for help. With close political connections with several governments in western Canada, the provinces have used this support to express their opposition to Kyoto and other federal initiatives in areas they consider to be exclusive provincial jurisdiction.

The oil- and gas-producing provinces, however, gained a new ally on January 23, 2006, when Canadians elected a minority Conservative government. Led by Stephen J. Harper (a one-time member of Parliament for the right-wing populist Reform Party and a past president of the National Citizens Coalition, a far-right lobby group), the Conservatives campaigned on a platform of accountability and transparency in government. Although the party's position was vague on a number of issues, including energy, Conservatives were understood to be opposed to the Kyoto Protocol and to any federal intrusion into areas of provincial jurisdiction, including oil and gas and other energy sources. The Conservatives made it clear, however, that they were committed to a free market in energy. In a July 2006 speech to a meeting of the Canada–United Kingdom Chamber of Commerce in London, Harper stated that investors "have recognized Canada's emergence as a global energy powerhouse—the emerging 'energy superpower' our government intends to build." He also reminded his audience that Canada has the second-largest oil reserves in the world—the oil sands. Harper made it clear that Canada was "a stable, reliable, producer in a volatile, unpredictable world." Canada's energy policy, he stated, was based on the idea of the free exchange of "products based on competitive market principles, not self-serving monopolistic political strategies." Oil and gas, Harper declared, was a commodity like any other, subject to the discipline of the free market (Harper 2006, FP15).

Whereas the first Conservative budget, in 2006, contained no reference to energy or to Canada's commitments under the Kyoto Protocol, the political landscape changed again in early 2007. The new federal Liberal leader, Stéphane Dion, had run his leadership campaign on the theme of environmental protection. Suddenly the environment—and especially global warming—was the most important issue for Canadian voters. The 2007 Conservative budget reflected the public's sudden concern for the environment with a focus on global warming. In his budget speech of March 19, 2007, the minister of finance, Jim Flaherty, also described Canada as an "emerging energy superpower." Canada is well positioned, he stated, "to take advantage of our significant natural resources in new, innovative and environmentally friendly ways that will provide significant benefits to the economy." The budget provided more than $1.5 billion in the Canada ecoTrust for Clean Air and Climate Change to support major environmental projects with the provinces and territories. As well, the Conservatives committed to clean energy technologies, such as carbon capture and storage, and to the phased end of accelerated capital cost allowance for general oil sands investment by 2015. The budget also provided measures to promote efficient, cleaner fuels, including incentives for renewable biofuels; a program to scrap older, less efficient vehicles; and a public transit tax credit (Flaherty 2007).

The Conservative minister of natural resources, Gary Lunn, a lawyer with experience in the resource sector, has also stated on a number of occasions the Conservative theme that Canada is an emerging energy superpower. Lunn also echoed Prime Minister Stephen Harper's comments concerning the Kyoto Protocol: "Trying to pretend that we can achieve Kyoto, it's not real; it's not being honest with Canadians." Even the far less ambitious GHG reduction targets set by the Conservatives are not, he claimed, without a price. "Nobody should be fooled that there is no cost to this. There is an economic cost." The federal government has taken an interest in wind, solar, and biomass power, despite its estimates that in the foreseeable future renewable energy will amount to only 4 percent of the energy supply. Fossil fuels will continue to be, in the view of the Conservatives, the most important part of the Canadian energy mix (Lunn 2007a).

While in opposition, the Conservatives had opposed the Kyoto Protocol for several reasons. First, many in the Conservative caucus, including the prime minister, had expressed skepticism that global warming was occurring and, if it were occurring, believed that human beings were not responsible for it. Second, the government had argued that the rejection by the Bush administration of the Kyoto Protocol made economically infeasible any effort by Canada to reduce greenhouse gas emissions. Meeting its commitments under the Kyoto Protocol would put Canada at a comparative economic disadvantage with its largest trading partner. Moreover, the oil- and gas-producing provinces of Newfoundland and Labrador, Saskatchewan, Alberta, and British Columbia believed they would suffer a disproportionate burden of the costs of reducing greenhouse gases if the Kyoto Protocol were implemented. These provincial governments were concerned that the added costs of greenhouse gas reduction would price non-conventional and offshore reserves out of the North American and world markets. Billions of dollars in planned investment could be lost and the future economic prosperity of the provinces could be threatened. In western oil- and gas-producing provinces, the Kyoto Protocol had been compared to the widely unpopular 1980 NEP.

In January 2007, Prime Minister Harper named John Baird minister of the environment to replace the inexperienced Rona Ambrose. Baird continued the federal government's opposition to the Kyoto Protocol while at the same time promising to produce a clean air policy. At the September 2007 Asia–Pacific Economic Cooperation (APEC) meetings in Australia, Harper announced that Canada would pursue a GHG-reduction plan based on the intensity of emissions rather than the absolute standards required by the Kyoto Protocol. According to Prime Minister Stephen Harper and his Australian counterpart, John Howard, Canada and Australia joined Russia, China, the United States, and India in agreeing that each country needed to make commitments to stop human activity from causing dangerous changes to the climate. Canada was criticized by some APEC members for setting GHG-reduction targets but doing little to achieve them. The Harper government was also singled out for choosing 2005 as the benchmark year for its targets instead of 1990, when emissions were much lower. Harper blamed the previous Liberal government's economic policies for Canada's skyrocketing emissions, which were more than 30 percent higher than its Kyoto Protocol target (De Souza 2007).

At a United Nations meeting called in late September 2007 to save the Kyoto Protocol, Harper announced that Canada would join the Asia–Pacific Partnership—an alternative climate change pact. Created in 2006 by Australia, China, India, Japan, Korea, and the United States, the Asia–Pacific Partnership has been criticized for lacking the mandatory targets contained in Kyoto. The seven countries—including Canada—account for nearly half the world's greenhouse gas emissions.

Another component of federal policy is an increased emphasis on North American energy integration. Conservative energy strategy was articulated at a North American energy ministers' meeting in Victoria, British Columbia, in July 2007. The energy ministers from Canada, the United States, and Mexico emphasized the importance of collaboration on energy technologies and facilitating energy markets to enhance security. Lunn argued that the meeting opened the door to a sustainable, affordable, secure energy future for North America. The agreement on energy science and technology also set an example for co-operation in other areas. The energy ministers committed to explore further opportunities to use the integrated nature of the North American energy market to the benefit of all three nations (Lunn 2007b).

CONCLUSIONS: OIL AND GAS AS MATURE STAPLES INDUSTRIES AT THE EDGE

The Canadian oil and gas industry is in a period of change. But what kind of change is not clear. The industry is divided between large and small producers and is being pulled in two competing and contradictory directions. On the one side are the large producers—those corporations producing more than 10,000 barrels of oil equivalent per day—that are fully integrated into the global market. They have the technology, knowledge, and financial resources to engage in an internationally competitive industry and develop unconventional sources of energy. On the other side are the small Canadian producers. They lack the resources to meet increasingly rigorous environmental, social, and market regulations. These corporations and individuals are dependent on the provinces for their survival. Any threat, such as increased regulation, becomes a federal–provincial issue.

The roles and responsibilities of the federal government—its international responsibilities and treaties, such as the Kyoto Protocol, the North American Energy Working Group, and the Canada–China Energy Working Group—are often in conflict with the interests of the oil- and gas-producing provinces that are dependent on petroleum revenues. But the Conservative government of Stephen Harper has set out to change this relationship. Abandoning Canada's Kyoto Protocol commitments, the Conservative government has removed itself from an active role in the oil and gas industry. Market forces will guide energy supply and demand.

The current federal energy and environmental initiatives are fundamentally different from the 1980 National Energy Policy and the multilateral environmental commitments of the Chrétien and Martin Liberal governments. The Conservatives have embraced North American energy integration and have announced Canada will not meet its commitments under the Kyoto Protocol. The result is a new dynamic among the continental strategy of the US Bush administration, the oil- and gas-producing provinces, the federal government, and the upstream oil and gas industry. Oil and gas are no longer viewed as strategic commodities to be regulated by the federal government. Instead, they are viewed as any other commodity, to be bought and sold in the free market, with little or no recognized strategic value. The result has been a federal retreat from environmental regulation and unrestrained development of oil and gas reserves. Yet a fundamental contradiction exists in the policies of the Harper government. Although large Canadian upstream oil and gas companies compete in global markets, they still rely on provincial and federal governments to protect them through international agreements, such as the Kyoto Protocol. Conservative rhetoric may proclaim a free market, but the industry still depends on the federal state for protection from an increasingly competitive and global environment. Despite the tensions in federal energy policy, signals indicate a post-staples petroleum industry is taking shape.

NOTES

1. These figures have only recently been considered by the International Energy Agency when calculating the totals of world reserves but are still not part of the annual surveys of world supplies prepared by the United States Department of Energy or BP Amoco.

2. The May 2001 United States National Energy Policy stimulated American interest in Alberta's oil sands as a safe and secure source for oil and other petroleum products. The continuing integration of the North American energy markets, especially in the oil and gas sector, is an important factor in the future viability of Alberta's oil sands and heavy oil development. Simply put, Alberta's oil and gas industry depends on increasing production of non-conventional sources of oil and natural gas and access to US markets.

3. Although these two administrative tribunals were successful in promoting the development and regulation of the Atlantic offshore areas, they have not been as successful in settling disputes between the Atlantic oil- and gas-producing provinces and the federal government or between the provinces. For example, an offshore boundary dispute exists between Nova Scotia and Newfoundland and Labrador, and the provinces have numerous complaints that they have been subject to unfair penalties in their revenue-sharing agreements with the federal government. Under existing

royalty-sharing agreements, the federal government has deducted equalization payments from the two provinces in proportion to the offshore petroleum royalties collected. Through its "Campaign for Fairness," Nova Scotia has waged a consistent battle with the federal government to have petroleum royalties excluded from the calculation of equalization payments. So far, the federal government has resisted Nova Scotia's request.

4. Several oil- and gas-producers groups have announced feasibility studies on a major natural gas pipeline from the Mackenzie Delta. Unlike the earlier attempt to construct a northern pipeline, this proposal has the support of the Northwest Territories government and Aboriginal communities. A consortium of oil and gas companies with interests in the Alaskan north slope has announced a proposal to bring natural gas to North American markets through a pipeline along the Arctic coast—the north slope—of Alaska, and a third group has proposed a natural gas pipeline along the Alaska Highway. The Bush administration and the US Congress have proposed loan guarantees and other non-cash measures worth US$20 billion as incentives for the construction of the Arctic shore and Alaska Highway lines (Brethour 2003, B7; Haggett 2003, D2).

5. Personal interview with Stephen Rodrigues, research manager, Canadian Association of Petroleum Producers, Calgary, September 12, 2002.

REFERENCES

Alberta Energy. 2005. Energy ministers agree to market western and northern Canada as a secure energy supplier (news release). Online at http://www.gov.ab.ca/acn/ 200502/17615E4FFA0AE-D507-48BE-A263A1685C0D833F.html.

Alberta Energy. 2007. *Energy annual report, 2006–2007*. Edmonton: Alberta Energy.

Alberta Energy and Utilities Board. 2004. *Momentum: Working for Albertans—2003 year in review*. Calgary: Alberta Energy and Utilities Board.

Breen, D.H. 1993. *Alberta's petroleum industry and the conservation board*. Edmonton: University of Alberta Press and the Energy Resources Conservation Board.

Bregha, F. 1979. *Bob Blair's pipeline: The business and politics of northern energy development projects*. Toronto: James Lorimer & Company.

Brethour, P. 2003. Deal on pipeline near for Mackenzie: Ottawa. *The Globe and Mail*, April 26: B7.

Canada, National Energy Board. 1999. *Canadian energy: Supply and demand to 2025*. Calgary: National Energy Board.

Canada, National Energy Board. 2007. *Canadian energy overview 2006: An energy market assessment—May 2007*. Calgary: National Energy Board.

Canadian Association of Petroleum Producers. 2000. *Annual survey 2000*. Calgary: Canadian Association of Petroleum Producers.

Canadian Association of Petroleum Producers. 2004. *Policy direction for Alberta's oil and gas industry*. Calgary: Canadian Association of Petroleum Producers.

Chase, S., and Mahoney, J. 2002. Albertans turn against Kyoto in poll. *The Globe and Mail*, October 8: 1.

De Souza, M. 2007. APEC declaration may undermine Kyoto Protocol: Wealthy nations accused of bullying at climate summit. *Vancouver Sun*, September 10: A4

Doern, G.B. 1999. Moved out and moving on: The National Energy Board as a reinvented regulatory agency. In *Changing the Rules: Canadian Regulatory Regimes and Institutions*, eds. G.B. Doern, M.M. Hill, M.J. Prince, and R.J. Shultz, 82–97. Toronto: University of Toronto Press.

Doern, G.B., and Toner, G. 1985. *The politics of energy: The development and implementation of the NEP*. Toronto: Methuen.

Fjell, O. 2000. President of the Norwegian state oil company, Statoil (news conference). Calgary: World Petroleum Congress, June 14.

Flaherty, J. 2007. *Budget 2007: Aspire to a stronger, safer, better Canada*. Ottawa: Department of Finance.

Fossum, J.E. 1997. *Oil, the state, and federalism: The rise and demise of Petro-Canada as a statist impulse*. Toronto: University of Toronto Press.

Foster, P. 1979. *The blue-eyed sheiks: The Canadian oil establishment*. Don Mills, ON: Collins.

Government of Canada. 2003. *Climate change plan for Canada: Climate change— Achieving our commitments together*. Ottawa: Industry Canada.

Haggett, S. 2003. Nault won't oppose US subsidies for Alaska pipeline. *Calgary Herald*, May 22: D2.

Harper, S. 2006. We intend to build "energy superpower." *National Post* July 29: FP15.

House, J.D. 1980. *The last of the free enterprisers: The oilmen of Calgary*. Toronto: Macmillan.

Lunn, G. 2007a. Notes for a speech by the Honourable Gary Lunn, minister of natural resources at the Trilateral North American Energy Ministers Meeting, Victoria, British Columbia, July 23.

Lunn, G. 2007b. Speech to the Calgary Chamber of Commerce luncheon, Calgary, Alberta, September 12.

Olsen, K., Collas, P., Boileau, P., Blain, D., Ha, C., Henderson, L., Liang, C., McKibbon, S., Morel-à-l'Hussier, L. 2002. *Canada's greenhouse gas inventory 1990–2000*. Ottawa: Environment Canada.

Polczer, S. 2007. Encana shatters profit record. Calgary energy giant earns $6.1B in 2006. *Calgary Herald*, February 16: A1.

Richards, J., and Pratt, L. 1979. *Prairie capitalism: Power and influence in the new west*. Toronto: McClelland & Stewart.

Stevenson, G. 1989. *Unfulfilled union: Canadian federalism and national unity*, 3rd ed. Toronto: Gage.

US, National Energy Policy Development Group. 2001. *National Energy Policy: Reliable, affordable, and environmentally sound energy for America's future*. Washington, DC: US Government Printing Office.

CHAPTER 13

Offshore Petroleum Politics: A Changing Frontier in a Global System

Peter Clancy*

Offshore oil and gas developments are among the new "unconventional" energy sources (see Brownsey, chapter 12) that have emerged in Canada over the last two decades as oil prices have risen and conventional domestic sources have declined. In the new millennium, activities in the offshore petroleum industry are unsettled, to say the least.

On the Atlantic coast, where investment has been mounting since 1995, petroleum operators and governments are negotiating regulatory change through an energy round table. On the Pacific coast, where a long-standing moratorium persists, corporate rights holders have made it clear that they will not return to offshore activity until federal and provincial authorities have resolved, to the satisfaction of all major stakeholders, First Nations title claims and jurisdictional overlaps. In the Arctic, a series of 1990s Aboriginal rights settlements opened the way for expanded resource project planning that included the offshore shelf. However, the settlements also raised questions of how the myriad planning and management authorities—federal, territorial, and Aboriginal—would interact in regulating major project initiatives.

In this chapter, the offshore petroleum sector is explored from a series of different perspectives. It is best understood as an emerging mature staple resource domain poised between local, national, and international forces. Because the petroleum industry operates on three coasts and under multiple state authorities, local conditions present significant variables; however, offshore petroleum is also very much a global domain. Although this sector's commercial roots are on the US Gulf coast, where Texas independents underwrote early exploration in the late 1940s, the international oil giants and their subsidiaries soon rose to prominence. By the time new offshore basins drew attention in Europe, Latin America, West Africa, Asia-Pacific, and Canada, a fully rounded multinational complex (including not just operators but service firms) had assumed a predominant competitive position.

So far, this description points to a classic mature staples sector, where hydrocarbons are extracted from a remote and physically challenging hinterland by highly capitalized enterprises to realize profit from sale and consumption in distant markets. This political economy of the offshore domain deserves a closer look, particularly from the perspective of Hutton's post-staples hypothesis (see chapter 3). To begin, offshore oil and gas is a relatively late arrival to the staples trade. Therefore, its regulatory regimes have been infused with social policy concerns that were not present in the formative eras of terrestrial petroleum. Other features arise from its "offshore" location, where a thrust toward an integrated oceans policy has emerged in recent decades and threatens to erode the sectoral autonomy of the petroleum domain.

OFFSHORE PETROLEUM AS A DISTINCT POLITICAL ECONOMY

Offshore petroleum can be treated, politically and commercially, as an industry *sui generis*. This is not a new proposition. Repeatedly during the 1950s, American oil interests pressed both Congress and the administration with arguments that the offshore petroleum industry was, by nature, qualitatively different from its onshore counterpart (Baxter 1993; Lore 1992). Government was urged to legislate, tax, and regulate accordingly. Realistically, of course, the offshore industry can never be detached completely from the land-based energy and hydrocarbon policies of sovereign states (Fant 1990; Richards and Pratt 1979). As Brownsey (see chapter 12) points out, the early legal and policy templates for industry development were forged in terrestrial contexts.

Over time, however, the divergences have become as pronounced as the similarities, in both corporate and state circles. To begin, offshore petroleum exists by virtue of complex engineering and technology systems that are among the most dynamic on the globe (Fee and O'Dea 1986; Kash et al. 1973). Moreover, the transfer of these technologies, from one hydrocarbon prospect or basin to another, is furthered by intra-firm and inter-firm transactions. Similarly, developments in the law of the sea have conferred crucial jurisdictions over continental shelf resources to national and regional authorities, enabling such states to fashion novel development strategies (Chircop and Marchand 2001; Cicin-Sain and Knecht 1987; Fitzgerald 2001; Hildreth 1986; Silva 1986; Stalport 1992).

Equally significant is the diffusion of public policy and regulatory practice (Nelsen 1991; Noreng 1980). The jurisdictional status and regime structures for offshore petroleum have diverged increasingly from their terrestrial counterparts

(Atlantic Canadian Petroleum Institute 2001; Fant 1990). The offshore petroleum sector has not functioned in policy isolation; a continuing thread of overlaps and intersections with other ocean businesses—marine transport, communication, and fishing, for example—complicates the rounded management of hydrocarbon resources. In addition, a new type of policy challenge has emerged in recent years in the form of ocean policy and governance. These frameworks are predicated on an integrated resource management of extensive ocean areas, usually in reference to ecosystem health and integrity. To date, they have no counterparts in terrestrial oil and gas administration, where a "pillared" regime normally distances petroleum from the related agriculture, forestry, wildlife, and water resources (Cicin-Sain and Knecht 2000; Goldstein 1982). Offshore, however, such emerging meta-frameworks complicate the political context for oil and gas capital in a variety of ways, as explored later in this chapter (National Research Council, Marine Board 1997).

THE HISTORICAL EVOLUTION OF THE CANADIAN OFFSHORE INDUSTRY

When offshore operations were pioneered in the Gulf of Mexico in the postwar period, the coastal states vied with Washington to claim legal jurisdiction. The resulting judicial settlement limited all coastal states, such as Louisiana, Texas, California, and others, to a coastal strip of three nautical miles, with the balance of the offshore continental shelf falling to the federal Department of the Interior (Gramling 1996; Lore 1992). When new offshore exploration began in the North Sea, in the late 1950s, the coastal nations had a different preoccupation. Negotiating boundary limits, they carved the region into a series of national sectors. Beginning in the southern waters adjacent to the Netherlands and England, the exploration frontier moved slowly across the North Sea. Because most of the world-class fields were found in the middle to northerly reaches, the major beneficiaries were the United Kingdom and Norway, both unitary states in which the central governments enjoyed exhaustive jurisdiction (Dunning 1989; Jenkin 1981; Nelsen 1991; Noreng 1980).

In Canada, the geopolitics of offshore claims paralleled the American pattern. In the early 1960s, both the coastal provinces and Ottawa asserted resource jurisdictions over the continental shelf. These actions resulted in parallel regulations and permitting systems, a highly unsatisfactory situation for explorationists, who often responded by taking out dual permits in order to fortify their legal positions. In arguments that foreshadowed later disputes, the provinces claimed an offshore jurisdiction as part of their pre-confederation powers, whereas Ottawa asserted its treaty power. The Supreme Court of Canada offered its first authoritative ruling in the *BC Offshore Reference* case of 1967, in which it found in favour of a federal jurisdiction. However, this decision proved to be only an opening salvo. The Pacific coast was again the battleground in the Strait of Georgia dispute concerning "inland" coastal waters, in which the BC Court of Appeal found in favour of the province in 1976. Eight years later, the Supreme Court of Canada agreed, confirming the distinction (on the west coast at least) between provincial subsea ownership of an "inner" shelf between the mainland and Vancouver Island and federal ownership of an "outer" shelf beyond the Strait (Townsend Gault 1983).

It is in this context that Ottawa's east coast strategy must be understood. Undeterred by the *Offshore Reference 1967*, and buoyed by the early drilling results off their own shores, the eastern provinces intensified their own jurisdictional claims. In addition, each province had colonial precedents that might point toward a Strait of Georgia outcome. Despite its prevailing legal advantage based on the 1967 Supreme Court ruling, Ottawa's constitutional position was far from unassailable. As a result, the Trudeau government entered negotiations with the Atlantic provinces toward an intergovernmental protocol on shared resource management. These negotiations led to an agreement in 1977, signed by the three Maritime provinces (but not Quebec or Newfoundland) that designated revenue-sharing and administrative arrangements for both the Gulf of St. Lawrence and the ocean continental shelf (Text of offshore agreement 1977).

Here the seeds were sown for a new approach to joint federal–provincial management; however, the prospects of joint management were far from assured at the time. In Newfoundland, Premier Brian Peckford had enacted a comprehensive regulatory regime of his own, inspired largely by the Norwegian experience (House 1985). In Nova Scotia, John Buchanan's Conservative government withdrew from the 1977 agreement soon after acceding to power. The dual 1979 discoveries of Hibernia oil (off Newfoundland's shores) and Venture gas (off Nova Scotia's shores) significantly heightened provincial ambitions. Here, however, the tactical paths of the two provinces diverged. In 1980, Nova Scotia enacted strong ownership and regulatory measures, though they were never proclaimed. Instead, Premier Buchanan joined Ottawa to strike the 1982 offshore accord, setting aside the ownership issue in favour of shared management controls. Dismissing this deal, Peckford launched a 1983 reference case on Newfoundland's offshore claims, which was trumped by Ottawa's separate reference to the Supreme Court of Canada. The federal victory did much to fortify its east coast jurisdictional base, concluding two decades of litigation over the spatial politics of Canadian offshore petroleum.

OFFSHORE PETRO-CAPITAL AS A POLITICAL FACTOR: THE ORGANIZATION OF OFFSHORE INTERESTS

This section follows the political economy tradition by exploring the organization and power quotient of ocean capital. The offshore petroleum industry displays sufficient uniqueness in its upstream operations to be considered a distinct sub-industry within the hydrocarbon sector. That being said, a plethora of intriguing questions remain. How does the offshore segment express its shared interests on political and policy questions? Is the "field" or "basin" a relevant political denominator? What are the prospects for coalition or alliance along the offshore value chain, from exploration to construction to production and beyond? The role of farm-ins (new investors sharing the costs of planned exploration work) and joint ventures has long been recognized as a source of industry solidarity (House 1980). Is the prevalence of farm-ins and joint ventures especially pronounced offshore, given the capital commitments and heightened risks involved?

Also needing to be addressed is the question of associational structures giving voice to offshore interests. This landscape is typically a complicated terrain of trade associations, business coalitions, technocrats, and consultants that can be expected to consolidate common interests and narrow the range of variance (Berry 1974). Relations between "petroleum" and other "ocean industries" are also pertinent, both as an indicator of potential alliances and an index of inter-industry rivalry.

These problems are more complicated than they first appear. Few if any oil companies restrict their operations to offshore waters alone. More commonly, a firm involved in upstream activities (exploration, extraction, and transport), in its efforts to acquire proven and commercially exploitable reserves, assembles a portfolio of properties and positions in properties of varying degrees of risk. This portfolio quite likely combines different fields, basins, and petroleum provinces within a single nation or beyond. Within such firms, an intricate internal process dictates where exploration and development funds will be spent in a given year. Consequently, regional and project managers bring a range of prospects to the corporate table, where they compete for annual appropriations. Relative attractiveness can change over time, according to exploration results, market conditions, and political contexts. Nevertheless, as long as a firm is committed to an exploration play, through the holding of exploration rights, farm-ins on wells, or equity in development projects, then that company bears a significant interest in the success of the play. Such a firm can, therefore, be expected to participate in industrial collective action to enhance that interest.

As long as the prospective sedimentary geology is confined to a single state jurisdiction, as in Alberta in the period from 1918 to 1958, the lines of political mobilization and intervention may be relatively straightforward. The upstream industry depended on provincial tenure and licensing policy, and the Alberta Petroleum Association (renamed the Canadian Petroleum Association in 1952) functioned as the collective voice of the major companies in dealing with the provincial government in Edmonton. However, as prospectivity proliferates into multiple state jurisdictions, the challenges of aggregating and articulating the concerns of shifting subsets mount. The Canadian Petroleum Association (CPA), like other trade associations servicing increasingly diversified memberships, opted for specialized internal sections or divisions where the relevant business constituencies could coalesce for their particular concerns and campaigns, while remaining part of the umbrella association and reporting through its board of governors. In this way, the CPA's Saskatchewan and British Columbia divisions were established.

A separate vehicle, the Independent Petroleum Association of Canada (IPAC), was formed to represent companies whose activities concentrated in the upstream (exploration and production) stages. This association sprang in part from postwar policy tensions with the foreign-owned "majors" over the shape of the Canadian oil market. For example, because the prairie independents had an interest in supplying the largest possible domestic market (at a time when oil exports were tightly controlled), they pushed for a coast-to-coast pipeline network. On the other hand, the foreign-owned majors, already supplying the Quebec and Maritime markets from their offshore sources, pushed for a west–east divide (House 1980). Although the CPA and the IPAC enjoyed similar membership numbers by the 1970s, the companies securing acreage on the east coast offshore were largely, though not exclusively, foreign-owned majors. This situation, together with the American precedent, may explain why the offshore corporate segment sought stand-alone representation at an early date.

In the United States, a specialized offshore association emerged shortly after the war. The Offshore Operators Committee (OOC) was organized before 1950, to speak for the offshore upstream segment of American petroleum. Over the past half century, the OOC has evolved to "consult with and advise … governmental entities concerning matters affecting the offshore petroleum industry" (Offshore Operators Committee n.d.). In particular, the OOC focuses on regulatory rule-making processes by government agencies. In 2002, the OOC numbered 70 operating companies and 25 service companies. Many if not most of these firms maintain parallel memberships in the omnibus voice of integrated oil, the American Petroleum Institute (API), and one or more of the more than dozen specialized industry associations.

In Canada, an analogue to the OOC appeared in two frontier regional associations. Their formation reflected the start of offshore drilling, with the first exploratory well drilled off the east coast in 1966 and the first exploratory well in the Arctic offshore drilled five years later (Gibbons and Voyer 1974; Keith et al. 1976). The offshore exploration permit holders banded together in two regional clusters in the early 1970s, each numbering about two dozen firms. For the federal northlands, this organization took the form of the Arctic Petroleum Operators Association (APOA.) On the Atlantic continental shelf, the parallel body was the East Coast Petroleum Operators Association (EPOA), where the costs of collective action were met by an assessment on the acreage-holding member companies (Offshore operators division strengthens east coast organizational structure 1984).

In 1983, the EPOA merged with the larger Canadian Petroleum Association as the Offshore Operators Division (OOD). Three years later, the Arctic producers followed suit. (This merging coincided with the mid-decadal market slump and massive industry retrenchment efforts.) The offshore group was renamed the CPA Frontier Division, with two parallel regional arms that shared a staff officer. This structure acknowledged both that the frontier members all operated under Canada Lands legislation and that the east coast regulatory boards and basins presented unique elements not found in the Arctic. The CPA went further by opening regional offices in Halifax and St. John's. Today this arrangement continues as the Atlantic section of the Canadian Association of Petroleum Producers (CAPP).

Even within the CAPP bloc, a uniformity of corporate interests in offshore matters cannot be assumed. To cite only the most recent development, the turn-of-the-century mega-mergers have created a new tier of international interests that dwarf, in scale, all other oil producers. The appearance of these "super majors" —Exxon Mobil, Chevron Texaco, Total-Elf-Fina, and Conoco-Philips—has altered the offshore business in a number of ways. First, it halved the number of giant players in the international petroleum game, curbing the amount of exploration rivalry. In addition, as these giants sought economies from their consolidation, their rationalization of budgets, staff, rights-holdings, and planned projects cut significantly the amount of exploration capital being directed to high-risk basins. This reduced investment in exploration has a knock-on impact in the offshore service and supply sector, which finds itself squeezed ever harder by these same tendencies. Furthermore, this approach reinforces the tendency of mega-firms to limit their interest to truly giant finds, passing over promising prospects whose profit potential fails to match their new-found scale. Of course, many other corporations can exploit this situation. Instead of targeting the global "elephant fields," they seek portfolios of more modest scale by specializing in prospects that the super majors decline or abandon or by concentrating on secondary or tertiary extraction from maturing fields that are being abandoned by their initial developers (Mitchell, Selley, and Morita 2001; Noreng 2002; Yedlin, 2004).

This strategy, however, does not exhaust the range of offshore corporate interests. Indeed, petroleum was a relative latecomer to business in the oceans sector, preceded by such major industry groups as shipbuilding, marine transport, cable and communications, and commercial fishing. Traditionally, the ocean was treated as open space in which separate core industries pursued independent operations. In the 1970s, however, this situation changed when "ocean industries" began to be recognized in government circles as a strategic growth sector (Beale 1980). The federal government's industrial strategy exercise of 1977 launched consultations in 22 designated sectors, including ocean industries (French 1980).

The possibility also existed for an umbrella grouping of marine-oriented firms and sectors that were in the business not of petroleum extraction per se, but of selling specialized goods and services to the offshore petroleum operators (Voyer 1983). In Nova Scotia, this possibility of related industries was realized in 1982 with the organization of the Offshore/Onshore Technologies Association of Nova Scotia (OTANS). That year, a delegation of Nova Scotia business people visited Aberdeen, Scotland, to better understand the potential for an offshore-linked industry. There, "the group saw tremendous potential, but they also learned that the oil and gas industry is a truly global business with plenty of natural barriers to entry" (Offshore/Onshore Technologies Association of Nova Scotia 2007a).

From the outset, OTANS combined advocacy ("to support the maximization of Atlantic Canadian participation in the supply of both goods and services" [Offshore/Onshore Technologies Association of Nova Scotia 2007b]), market intelligence on business opportunities (meetings with industry leaders and information bulletins, for example), and member networking (with one another and with the lead offshore operators). The original membership of 30 grew to 200 within a few years. Whereas the offshore supply and service sector has waxed and waned along with the offshore business cycle, OTANS numbered more than 500 members in 2004 and now describes itself as Canada's largest oil and gas industry association.

Looking beyond these patterns of sectoral affinity, a series of market factors will inevitably shape the timing and intensity of political representations. Offshore developments cannot proceed without assured markets, which are integral to political coalition building. Also, the so-called "cycle" factors stem from the project development phase. Room for considerable ambiguity exists here. On one hand, industry political agendas can be expected to reflect the changing imperatives of the field life cycle, and the "basin development" hypothesis deserves sustained attention. At the same time, however, fields are likely to include multiple projects at different stages of development. Today on the Scotian Shelf, for example, the Cohasset oil field has been decommissioned, Sable gas is in production, and Deep Panuke is in an early development stage. The muting or offsetting impact of such multi-phase priorities can provide state authorities with considerable room to manoeuvre.

Several possible trajectories can be seen here. Over time, offshore petroleum networks can shift their shapes. These networks may begin as a classical industrial clientelism, in which state agents bargain with petroleum operators and the offshore service sector over the terms of development for the resource. With time, however, these networks evolve toward something new, whose outline is not yet entirely clear. They may evolve to a form of business–government concertation, driven by high-level elite accommodation, as illustrated by the Atlantic Energy Roundtable. Already an evident drive exists to restructure the regulatory regime toward a simplified, flexible, and discretionary form of performance-based regulation. Alternatively, these networks may evolve toward a broader ocean pluralism, in which the offshore petroleum bloc finds its public policy concerns being settled by a diverse network of stakeholder interests. The sections below help to clarify these possibilities.

Technology as a Political Variable

One of the strong sources of business and political solidarity for offshore petroleum has been its reliance on advanced technology. After all, these advances were instrumental in creating the offshore industry (Gurney 1997; National Research Council, Marine Board 1980). It is worth recalling the primitivity of early offshore exploration in the Gulf of Mexico region and the dramatic changes that followed. In the 1940s, drilling barges were dragged into shallow, swamp water positions and submerged. As ambitions turned toward open water, military-surplus landing ships were refitted with derricks and drill support systems (Szell 1979). The first authentic "standing" rig, the Kerr-McGee 16, went a dozen miles offshore in 1947 to drill in 18 feet of water. In the half century since, the Gulf of Mexico geological province (and its industrial and political regimes) has been transformed repeatedly.

Successive waves of innovation have been dramatic, as evidenced each year at the Offshore Technology Conference (OTC) in Houston (Offshore Technology Conference 2007). The results have improved the prospects for locating petroleum deposits; opened access to ever more remote sites; altered the techniques of collection, storage, and transport of products; and (through resurvey and rediscovery processes) turned apparently mature and exhausted sites and basins into new, high-growth prospects (US Department of Energy, Office of Fossil Energy 1999; US Department of Energy, Office of Natural Gas and Petroleum Technology 1997).

These transformative technologies have affected various facets of offshore development. In exploration, three- and four-dimensional seismic image measurements have dramatically refined the accuracy of pre-drill intelligence. This technology, incidentally, has a major implication for offshore regions that have been "inactive" in recent decades, either because of formal moratorium policies (as in British Columbia and the Northwest Territories) or because of lapses in exploration rights-holdings. The reopening of such areas facilitates qualitative reappraisals through new seismic campaigns. Second, directional drilling has become far more sophisticated, allowing both angular and horizontal access to reservoirs and the sub-surface linkage of small, complex deposits. In offshore environments, this technology provides great flexibility in drilling multiple wells in significantly dispersed configurations from a single platform and in utilizing seabed lines to gather the product together. Finally, techniques of "measurement while drilling" allow ongoing well data to be compiled in a single step during the drilling process. In super-high-cost environments, where single wells can cost $50 million to $75 million in shallow water and twice that amount in the greater depths of the continental slope, these technologies represent dramatic economies.

In production, the most visible evidence of technology are the new structures above the surface, including a variety of production platforms, ranging from jacket towers to semi-submersibles to compliant towers and floating systems for production, storage, and offloading (FPSOs) that offer an alternative to pipeline transit. Until recently, the FPSO option was restricted to oil field development. However in the past few years, this option has been extended to gas fields, with ship-based plants being used to liquefy and store natural gas (the so-called FLNG systems) before offloading to LNG tankers.

For its part, the offshore industry has expressed frustration that step-changes in technological advance have not been adequately recognized or appreciated by either the policy establishment or the interested public. This lack of recognition is a cause of corporate frustration because many such advances have altered, sometimes decisively, the risk equations of offshore activities. The impact of these changes is especially pertinent to a sector whose periodic political crisis moments—the Santa Barbara blowout of 1968, the Mexican Ixtoc 1 blowout in 1979, the Ocean Ranger loss in 1982, and the Piper Alpha platform fire of 1988—are 20 to 40 years in the past.

At the same time, the relentless drive toward new technologies raises questions of reliability, transferability, and risk of unintended consequences. In western states, the organized public will continue to pose such questions as long as offshore operations are underway (Coalition to Restore Coastal Louisiana 1989; Freudenburg and Gramling 1994; Jenkins-Smith and St. Clair 1993). Indeed, with offshore operators seeking and obtaining permission to drill in 10,000 feet of water and to sub-floor depths of 25,000 feet, it could hardly be otherwise (Oynes 2003; US Minerals Management Service 2003). As a result, project assessment (both environmental and socio-economic) remains a central and politically charged terrain. It has precipitated familiar policy debates on the roles of "prescriptive" versus "performance-based" regulations, varieties of industry self-regulation, or third-party certification (Pratt, Becker, and McClenahan 2002).

THE POLITICS OF OFFSHORE OIL AND GAS PRODUCTION IN CANADA

As was discussed previously in this chapter and by Brownsey (see chapter 12), the history of commercial petroleum in federal systems is, in significant part, a history of intergovernmental conflict (Fitzgerald 2001; Hunt 1989; Laendner 1993). The development of commercial offshore oil and gas reserves has pitted national governments against provinces and states, and provinces against one another, in struggles over issues of jurisdiction, resource ownership, fiscal policy, environmental security, and domestic industrial and employment benefits, to name only the most prominent issues. What began on land has carried over to the water, where Washington faces coastal states from Maine to Alaska, and Ottawa faces provinces from Newfoundland to British Columbia.[1] In such cases, a strong proclivity seems to exist for constitutional litigation, in which central and regional governments advance sovereign claims that are determined by judicial review. In both the United States and Canada, central authorities emerged legally dominant from this phase. Supreme Courts generally found the national case for sovereign powers over continental shelf resources to be superior to provincial and state arguments for historical (colonial) entitlements.

In the opening decades of offshore petroleum (1950–1970), such jurisdictions may well have appeared to be self-contained and exhaustive. That is, all political questions pertaining to offshore petroleum were considered to fall under national jurisdiction. If continental shelf regions were valued economically for their petroleum reserves alone, this arrangement might have been sustained indefinitely, with federal authorities administering leases, collecting royalties, and regulating extractive projects in much the same way as did Texas and Alberta on land.

However, the very fact of ocean jurisdiction introduced complicating factors. One was the presence of coexisting and potentially rival industries, such as fishing, marine transport, and coastal tourism, which had substantial (and historically prior) claims to ocean use (Doyle 1978; Goldstein 1982). Their effective political mobilizations not only challenged offshore resource administrators to expand their policy repertoires but also provided avenues for provincial and state authorities to reassert an offshore presence. The fishing resource offers a prime example. Apart from the internal waters of bays, estuaries, and the coastal strip, Canadian provincial involvement in marine fisheries centres on land-based processing and sale (Pross and McCorquodale 1990). However, this arrangement has been more than sufficient to enable provincial authorities to champion the economic interests of their fishing sectors in the face of risk or threat from oil interests. On the Atlantic coast, programs to compensate the fisheries for oil and gas disruption became pressing concerns following the Hibernia and Sable discoveries of the late 1970s (Heber 1986). Moreover, after the joint federal–provincial management board structure emerged in 1982, the provinces enjoyed direct leverage over key petroleum management decisions, by virtue of the ministerial veto. Thus, Nova Scotia was able to trigger, unilaterally, the 1987 moratorium on petroleum exploration on Georges Bank, in the name of protecting one of the region's richest fisheries (Baetz 1993).

Another key political conditioning issue was the heightened awareness of ocean ecology beginning in the 1970s. This issue owed much to the damaging environmental episodes mentioned earlier, together with tanker spills, marine mammal welfare campaigns, and a growing appreciation of the scale of shore-based pollution. The ocean commons were revealed as a profoundly complex yet fragile environment that was in desperate need of integrated and effective governance (Silva

1986). Here, policy issues are linked, overlaps abound, and intergovernmental and inter-agency conflicts are latent in all commercial and regulatory actions (Dauterive 2000; Mann Borghese 1998; Wilder 1998). Such recognition hastened the breakdown of the traditional sectoral approach to ocean resources (Andersen 1993). Previously separate domains—of oil, fish, transport, communications, parks, and protection—are now increasingly aggregated, creating a new era of ocean politics. In Canada, the new guiding principles include ecosystem management, the precautionary approach, and integrated decision making (Fisheries and Oceans Canada 2002). An emerging new repertoire of policy instruments and planning tools now addresses coastal management areas, large ocean management areas, and protected marine areas.

Although the institutions of ocean governance are still rudimentary, they do provide a new political space that is being actively contested by an expanding range of interests. The risks of this situation have not been lost on the offshore petroleum bloc, which recognizes the potential of holistic ocean policies to erode or even displace sectoral resource regimes (Atlantic Canadian Petroleum Institute 2001; Public Review Commission 2002). Much will depend on how the existing regulatory arrangements are reconciled with new initiatives and where the seats of ministerial and bureaucratic authority are lodged. As a result, the interface between the respective management regimes will likely continue to be politically contested for the foreseeable future.

State Strength and Capacities

Another key dimension of offshore politics involves the capacities of coastal states to manage hydrocarbon resources. A panoply of policy instruments figure in any effort at offshore management (see figure 13.1).

Particularly intriguing, however, is the application of this perspective to the offshore development area. In Atlantic Canada, for instance, a curious institutional hybrid has emerged over the past 25 years. Its roots lay in the federal–provincial disputes over offshore resource ownership, and its stakes were exacerbated by the energy price spikes of the 1970s brought about by the Organization of Petroleum Exporting Countries (OPEC). As Atlantic offshore exploration began to yield significant discoveries (particularly the twin Hibernia oil and Venture gas strikes of 1979), the need to resolve uncertainties over state jurisdiction became more urgent, with industry interests hesitating to move forward so long as their tenures remained cloudy. At this point, the dual "ownership" dispute was transformed into a joint "management" regime, by virtue of a series of negotiated intergovernmental accords.

The concept of the joint federal–provincial offshore management board has a mixed provenance originating in the 1970s.[2] In petroleum, the prototype was the tri-province Maritime Offshore Agreement of 1977. It was succeeded by the

Figure 13.1   Offshore Petroleum Management Issue Areas and Instruments

Offshore policy issue areas	Policy instruments
1. Determining jurisdiction	Continental shelf jurisdictions; international conventions; constitutional powers; boundary and federalism litigation; joint management boards.
2. Allocating rights to explore and extract	Auctions or concessions; exploration, commercial discovery, production licences; moratoriums; state "back-in" provisions.
3. Project assessment/approval	Project proposals; panel reviews; public hearings; project licensing; terms and conditions; discretionary deviations.
4. Royalty and taxation	Cash royalties; royalties-in-kind; royalty relief; depletion allowances; state oil companies.
5. Health and safety	Statutory prescriptions; codes of conduct; operator management systems; third-party standards and audits.
6. Environmental security	Project environmental assessments; statutory prescriptions on equipment or processes; environmental effects monitoring; operator management systems; third-party standards and audits.
7. Industrial and employment benefits	Procurement plan reviews (undertakings, bid lists, award pre-screening, designated items, domestic-content levels); employment plan reviews (training, hiring levels); audits; performance links to future rights allocation.
8. State regulatory reform	Streamlining of multi-agent processes; joint project assessments; statutory incorporation of private industry standards; use of performance-based standards; reduced regulatory cycle times.

Source: Adapted from Fee, D. 1988. *Petroleum exploitation strategy*. London: Belhaven Press.

Canada–Nova Scotia offshore petroleum deal of 1982, which was transcended, in turn, by the 1985 (Canada–Newfoundland) Atlantic Accord and the revised Canada–Nova Scotia deal a year later (Crosbie 2003). Talks on a parallel Pacific Accord between Ottawa and British Columbia were underway after 1987, but halted, as mentioned earlier, with the decision not to lift the long-standing west coast moratorium on offshore drilling. However, the prospects for inter-basin policy learning remain strong (House 2002).

A new template for offshore management was established by the east coast accords—of jointly appointed petroleum boards supported by professional staff, exercising delegated regulatory powers under federal and provincial statutes and mandated to coordinate the essential administrative functions for the oil and gas sector. Although the boards enjoy substantial autonomy as Crown agents, they are responsible to designated federal and provincial ministers, who also exercise powers of review, confirmation, and the overriding of select types of decisions through "an elaborate series of trumping arrangements" vis-à-vis the boards (Brown 1991). At each level of government, a range of bureaus and agencies are bound into the board structure by formal memorandums of agreement, whereas industry and public interests seek access through a shifting network of advisory committees.

OFFSHORE PETROLEUM REGULATION IN THE NEW MILLENNIUM

In the years since 2000, the offshore regulatory system has come under wholesale political challenge of a sort not seen for a generation. This challenge is evident on all three coasts, though the configurations of players, interests, and processes are distinct in each case. A common signifying theme, however, is that the offshore regulatory regimes—those broad state structures of rules and values—are past their time for review and overhaul. Although this case is advanced most frequently by offshore petroleum capital, it is not necessarily resisted by federal or provincial state agents, who themselves strain against strictures of the 1980s "joint" political settlement.

The case for regulatory change is concise. Offshore resources administration is a multi-layered construct whose elements are not well integrated. Consequently, its workings are slow, repetitive, and often working at cross-purposes (Canadian Association of Petroleum Producers 2002). This balkanized character is due partly to the ambitious scope of offshore regulation, which covers sectors from environmental protection to health and safety to rights and royalties and business benefits. It is also due to the incremental growth of these functions, normally in separate policy silos, over a period of 30 years and longer. The result is not rational, from either the industry or the public service perspective. Regulatory change is expensive to comply with and unpredictable in its results. Furthermore, it presents huge challenges of coordination, across two (sometimes three) levels of government and more than a dozen major departments and agencies. This difficulty has been acknowledged in the state realm by the design of offshore energy accords, joint federal–provincial management authorities, and memorandums of agreement between lead departments and agencies. Yet the memorandum of agreement (MoA) process has been glacial, remains incomplete, and reveals at best a mixed record of achievement.

What, then, is the alternative? The offshore petroleum operators talk of regulatory simplification or rationalization, limiting the range of policy goals, shortening the length of regulatory cycles, shifting from prescription to performance-based regulation, or achieving regulatory efficiency as an industry competitive advantage. The overarching theme is the need for greater predictability and greater certainty in relations between the state and the stakeholders. Such a policy discourse causes alarm in other reaches of the offshore policy network, most visibly in the environmental non-governmental organizations (NGOs) but also in offshore business supply circles, the fishing sector, and the coastal public domain. Perhaps for these reasons, the recent review initiatives have resulted in varying degrees of political visibility. The three major initiatives are briefly described below.

On the Atlantic coast, the process kicked off in November 2002, when a high-level business–government conference was convened in Halifax under the name of the Atlantic Canada Energy Roundtable (AER). The catalyst was the Canadian Association of Petroleum Producers, which had already flagged "regulatory efficiency and effectiveness" as a pressing public policy concern. However, more immediate driving pressures came from the disappointing results of early drilling on the deepwater continental slope (depths exceeding 200 metres) and the regulatory "time out" declared by leading operator EnCana, in suspending its Deep Panuke project application early in 2003.

The AER brought together senior leaders and staff from four federal departments (Industry Canada, the Department of Fisheries and Oceans, Natural Resources Canada, and the Atlantic Canada Opportunities Agency); energy ministers from Nova Scotia, New Brunswick, and Newfoundland and Labrador; and chief executive officers from 25 leading petroleum companies. The industry premise was that "the Atlantic Canada regulatory framework is dated and inefficient; this increases costs and cycle times" (Protti 2002). Of particular concern was the new burden imposed by the Canadian Environmental Assessment Agency (CEAA) process, which was extended to the Atlantic offshore region after 2001. Government representatives were certainly willing to enter the dialogue. Ottawa embraced the discourse of "smart regulation" in its fall 2002 throne speech, and the offshore provinces recognized that the exploration bubble of the late 1990s had deflated if not burst. Thus, this inaugural round table meeting was propelled by a confluence of commercial and political concerns.

The structure of this exercise is one of its most notable features. First, it drew representation from the most senior levels of the respective organizations. As a result, their endorsement of a continuing work program, with agreement to review the results at regular intervals, ensured not only that follow-up would occur but that tangible progress was expected. Second, under guidance from discussion papers from CAPP and the Atlantic Canada Economic Council, among others, two leading themes were identified for future work by middle-level and technical officials. One theme dealt with "regulatory issues," with the goal of broad spectrum regulatory renewal along streamlined, performance-based criteria. The second theme involved "industrial opportunities" and the need for a competitive contracting environment in which current international project procurement practices would form the basis for a new benefits regime and pave the way for an export-oriented Atlantic supplier base (Atlantic Energy Roundtable 2003). In 2005, the AER reported mixed progress in delivering results. Firm commitments have been agreed on for coordinated regulatory review of future offshore projects, within significantly shorter time frames. Consensus was not reached, however, on a series of industry cost concerns: more discretionary rules on safety and environmental protection, the flow testing of new discoveries, the formal environmental assessment of exploratory wells, and reporting protocols for industrial benefits .

In the North, the time frame is similar but the process is different. A major pipeline infrastructure will be required to sustain long-term natural gas activities. At least two possible projects were evident by the year 2000. The Mackenzie Valley Project proposed to link three major gas fields in the Mackenzie Delta to the Alberta trunk system through a large-diameter pipeline with an initial capacity of approximately 1 billion cubic feet (bcf) per day. The Alaska Gas Producers pipeline project proposed to connect the north slope gas "over the top" of the Arctic coast and down the Mackenzie Valley, with a capacity four times that of the Mackenzie pipeline.

With such major projects in the offing, and the Aboriginal groups in settled claim areas indicating their interest in joint ownership, the issue of the regulation of a northern pipeline project was back on the agenda after almost 25 years. In November 2000, a committee of regulatory agency heads was convened to explore ways of coordinating the regulatory processes that mandated at least eight separate public hearings. Eighteen months later, the Northern Pipeline Environmental Impact Assessment and Regulatory Chairs' Committee released a co-operation plan endorsed by three federal agencies, the Government of the Northwest Territories and two of its boards, and four Aboriginal settlement boards. This plan sets out general terms for a joint environmental assessment process, a coordinated regulatory process, consolidated information requirements, shared technical support resources, and a public involvement plan. In addition, an estimated three- to four-year template of phases and outputs was forecast, covering the time from the filing of a preliminary information package (PIP) to complete certification and permitting (Northern Pipeline Environmental Impact Assessment and Regulatory Chairs' Committee 2002). Notably, this plan was agreed to prior to the filing of any project applications. Since then, the Mackenzie Valley group triggered a formal regulatory review by filing its preliminary plan in June 2003.

The west coast situation offers a different face again. As seen earlier, British Columbia showed several signs of framing a regulatory and management system that meets or exceeds the streamlining features described above. The moratorium offered an umbrella under which such preparations could occur.

Whatever the outcomes, this proliferation of review and redesign initiatives speaks to the degree of political flux in offshore regulatory regimes. The range of political agendas and policy priorities is broad. Obviously these initiatives are advanced in differing scales, and they should be interpreted accordingly. Restructuring a multi-agency, consolidated regulatory process is a massive undertaking, as would be seeking to tighten the permitting procedures within a single agency. In the Arctic and Pacific, opportunities exist to build or restructure the regime in periods of comparative political calm, while capitalizing on the experience of the Atlantic coast. Equally, the new bargains are being negotiated in settings of varying political and commercial urgency. The reality of competition between Canada's three offshore coastal regimes cannot be denied, given the shared involvement of the offshore corporate sector. Each regime exhibits its own sources of comparative political and commercial advantage. Only the east coast has reached the offshore production threshold. Only the North has made significant progress in accommodating Aboriginal title and treaty interests. Only the west coast is in a position to fashion new arrangements on a relatively blank canvas. On each coast, agencies have histories of interaction that can be alternately emancipating or paralyzing.

CONCLUSIONS

In Canada, offshore petroleum politics reflect many of the classic staple resource features. Clearly, the possibility exists for a petroleum staple trade in all of Canada's continental-shelf regions. Capital seeks to appropriate a valued product and draws upon extensive technical and organizational capabilities to achieve this end. The vitality of this staple trade depends on market conditions external to the host economy—in this case, the notoriously volatile markets for oil and gas.

As with most staples, the host states play a co-determining role in development prospects. State agencies can impinge on the industry through a variety of elements that make up an offshore petroleum strategy, including regulatory measures aimed at Crown rights, royalties, health and safety issues, environmental concerns, and industrial and employment benefits. Mature staple states often adopt quasi-mercantilist outlooks, utilizing Crown ownership to stipulate the terms of access while seeking to lever maximum commercial linkages and domestic surplus retention.

Whatever the state presence, its interests in managing field and basin development on a rounded basis are, at some point, likely to collide with the narrower extractive project focus of corporate sponsors. Finally, it should be remembered that the commercial and political underpinnings of staple industries are likely to change over time. The Canadian joint offshore boards are institutional products of the 1975–1985 era of the energy crisis. Their capacities to adapt to subsequent regime changes, including energy price decontrol, new technological capabilities, and shifting paradigms of project regulation, will co-determine the pace and scale of staple growth. Increasing pressures encourage policy convergence, and Canada's offshore future may yet involve a single cluster of offshore capital (indigenous or external) in a dominant investment position, facing a single (unitary or joint) regulator.

Despite the cluster of "mature staple" properties mentioned above, the offshore petroleum sector exhibits "post-staple" attributes in a number of striking ways, which are particularly evident in the growing influence of metropolitan or post-material political forces in the offshore sector. This influence may stem, in part, because the industry in question does not occupy a spatial hinterland in the classic sense of a social formation resident in a material-extraction zone. Indeed, the offshore petroleum shelves are strikingly socially uninhabited. This situation creates a context of ambiguity on matters of stakeholders and representation. The petroleum staple "community" is restricted in size (by the capital intensity of its operations) and transitory in its presence (rotating in and out of offshore workplaces). Meanwhile the shore-based "community" that might claim a stake based on physical proximity (coastal residence) or livelihood (fisheries) is, as we have seen, largely disconnected from the petroleum staple.

Second, the political templates for offshore regulation have been forged over three decades of dramatically shifting public and governmental values. Whereas industry regulation was traditionally aimed at stabilizing the conditions for production and profit, the new trajectories of social regulation deal with the externalities of material production, for workplace health, safety, and environmental security. As we have seen, these fields are now central arenas of political conflict between offshore capital and state authorities. Corporate resistance to offshore social regulation mounted rapidly through the 1990s and is now reflected in a series of concerted business–government initiatives, such as the Atlantic Energy Roundtable (with parallels in the North Sea and the Gulf of Mexico), aimed at reducing the social costs of offshore operations while redefining the locus of regulatory initiative. This is the world of harmonized and coordinated reviews, performance-based standards, and the so-called smart regulation, where the private–public interface is being presently redefined.

Finally, the offshore petroleum sector is clearly far from insulated, politically, from the spillover impacts of other fields. Of particular interest are the potential challenges from new, holistic resource management paradigms and new social group claims. Ocean governance strategies that seek to marshal a wider array of stakeholders under the banners of integrated management, ecosystem modelling, and sustainable development pose a potential threat to resource management regimes (offshore petroleum, for example) based on single-sector extraction. On the other hand, the recent legal claims by Aboriginal peoples to offshore resource ownership, which have won some degree of judicial recognition, stand to insert yet another policy template onto the offshore domain.

In so many respects, offshore petroleum is poised at a sensitive juncture. Perhaps the most significant political chapters remain to be written.

NOTES

    *   The author acknowledges financial support from the Social Sciences and Humanities Research Council of Canada, under the project "Policy innovation and management on the eastern continental shelf: The politics of offshore petroleum development in Nova Scotia and Louisiana."

    1. A similar dynamic occurs in Australia (Cullen 1990; Haward 1989).

    2. Note the parallel negotiations over power-sharing relations, at Aboriginal land claims discussions and through co-management schemes put forward in other renewable resource fields (Clancy 1990, 1999).

REFERENCES

Andersen, S.S. 1993. *The struggle for North Sea oil and gas: Government strategies in Denmark, Britain and Norway.* Stockholm: Scandinavian University Press.

Atlantic Canadian Petroleum Institute. 2001. *Offshore oil and gas approvals in Atlantic Canada.* Halifax: Erlands and Associates.

Atlantic Energy Roundtable. 2003. Submission to Atlantic Energy Roundtable II. Online at http://www2.nrcan.gc.ca/es/erb/CMFiles/Roundtable_Submission_-_EN192PIE-05112003-3212.pdf.

Baetz, M.C. 1993. Texaco and Georges Bank (A). In *Readings and Canadian Cases in Business, Government, and Society,* ed. M.C. Baetz, 305–25. Scarborough, ON: Nelson Canada.

Baxter, V. 1993. Political economy of oil and exploitation of offshore oil. In *Impact of Offshore Oil Exploration,* ed. S. Laska, 15–76. New Orleans: Mineral Management Service.

Beale, B. 1980. *Energy and industry.* Toronto: Canadian Institute for Economic Policy.

Berry, G.R. 1974. The oil lobby and the energy crisis. *Canadian Public Administration* 17(4): 600–35.

Brown, D.M. 1991. Sea-change in Newfoundland: From Peckford to Wells. In *Canada: The State of the Federation, 1990,* eds. R.L. Watts and D.M. Brown, 199–229. Kingston: Institute of Intergovernmental Relations.

Canadian Association of Petroleum Producers. 2002. Submission: Atlantic Energy Roundtable. Online at http://www.capp.ca/raw.asp?x=1&dt=NTV&dn=40286.

Chircop, A., and Marchand, B.A. 2001. Oceans Act: Uncharted seas for offshore development in Atlantic Canada? *Dalhousie Law Journal* 24(1): 23–50.

Cicin-Sain, B., and Knecht, R. 1987. Federalism under stress: The case of offshore oil and California. In *Perspectives on Federalism,* ed. H.N. Scheiber, 149–76. Berkeley: University of California Press.

Cicin-Sain, B., and Knecht, R. 2000. *The future of US ocean policy: Choices for the new century.* Washington, DC: Island Press.

Clancy, P. 1990. Political devolution and wildlife management. In *Devolution and Constitutional Development in the Canadian North*, ed. G. Dacks, 71–120. Ottawa: Carleton University Press.

Clancy, P. 1999. The politics and administration of Aboriginal claims. In *Public Administration and Policy*, eds. M.W. Westmacott and H. Mellon, 55–72. Scarborough, ON: Prentice Hall Allyn & Bacon.

Coalition to Restore Coastal Louisiana. 1989. *Coastal Louisiana: Here today and gone tomorrow?* Baton Rouge, LA: The Coalition.

Crosbie, J.C. 2003. *Overview paper on the 1985 Canada–Newfoundland Accord Act.* Prepared for the Royal Commission on Renewing and Strengthening Our Place in Canada. St. John's: Queen's Printer.

Cullen, R. 1990. *Federalism in action: The Australian and Canadian offshore disputes.* Sydney, Australia: The Federation Press.

Dauterive, L. 2000. *Rigs-to-reefs: Policy, progress and perspectives.* New Orleans: Minerals Management Service.

Doyle, R.G. 1978. *Maine and the search for OCS oil and gas.* Bangor, ME: Maine State Planning Office.

Dunning, F. 1989. *Britain's offshore oil and gas.* London: UK Offshore Operators Association.

Fant, D.V. 1990. *An analysis and evaluation of rules and procedures governing OCS operations.* Washington, DC: American Bar Association.

Fee, D.A. 1988. *Petroleum exploitation strategy.* London: Belhaven Press.

Fee, D.A., and O'Dea, J. 1986. *Technology for developing marginal offshore oilfields.* London: Elsevier Applied Science.

Fisheries and Oceans Canada. 2002. *Canada's ocean strategy.* Ottawa: Fisheries and Oceans Canada.

Fitzgerald, E.A. 2001. *The seaweed rebellion: Federal–State conflicts over offshore energy development.* Lanham, MD: Lexington Books.

French, R. 1980. *How Ottawa decides: Planning and industrial policy-making 1968–1980.* Toronto: Canadian Institute for Economic Policy.

Freudenburg, W.R., and Gramling, R. 1994. *Oil in troubled waters.* Albany, NY: State University of New York Press.

Gibbons, M., and Voyer, R. 1974. *A technology assessment system: A case study of east coast offshore petroleum exploitation.* Ottawa: Science Council of Canada.

Goldstein, J. 1982. *The politics of offshore oil.* New York: Praeger.

Gramling, R. 1996. *Oil on the edge: Offshore development, conflict, gridlock.* Albany, NY: State University of New York Press.

Gurney, J. 1997. *The Gulf of Mexico: Revival and opportunity in the oil industry.* London: Financial Times.

Haward, M. 1989. The Australian offshore constitutional settlement. *Marine Policy* 13(October): 334–48.

Heber, R.W. 1986. Fish and oil: The cultural ecology of offshore resource activities in Nova Scotia. In *Fish versus Oil: Resources and Rural Development in North Atlantic Societies*, ed. J.D. House, 162–75. St. John's: Institute for Social and Economic Research.

Hildreth, R. 1986. Ocean resources and intergovernmental relations in the 1980s: Outer continental shelf hydrocarbons and minerals. In *Ocean Resources and US Intergovernmental Relations in the 1980s*, ed. M. Silva, 155–96. Boulder, CO: Westview Press.

House, J.D. 1980. *The last of the free enterprisers*. Toronto: McClelland & Stewart.

House, J.D. 1985. *The challenge of oil: Newfoundland's quest for controlled development*. St. John's: Institute for Social and Economic Research.

House, J.D. 2002. Myths and realities about petroleum-related development: Lessons for British Columbia from Atlantic Canada and the North Sea. *Journal of Canadian Studies*, 37(4): 9–32.

Hunt, C.D. 1989. *The offshore petroleum regimes of Canada and Australia*. Calgary: Canadian Institute of Resources Law.

Jenkin, M. 1981. *British industry and the North Sea: State intervention in a developing industrial sector*. London: Macmillan.

Jenkins-Smith, H.C., and St. Clair, G.K. 1993. The politics of offshore energy: Empirically testing the advocacy coalition framework. In *Policy Change and Learning*, eds. P. Sabatier and H.C. Jenkins-Smith, 149–76. Boulder, CO: Westview Press.

Kash, D.E., White, I.L., Bergey, K.H., Chartrock, M.A., Devine, M.D., Salomon, S.N., and Young, H.W. 1973. *Energy under the oceans: A technology assessment of outer continental shelf oil and gas operations*. Norman, OK: University of Oklahoma Press.

Keith, R.F., Fischer, C.E., De'Ath, E.J., Farkas, G.R., and Francis, S.C. 1976. *Northern development and technology assessment systems: A study of petroleum development programs in the Mackenzie Delta-Beaufort Sea region and the Arctic Islands*. Ottawa: Science Council of Canada.

Laendner, G. 1993. *A failed strategy: The offshore oil industry's development of the outer continental shelf*. New York: Garland.

Lore, G. 1992. *Exploration and discoveries, 1947–1989: An historical perspective*, Report 91-0078. New Orleans: Minerals Management Service, Gulf of Mexico Region.

Mann Borghese, E. 1998. *The oceanic circle: Governing the seas as a global resource*. Tokyo: United Nations University Press.

Mitchell, J., Selley, N., and Morita, K. 2001. *The new economy of oil: Impacts on business, geopolitics and society*. London: Royal Institute of International Affairs.

National Research Council, Marine Board. 1980. *Outer continental shelf frontier technology*. Washington, DC: National Academy of Sciences.

National Research Council, Marine Board. 1997. *Striking a balance: Improving stewardship of marine areas*. Washington, DC: National Academy Press.

Nelsen, B.F. 1991. *The state offshore: Petroleum, politics and state intervention on the British and Norwegian continental shelves*. New York: Praeger.

Noreng, O. 1980. *The oil industry and government strategy in the North Sea*. London: Croom Helm.

Noreng, O. 2002. *Crude power: Politics and the oil market*. London: I.B. Tauris.

Northern Pipeline Environmental Impact Assessment and Regulatory Chairs' Committee. 2002. Cooperation plan: For the environmental impact assessment and regulatory review of a northern gas pipeline project through the Northwest Territories. Online at http://www.ngps.nt.ca/docs/coop_plan_FINAL.pdf.

Offshore/Onshore Technologies Association of Nova Scotia. 2007a. History. Online at http://www.otans.com/history.asp.

Offshore/Onshore Technologies Association of Nova Scotia. 2007b. Welcome to OTANS. Online at http://www.otans.com/index.asp.

Offshore Operators Committee. n.d. Who is the Offshore Operators Committee? Online at http://www.offshoreoperators.com/who_is.shtml.

Offshore operators division strengthens east coast organizational structure. 1984. *Eastern Offshore News*, June: 18–19.

Offshore Technology Conference. 2007. About OTC. Online at http://www.otcnet.org/otcnet/about_otc/index.html.

Oynes, C.C. 2003. *The role of deep gas from the shelf*. New Orleans: Minerals Management Service, Gulf of Mexico Region.

Pratt, J.A., Becker, W.H., and McClenahan, W.M. 2002. *Voice of the marketplace: A history of the National Petroleum Council*. College Station, TX: Texas A&M University Press.

Pross, A.P., and McCorquodale, S. 1990. The state, interests, and policy making in the east coast fishery. In *Policy Communities and Public Policy in Canada*, eds. W.D. Coleman and G. Skogstad, 34–58. Toronto: Copp Clark Pitman.

Protti, G. 2002. *Atlantic energy roundtable*. PowerPoint presentation. November 22.

Public Review Comission. 2002. *Report on the effects of potential oil and gas exploration offshore Cape Breton*. Halifax: Canada–Nova Scotia Offshore Petroleum Board.

Richards, J., and Pratt, L. 1979. *Prairie capitalism: Power and influence in the new west*. Toronto: McClelland & Stewart.

Silva, M. 1986. *Ocean resources and United States intergovernmental relations in the 1980s*. Boulder, CO: Westview Press.

Stalport, N. 1992. Canadian offshore renewable resources: Law and policy issues. In *Canadian Ocean Law and Policy*, ed. D. VanderZwaag, 192–234. Toronto: Butterworths.

Szell, J.S. 1979. *Innovations in energy: The story of Kerr McGee*. Norman, OK: University of Oklahoma Press.

Text of offshore agreement. 1977. *Halifax Chronicle-Herald*, February 2: 1, 34.

Townsend Gault, I. 1983. *Petroleum operations on the continental margin: The legal issues in a modern perspective*. Calgary: Canadian Institute of Resources Law.

US Department of Energy, Office of Fossil Energy 1999. Environmental benefits of advanced oil and gas exploration and production technology. Online at http://www.fossil.energy.gov/programs/oilgas/publications/environ_benefits/env_benefits.pdf.

US Department of Energy, Office of Natural Gas and Petroleum Technology. 1997. Oil and gas R&D programs. Online at http://www.osti.gov/bridge/servlets/purl/653604-98Wo17/webviewable/653604.pdf.

US Minerals Management Service. 2003. *Dynamics of the oil and gas industry in the Gulf of Mexico: 1980–2000—Final report.* New Orleans: Gulf of Mexico OCS Region.

Voyer, R. 1983. *Offshore oil: Opportunities for industrial development and job creation.* Ottawa: Canadian Institute for Economic Policy.

Wilder, R.J. 1998. *Listening to the sea: The politics of improving environmental protection.* Pittsburgh: University of Pittsburgh Press.

Yedlin, D. 2004. Oil patch sale. *The Globe and Mail,* May 31: B2.

CHAPTER 14

From Black Gold to Blue Gold: The Emerging Water Trade

John N. McDougall

INTRODUCTION

Canada has 7 percent of the world's renewable freshwater supply and only 0.5 percent of the world's population, but its per capita consumption of the commodity is the second highest in the world (Boyd 2001). Moreover, more than half of Canada's total water supply flows northward into the Arctic Ocean and Hudson Bay. Thus, neither the practical availability nor the "renewability" of freshwater resources can be taken for granted in the places where most Canadians live and most Canadian industries operate. As a result, proper water management is receiving closer attention today than during most of the country's past (Environment Canada 2007). A majority of Canadians are, therefore, unlikely to ever be persuaded that their lakes and rivers are "surplus" to their needs. Canada's waterways also played a crucial role in the formation and evolution of the Canadian economy—most notably, the fur trade and the early logging industry—to the extent that they helped to shape the Canadian identity. In short, the idea of treating bulk water (as opposed to bottled water) as an "exportable good" has a very low probability of wide acceptance among the Canadian public.

Water resources in Canada are "potential staples" or, as Netherton suggests (see chapter 15), "quasi-staples." That is, although the exploitation of water resources features many of the aspects of a staples industry, such as large-scale, technologically influenced, rural-based, bulk-commodity characteristics, it lacks other characteristics, especially a traditional staples export orientation. However, this situation is changing. In the case of electricity, deregulation in both Canadian and US markets has resulted in the emergence of a new production regime in Canada, one that is approaching a typical "mature" staples industry, albeit with new environmental regulations and conditions for participation of a much broader spectrum of "stakeholders," which bears some resemblance to a "post-staples" model (see Netherton, chapter 15). The same is true of water resources as a whole. For almost two decades, one of the most controversial concerns raised by Canadian opponents of free trade with the United States was that free trade would lead to the large-scale export of water from Canada, in which case, the commodity of water would become a "staple," and the water industry that would then emerge in Canada would move from a "potential" staple industry to an "actual" staple industry.

The main point of this chapter is to describe recent developments regarding water in relation to free trade between Canada and the United States. As will be detailed below, currently—even with the North American Free Trade Agreement (NAFTA) in effect—both the economics of bulk-water transmission and the existing federal–provincial water policy regime place prohibitive obstacles in the way of bulk-water exports. However, the emerging international trade regime with respect to investor rights and trade in services creates considerable potential for major foreign investments in, and hence control of, water services. In other words, contrary to the expectation of many observers, the "trade in goods" aspects of market liberalization may have substantially less impact on the use of Canada's water resources than those provisions of the trade agreement relating to rights of establishment and trade in services.

This development has many interesting parallels with the current situation in the petroleum sector in which exports of oil and gas services have become increasingly important in recent years. These parallels will be explored to determine what they can tell us about the future development of a potential water staple. Thus, the remainder of this chapter is devoted to a closer examination of the political economy of bulk-water exports from Canada in the light of the history and future prospects for the country's petroleum industry. In particular, this chapter draws out the similarities and differences between the emerging trade regime with respect to water and the past and present trade regimes with respect to oil, natural gas, and the construction of pipelines to carry both.

Accordingly, this chapter will examine the costs of transporting bulk water; the regulatory constraints bearing on cross-border transmission projects; the evolution of the international trade regime with respect to oil and gas; the free trade provisions governing bulk-water exports and prospective international investments in Canadian water services; and finally, the growing role of multinational corporations in the provision of water services worldwide.

THE ECONOMICS OF BULK-WATER TRANSMISSION

Fresh water in its natural state of rivers, lakes, and glaciers presents a particularly striking range of potential alternative economic uses. Some fundamental economic questions emerge about the optimal form in which to "export" bulk water: as the commodity itself, embedded in foods or in manufactured items, or as services. For example, should it enter "trade" as a bulk export; as a power export via hydroelectricity generation; as embodied in agricultural or fisheries exports; in manufactured products using either hydro resources, such as aluminum, or large-scale water inputs, such as steel; or, left in place, as ecological or other forms of tourism? Similar to all staples, in addition to the export of bulk-commodity water itself, the possibly higher range and value of potential and existing "water-based exports" should be considered. The international trade in food grains provides one example of existing higher-value-added exports based on water resources, as do most other agricultural crops, along with exports of industrial products, from beer to aluminum ingots, cans, car parts, and jetliner bodies (Scott, Olynyk, and Renzetti 1986, 164).

Although exporting water as a bulk-commodity staple might not be an optimal use for Canadian water, such schemes have been a constant feature of water resource discussions for many years. However, these schemes may never make economic sense.

That is, similar to the case with oil or gas, the cost of transporting large volumes of water by land or sea is considerable. For example, in their heyday, oil and gas pipelines represented some of the largest and most expensive infrastructural projects in history, rivalled perhaps only by the transcontinental railways and some of the largest electrical power facilities. Similarly, although the cost of energy transmission systems is not part of this discussion (see Netherton, chapter 15), by most accounts, the systems constructed to export such commodities often absorb a substantial portion of their delivered cost. Thus, for all of these industries, a traditional staples concern for geography (that is, the distances between major sources and major markets) has played an important role in the marketing of these resources. As Brownsey has discussed (see chapter 12), this concern largely explains why, in the North American oil and gas market, cross-border regional market structures prevailed over national market structures for most of the post–Second World War period.

As a result of these geographic realities, the economics of international bulk-water transmission does not appear to be very positive, substantiated by the simple observation that very little bulk-water transmission takes place anywhere in the world. Except for a few small-scale operations—generally involving the bulk shipment of water from one country to bottling plants in another country—practically no municipal water services anywhere in the world distribute internationally traded water.[1] In an even more convincing example, although various schemes have been touted over the last few decades to move Alaskan water by tanker to ports on the west coast of the United States, to date, none of these schemes has come to fruition. Moreover, although a few Canadian provinces (Newfoundland and Labrador, British Columbia, and Ontario) have at times granted export permits for the export of water by tanker, a combination of economics and regulatory impediments have killed these initiatives or placed them on hold for the foreseeable future.

Moving large quantities of water on a sustained basis and over large distances is a very expensive business, probably prohibitively so, and is physically possible in only five known ways: by ocean-going tanker; by tanker trucks carried by barge; by pipeline; by huge floating bags towed by ship; and by water diversions (Feehan 2001, 12). The best-known and most fully costed of these methods is that of ocean-going tankers (converted from their more conventional function of shipping crude oil), but the economics of tanker shipments of water is not very attractive. The lowest estimated cost of tanker shipments is approximately US$1.14 per cubic metre for a 15-day return trip, and the cost could easily run as high as US$3.60 per cubic metre (Feehan 2001, 13–15).[2] Meanwhile, in 2001, the wholesale cost of treated water in California, for example, was reported to range from US$400 to US$600 per acre foot, or approximately US$0.32 to US$0.49 per cubic metre (Feehan 2001, 21).[3] In some of the driest regions of the United States, these prices can double. Nevertheless, even the highest of these prices is currently insufficient to make tanker shipments competitive.

Bulk-water pipelines have also been considered and, in a few instances, have been costed as a means of transmitting water. Again, the economics of such projects is not encouraging. For example, in 1971, the Libya pipeline project was conceived to pump water a distance of more than 1,000 kilometres from the southern Nubian desert to cities on the Mediterranean. At maximum scale, this project was anticipated to supply 730 million cubic metres per year, the equivalent of a good-sized river. However, because the estimated cost was $25 billion, and the sources of groundwater involved were expected to run out in 40 to 60 years, the project was abandoned (Judd 2000, 113).[4] Meanwhile, at approximately the same time, and closer to home, a pipeline was proposed to transport water from Alaska to Lake Shasta in California, a distance of 2,200 kilometres. The estimated cost was US$110 billion, yielding unit costs of delivered water at an estimated US$2.40 to US$3.25 per cubic metre (Judd 2000, 13).[5]

In light of these figures, water diversions may be the only economically viable mode of exporting water in the quantities envisaged by both the proponents and detractors of bulk-water exports in North America. However, economic fundamentals—not to mention significant potential for political and regulatory impediments—seem certain to deter proposals for water diversion. For example, Scott, Olynyk, and Renzetti (1986, 164–65) point out that the feasibility of these projects can be undermined by such factors as overall distance, water losses in transit due to seepage, watershed storage capacity, elevation (and therefore the need for pumping facilities), and exhaustible returns to scale. Their main point is that, by increasing prospective capital costs, such factors threaten to raise significantly the overall debt that the projects must carry and thereby would increase the delivered unit cost of the water.

THE POLITICS OF BULK-WATER EXPORTS: LESSONS FROM THE OIL AND GAS EXPERIENCE

Despite the physical differences between pipelines and water diversions, the political economy of cross-border natural gas pipelines sheds light on the economic, political, and regulatory constraints that are likely to affect the cost and overall feasibility of large-scale transshipments of water. During the 1950s and 1960s, the governments of Canada and the United States encountered significant difficulties in achieving the international regulatory coordination required to undertake major cross-border pipeline projects. Both countries had a system for approving "certificates of public convenience and necessity," which empowered the companies engaged in such transcontinental projects to prevail over the other economic and social interests they impinged upon. The difficulty of the project was in coordinating the requisite authorities on both sides of the border to grant such certificates on the same—or even compatible—terms and conditions (McDougall 1982, chapters 4–6).

The promoters of such projects also encountered difficulty matching available suppliers with eventual consumers on sufficiently favourable terms—and in sufficient time—to ensure the economic viability of specific pipeline ventures. Scott, Olynyk, and Renzetti (1986, 179), for example, point to the manner in which regulatory and economic factors combined to undermine the viability of the Alaskan natural gas pipeline project aborted in the late 1970s: "This $40 billion project was half built when the US importers belatedly discovered in the late 1970s that gas from contiguous states would be less expensive than Alaskan or Canadian supplies. This discovery has led to financing difficulties and project delays so that it is now uncertain when, or even if, the pipeline will be completed." Recently, of course, similar problems have befallen contending projects aimed to link northern Alaskan and Mackenzie Delta gas reserves to markets in the United States.

The fundamental economic problem is that in order to pay for the construction of such massive projects, the prices earned on gas delivered through these pipelines need to be high enough that they promise to both depress current demand and promote an alternative supply of the commodity in the intended market, to the point where the projected need for the delivered commodity disappears. Scott, Olynyk, and Renzetti (1986, 178–79) point out that, with respect to potential

Canadian water exports to the United States, "the delivery of Canadian water ... would be a very unattractive alternative to developing the political will to make better use of the water supplies already available in the south and southwestern United States." In other words, if water was priced at its market value, especially for agricultural uses, the United States would not have to worry about importing it.[6]

Meanwhile, this economic obstacle is exacerbated by mandated regulatory approval processes, which often entail allocation of burdens and benefits among suppliers, transmitters, and consumers, all of whom are subject to different economic and political priorities of the governments involved. Regulatory conflicts in such situations are very common and can lead to long delays in attaining approvals, adding another level of uncertainty and financial risk for project developers. Nation-to-nation diplomacy—and issue linkages—will likely be necessary to achieve resolution of these kinds of problems, but these processes, too, are extremely lengthy and difficult, involving negotiations and ratification of international agreements and accords that, once in place, are also very difficult to change if market conditions alter.

THE TRADE REGIME AFFECTING OIL AND GAS: LESSONS FOR WATER EXPORTS

Despite the difficulties involved in their negotiation, some major international agreements exist that affect large-scale bulk-water exports. Most notable among these are the Canada–US Free Trade Agreement (FTA) and its successor North American Free Trade Agreement (NAFTA), whose terms affect trade in most major Canadian staple exports. Despite all the attention paid to the pricing, marketing, and security of energy supplies in both the FTA and the NAFTA, scarcely a word appears in either agreement about the regulatory approval of cross-border transmission projects (see McDougall 1991). (The NAFTA provisions concerning energy regulation are discussed later in this section.)

No analogous "case law" exists under these trade agreements that can simply be reused or applied to large-scale projects designed for the transmission or redirection of bulk-water exports. However, some lessons can be derived by first comparing the development and evolution of the old protective trade regime governing oil and gas with the more recent, liberalized trade regime and then by examining the extent to which these differences may serve to guide the salient dimensions of any future liberalized international trade regime pertaining to bulk water.

The value and validity of this comparative exercise largely depends, of course, on the idea that some of the more fundamental similarities between the two types of commodities outweigh their differences. Among the most important similarities between petroleum and water as subjects of public policy—including international trade and investment policies—is their *indispensability*. Both resources can be categorized as vital. That is, living without petroleum is extremely difficult, and living without water is literally impossible. Both are almost equally necessary for the production of a wide range of highly desirable goods and services and for the enjoyment of a tolerable life in most societies. In addition, because these two commodities meet the fundamental human need for heat and/or motive power in a wide variety of ways, some of the most valuable uses of water (as hydroelectric power, for example; see Netherton, chapter 15) and petroleum products intersect or overlap with one another, and therefore both play a part in the various mixes of energy sources consumed by different industrialized societies. (Exploration of this link, which is beyond the scope of this chapter, is discussed by Netherton in chapter 15.) Some direct overlap also occurs between the two commodities in the production methods for unconventional oil and gas sources, such as tar sands extraction (see Brownsey, chapter 12), which requires access to enormous quantities of water to generate steam to separate oil from sand. Similarly, advanced forms of agricultural production require large quantities of both water and energy as inputs.

These points have all featured in recent international environmental and trade talks and agreements. For instance, both the production of synthetic crude oil ("syncrude") in Alberta and the provision of municipal water services in Ontario surfaced as major focal points during the recent political controversy over Canada's ratification of the Kyoto Protocol. The export of both water and oil and gas became even more controversial during the country's free trade debate in the mid-1980s (and, as will be discussed later in this section, a debate continues over whether NAFTA obligates Canada to export water in bulk to the United States).

However, some major differences exist between the politics and policy regimes relating to oil and gas and those relating to water. These differences have affected treatment of both products in both the pre–free trade era and the current free trade era. In the pre–free trade era, water exports and imports were simply not an issue, owing mostly to the economic impediments to the large-scale transmission of water. Also during the pre–free trade era, considerably less international trade was conducted in oil and natural gas than otherwise might have been expected. This gap between trade potential and actual trade was in part a consequence of the kinds of national policy restrictions on such trade permitted under the then reigning quasi-protectionist international trade regime that allowed countries to reserve supplies for themselves for energy self-sufficiency purposes.

Although substantial international trade in oil took place throughout most of the 20th century, national oil and natural gas markets were heavily regulated. The national market regulation had four common instruments:

1. Quantitative trade restrictions (import/export quotas)
2. Discriminatory price structures
3. Restrictions on foreign ownership
4. Investment and regulation of infrastructural development

Space permits only the briefest review of how the new North American free trade regime has constrained the use of nearly all of these instruments used to control and shape national energy markets. Broadly speaking, however, under the current regime of market liberalization, the first three of these four national policy instruments are explicitly ruled out for oil and gas, and by extension are no longer available for application to the case of water. In addition, chapter 11 of NAFTA provides foreign investors in all resource sectors with the right to legal action against any future national policies and regulations that might have the effect of denying them the opportunity to realize a financial return on previous or prospective investments, severely restricting the applicability for the fourth policy instrument.

More specifically—to begin with the first instrument of quotas and preferential prices—it may be simplest to say that North American free trade completely ruled out another National Energy Program (NEP) (on the NEP, see Brownsey, chapter 12). That is, the trade agreements specifically forbid two of the key pillars of the NEP program: the diversion of Canadian energy supplies from existing American markets in favour of expanded Canadian markets and the imposition of higher prices on remaining exports than the price charged to domestic consumers (NAFTA, articles 603, 604, and 605).

Similarly, the kinds of preference that the NEP extended to Canadian-owned firms over foreign-owned firms in the exploration and development of "Canada Lands" (territory under federal jurisdiction) would today be in violation of several NAFTA provisions in the investment chapter of the agreement. Generically, these provisions fall under the "national treatment" principle, which specifies that, in the wording of one section of that chapter, "each Party shall accord to investors of another Party treatment no less favorable than that it accords, in like circumstances, to its own investors with respect to the establishment, acquisition, expansion, management, conduct, operation, and sale or other disposition of investments" (ibid., article 1102.1). In other words, the NEP's provisions of special tax, subsidy, regulatory, and other advantages to oil and gas companies with more than 50 percent Canadian ownership—as an incentive both to encourage those firms to engage in particular kinds of performance and to encourage the "repatriation" of existing firms operating under federal jurisdiction—are now out of the question.

In terms of regulation, the NAFTA text is remarkably vague, especially given the backdrop of the enormous controversies surrounding the fate of major northern pipeline proposals during the 1970s and early 1980s. Article 606, titled "Energy Regulatory Measures," creates no precise legal obligation on the part of its members to extend national treatment to the regulation of the construction of energy facilities (although section 1 of that article explicitly extends national treatment to government action with respect to exports and export taxes). Instead, section 2 of the article stipulates that each member must ensure that "in the application of any energy regulatory measure, energy regulatory bodies within its territory avoid disruption of contractual relationships to the maximum extent practicable, and provide for orderly and equitable implementation appropriate to such measures" (ibid., article 606). As NAFTA obligations go, this one seems to fall considerably short of a precise or firmly binding commitment.

Free Trade Agreements and Water Exports and Investments

Before extrapolating these changes in the new trade regime with respect to oil and gas to the emerging regime with respect to water, it is worth noting the considerable controversy in Canada (and elsewhere) concerning the extent to which NAFTA is applicable to water exports. Given the kinds of arguments that have taken place on the matter of trade agreements and water exports, the member governments of the FTA and NAFTA have, unsurprisingly, gone out of their way to provide frequent public assurances that these agreements establish no obligation to export water. The chapter and verse of these repeated assurances will not be reviewed here. However, a 1999 study presented an objective summary of both sides of this apparently endless debate:

> [T]he three NAFTA countries clearly stated in their joint declaration of December 1993 that the NAFTA does not apply to water in its natural state in lakes, rivers, etc., since the water has not at that point "entered into commerce and become a good" for the purposes of the NAFTA. The [Canadian] federal government has taken this position all along with respect to the NAFTA and its predecessor, the FTA. Nevertheless, critics of the government position remain adamant that water in its natural state is covered by the NAFTA and that nothing short of an amendment to the agreement, accompanied by federal legislation banning large scale water exports, will protect our water resources adequately. Hence, the concerns of critics have not been appeased by the federal government's recent announcement of a strategy for seeking a commitment from all jurisdictions across Canada to prohibit the bulk removal of water, including water for export, from Canadian watersheds. Thus, the debate concerning water exports continues. (Johansen 1999, 10)

However, the joint federal–provincial strategy referred to above did not succeed, owing to the reluctance of provincial governments to cede or compromise their constitutional jurisdiction over any of their natural resources. Nevertheless, all but one of the provinces (New Brunswick) subsequently passed unilateral legislation to effectively ban the "bulk removal" of water outside their borders or between their major watersheds. In framing such prohibitions, all governments in Canada seemed to exercise great care to avoid using the term "water exports," apparently out of a concern that to do so would subject their attempts to regulate this matter to appeals under existing trade agreements (Heinmiller 2004, 20).

More recently, the government of Newfoundland and Labrador received an opinion on this matter that closely resembles the federal government's position summarized in the preceding quotation. According to this opinion:

> NAFTA and the WTO [World Trade Organization] place obligations on Canada in respect of trade in goods and in respect of investment by the investors of NAFTA parties. These obligations apply to bulk water only if the sale of bulk water is permitted and bulk water is placed into commerce. Nothing in NAFTA or the WTO requires a state to exploit its natural resources. There is, thus, no obligation on Canada to permit the sale of bulk water. It can do so if it chooses. Since natural resources, including fresh water, fall within provincial jurisdiction, any decision on the sale of bulk water is a matter for each province. (McRae 2001, 21)

This opinion goes on to make the case, however, that should a province authorize the sale of bulk water, then the relevant rules of NAFTA and the WTO would apply, with two major consequences. First, barring legitimate environmental grounds for doing so, the sale of bulk water could not be restricted to the domestic market within Canada. Second, any subsequent decision to stop selling bulk water might involve liability to foreign investors for denying them expected commercial benefits of any investments they had made (McRae 2001, 21).[7]

Worthy of exploration in greater detail is the role of NAFTA's chapter 11 in protecting the rights of investors in relation to the possible export of water, potentially to the detriment of the planning and regulation of Canada's water resources. Article 1102 can obligate Canadian governments to permit the export of water under two different scenarios. Both scenarios involve national treatment, but they differ with respect to whether the potential adverse discrimination in violation of national treatment injures either the investors in the water project or the potential consumers of the water delivered by the project. The first possibility might occur if both a Canadian and an American investor were seeking separate bulk-water export licences or water diversion approvals. The government in question would then be constrained by article 1102 from granting a licence to a Canadian investor while denying one to an American investor, which would constitute a denial of national treatment to the American investor. The implication is that Canadian governments retain the power to deny water export projects as long as such a prohibition applies to both national and foreign investors (Shrybman 2002, 7).

The second possibility, that of injury to a consumer, might occur if one company (domestic or foreign) is seeking to provide domestic water services to Canadian municipal consumers from a watershed within a Canadian province, and another company (domestic or foreign) seeks to also provide water services (from the same watershed) on behalf of municipal consumers in an American state. In other words, the comparison is not between licensing a domestic-based proposal versus a foreign-based proposal for exports but between licensing "in like circumstances" two very similar projects for the delivery of water services, with the only difference being the nationality of the beneficiaries of the investment. Here, the implication is that, after certain types of exploitation of Canadian water resources are permitted at all, their benefits cannot be restricted to Canadians. As a corollary of this, and as discussed earlier in connection with the government of Newfoundland and Labrador, no obligation seems to exist under NAFTA to grant proposals to exploit water resources for export as long as no proposals are granted to exploit bulk water commercially within Canada.

However, Steven Shrybman (2002, 8) has argued that plausible court interpretations of NAFTA's chapter 11 cast a shadow over even this conclusion. Shrybman cites the possibility that foreign investors holding riparian rights or licences under federal or provincial permits and attempting to exercise them for purposes of bulk-water exports "might assert a claim that any denial of the opportunity to do so represents expropriation under the expansive terms of article 1110. Alternatively, water use permits, which are silent with respect to the particular purpose for which the license was granted, might also give rise to claims under Chapter 11."

However, it may be that none of the possibilities raised in this discussion of NAFTA's chapter 11 represents, at this stage in NAFTA's history, a legal or political certainty. Shrybman's opinion itself notes and echoes a number of widely shared concerns about the open-ended and untested implications of chapter 11. For example, he writes (Shrybman 2002, 8) that the investment provisions of this chapter represent a "very significant innovation in the sphere of international trade agreements, and many of the terms and concepts engendered by the provisions of this chapter are entirely untested by trade dispute of [sic] judicial determination. Making predictions about the likely outcome of prospective litigation arising under these rules is a highly uncertain enterprise." Worse still, the nature of the dispute-resolution process contained within NAFTA's chapter 11 may not even produce clarification of key issues as time passes and cases potentially proliferate, because no process of judicial precedent exists under these procedures to bind any tribunal to adopting the same interpretation as another, even if a tribunal had considered the same issues. For this reason, Shrybman (ibid., 9) writes, "it will be impossible in our view for Canada to develop water policy or regulatory initiatives with any certainty that these would withstand the rigours of investor–state litigation or for that matter, trade challenge."

What can be predicted with some certainty, however, is that even if—for reasons argued earlier in this discussion—few or no proposals come forward in the near future for bulk-water exports, pressures from multinational corporations to expand into the provision of municipal water *services* in Canada will grow significantly over the foreseeable future. Hence bulk-water exports may soon become a less pressing issue for its opponents than the preservation of government ownership of critical public water services.[8]

Water Service Investments

Barlow and Clark (2002) have painted a disconcerting picture of the potential impact of water services investment on future bulk-water export plans. They describe how economic globalization is driving what they depict as a world water crisis, first by looking at the World Water Forum in March 2000, at which business organizations (such as the Global Water Partnership), the World Bank, and some of the world's largest for-profit water corporations discussed how companies could benefit from selling water around the world. The authors then consider three ways in which the delivery of water, traditionally provided by municipal governments in most countries, is gradually being taken over by multinational corporations: first, the complete selling off by governments of public water delivery and treatment systems to corporations, as has happened in the United Kingdom; second, the model developed in France, whereby water corporations are granted concessions or leases by governments to take over the delivery of the service and carry the cost of operating and maintaining the system, while collecting all the revenues for the water service and keeping the surplus as a profit; and third, a more restricted model, in which a corporation is contracted by the government to manage water services for an administrative fee, but is not permitted to take over the collection of revenues.

To date, the most prevalent of the three models is the second, often referred to as "public–private partnerships." When privatization schemes are implemented, public controls diminish substantially—even though typically the public will have provided financial guarantees to the investing firm. Most privatized water systems involve long-term concession contracts lasting between 20 and 30 years, which are extremely difficult to cancel, even when unsatisfactory performance can be demonstrated. Meanwhile, some international observers have noted that the big water corporations have developed a close working relationship with the World Bank and other global financial agencies. This relationship allows these corporations to position themselves to play a strategic role in the World Trade Organization, especially in negotiations to establish a new set of global rules for cross-border trade in water services (Finger and Lobina 1999). As a result, both the prospects of diversification and expansion of "water transnational corporations" (TNCs) and the concentration in the global water industry are added to existing concerns about the future political economy of water.

TNCs thus appear to be gaining access to a wide range of previously protected sectors of public utilities, including water. The typical oligopolistic structure of the

French market seems to be reproducing itself on a global scale as a result of trade liberalization and privatization. Collusive behaviour among TNCs is both a cause and a consequence of their excessive market power, dramatically restricting competition in water supply and sanitation. Therefore, the adoption of appropriate legal instruments may be required to bind TNCs to fair conduct and consequently to fairly manage the global trade in water services.

However, the overall conclusion remains that nothing in NAFTA, the WTO, or the General Agreement on Trade in Services (GATS) can compel any level of government to privatize local water works or to force them to contract with a global firm to do so. However, a move toward any form of privatization means that governments cannot discriminate against foreign-based firms in the provision of such services, consistent with those conclusions arrived at with respect to water exports and trade treaties.

EVALUATING THE POTENTIAL FOR WATER SERVICE DEVELOPMENT

It remains to be seen whether Canadian governments will be tempted to take advantage of the interest of the global water giants in operating or fully taking over the country's water services, especially the municipal water systems. In attempting to anticipate whether this phenomenon might be adopted and how far it might spread, some background factors may facilitate a higher rate of acceptance of this model. In the first place, such moves would need to be consistent with the recent tendency of local governments to substitute private investment—including foreign direct investment—for taxation in meeting both capital and operating budget requirements. Selling off erstwhile public assets seems a more attractive option for municipal politicians than facing the flack associated with raising taxes. At a more profound level, however, the grip that neo-conservatism seems to have on the Canadian business community seems more likely to smooth the way for more foreign direct investment (FDI) in Canadian water services.

In fact, the extent to which the orientation of Canadian business has become transformed in the neo-conservative and free trade era is quite striking. Free trade would likely not have come about if dominant Canadian business interests had not abandoned their traditional insistence on the preservation of a national economy and instead embraced the free trade option. However, matters have moved well beyond that initial repudiation of national protectionism. Today, Canadian business not only places a higher priority on market forces than on state intervention but also is beginning to place a higher priority on the American market than on the Canadian market. Although foreign direct investment flows were once almost entirely one way—from south to north—they recently have evened out, and during the past few years they have begun to flow heavily from north to south. Thus, according to the Department of Foreign Affairs and International Trade (Canada, Department of Foreign Affairs and International Trade 2003, 31, table 2.4.1), the compound annual growth rate of outward Canadian foreign direct investment into the United States has risen from 0.35 percent in 1989–1994 to 16.38 percent in 1994–2002. Meanwhile, the comparable figures for inward US investment into Canada have fallen over the same period from 26.33 percent to 16.63 percent. Because of this growing desire of Canadian businesses to penetrate the American (and other foreign) markets with investments, as opposed to simply through exports, these transactions have taken on an even greater hostility to what remains of Canadian economic protectionism, especially with respect to investor rights.

Because investors' access to foreign markets is generally available only on a reciprocal basis, a substantial proportion of the Canadian business community now lobbies the Canadian government to make the country more open to trade in services (for example) so that businesses can more effectively acquire more open access for similar investments in other countries. As a result, according to Stephen Clarkson, "Now thinking of Canada more as a home than as a host country for foreign investment, Ottawa's trade officials welcomed the tough rules that the United States wanted to impose on the world" (Clarkson 2002, 119). Having grown to enjoy their recent status as free-traders, it seems, Canadian business people now fancy themselves as footloose international investors.

The potential economic benefit to Canadian industries, such as water services, from such reciprocally liberalizing changes is difficulty to quantify precisely. However, from occasional coverage in the business pages of the country's major newspapers, the Canadian oil patch, for example, seems to be increasingly populated by firms with less interest in exporting oil and gas to the United States than in exporting worldwide their technological and managerial knowledge with respect to the discovery and optimal exploitation of oil and gas reserves.

Alberta's oil and gas firms—with much encouragement from the Alberta government—are striving more and more to add earnings associated with the export of oil and gas services, technology, and managerial expertise to earnings deriving from the export of oil and gas themselves. In fact, from 1998 to 2000, between 27 and 30 percent of the overall revenues flowing to Canada's oil and gas equipment and services industry were generated by service exports (Statistics Canada, Energy Section 2002, 2–3). More broadly, the average annual growth of Alberta's export of services in all sectors between 1989 and 1999 was 7.9 percent, an increase from $1.7 billion in 1989 to $3.6 billion in 1999 (Alberta Economic Development 2001, 11). Accordingly, a recent review of the Canadian oil and gas industry (Industry Canada 2006) reports that the oil and gas services sector "is not expected to slow down in the foreseeable future." Specifically, this sector expects annual growth rates of 12.7 percent per year (compared with expected annual growth rates of 9 percent for the oil and gas manufacturing sector) (ibid.).

These developments in the oil patch may be a good example of some of the dynamics of the post-staples state in "Schumpeterian competition mode," as described by Wellstead (see chapter 2). The city of Calgary shows signs of such a transformation, as it appears to be moving from an industrial (albeit predominantly extractive) economy to a knowledge-based economy focused on the provision (including export) of specialized services instead of the natural resources themselves. Calgary also appears to conform to the emerging model of "metropolitanization" described by Hutton (see chapter 3), in which immigration and other sources of social change combine with industrial transformations to create a shift in economic orientation. As Hutton (ibid., 50) informs us, "Increasingly, Canada's metropolitan cities ... foster engagement with international and global markets, cities, and societies, and, in the process, promote a greater measure of divergence from traditional regional resource regions and communities."

Moreover, as Stephen Clarkson anticipated, these developments have encouraged the Alberta government to press for an intensely liberalizing stance at international trade negotiations, whether at the WTO, the GATS, or the Free Trade Association of the Americas. This link is drawn explicitly in the *Alberta Service Exports Survey* (Alberta Economic Development 2001) and is elaborated in more detail in this passage from an earlier provincial study:

> For purposes of the GATS negotiations, the federal government requires an accurate assessment of the trade barriers encountered by service exporters in this country. In coordination with the Department of Intergovernmental and International Relations, who will provide the Federal Government with Alberta's position regarding the GATS negotiations, Alberta Economic Development [AED] has initiated this research to provide updated and reliable information on trade barriers faced by the province's services exporters by market, sector, mode of supply, and type of barrier. (Alberta Economic Development 1999, 5)

This undertaking was part of a wider initiative on the part of AED "to support government efforts in developing trade initiatives and in reducing trade impediments in key markets and be an advocate for open competition" (ibid.). Ample evidence indicates that a substantial portion of this initiative was aimed to persuade the federal government to "schedule" substantial commitments of its own toward the further liberalization of the domestic market for foreign-based service providers across a wide spectrum of industries. In keeping with the overall linkages explored in this discussion, such an appeal seems almost inevitably to point in the direction of trade-offs between the interests of the maturing oil patch in search of foreign markets and those of multinational water-service providers seeking access to the Canadian market.

CONCLUSION: THE EFFECTS OF FREE TRADE AGREEMENTS ON NATIONAL RESOURCE POLICIES

The foregoing analysis of changes in trade regimes and their possible application to emerging water trade supports three principal conclusions. First, actual trade in bulk water is unlikely very soon, due to the constraints imposed by the very high cost of the long-distance transmission of bulk water. Thus, interestingly enough, even under the new free trade regime, bulk-water trade is highly unlikely to ever replicate the continental pattern of oil and gas trade and transmission.

Second, for this reason—plus the fact that NAFTA does not significantly alter the exercise of national regulatory powers over the construction and operation of major transmission facilities—the most consequential characteristics of the new free trade regime with respect to water are *not* those pertaining to commodity trade and transportation but are those characteristics pertaining to the rights of investors. As a result, the principal policy challenge associated with water in contemporary North America is not to prevent the large-scale alienation of the commodity to foreign consumers—the hew and cry of an earlier generation of "nationalists" in relation to oil and natural gas as tradable commodities—but to avert the wholesale takeover of local water services by foreign investors, particularly in the form of mammoth TNCs.

Third, as a consequence of this possibility, the relative shift in the focus of political controversy from oil and gas in the 1970s and 1980s toward water in the present decade neatly parallels a more general shift in the relative significance of the investment as opposed to the trade provisions of the emerging market liberalization process, both continental and global. From the vantage point of the evolving balance between state and market, the regime constructed by the General Agreement on Tariffs and Trade (GATT)—primarily in order to reduce tariffs on manufactured goods—left plenty of room for interventionist and protectionist resource policies of the kind adopted by both Canada and the United States during the Cold War era. Today, the more comprehensive and ambitious free trade regime dominated by the WTO—including GATS and the Agreement on Trade-Related Investment Measures (TRIMS)—is aimed at severely constraining national governments from framing or retaining policies that impede TNCs from encroaching on national, provincial, and local government delivery of important public services, ranging from health care through municipal water services to education and a host of environmental management functions. This regime, as we have seen, has consequences both for services and for commodity exports.

Meanwhile, the political side of Canada's political economy of resource policy is changing according to the entrepreneurial priorities of Canadian-based resource companies. Just as during the 1950s, '60s, and '70s, domestic groups had a strong economic interest in wider continental markets for Canada's oil and gas—and therefore were pressing for less restrictive Canadian policies toward both exports and imports—today, similar domestic groups have a strong economic interest in expanding Canada's share of the growing world market for commodity-based service industries—and therefore press for national policies that are less restrictive toward foreign investment and rights of establishment. The extent to which they succeed will affect the development of many staples, including propelling a potential staple, water resources, to the status of a true staple industry.

NOTES

1. As a minor exception to this statement, small delivery systems carry small volumes of Canadian municipal water a few miles to adjacent American towns across the border. Two examples are the sale of water by the town of Coutts, Alberta, to the nearby community of Sweetgrass, Montana, and a similar relationship between Delta, British Columbia, and the US Point Roberts enclave in Washington state (see Scott, Olynyk, and Renzetti 1986, 184). It is worth noting, in the context of the discussion of delivered water prices that follows, that the price charged for these exports (in 1982) was Cdn $0.42 per cubic metre.

2. Costs vary depending principally on the capacity of the tanker, the number of days consumed by the round trips, and the state of the oil tanker market. Moreover, these estimates do not include the cost of on- and off-loading facilities. (For all of the foregoing estimates, see Feehan 2001, 13–15.)

3. These figures compare reasonably well with other sources on water prices in the western United States. For example, the Canadian Environmental Law Association (1993, 99), reported that "prices paid for water in the Los Angeles area by various categories of water users in 1990 ranged from $362 to $857 per acre foot." For a more recent comparison, the NUS Consulting Group (2001) records "national" (presumably average) prices (in US$ per cubic metre) in selected countries, including US$0.52 per cubic metre for the United States, US$1.11 per cubic metre for the United Kingdom, and US$0.37 per cubic metre for Canada.

4. Allowing for the broad-brush character of these estimates, the unit cost of delivery for this project over a 50-year lifespan has been calculated by the author at US$0.68 per cubic metre (based on data provided by Judd 2000).

5. The plausibility of this cost estimate may be measured against the cost projections in 1982 for a much more modest plan to transfer water from the Mississippi/Missouri drainage to the high plains region from Texas to Nebraska, which the US Army Corps of Engineers estimated could run as high as US$0.64 per cubic metre (Scott, Olynyk, and Renzetti 1986, 177). Meanwhile, Judd (2000) also provided figures for the cost of agricultural water in the California market at the time at 5 to 10 times below the prevailing cost of urban water of only US$0.25 to US$0.50 per cubic metre—in other words, pennies or fractions of pennies per cubic metre.

6. Scott, Olynyk, and Renzetti (1986, 205–24) provide a good overview of the cost–benefit calculations bearing on major water transmission systems, some of which touch on this conundrum.

7. The obligation of the government of Canada to extend an international minimum standard of treatment and expropriation to foreign investors is contained in articles 1105 and 1110 of NAFTA. In addition, NAFTA includes a "proportionality clause" (article 315), which specifies that the government of a member country cannot reduce or restrict the export of a resource to another member country after the export flow has been established.

8. Interestingly, a similar parallel is at work in the oil and gas sector. Alberta's oil patch is beginning to realize a larger and larger share of its total returns on the export of oil and gas services, as compared with its traditional export of basic petroleum commodities, thus creating a strong interest on the part of at least one major Canadian industry in promoting stronger international protections for its own and others' foreign direct investment in services industries.

REFERENCES

Alberta Economic Development. 1999. Alberta service exports study 1999. Online at http://www.iir.gov.ab.ca/about_us/documents/AB_ServiceExportsStudy_1999.pdf.

Alberta Economic Development. 2001. *Alberta service exports survey*. Edmonton: Alberta International and Intergovernmental Relations; Alberta Economic Development, Investment & Trade.

Barlow M., and Clarke. T. 2002. *Blue gold: The battle against corporate theft of the world's water*. Toronto: McClelland & Stewart.

Boyd, D.R. 2001. Water: Water consumption. Online at http://www .environmentalindicators.com/htdocs/indicators/6wate.htm.

Canada, Department of Foreign Affairs and International Trade. 2003. *NAFTA @ 10: A preliminary report*. Ottawa: Minister of Public Works and Government Services Canada.

Canadian Environmental Law Association. 1993. *NAFTA and water exports*. Toronto: Canadian Environmental Law Association.

Clarkson, S. 2002. *Uncle Sam and us: Globalization, neoconservatism, and the Canadian state*. Toronto: University of Toronto Press.

Environment Canada. 2007. Frequently asked questions. Online at http://www.ec.gc.ca/ water/en/info/misc/e_FAQ.htm#1.

Feehan, J. 2001. Export of bulk water from Newfoundland and Labrador: A preliminary assessment of economic feasibility. In *Report of the Ministerial Committee Examining the Export of Bulk Water*. St. John's: Government of Newfoundland and Labrador.

Finger, M., and Lobina, E. 1999. Managing trade in a globalizing world: Trade in public services and transnational corporations—The case of the global water industry. In *Global Trade and Global Social Issues*, eds. A. Taylor and C. Thomas, 170–96. New York: Routledge.

Heinmiller, T. 2004. Harmonization through emulation: Canadian federalism and water export policy. Paper presented to Questioning the Boundaries of Governance: A Graduate Workshop on the Theory and Practice of Federalism, Decentralisation and Multilevel Governance, Munk Centre for International Studies, University of Toronto, Toronto, February 14–15.

Industry Canada. 2006. Oil and gas equipment and services industry report—October 2006. Online at http://strategis.gc.ca/epic/site/ogt-ipg.nsf/en/og00187e.html.

Johansen, D. 1999. *Water exports and the NAFTA.* Online at http://dsp-psd.pwgsc.gc.ca/Collection-R/LoPBdP/EB/prb995-e.htm.

Judd, O. 2000. A future basis for national security and international policy: Fresh water. In *Essays on the Future in Honor of Nick Metropolis*, eds. S.S. Hecker and G.-C. Rota, 107–22. Boston: Birkhauser.

McDougall, J. 1982. *Fuels and the national policy.* Toronto: Butterworths.

McDougall, J. 1991. The Canada–U.S. free trade agreement and Canada's energy trade. *Canadian Public Policy* 17(1): 1–13.

McRae, D. 2001. Opinion presented in a letter to the ministerial committee, as reproduced in *Report of the Ministerial Committee Examining the Export of Bulk Water*, Government of Newfoundland and Labrador, 21. St. John's: Government of Newfoundland and Labrador.

NUS Consulting Group. 2001. Cost of water goes up worldwide, with larger increases expected. Online at http://www.greenspun.com/bboard/q-and-a-fetch-msg.tcl?msg_id=0067gs.

Scott, A., Olynyk, J., and Renzetti, S. 1986. The design of water export policy. In *Canada's Resource Industries and Water Export Policy*, vol. 14, ed. J. Whalley, 161–246. Toronto: University of Toronto Press.

Shrybman, S. 2002. Water export controls and Canadian international trade obligations. Online at http://www.waterbank.com/Newsletters/nws15.html.

Statistics Canada, Energy Section. 2002. *Oil and gas equipment and services incidental to oil and gas extraction and production survey 1998–2000.* Online at http://strategis.ic.gc.ca/epic/site/oges-msepg.nsf/vwapj/IndCanReport-Nov02.pdf/$FILE/IndCanReport-Nov02.pdf.

CHAPTER 15

The Political Economy of Canadian Hydroelectricity

Alexander Netherton*

INTRODUCTION: HYDRO AS A STAPLE—SYSTEM AND REGIME

Thinking of hydro as a staple is a little like assuming that a whale is a big fish. They share great similarities but also possess significant differences. Hydro, thought of as "water power," is a resource that has played an important role in Canada's economic and social development, and hydro megaprojects have many "staples-like" features. Water power was once used to run grist mills and motor machinery; however, since the late 19th century, the term *hydro* has referred to water power as a renewable resource used to generate electricity, one of the most important modern forms of energy. Hydro refers to a staples resource, a form of manufactured energy, and a related system of technology. Indeed, Canadians often interchange the words *hydro, electricity,* and *utility.* But unlike other industrial staples, hydroelectricity was not developed primarily for export markets, and limited international trade can actually lower Canadian energy costs. John Dales (1957) argued that hydro's energy can contribute a significant portion of the value of other resources and manufactured items heading for export. For these reasons, he considered hydro a "quasi staple."

Hydroelectric systems are prone to the classic staples problem of excess capacity. Economic rents and linkages integral to staples analysis are also extraordinarily important to hydro. Simply put, because of the high costs of hydro megaprojects and infrastructure, utilities experience inordinately high financial costs when market demand is low—and conversely can make significant returns when markets grow to utilize the full capacity of a system. To address this problem, electricity producers manage the costs of hydro by gradually developing all of the energy potential, or "capacity," of a dam over time (Bernard 1989) and are at the forefront of initiating economic strategies to cultivate energy consumption or conservation, as needed.

Neither technology nor staples are void of politics. Yet the staples approach is often associated with deterministic analyses in which the state and politics are reduced to geography, economics, and the interests of dominant classes (Albo and Jenson 1989; Laxer 1991). The study of technology is marked by approaches that emphasize its social construction, not a "hard" or "soft" technological determinism (Bijker, Hughes, and Pinch 1989). Yet when it comes to electrical systems, Thomas P. Hughes (2001), perhaps the foremost student of the history of technology and electrification, coined the term *technological momentum* to unite the two trends. He argues that in the early stages, technology systems are socially constructed, but as they grow, they gain a momentum that distances them from social and political forces.

Comparative energy policy studies reveal similar findings. Herbert Kitschelt's (1986a) comparative study of the development of fast breeder nuclear reactor systems concludes that causal variables shifted over time. Initially the regimes were shaped by social class and domestic policy coalitions. As policies solidified into regimes, the structure of the regimes themselves had particular "regime" effects on policy innovation and change. Lastly, the international system was a source of policy change. In another study, Kitschelt (1986b) refines the idea of regime effects by arguing that the open or closed nature of political opportunity structures are critical to ensuring that innovation follows from social and political pressure.

Langdon Winner (2003) argues that each technology has its own politics and effects in ordering society. For example, the supply of hydro depends on the vagaries of the natural water cycle. To overcome the adverse effects of a fluctuating water supply and to make the most from the resource, water needs to be managed by dams, reservoirs, river diversions, control works, and mitigative engineering, which require significant alterations and ongoing environmental management of vast drainage systems. Other staple resources and technologies used to generate electricity, from large-scale nuclear-thermal and coal-thermal technologies to wind farms, have their own particular politics, policy agenda, and set of policy linkages.

Electrical energy policy does not centre exclusively on production. Electricity systems also have a complex network of transmission and distribution lines connecting energy production to its point of use. Unlike a train or pipeline, in which a particular resource is shipped from point A to point B, an electricity network or grid is a balancing act, requiring managers to balance the input of energy at one point with the loss of energy at other points. Since electricity cannot be stored (except in the form of water reservoirs or alternative fuels), grids need constant management to meet daily and seasonal peaks and troughs of demand.

Hughes (1982) used the term *cultures of power* to bring together the various elements of an early hydroelectric system. This analysis relies on the concept of "regime," which includes paradigmatic ideas, political structures and processes, and a social and political network in the policy field. As will be discussed later in this chapter, hydroelectric energy policies have changed over time, as the result of having been governed by three succeeding policy regimes: a formative mixed regime, a postwar provincial hydro and megaproject regime, and an emerging sustainability/regionalization regime.

THE MIXED REGIME: ELECTRIFICATION AND INDUSTRIALIZATION TO 1945

Canada's formative hydro regime was the site of conflict regarding the control of hydro utilities for the process of electrification. Public policy was geared toward producing energy for manufacturing, resource industrialization, and urban modernization. Utilities were considered natural monopolies, and the big question centred on the distribution of rents and linkages. According to the leading historians in this field, John Dales, H.V. Nelles, and Christopher Armstrong, the "story" surrounding the formative electrical energy policy regimes was the struggle over the control and use of hydro. Public power movements, which advocated for power to be supplied at cost, squared off against power's financial interests. The result was a mixed regime of private and public (primarily municipal) utilities, except in the case of Ontario, where an exceptional set of circumstances led to the establishment of a province-wide hydro commission that initially bought power and then delivered it to municipal distribution utilities. Eventually this hybrid turned into a powerful producer and wholesale distributor of energy.[1] Where possible, other utilities also tried to overcome the uncertainties of staples development by vertical integration. A vertically integrated utility is one that has its own generating capacity, transmission networks, and geographically defined distribution area. Armstrong and Nelles (1986) aptly termed the historical period "Monopoly's Moment."

Decisions on public ownership during this period depended on, among other things, the ideology of government elites, the characteristics of public power movements, the strength and cohesiveness of utility capital, the fiscal resources of governments, the disposition of intergovernmental relations, and the relative scarcity of hydro resources (Dales 1957; Nelles 1974; Armstrong 1981; Armstrong and Nelles 1983, 1986). The mixed nature of the regime illustrated a novel Canadian culture of power in which hydro was seen as a legitimate extension of the public (as opposed to the private) sphere.

Major electricity networks were defined by urban regions, and as hydro resources were developed, these networks were also involved in regional industrialization. In Quebec, the abundance of hydro resources led utilities to advance the industrial development of hydro-rich regions, such as the Saguenay (Dales 1957). In more remote regions, industrial producers emerged to develop hydro resources for local mines, the pulp and paper industry, and, later, for aluminum-smelting facilities. The end result was a fragmented set of electricity networks. The operating assumption was regional network self-reliance, characterized by each network standing on its own and relationships between networks being ad hoc rather than systemic.

The ecological impact of early hydro regimes was concentrated on rivers (and their associated drainage systems) that were close to urban populations. Some hydro sources, such as the Niagara, Winnipeg, and Ottawa rivers, were part of international and interprovincial boundaries and drainage basins. Remote hydro resources were unsuitable for exploitation for urban networks because long-distance transmission technologies were relatively inefficient. Initially, hydro investments were ad hoc, but with time the planning and conservation regimes played a larger role in determining the most rational and efficient use of resources and thus capital. Provincial governments played a key role in shaping these conservation strategies through a licensing procedure. Although the rights to hydro resources were first sold as private property, over time, provincial governments instituted a rentier regime by claiming ownership of these resources and then licensing their use in return for a form of royalty. Investment was sequenced through the timing and terms of licences.

Canada and the United States established an enduring process for binational resource conservation and dispute resolution. The 1909 Canada–United States Boundary Waters Treaty established the International Joint Commission (IJC), itself a framework to provide equal rights in boundary water resources and a consensual binational process for settling disputes. The IJC then provided the framework to establish conservation boards to ensure the equitable sharing of hydro resources for Niagara Falls (the linchpin of early Ontario energy policy) and the Lake of the Woods–Rainy River–Winnipeg River system (central to the Manitoba energy strategy). In time, the IJC process spread to all boundary waters.

Ottawa did not have the same success carving out a national electricity policy. Christopher Armstrong (1981) details how the jurisdictional ambiguity of hydro left the determination of federal and provincial roles more to the play of politics than to the constitution. Although provinces generally claimed ownership of resources and Crown lands, hydro resources were not enumerated in the constitutional division of powers. Ottawa had clear responsibilities for fisheries and navigation (even in inland waters) and powers to regulate international and interprovincial trade. Ottawa also managed the water resources of the three Prairie provinces until 1930. But the waning years of the National Policy were also a nadir of federal power. Prime Minister Mackenzie King's successive attempts to outline a federal role in hydro were a failure, largely due to opposition in Quebec and Ontario. Even a constitutional reference did not resolve the issue. Thus, hydro development became a provincial affair.

National electricity policy eventually centred on protecting hydro for domestic markets by discouraging long-term exports, but did little else. Ottawa did not, for example, establish interprovincial water conservation agreements or regulate interprovincial trade in electricity. Protecting hydro for the domestic market really meant protecting it for provincial purposes. Hydro regimes were effectively centred in provincial capitals. Even in the Prairie provinces, federal hydro planning and licensing would need the consent of the junior provinces.

Provincial hydro regimes did, however, have substantial economic impact and success. Electricity networks spread throughout urban Canada, and a "cheap power policy" was used to fuel industrialization and social and technological modernization. Peter Wylie (1990, 856–58) estimates that the technological adaptation and restructuring of Canadian manufacturing during the 1900–1929 period led to a more than fivefold increase in production and to significant decreases (up to 15 percent) in manufacturing costs. He argues that the low-cost domestic energy helped offset the relatively higher costs of other factors, such as imported technology. Certainly, the 1929–1939 Depression and the subsequent Second World War acted as "perturbations" that substantially affected the development of the formative energy regime. The only complete failure of a hydro utility during the period occurred in Manitoba, where the collapse of key industrial markets forced Winnipeg Electric, the Nesbitt-Thomson affiliate and the province's major private utility, into "financial reorganization" (Netherton 1993).

Over time, however, the formative regime revealed several limitations. First, the regime assumed that private utility capital shared the public policy goals of supplying cheap and abundant power. In what appears to be a case of monopolies gone wild, John Dales (1957) chronicled the efforts of the five regional Quebec monopolies to foster industrialization and concluded that they had stifled the economic development of the province. At issue were the high rates that weakly regulated monopolies charged urban domestic consumers, in contrast to the cheap commercial and industrial rates offered business, a de facto tax that Dales considered a drag on the economy. The regulatory issue was significant because, although Canada's political culture was more accepting of regulation than the US political culture, the actual form of regulation was generally not particularly effective (Currie 1946; Dupré and Party 1998). Dales (1957) was also critical of the complacency of the Montreal monopolies with respect to St. Lawrence hydro resources, energy that Dales contends would have substantially aided the development of the region. Research suggests similar problems on the Prairies, where the lack of surplus power in Manitoba during the Second World War hindered war-related industrialization and economic development (Netherton 1993). Indeed, during the war, all provinces were under pressure to renew their investment in electrical energy infrastructures, yet it was unclear whether municipalities or private utility capital were up to the task or wanted to play by the same old rules.

Lastly, these formative regimes institutionalized social inequality, particularly between rural and urban societies. The latter had the population density that made its inclusion within electrical networks economically viable for public and private utilities. But the low density of rural populations, and especially the lack of agricultural income on the Prairies during the 1930s, made rural electrification conventionally impossible.

THE KEYNESIAN REGIME: PROVINCIAL HYDROS AND MEGAPROJECTS, 1946–1992

After having faced the exigencies of the Depression and the war effort, when public leaders thought of postwar energy needs, they began to see the role of the state in more systematic and social terms than previously. The new overall policy objective was not the pursuit of and control over electrification but the need to ensure both that sufficient investment could be made to meet postwar needs and that equity existed among the various fragmented electrical networks. The emerging energy policy regime conformed to Keynesian welfare state principles, or the Canadian technocratic variety (Campbell 1987), in that it necessitated a massive state-assisted investment program for electrical energy and, at the same time, the systematic continuation of promotional rates.

The historical disparity between rural and urban energy costs was reduced by the development of "postage stamp" rates that ensured all consumers in similar classes (industrial, commercial, and domestic) shared a common price structure. This broader "cheap power" policy was consistent with Keynesian principles of subsidizing demand management. In a broader sense, this policy also facilitated the mass production and consumption of electrical goods, a system of production and economic regulation often termed "Fordism." Jane Jenson (1989) terms the Canadian variation "permeable Fordism," partly because of the importance of provinces in shaping staples-related continental economic relations. Although the ideas and conditions that propelled the regime dissipated in the 1980s, regime change would not occur until the early 1990s.

With much attention turned to supply issues, it is easy to forget that postwar electricity policy began with policy links to consumption. A.W. Currie's postwar review of Canadian utility regulation (1946, 153–55) points out that in Ontario (the province with the most developed electricity market), the cost of appliances, not the cost of electricity, had become the impediment to the continued electrification of society. The viable corporate strategy for utilities, therefore, was to help cultivate the mass consumption of appliances. For example, public utilities sometimes subsidized the costs of electric stoves, refrigerators, and washing machines. In rural electrification programs, some utilities offered prospective customers a complete set of appliances in five-year financial packages (Netherton 1993). Eventually, popular utility demonstration programs, such as "live better electrically," were indicative of the convergence of electricity policy to that of the mass production and consumption of electrical wares—from the energy-guzzling big appliances to the transformation of "hand tools" into "power tools."[2]

Once set in motion and given continued economic growth, the combination of cheap power and permeable Fordism produced pressures that led to a new regime of "provincial hydros" and "megaprojects." As a result of the annual growth of energy demand at between 6 and 7 percent, utilities looked at doubling their generation capacity each decade. Accordingly, provincial utilities commenced massive investment programs into coal, nuclear, and hydro—stretching provincial financial capacity to its limits.

The shape of the new regime came from several sources. First, vertical integration was the most important institutional innovation developed from the pre-war period. Public ownership and vertical integration then provided means for the top to bottom rationalization of the previously fragmented or investment-starved sector. Both the scale of the projected capital investments and the level of long-term risk associated with these investments necessitated substantive public involvement. Provincial governments stepped in to plan and implement these investments. Instead of institutionalizing the myth of municipal ownership—as in the old Ontario Hydro-Electric Power Commission—the new public ownership model was legally controlled by the provincial executive, as in the postwar British model of a nationalized firm (Murphy 1952).[3]

Why the provincial state? Private utility capital lost its leading role in the first regime. No politically cohesive grouping of private utility capital existed to redefine the regime to include its long-term needs, and the general thrust of creating provincial or public hydro utilities had broad political support. Private capital could not be the instrument to carry out an expanded program of investment, reorganize networks to eliminate inequities, and, at the same time, push the cheap power policy to its very limits.[4]

The provincial hydro utilities dominated the new policy regime. Equipped with easy access to financial markets (because provincial governments guaranteed their bonds), these utilities turned the regime into an investment machine. Indeed, during the boom in public energy investment, many hydro utilities' annual investment expenditures rivalled those of the provincial governments that owned them. A second source of authority for the utilities in the policy regime was simply that they monopolized the policy expertise to manage the design and construction of the new energy systems. In particular, new developments in transmission technology were instrumental in incorporating remote hydro resources as sources for urban Canada's energy needs.

Regime development occurred in stages. The provinces of Manitoba, Quebec, British Columbia, and Newfoundland became more concerned with planning and implementing long-term hydroelectric development strategies. This development included taking over the fragmented local networks, integrating them into a wider provincial network, and gradually investing in electricity generation capacity. A second stage saw the major hydro-producing provinces place existing private hydro producers under public ownership (Blais and Faucher 1979; Froschauer 1999). There were, however, exceptions. For example, provincial governments, for the most part, did not expropriate the assets of private industrial producers, and aluminum producers, which were often isolated from the emerging provincial networks, were allowed an expansion of private hydro development for industrial purposes.

In provinces that relied on diverse fuels and technologies (hydro, thermal generation from coal, petroleum, natural gas, and later nuclear power), such as Ontario, Nova Scotia, New Brunswick, and Saskatchewan, the provincial energy policy regimes were variations of the universal postwar model, retaining their provincial boundaries and assumptions of provincial self-reliance.

Three provinces continued the development of older regimes. Perhaps due to resource and fiscal limitations, Prince Edward Island nominally kept an older private monopoly, but eventually relied on imported energy to supply its needs. The private distribution utility on the island of Newfoundland kept its monopoly, though the provincial government undertook tasks of power development and fostering rural electrification. In contrast, the hydro export policy regime for Labrador was dominated by provincial state ownership, although with mixed (Quebec and Newfoundland) ownership. Alberta continued to develop the regionally based mixed private and municipally owned system developed in the formative regime.

The Keynesian regime began to change in the context of developing hydro megaprojects: the Peace River in British Columbia, the Churchill River Diversion and Nelson River projects in Manitoba, the James Bay project in Quebec, and the Churchill Falls project in Labrador. The scale of these projects amplified traditional staples concerns with markets and excess capacity because the energy produced would be well beyond the immediate needs of each of the hydro-producing provinces. The government of Canada wanted new hydro resources to serve national markets by means of a national power grid, but lack of provincial support put an end to this idea (Cass-Beggs 1964; Froschauer 1999). To facilitate the economic and financial grounding of remote hydro projects, Ottawa abandoned its traditional discouragement of exports and published a 1963 National Power Policy that encouraged provincial utilities to build hydro projects that would be dedicated to supplying energy to export markets, with the idea that the energy produced would eventually be reclaimed by Canadian markets as domestic demand grew. We can call this policy a "prebuild" strategy, whereby the provinces used continental markets to offset the risks of excess capacity.

During the 1970s, the political discourse about hydro and electricity exports changed. Instead of necessitating policies to offset their perceived marginal status, hydro became linked to the debate on economic nationalism versus continental integration (Howlett, Netherton, and Ramesh 1999). Although Ottawa changed policy direction with respect to hydro, no other electricity-related staple followed suit. The idea of building CANDU nuclear energy plants was loaded with sufficient economic, environmental, and political risk that no government seriously entertained the idea. A proposal to replace US power lost as a result of the nuclear accident at Three Mile Island with coal-generated power from Ontario failed for the same reasons. And, despite persistent rumours of a coal export option emerging from the Maritimes, no such initiative materialized. Political and economic conditions limited the staples development to hydro (Battle, Gislason, and Douglas 1984; Poch 1987).

The official planning and initial implementation of hydro megaprojects at first highlighted the provincial and national economic development and the technological challenges associated with such projects—a discourse that reflected the absence of a broad-based concept of development and the racism of resource policy and Aboriginal–state relations of their day (Rea 1976; Waldram 1988). Given these influences, the emerging hydro strategies inevitably produced considerable opposition from Aboriginal peoples and from social and environmental interests opposed to or negatively affected by hydro megaprojects. The Aboriginal peoples displaced by reservoirs, river diversions, and other changes attributable to hydro megaprojects were the only societal group targeted to pay directly for energy strategies that had been designed to benefit the majority. Opposition to hydro projects then began to focus on regimes of compensation and mitigation and were closely associated with broader struggles for the recognition of Aboriginal rights.

Initially, Aboriginal communities were authoritatively marginalized by being "relocated" to locations chosen by bureaucrats and hydro officials. Then, in the early 1970s, the James Bay Cree asserted their rights by using the judiciary to force Quebec Premier Robert Bourassa to negotiate a comprehensive settlement of their claims during construction of the James Bay Hydro project. In Manitoba, a similar process of "negotiating with a bulldozer in the backyard" resulted in the 1978 signing of the Northern Flood Agreement (Waldram 1988). In these political struggles, Aboriginal political movements and their allies in political parties, churches, the New Left, and nationalist and environmental groups used political and legal resources to open a crack in the notoriously closed and powerful hydro regimes.

After the first "oil crisis," federal and provincial governments split on the nature of hydro development. Constitutional responsibility for Aboriginal peoples and an increased environmental awareness split the interests of the power developers from federal authorities. Western oil and gas producers also squared off with Ottawa on issues relating to economic rents and their use for provincial economic development strategies (Howlett, Netherton, and Ramesh 1999). Ottawa began to see hydro not as a marginal resource but as the source of considerable economic rents that ought to be more fairly distributed among Canadians (Zuker, Jenkins, and the Economic Council of Canada 1984). Federal–provincial conflict and the collapse of the oil boom ended this form of analysis. After a change of power in Ottawa, federal authorities promoted their view that the public interest would be better served by a more market-disciplined electricity regime (Economic Council of Canada 1985). Canadian utilities scrambled to adjust to a new economic climate.

Environmental objectives were represented unevenly in the policy regime and were not immediately successful. Environmental impact assessments emerged slowly and diffused into provincial decision making unevenly, but addressed a wider range of issues than provincial energy strategies had heretofore considered. New environmental policy initiatives emerged as clearer legislative mandates and new regulatory regimes were put in place in some Canadian provinces (Jaccard, Nyboer, and Makinen 1991). Policy-makers moved away from pursuing new energy supplies to focus on the possibility of gains from better use of resources. Vertically integrated utilities experimented with new policy concepts, such as integrated resource planning and demand side management (DSM) programs. For example, Power Smart and other conservation and energy-efficiency programs initiated policies ranging from subsidizing improvements in housing technology to the creation of energy-efficiency standards for public lighting, electrical appliances, and electronic components.

In the 1980s, utilities also experimented by seeding the use of more environmentally benign "green" technologies and encouraging non-utility industrial producers of electricity and small producers of more expensive alternative-energy technologies (now generally termed "independent power producers," or IPPs) to sell to major utilities. The policy logic was that seeding small amounts of alternative-energy technologies into the supply at uneconomic prices would eventually lead to a significant diversity of supply. The policy assumed that continually increasing energy prices would ensure that the new energy supplies would eventually be economically viable. Eventually, natural gas producers, relying on a new and significantly more efficient and small-scale combined-cycle turbine technology, used provisions of the US legislation to gain a foothold in the electricity market, a process that took the pressure off utilities to pursue megaprojects.

Eventually, the concept of sustainable development replaced the Keynesian concept of abundant low-cost energy, thereby linking competitive market efficiency and long-term environmental protection. Energy policy was evolving to meet post-industrial and global exigencies.

Hydro and Postwar Continental Integration

The emergence of the provincial hydros and megaprojects regime occurred within the parameters of a highly contested national economic strategy that facilitated a regulated continental integration, including branch plant industrialization and the production of industrial staples for export (Howlett, Netherton, and Ramesh 1999). Because the constitution granted provincial jurisdiction over natural resources, under this economic strategy the provinces assumed the roles of central actors in shaping the development of resource export strategies. In Canada's "permeable" Fordism, the politics of nationalism became tied to questions of federalism and contested patterns of continental integration. Yet the regime also witnessed the rise of the federal government as a central mediator and regulator of continental integration.

Canada–United States and federal–provincial collaborations began with the shared goal of gaining the most from shared resources during the energy shortage that followed the Second World War. During the 1950s, Ottawa worked with the US government and the provinces of Ontario and Quebec to reach an agreement on the St. Lawrence River hydro development—in parcel with an emerging pact on the construction of an international seaway system extending Canada's inland ocean ports from Montreal to Lake Superior's Thunder Bay. Although these projects appear to be remnants from the prewar National Policy of east–west integration, their status as shared infrastructure spoke to the Canada–US continental partnership (Smiley 1975, 46–47). Similarly, through the IJC, Ottawa coordinated the negotiation of the Columbia River Treaty, an agreement whereby stabilization of the Columbia River's tributaries in Canada, by means of dams and reservoirs, allows for greater power development in the lower Columbia River and, eventually, the Peace River (Swainson 1979). Similar initiatives led to conservation regimes on the Saint John River and the sharing of the costs of New Brunswick's diesel electric-generating capacity with the state of Maine.

The functional integration between Canada and the United States also tackled the problem of reliability. In 1965, a major ice storm in Quebec tripped a prolonged blackout throughout northeastern North America. Three years later, the United States responded by launching a voluntary non-profit corporation, the National Electric Reliability Council (NERC), to promote, educate, assess, and monitor system reliability issues. To aid in this process, NERC set up a system of regional reliability councils throughout the United States, which evolved into regional groups of co-operating utilities. These groups became institutional stepping stones for Canadian utilities seeking greater continental market and reliability integration.

Ottawa established the National Energy Board (NEB) to regulate international and interprovincial energy trade. As in the formative regime, Ottawa, through the NEB, did not exercise authority over interprovincial electricity trade. Yet it did become the central regulator of international electricity trade and international transmission facilities. To allay traditional nationalist concerns, NEB regulations confined exports to energy that was surplus to domestic needs and placed price constraints and time limitations on export licences. Eventually, the NEB began to consider the social, environmental, and traditional economic impacts of energy export projects—including hydroelectric projects built for export purposes—though in many ways its close collaboration with industry made it a de facto representative of corporate thinking (Robinson and Hooker 1987; Poch 1987; Averyt 1992).

By the 1970s, electricity trade and interconnections in many provinces represented an equitable functional integration in which benefits were shared by all participants (Perlgut 1978). In the Maritimes, New Brunswick Hydro had one small interconnection with the state of Maine—and would continue its agreements, sharing capacity with interconnected US utilities. The Ontario network became functionally integrated with the networks of New York and Michigan, and power flowed through their interconnected grids clockwise around Lake Ontario and Lake Erie.[5]

Slightly different trading relationships emerged in several of the large hydro-electricity-producing provinces. The proliferation of small international interconnections that characterized the formative regime in Quebec had been eliminated, and instead, Hydro-Québec built large-capacity interconnections with the Power Authority of the State of New York (PASNY), exporting energy in a form of seasonal diversity exchange to offset costs of financing the James Bay development.[6] Similarly, new international connections between Manitoba and Minnesota reflected a "prebuild" export strategy for energy flowing from megaprojects on Manitoba Hydro's Nelson River power corridor. British Columbia developed several interconnections with Bonneville Power Authority (BPA), the US federally owned utility (based on the Ontario Hydro model) that was charged with developing the hydro potential of the Columbia River.

Despite these new trade relations, Canadian electricity did not take an overall staples-export structure similar to that displayed by oil and natural gas industries. Total exports to the United States were less than 7 percent of total Canadian production, and US exports reached only 0.25 percent of US production. Clearly the staples relationship envisaged by provincial power planners and the National Power Policy did not materialize. When seeking explanations, note that trade in electricity was an administered practice in which pricing schemes and quantities were set by national regulators.

By the late 1970s, falling demand and excess capacity in Canada, coupled with high energy costs in the United States, provided the context for a renewed interest in Canada–US energy trade. At that point, utilities and national governments came to the conclusion that the regulatory framework was stifling trade (Canada, Energy, Mines and Resources and US, Department of Energy 1978; DeVaul, Keating, and Sugarman 1984).

Canadian utilities could not place energy on export markets because interconnected US utilities refused to "wheel" or transmit power across their network. US utilities were concerned that Canadian price regulations barred them from making the most from import opportunities. Also, US regulatory policy prohibited utilities from making profits importing Canadian energy. Even during the Canada–US free trade negotiations, the Reagan administration (US, Department of Energy, Office of Policy Planning and Analysis 1987) viewed exports as unfair competition because of subsidies associated with public ownership and predicted that as prices came to market levels, Canadian supply would have only minimal impact on US supply. At mid-decade, even Canadian observers concurred that export prospects looked bleak (Helliwell, MacGregor, and Plourde 1984)

The 1980s witnessed the rise of neo-conservatism and a shift to more market-disciplined, or neo-liberal, economic and energy strategies. Important to this process was an intellectual and political critique and an abandonment of the Keynesian strategy. The collapse of the postwar boom left the hydros in difficulties. Many began to argue that the provincial hydro regime had lost its way. For economists such as Jean-Thomas Bernard and R.D. Cairns (1987), the inability of publicly owned utilities to set prices at marginal costs meant that these regimes could not collect or redistribute rents efficiently, whereas other economists, sociologists, and historians argued that the regime was out of control (Cairns and Heyes 1993; Hargrove 1994; Mackay 1983; Tritschler 1979; Young 1982).

Others questioned more openly the older paradigmatic assumptions, arguing that public ownership led to overinvestment and economic waste—inappropriate consequences in light of the sustainable development and environmental policy objectives that emerged during the 1970s. Glen P. Jenkins (1985) opened a national debate on public ownership by arguing that the financial and tax advantages given to provincially owned public utilities created distortions and massive economic waste of the capital invested in them—a waste that represented up to 60 percent of the cost of Canadian electricity. Although economists criticized Jenkins's method, the extent of the distortion, and the alternative remedies, and in turn defended the potential of provincially owned utilities as instruments to capture rents from hydro resources, no economist defended the regime as it was (Bernard and Cairns 1987; Jenkins 1987; Spiro 1987).

Thinking of hydro in terms of rents provides a fitting end to the discussion of the postwar regime. Because the government of Quebec began taking annual dividends from Hydro-Québec, it is fair to conclude that Quebec was able to gain economic rents—though some debated whether the first stages of Quebec's "prebuild" produced meaningful export returns (Bernard 1982). The same cannot, however, be said of the government of Newfoundland's Churchill Falls project, which, during the 1970s, supplied approximately one-third of Quebec's electricity needs (Bernard 1989). According to Quebec and Newfoundland's infamous 1969 contract, the lion's share of the Churchill Falls power would be sold to Quebec for up to 65 years at declining prices. In a similar long-term contract, the government of British Columbia assigned a monetary value on its share of the downstream benefits after completing Canada's obligations in the Columbia River Treaty. As in the Churchill River case, the contract price turned out to be well below the actual market power of the energy. Finally, the first stages of Manitoba's Nelson River hydro strategy left the provincial utility technically bankrupt and politically disgraced, while surplus energy was dumped on the export market (Netherton 1993).

Provincial regimes with mixed technologies and resources were also in trouble, particularly Ontario and New Brunswick, which relied on nuclear energy and the CANDU technology, and those provinces that relied heavily on coal, such as Alberta, Saskatchewan, Ontario, New Brunswick, and Nova Scotia. Clearly the regime was prone to failure. Summing up this situation, Mark Jaccard (1995) argued the case for change by asking whether electricity ought still to be considered an important public good, whether its production and distribution were natural monopolies, and whether vertically integrated public utilities were an appropriate agent to carry out public objectives. In concluding the negative for each question, Jaccard made his case for completely changing the existing regime.

THE SUSTAINABILITY/REGIONALIZATION REGIME, POST-1992

After concluding the Canada–United States Free Trade Agreement (FTA), the Canadian government established a new electricity policy in which the National Energy Board export regulations were revised to conform to the terms of the new trade regime. The security of the older supply and price protection regulations was replaced by concerns about third-party effects, environmental standards, and fair market access by other potential Canadian customers. Although the NEB would still not regulate interprovincial electricity trade or interconnections, it indicated that it would consider objections from other provinces before agreeing to any new international power lines (Energy, Mines and Resources Canada 1988). Although these provisions were significant, they were very timid steps toward eroding provincial autarky and facilitating interprovincial integration, but did not seriously challenge the limits of provincialism.

Neither the FTA nor the new NEB regulations opened up floodgates of electricity trade between Canadian and US utility networks or among provincial utilities. At issue was the fragmented nature of the US markets and the domestic trade barriers that discouraged intersystem trade. Electricity trade within the United States was blocked because utilities were not obliged to wheel a third party's energy along their lines. Canadian exporters considered this wheeling problem the major obstacle to developing long-term inter-regional trade. The US domestic energy policy regime would have to change in order for trade to occur.

In 1992, a new US energy policy emerged that was founded on the assumption of internal market failure—that the United States had a great deal of generation capacity but it was inefficient, and energy was unevenly distributed. In contrast to the Canadian case, the US federal government has both expansive powers over interstate and international trade and a long history of using federal powers to manage the electrical energy sector. The US Federal Energy Regulatory Commission (FERC), the major federal energy authority, was authorized by the new policy to embark on a bold initiative to establish competitive markets for the supply, transmission, and distribution of electricity throughout the United States. The United States was to be organized into a set of regional trading organizations, or RTOs. The RTO structure is defined as a "functioning voluntary organization (of transmission owners, transmission users and other entities approved by FERC) to efficiently coordinate transmission planning and expansion, operation, and use on a regional and inter-regional basis"—in other words, interconnected regional electricity networks (Canada, National Energy Board 2005, 88).

Four initial FERC regulatory orders and policies had significant extraterritorial impact on Canadian exporters. In 1996, FERC authored order 888, commonly known as the "open access" or "reciprocity" provision. This provision ordered utilities that wanted access to US markets to allow access of US utilities to their own markets. Each utility could therefore outline a series of consistent market prices for the use of its transmission system. These open access transmission tariffs (OATTs) were the costs that the utility would charge others for wheeling their energy. The condition of open access meant a utility that wanted to trade in the United States could not bar other utilities access to its own system.

Following order 888 was order 889, demanding that the utilities use the same time-sharing data system (creating a market for electricity depends on the ability to provide instantaneous price signals using advanced levels of information technology). In 1997, in response to the wave of mergers and acquisitions as a result of deregulation, FERC issued order 592, a policy that attempted to ensure that corporate mergers and restructuring did not thwart the intent to establish competitive markets. Finally, in December 1999, FERC issued order 2000, which asked that all utilities wanting to trade in US markets apply to join an RTO. FERC could not directly require this condition from Canadian utilities, which were not under its direct legal authority; however, interconnected Canadian utilities had to weigh their costs of entry and exclusion.

In Canada, by the early 1990s, neo-liberal reformers advocated variations of the new epistemic energy regime, one initially developed in the United Kingdom, in international organizations, and especially in the United States. The proposed regime would first unbundle the vertically integrated utilities into functional parts: separate producers, system (grid) operators, distributors, and specialized service companies. The idea was that distributors would buy energy from competing producers through a neutral and independent system operator. The proposed regime necessitated the legal and regulatory framework to create and regulate competitive energy markets. This regime was not simply a means of attacking inefficiencies of state monopolies but an architecture to establish secure markets for energy infrastructure and services throughout the developing world and post-communist economies (Kessides and the World Bank 2004; US, Energy Information Administration 1997). The proposed regime provided opportunity structures for the growth of private capital (US, Energy Information Administration 1996).

Neo-liberal energy policy alternatives gained currency in governing circles—though attempts to implement these alternatives were highly contested, particularly by political and social forces organized around a defence of public institutions and a social democratic critique of markets. The first political struggle was over privatization.

In 1992, Nova Scotia Power was the first provincial hydro to be privatized. Privatization was justified as a method to attract new capital into the energy sector without increasing public costs (Webster 1993). But the privatization did not mean the adoption of a neo-liberal regime, as the new company remained a vertically integrated monopoly. Premier Clyde Wells attempted to privatize Newfoundland and Labrador Hydro in 1994, as a means of forcing a renegotiation of the Churchill Falls power contract, but backed down in the face of mobilized popular opposition.

In Ontario, the contestation took the form of a complex struggle among the government, business, free market environmentalists, trade unions, and leftist forces. The Ontario government began utility market reform with a public discussion led by an Advisory Council on Competition, followed by a white paper and the 1998 *Energy Competition Act*, which would disintegrate and privatize the highly indebted, crisis-ridden Ontario Hydro (MacDonald and the Advisory Committee on Competition in Ontario's Electricity System 1996; Ontario, Ministry of Energy, Science and Technology 1997). The older nuclear facilities were taken out of active service, and after a damning assessment of Ontario Hydro's nuclear management performance, one of three nuclear complexes was leased to a British transnational energy firm.

In 2002, after several years of open contestation, the Ontario government came to the brink of privatization just as the new system began to operate. However, at the eleventh hour, an anti-privatization coalition led by organized labour launched a successful legal challenge to the privatization legislation. Faced with prospects of remaking the privatization coalition, the Ontario government withdrew the initiative (Swift and Stewart 2005). Even in Alberta, Canada's most "extreme" market experiment, no major generating utilities have been privatized, and the new market includes both major municipal utilities and IPPs—clearly a mixed system. The "market system" would be predominantly state-owned.

A second set of political conflicts was fought over the exact form of the new regime that would replace the old. These conflicts did not lend themselves to mass mobilization, but nevertheless produced critical review and conflict with policy networks. The "market design" debate centred on the degree of competition to be placed into the regime and its organization and redistributive implications. For example, large hydroelectric systems could not be broken up into competing power producers, so that the idea of restructuring to lose monopoly control was not a real possibility. Debt and equity were other key issues. Utilities with expensive technologies, such as old coal or problematic nuclear plants, would find such plants valueless in a competitive market—hence the term "stranded assets." Conversely, hydro systems' older hydro assets provided a province's consumers with a legacy of low-cost energy that had to be protected, or those benefits would be distributed to all consumers through a larger cross-border market integration. Many initiatives to change the existing system were hotly contested (Cohen 2001, 2002; Dewees 2002; Dunsky and Raphals 1998; Plourde 2002).

By 2000, several different models of the new energy regime had emerged in the United States, but the most symbolic new starts, such as California and its Enron-related energy debacle, were costly failures (Jaccard 2002; Woo, Lloyd, and Tishler 2003). Energy policy debate turned toward establishing a standard market design (SMD) that would guide utilities in forming the market rules within newly formed RTOs.[7]

In this context, Canadian utilities faced three broad choices. One option was to embrace the new regime through the design and implementation of a form of electricity market—with all its intended effects. The second option was to simply undergo a minimal restructuring that would allow the utility to become an integrated part of a larger market area, allowing third parties to sell power to provincial distributors and to wheel wholesale power across provincial grids. The third option saw provincial utilities themselves take on the new roles within the regime's expanded opportunity structure. The results are summarized in figure 15.1.

Provinces with mixed-fuels systems have been the centre of active market design and implementation (Canada, National Energy Board 2005). Reliance on expensive and highly environmentally difficult coal technologies or reliance on a set of aging, expensive CANDU nuclear reactors provided ample incentive for a regime shift. Ontario and Alberta, the two jurisdictions that pursued full-market integration, have also corrected initially volatile markets by implementing forms of rebates, contract alternatives, and other interventions to correct market failure. Learning from these lessons, New Brunswick maintained price caps on domestic energy consumption. Prince Edward Island made a de facto regime integration with New Brunswick through interconnections and by adopting the New Brunswick rates for its regulated distribution utility. Nova Scotia adopted the minimum restructuring

Figure 15.1 Characteristics of Emerging Sustainable Regimes in Canadian Provincial Utilities

	Systems with mixed resources and technologies	Hydro-based systems
No regime change or isolated systems		Newfoundland and Labrador
Trade-related restructuring, primarily to meet US Federal Energy Regulatory (FERC) orders to enable North American trade	Nova Scotia Saskatchewan	British Columbia Manitoba Quebec
Adoption of "managed competition" variations of the epistemic neo-liberal model	Alberta New Brunswick–Prince Edward Island[a] Ontario	

[a] Prince Edward Island has effectively integrated with the New Brunswick regime.

possible. Doern and Gattinger (2003) term this approach a system of "managed" competition that seeks to establish workable systems, not unfettered markets.

With the exception of Newfoundland and Labrador's Churchill system, hydro utilities enjoyed years of success simply because they could trade effectively on continental markets. At the same time, the four major hydro-based utilities all chose different directions. The British Columbia NDP government's hydro strategy took a path of minimal change and, at the same time, considered hydro a tool of industrialization. The province's subsequent Liberal government oversaw restructuring, then purposely stifled the growth of the former provincial utility by relying solely on independent producers to supply new power (British Columbia, Ministry of Energy and Mines 2002; Cohen 2002).

In Manitoba and Quebec, utilities took the opportunity to purchase natural gas distribution utilities, resulting in the convergence of gas and electrical markets. This strategy was part of a broad "rush to gas" convergence originally sparked by innovative energy-efficient gas turbines and cheap and abundant supplies of gas. Now, however, gas is neither cheap nor plentiful (Canada, National Energy Board 2005). Quebec also used the opportunity to invest in hydro and natural gas energy assets in the United States, Brazil, and Latin America, making it both a major regional player and one of the world's largest energy companies. No other provincial hydro has followed a similar growth path.

The isolation of Newfoundland's electrical system provided conditions that enabled provincial political forces to shape a unique policy regime. One private distribution monopoly covers most of the island, and the provincial hydro develops the energy. Finally, Newfoundland and Labrador's Churchill Falls resources and system lie stranded.

Both Manitoba and Quebec took steps for reconciliation with Aboriginal peoples. Manitoba Hydro negotiated approximately 14 agreements with Aboriginal peoples affected by the Nelson River hydro developments, and the government of Quebec finally made a historic "Peace of the Brave" with the James Bay Cree. It is too early, however, to evaluate this new relationship between Aboriginal peoples and the state with respect to hydro regimes (Manitoba Hydro's perspectives 1999; Hydro signs historic agreement 2000; Fox Lake agreement 2004; Ha 2007).

Finally, electricity policy has been marked by a debate on how best to maintain markets and sustainability. By default, sustainability is not a key issue for hydro systems because water is a renewable resource that does not produce GHGs—except for the ethanol produced by flooding forests. The neo-liberal model assumes that competitive markets will deliver sustainable energy, but the practice has been much different. Markets have retarded demand side management and integrated resource planning. Moreover, IPPs cannot deliver "green" energy at competitive prices.

These issues emerged in 2002, when Canada ratified the Kyoto Protocol. Provincial electrical energy regimes then tied their sustainability agenda to Kyoto Protocol obligations—particularly since the treaty was to come into force by 2005. In anticipation of some of these challenges, the federal government subsidized provincial investments in wind power and other forms of renewable or green energy. Provinces adopted legislated portfolios of sustainable energy that required a percentage of total power to originate from sustainable or green sources. Some jurisdictions, such as Ontario, faced a set of environmentally difficult choices, such as either continuing to use coal or refurbishing their aging nuclear systems. Indeed, Canadian nuclear proponents advanced the idea of a new generation of CANDU reactors as a solution to both global warming and meeting Kyoto Protocol obligations. All provinces needed to abandon their markets in the short run to foster the development of green energy (Rowlands 2007). On the whole, these policy initiatives failed to deliver the goods.

In 2006, a change of national government brought into power the Conservative minority government of Stephen Harper, an opponent of the Kyoto Protocol. Under Harper, the federal government voiced its opposition to the standards set by the Kyoto Protocol, agreeing instead to pursue a GHG-reduction plan based on the intensity of emissions (see Brownsey, chapter 12, under the heading "The New National Energy Program and the Kyoto Protocol"). These developments split the provinces. The government of Quebec was committed to maintaining Kyoto Protocol obligations, and other hydro provinces were similarly "Kyoto-ready." The coal- and nuclear-based hydro regimes, however, faced a much greater challenge. A 2006 David Suzuki Foundation assessment of provincial climate change policies (Marshall 2006) sums up the problem with the title *All Over the Map*.

The new regime has spurred the growth of private energy capital. The largest new actor is TransAlta Corporation, based in Alberta. TransAlta claims control over 10,000 megawatts of coal, hydro, and alternative-energy sources in Canada, the United States, and Australia, giving it about twice the capacity of Manitoba Hydro (TransAlta Corporation 2007). Fortis, the owners of Newfoundland's distribution monopoly, has also grown to become a major private-utility holding company, owning major regulated distribution utilities in Newfoundland and Labrador, the provincial monopoly in Prince Edward Island (Maritime Electric), minor equity in New Brunswick's nuclear capacity, and major distribution assets in Alberta (the former TransAlta distribution system) and British Columbia (the former West Kootenay Power). Fortis has also acquired Terasen Gas, BC's major gas distribution company. Outside of Canada, Fortis owns transmission and generation assets in New York, Belize, and Grand Cayman (Fortis 2007).

Emera, a smaller Maritime energy services company, has taken a broader convergence strategy that links regional electric utilities with natural gas pipelines (Emera 2007). Emera currently owns Nova Scotia Power, Bangor Hydro-Electric (a small hydro-based utility in Maine), a minority stake in the Sable Island Gas Pipeline, a regional heating fuel company, and the largest utility service corporation in the region.[8] Emera's major problem is that regional gas supply will soon be depleted. The company has taken an equity position in the proposed pipeline to service a new liquefied natural gas terminal (Hughes 2007). Beyond that, Emera and Nova Scotia face pressures for greater regional integration, particularly with the New Brunswick and New England utilities.

To what extent has the new regime changed patterns of interprovincial and international trade? The answer appears in some ways paradoxical. The regime has raised expectations with its primary goal of increasing market efficiency and integration. Predictably, all Canadian utilities with US interconnections were fairly quick, despite some regulatory challenges, to meet the minimal FERC reciprocity demands through organizational restructuring and adoption of OATTs.[9] Ontario is joining the two RTOs on its borders. To protect its regional market access, Manitoba worked out an agreement to be an "external participant" within the Midwest Independent System Operator (MISO), a fully market-based RTO. British Columbia was also involved in the negotiations concerning GridWest, the RTO for the Pacific Northwest. Other western Canadian stakeholders are looking primarily to increase the transmission infrastructure for electricity from Alberta through BC into the California market.

On the other hand, the regime has not been powerful enough to break down interprovincial barriers or to significantly develop regional or national grids. Despite the regime change, Quebec is the only likely market for Labrador power in the foreseeable future, and this monopsony power (being the only feasible buyer) gives Quebec enormous leverage in price negotiation. Although both governments have started negotiations, no acceptable deal has been reached. Similarly, the governments of Newfoundland and Ontario have discussed the construction of an east–west grid to develop and transmit Labrador power to needy markets. But no action has been taken. Manitoba has tried to sell Nelson River energy to Ontario since the early 1960s—only to be repeatedly disappointed by last-minute cancellations. In the latest round, this old idea has been dressed in Kyoto garments as the "The Clean Energy Transfer Initiative" (Chliboyko 2005).

The contemporary energy strategies of Alberta, Nova Scotia, and New Brunswick depend upon future regional electricity market integration. Economic pressures are bringing the two larger Maritime provinces toward convergence. New Brunswick needs greater regional markets to pool the costs of its older coal and nuclear assets, and Nova Scotia and PEI need energy. Development of the oil sands will be energy intensive, and regional integration will also allow Alberta to make related large-scale cogeneration projects viable (Canada, National Energy Board 2005).

Explanations for this paradox of raised expectations and slow delivery can reasonably take two forms. First, Canadian federalism has worked to discourage any meaningful federal initiative in energy market integration. Canadian neo-liberalism has been associated with significant decentralization, and federal initiatives in hydro, a symbolically important provincial jurisdiction, would be untenable to both Quebec and other powerful provinces. Given this situation, Ottawa's strategy has been to avoid taking roles that would infringe on provincial jurisdictions (Canada, National Energy Board 1992). Ottawa has funded alternative-energy sources and promoted green consumption as part of its climate change mandate, and worked with governments and corporate interests to foster the idea of North American energy integration (Canadian Electrical Association 2004). Interprovincial integration, however, still lacks systemic coordination or political leverage.

Without a meaningful federal role, regime articulation occurs within the context of FERC as a quasi-supranational North American regulator. Here, dynamics within the US political economy preclude any fast or unilateral policy thrusts. Clearly, one regime effect has been that the increased importance attached to interconnections has not been matched by systemic investment in hydro grids. As a result, the North American grid has experienced increasing reliability problems. The issue came to a head with the August 2003 blackout, when a regional US electrical system experienced a succession of problems that caused a series of cascading power failures, eventually putting 50 million Canadians and Americans in the dark. A binational report on the incident (US–Canada Power System Outage Task Force 2004) recommended replacing NERC with a new electrical reliability organization with the authority to enforce standards on utilities. The most recent institutional development has seen FERC take effective jurisdiction over North American system reliability. Lastly is the issue of whether the present policy regime provides an adequate structure for hydro investments. Each of the major Canadian jurisdictions faces an impending supply problem. Hydro projects in the past have been negotiated with long-term take or pay contracts. It is not clear whether the short-term horizons within contemporary hydro regimes can deliver the goods.

CONCLUSIONS

The "quasi-staples" status of hydro needs to be reflected in any summation of its "post-staples" trajectory. Staples analysis has always focused on the creation and redistribution of economic rents, technological change, and trade issues. These features have been prominent in each of the three regimes of hydroelectricity described in this chapter. Additionally, because it is a fuel, hydro is subject to natural cycles.

In the formative period, the two key rent-related issues were the distribution of rents to subsidize industrialization and urban electrification. As far as technology is concerned, in the first regime, electricity was sourced from a variety of technologies and the most readily available resource—the most important being hydro. A fragmented set of networks or systems had fixed borders—and the largest were defined by urban regions. The utilities that controlled these networks competed to extend their control over resources and urban populations. This regime was initially shaped by complex political struggles involving federal, provincial, and municipal levels of the state; private utility capital; and populist public power movements. The result was a policy regime dominated by provincial and local interests and involving competition between public and private sectors. To a large extent, this regime was successful. The Depression and war changed the context of electricity energy policy, however, and the formative regimes were simply not adequate to the exigencies of the postwar period.

In the second regime, hydro investments were promoted as a form of public good. The regime centred on a set of powerful state-owned vertically integrated utilities—monopolies that minimized the risks of hydro development. Hydro rents were distributed through "cheap rates" to subsidize regional economic development and facilitate the development of mass production and mass consumption. In its final stages, economic rents were taken from public utilities as sources of public revenue. The second regime ushered in the era of "big" technologies and megaprojects—increasingly larger hydro, nuclear, and coal plants—with the attendant political, social, and environmental agendas particular to each. Curiously, the rise of the provincial hydro regimes was the product of the provincial political and economic elites—not the mass mobilization of public power movements. Networks were reorganized into provincial grids, and in a process fraught with contestation, provincial hydro networks extended their reach into northern peripheries.

This regime saw the rise of limited functional integration between Canadian provincial networks and US regional networks and the development of large-scale export relations among the hydro-producing provinces and between Canada and the United States. But not all of these were successful. A critical weakness of the regime was that integration was limited by the general assumption of network or system self-reliance. Although the regime was generally politically popular, the notoriously closed nature of hydro regimes sparked systemic conflict with Aboriginal peoples and environmentalists. The provincial hydros and megaprojects regime was essentially a growth and investment machine that would be challenged to respond to the uncertain dynamics of the post-Keynesian economy. Increasingly, this regime lost political support from the economic elite and forfeited intellectual legitimacy from both environmentalists and an increasing cadre of neo-liberal policy experts who promoted market alternatives. This regime's fate was sealed by the Canada–United States Free Trade Agreement.

The sustainability/regionalization regime has abandoned the focus on rents and linkages that were at the centre of the previous hydro strategies. By either disciplining or replacing hydro as a public good with the market, it assumed that economic efficiencies would provide widely diffused benefits. The policy challenge has been to ensure that the legacy of low-cost hydro remains the entitlement of Canadian consumers and not broadly distributed to trading partners. For new investments, rents and linkages are oriented toward sustainable development. Hence "smart" consumption has replaced "mass" consumption, and "demand-side management" has replaced the "cheap power" policy. In theory, a series of benign and/or sustainable technologies has been developed and can be further developed for energy production, such as wind farms, photovoltaic solar power, and small-scale hydro systems. Natural gas has also entered into the generation technologies with the efficient "combined-cycle gas turbine."

The implementation of this regime has been shaped by significant political conflict. First, regionally based class conflicts pitted neo-liberal "reformers" advocating privatization of provincial hydros against the labour movement and social movements defending publicly owned power companies. A second set of conflicts within policy networks revolved around the form of the new regime and details of its configuration. A third set of conflicts centred on tensions between federal and provincial governments and the rise of Washington, through FERC, as a supranational North American utility regulator. Because the third regime emerged during a recent nadir of federal power, critical weaknesses in the regime were limited interprovincial trade, the absence of a federal role in shaping international trade, and limited commitments toward sustainability.

Although sustainable development interests began the regime with an implicit alliance with neo-liberal forces, these interests have ended up disenchanted by the new regime's poor performance on environmental issues. Environmental and sustainability issues have changed. The most important agenda centres on defining sustainability relative to global warming. Here, hydro systems have substantial advantages over coal- or nuclear-based systems and technologies. Although hydro has dominated electrical energy regimes in the past, the future for many Canadian provinces appears to be a difficult set of choices and trade-offs. And even hydro policy regimes will need to adapt in the face of changes to the water cycle.

The third regime has not worked out as planned. Although advocates for change sought a neo-liberal revolution, they ended up with an uncertain system of managed competition and increasingly transnational regional electricity grids. Privatization has not generally taken place, and provincial governments are carefully seeking ways to legitimate the new regime. The evolving regime is highly influenced by the supranational role the US government has played in structuring continental markets. As a result, electrical energy policy is increasingly a North American game. Although this sector may not have been considered a "full" staple industry in the past, it has shared the form and agenda of a mature staples industry, and more recently, the characteristics reveal features of a post-staples industry. Yet, provincial electrical energy policy regimes are now marked by significant differences stemming from the economic, environmental, and political attributes of major hydro, coal, nuclear, and natural gas resources and technologies. Nowhere are these differences more apparent than in provincial attempts to fashion sustainable energy strategies. In this era, hydro still trumps all. In other words, staples count.

NOTES

* The author thanks Michael Howlett and Keith Brownsey for their comments and suggestions. Thanks also to the anonymous reviewers who commented on earlier versions of this chapter.

1. The province-wide (as opposed to urban or regional) outcome for Ontario was the result of an overall energy scarcity, inter-regional competition, and the historic loss of authority over Canadian Niagara hydro resources. Additionally, Ontario's broadly based municipal public power system had business support and leadership. The ability to deliver energy at cost precluded financial interests from extracting rents from the natural monopolies.

2. Indeed, as the work of Joy Parr, Gunilla Ekberg, and James Williams illustrates, domestic technology, particularly in the kitchen, which marks the intersection of the market, the state, and the domestic sphere, took on extraordinary importance in postwar culture and design, economic policy, utility business incomes, and mass manufacturers (Parr and Ekberg 1996; Parr 1999, 2002; Williams 1998).

3. American utilities also became vertically integrated. During the Depression, the US federal government used the Ontario Hydro model in its New Deal program to

create the Tennessee Valley and Bonneville power authorities. But this federal role in hydro was not the rule. The difference between the two political communities was that most US private utilities were regulated, as opposed to being publicly owned, so there was no wholesale postwar rationalization.

4. The provincial state rose to dominance over formerly private utility capital and former municipal structures. So important was the idea of the primacy of states over capital that the government of Manitoba was able to successfully rewrite the terms of the Natural Resources Transfer Agreements so that the province could unilaterally change the historical resource claims of capital. This move would substantially leverage the ideologically conservative Liberal-Progressive government in its plan to take over the Nesbitt-Thomson affiliate that dominated the provincial hydro sector. This strategy was a quasi-constitutional change that was justified in terms of provincial equality: if the Hydro-Electric Power Commission of Ontario could use its dominance to break or change supply contracts as leverage to drive private and foreign capital out of the sector, then Manitoba could use powers to expropriate resource rights for the same purposes (Netherton 1993).

5. Additionally, a great deal of economy energy was exchanged with Michigan. Indeed, US auto interests worked out a set of US regulatory exceptions that allowed automakers unregulated access to Ontario electricity (Perlgut 1978).

6. Although Quebec would eventually develop more hydro capacity than any other province, the excess energy has been used primarily for domestic markets, not for export (Laundry 1984).

7. In July 2002, FERC issued a notification that it would establish rules to address a standard market design. This notification was followed in 2003 with a white paper and a consultation process (US, Federal Energy Regulatory Commission 2003). However, at the time of writing, FERC has not finished this process, and significant opposition to the FERC model has developed in the southern states and in California.

8. An interesting development, from a staples perspective, is the growth of Cameco and Bruce Power. During the mid-1990s, the Harris government effectively privatized Ontario Hydro's oldest nuclear facilities in the Bruce Peninsula, known as the Bruce Power Complex. Four of the installation's eight reactors had been laid up by Ontario Hydro. The privatization took the form of a long-term lease to a British firm, which for other reasons shortly wanted out of its Canadian operations. The Canadian replacement was Bruce Power, a partnership among Cameco, the Saskatchewan uranium supplier; TransCanada Pipelines; and the two unions working at the Bruce Power Complex. Privatization has been a success, with substantially greater efficiency and power production from operating units and refurbishment of two older installations. Cameco, over time, has increased its ownership and has, therefore, emerged as both a staples supplier and a high-technology consumer of its own product.

9. In a useful comparison of international electricity trade, Pineau, Hira, and Froschauer (2004) indicate that Canada and the United States have the most integrated electricity markets in the world. Although total Canadian exports vary, they do not exceed 9 percent of total generation, whereas imports from the United States are less than

1 percent of US total generation. Significantly, the capacity of international inter-connections is about 17 percent of total Canadian generation capacity, implying that short-term trade remains an integral part of managing the Canadian energy supply. An overall picture emerges of a complex regional integration, not a staples export relationship or a profound market dependence.

REFERENCES

Albo, G., and Jenson, J. 1989. A contested concept: The relative autonomy of the state. In *The New Canadian Political Economy*, eds. W. Clement and G. Williams, 180–211. Montreal and Kingston: McGill-Queen's University Press.

Armstrong, C. 1981. *The politics of federalism: Ontario's relations with the federal government, 1867–1942.* Toronto: University of Toronto Press.

Armstrong, C., and Nelles, H.V. 1983. Contrasting development of the hydro electric industry in the Montreal and Toronto regions, 1900–1930. *Journal of Canadian Studies* 18(1): 5–27.

Armstrong, C., and Nelles, H.V. 1986. *Monopoly's moment: The organization and regulation of Canadian utilities, 1830–1930.* Philadelphia: Temple University Press.

Averyt, W.F. 1992. *Canada–U.S. electricity trade and environmental politics.* Orono, ME: Canadian–American Center, University of Maine.

Battle, E.F., Gislason, G.S., and Douglas, G.W. 1984. Potential benefits and costs of Canadian electricity exports. *Canadian Public Policy* 10(3): 363.

Bernard, J.-T. 1982. L'exportation d'électricité par le Québec. *Canadian Public Policy* 8(3): 321–33.

Bernard, J.-T. 1989. A Ricardian theory of hydroelectric power development: Some Canadian evidence. *Canadian Journal of Economics* 22(2): 328–39.

Bernard, J.-T., and Cairns, R.D. 1987. On public utility pricing and forgone economic benefits. *Canadian Journal of Economics* 20(1): 152–63.

Bijker, W.E., Hughes, T.P., and Pinch, T.J., eds. 1989. *The social construction of technological systems: New directions in the sociology and history of technology.* Cambridge, MA: MIT Press.

Blais, A., and Faucher, P. 1979. Les enjeux économiques de la nationalization d'électricité (book review). *Canadian Journal of Political Science* 12(4): 809–15.

British Columbia, Ministry of Energy and Mines. 2002. *Energy for our future: A plan for BC.* Victoria: Ministry of Energy and Mines.

Cairns, R.D., and Heyes, A.G. 1993. Why do we price electricity the way we do? Canadian policy in the light of political-economic theories of governmental behaviour. *Canadian Public Administration* 36(2): 153–74.

Campbell, R.M. 1987. Grand illusions: The politics of the Keynesian experience in Canada, 1945–1975. Peterborough, ON: Broadview Press.

Canada, Department of Energy, Mines and Resources and US, Department of Energy. 1978. *Electricity exchanges.* Ottawa: Department of Supply and Services.

Canada, National Energy Board. 1992. *Inter-utility trade review: Transmission access and wheeling.* Calgary: National Energy Board.

Canada, National Energy Board. 2005. *Outlook for electricity markets, 2005–2006: An energy market assessment.* Calgary: National Energy Board Publication Office.

Canadian Electrical Association. 2004. *The integrated North American electricity market: A bi-national model for securing a reliable supply of electricity.* Montreal: Canadian Electrical Association.

Cass-Beggs, D. 1964. How might one administer a Canadian power grid. *Canadian Public Administration* 7(3): 333–42.

Chliboyko, J. 2005. Ontario, Manitoba may revisit power project: Provinces take first step to send electricity east. *Business Edge* 1(23). Online at http://www.businessedge.ca/article.cfm/newsID/11296.cfm.

Cohen, M.G. 2001. *From public good to private exploitation: GATS and the restructuring of Canadian electrical utilities.* Orono, ME: Canadian–American Center.

Cohen M.G. 2002. *Public power and the political economy of electricity competition: The case of BC.* Vancouver: Canadian Centre for Policy Alternatives.

Currie, A.W. 1946. Rate control on Canadian public utilities. *Canadian Journal of Economics and Political Science* 12(2): 148–58.

Dales, J. 1957. *Hydroelectricity and industrialization: Quebec, 1898–1940.* Cambridge, MA: Cambridge University Press.

DeVaul, D., Keating, T., and Sugarman, R.J. 1984. *Trading in power: The potential for Canadian electricity exchange.* Washington, DC: Northeast-Midwest Institute; Canadian Institute of International Affairs.

Dewees, D.N. 2002. Electricity restructuring in Canada. Paper presented to the CRUISE Conference on Canadian Energy Policy in the Sustainable Development Era, Carleton University, Ottawa, October 17–18.

Doern, G.B., and Gattinger, M. 2003. *Power switch: Energy regulatory governance in the twenty-first century.* Toronto: University of Toronto Press.

Dunsky, P., and Raphals, P. 1998. Challenges for effective competition in large-hydro dominated markets: The case of Quebec. In *Deregulation of Electric Utilities*, ed. G. Zaccour, 101–17. Boston: Kluwer Academic.

Dupré, R., and Party, M. 1998. Hydroelectricity and the state in Quebec and Ontario: Two different historical paths. In *Deregulation of Electric Utilities*, ed. G. Zaccour, 119–47. Boston: Kluwer Academic.

Economic Council of Canada. 1985. *Connections: An energy strategy for the future.* Ottawa: Economic Council of Canada and Supply and Services Canada.

Emera. 2007. *2006 annual financial report.* Online at http://www.emera.com/investors/AR/Emera06financial.pdf.

Energy, Mines and Resources Canada. 1988. *Canadian electricity policy.* Ottawa: Energy, Mines and Resources.

Fortis Inc. 2007. *2006 annual report.* Online at http://www.fortisinc.com/InvestorCentre/FinancialReports/AnnualReport/.

Fox Lake settlement agreement addresses past hydro development in Nelson River area. 2004. *Insights* 14(2). Online at http://www.hydro.mb.ca/news/insights/insights _04_08.shtml#story4.

Froschauer, K. 1999. *White gold: Hydroelectric power in Canada.* Vancouver: University of British Columbia Press.

Ha, T.T. 2007. Ottawa, Cree reach "historic" $1.4-billion accord. *The Globe and Mail* July 17: A1.

Hargrove, E C. 1994. *Prisoners of myth: The leadership of the Tennessee Valley Authority, 1933–1990.* Princeton, NJ: Princeton University Press.

Helliwell, J.F., MacGregor, M.E., and Plourde, A. 1984. Changes in Canadian energy demand, supply, and policies, 1974–1986. *Natural Resources Journal* 24(2): 297–324.

Howlett, M., Netherton, A., and Ramesh, M. 1999. *The political economy of Canada: An introduction.* Don Mills, ON: Oxford University Press.

Hughes, L. 2007. *Security in Nova Scotia.* Halifax: Canadian Centre for Policy Alternatives.

Hughes, T.P. 1982. *Networks of power: Electrification in western society, 1880–1930.* Baltimore: Johns Hopkins University Press.

Hughes, T.P. 2001. Technological momentum. In *Technology and the Future,* 8th ed., ed. A.H. Teich, 26–43. Boston: St Martin's Press.

Hydro signs historic agreement on future development in the north. 2000. *Insights* 10(3). Online at https://www.hydro.mb.ca/news/insights/insights_00_11.shtml.

Jaccard, M. 1995. Oscillating currents: The changing rationale for government intervention in the electricity industry. *Energy Policy* 23(7): 572–92.

Jaccard, M. 2002. *California shorts a circuit: Should Canadians trust the wiring diagram?* Toronto: C.D. Howe Institute. Online at http://www.cdhowe.org/pdf/commentary _159.pdf.

Jaccard, M., Nyboer, J., and Makinen, T. 1991. Managing instead of building: BC Hydro's role in the 1990s. *BC Studies* 91–92(Winter): 98–226.

Jenkins, G.P. 1985. Public utility finance and economic waste. *Canadian Journal of Economics* 18(3): 484–98.

Jenkins, G.P. 1987. Public utility finance and pricing: A reply. *Canadian Journal of Economics* 20(1): 172–76.

Jenson, J. 1989. "Different" but not "exceptional": Canada's permeable Fordism. *Canadian Review of Sociology and Anthropology* 26(1): 69–94.

Kessides, I.N., and the World Bank. 2004. *Reforming infrastructure: Privatization, regulation, and competition.* Washington, DC: World Bank; New York: Oxford University Press.

Kitschelt, H.P. 1986a. Four theories of public policy-making and fast breeder reactor development in France, the United States, and West Germany. *International Organization* 40(1): 65–104.

Kitschelt, H.P. 1986b. Political opportunity structures and political protest: Anti-nuclear movements in four democracies. *British Journal of Political Science* 16(1): 57–85.

Laundry, R. 1984. L'hydro-electricité du Québec: Produire pour consumer ou produire pour exporter? *Revue Études Internationales* 15(1): 95–119.

Laxer, G. 1991. *Perspectives on Canadian economic development: Class, staples, gender and elites.* Toronto: Oxford University Press.

Macdonald, D., and the Advisory Committee on Competition in Ontario's Electricity System. 1996. *Final report: A framework for competition.* Toronto: Advisory Committee on Competition

Mackay, P. 1983. *Electric empire: The inside story of Ontario Hydro.* Toronto: Between the Lines.

Manitoba Hydro's perspectives on NFA implementation. 1999. *Insights* 9(2). Online at http://www.hydro.mb.ca/news/insights/insights_99_08.shtml#story2.

Marshall, D. 2006. *All over the map: 2006 status report of provincial climate change plans.* Vancouver: David Suzuki Foundation.

Murphy, M.E. 1952. Nationalization of British industry. *Canadian Journal of Economics and Political Science* 18(2): 146–62.

Nelles, H.V. 1974. *The politics of development: Forests, mines and hydro-electric power in Ontario, 1849–1941.* Toronto: Macmillan.

Netherton, A. 1993. From rentiership to continental modernization: Shifting policy paradigms of state intervention in hydro in Manitoba, 1922–1977. Doctoral thesis, Faculty of Political Science, Carleton University, Ottawa.

Ontario, Ministry of Energy, Science and Technology. 1997. *Directions for change: Charting a course for competitive electricity and jobs in Ontario.* Toronto: Ministry of Energy, Science and Technology.

Parr, J. 1999. *Domestic goods: The material, the moral and the economic in the postwar years to 1999.* Toronto: University of Toronto Press.

Parr, J. 2002. Modern kitchen, good home, strong nation. *Technology and Culture* 43(4): 657–67.

Parr, J., and Ekberg, G. 1996. Mrs. Consumer and Mr. Keynes in postwar Canada and Sweden. *Gender and History* 8(2): 212–30.

Perlgut, M. 1978. *Electricity across the border: The US–Canadian experience.* Montreal: C.D. Howe Research Institute and National Planning Association.

Pineau, P.-O., Hira, A., and Froschauer, K. 2004. Measuring international electricity integration: A comparative study of the power systems under the Nordic Council, Mercosur, and NAFTA. *Energy Policy* 32(13): 1457–75.

Plourde, A. 2002. The changing nature of national and continental energy markets. Paper presented to the CRUISE Conference on Canadian Energy Policy in the Sustainable Development Era, Carleton University, Ottawa, October 17–18.

Poch, 1987. Regulating the export of environmental quality: The case of electricity exports. In *Trading Canada's Natural Resources: Essays from the third Banff Conference on Natural Resources Law,* ed. J.O. Saunders, 309–23. Calgary: Carswell.

Rea, K.J. 1976. *The political economy of northern development.* Ottawa: Information Canada.

Robinson, J.B., and Hooker, C.A. 1987. Future imperfect: Energy policy and modeling in Canada—Institutional mandates and constitutional conflict. In *The Politics of Energy Forecasting*, eds. T. Baumgartner and A. Midttun, 211–39. Oxford: Clarendon Press.

Rowlands, I.H. 2007. The development of renewable electricity policy in the province of Ontario: The influence of ideas and timing. *Review of Policy Research* 24(3): 185–207.

Smiley, D.V. 1975. Canada and the quest for a national policy. *Canadian Journal of Political Science* 8(1): 40–62.

Spiro, P.S. 1987. Public utility finance and the cost of capital: Comments on Jenkins. *Canadian Journal of Economics* 20(1): 164–71.

Swainson, N.A. 1979. *Conflict over the Columbia: The Canadian background to an historic treaty*. Montreal and Kingston: McGill-Queen's University Press.

Swift, J., and Stewart, K. 2005. Union power and the charged politics of electricity in Ontario. *Just Labour* 5(Winter): 14–21.

TransAlta Corporation. 2007. *2006 annual report*. Online at http://www.transalta.com/ transalta/webcms.nsf/AllDoc/0CE524B035476001872572DE0058F2A5/$File/ TA%2006ARWebOption.pdf.

Tritschler, G.E. 1979. *Final report of the Commission of Inquiry into Manitoba Hydro*. Winnipeg: Queen's Printer.

US–Canada Power System Outage Task Force. 2004. *Final report on the August 14, 2003 blackout in the United States and Canada: Causes and recommendations*. Ottawa and Washington, DC: The Task Force.

US, Department of Energy, Office of Policy Planning and Analysis. 1987. *Northern lights: The economic and practical potential of imported power from Canada*. Washington, DC: US Department of Energy, Office of Policy, Planning and Analysis.

US, Energy Information Administration. 1996. Privatization and the genesis of the multinational power company. In *Privatization and the Globalization of Energy Markets*, 37–56. Washington, DC: Energy Information Administration, Office of Energy Markets and End Use, US Department of Energy.

US, Energy Information Administration. 1997. *Electricity reform abroad and US investment*. Washington, DC: Energy Information Administration, Office of Energy Markets and End Use, US Department of Energy. Online at http://www.eia.doe.gov/emeu/ pgem/electric/contents.html.

US, Federal Energy Regulatory Commission. 2003. *White paper wholesale power market platform*. Washington, DC: Federal Energy Regulatory Commission.

Waldram, J.B. 1988. *As long as the rivers run: Hydroelectric development and Native communities in western Canada*. Winnipeg: University of Manitoba Press.

Webster, P. 1993. Nova Scotia: Where's the power? Power for money for votes: The privatization of Nova Scotia Power. *New Maritimes* 11(4): 6–14.

Williams, J.C. 1998. Getting housewives the electric message: Gender and energy marketing in the early twentieth century. In *His & Hers: Gender, Consumption, and*

Technology, eds. R. Horowitz and A. Mohen, 149–70. Charlottesville, VA: University of Virginia Press.

Winner, L. 2003. Do artifacts have politics? In *Technology and the Future*, 9th ed., ed. A. Teich, 148–64. Belmont, CA: Wadsworth.

Woo, C.K., Lloyd, D., and Tishler, A. 2003. Electricity market reform failures: UK, Norway, Alberta and California. *Energy Policy* 31(11): 1103–15.

Wylie, P.J. 1990. Indigenous technological adaptation in Canadian manufacturing, 1900–1929. *Canadian Journal of Economics* 23(4): 856–72.

Young, R.A. 1982. Planning for power: The New Brunswick Electric Power Commission in the 1950s. *Acadiensis* 12(1): 73–99.

Zuker, R.C., Jenkins, G.P., and the Economic Council of Canada. 1984. *Blue gold: Hydro-electric rent in Canada*. Ottawa: Minister of Supply and Services Canada.

Index